WINDOWS
NT
Professional
Library

Windows NT & UNIX
Integration Guide

About the Authors . . .

David Gunter is an information technology consultant and author based in Cary, NC. In addition to software development, he has been involved with supporting and managing diverse systems and networks for more than 10 years. David has a master's degree in Computer Science from the University of Tennessee. He has worked as both a lead and contributing author on several computer books, including the best-selling *Special Edition Using Linux* series. His publication credits include *Using Linux*, First, Second, and Third Editions; *Using the Internet*, Third Edition; *Netscape Starter Kit*; *Using Netscape 3*; *Using Netscape 2*; *Client/Server Programming with RPC and DCE*; *Using UNIX*, Second Edition; and *Using Turbo C++ 4.5*. When not writing, consulting, researching, or surfing the Net, David spends as much time as possible with his wonderful wife, their dog, and two cats.

Steven Burnett is an information technology consultant whose interests for the last several years have focused around heterogeneous system management and modular documentation. A member of USENIX and SAGE, he holds a Master's degree in technical communication from North Carolina State University, and has contributed to the following books: *Using Linux*, Third Edition; *Client/Server Programming With RPC and DCE*; *Using Netscape 2*; *Using Netscape 3*; and *Netscape Starter Kit*. In his spare time, Steven enjoys spending time with his wonderful wife Merrie, listening to music, extending the home LAN, and trying to play a Chapman Stick.

Lola Gunter is a technical consultant in Cary, NC. She has worked in Web and multimedia software development as a computer consultant and as a manager of technical documentation. Her publication credits include *Using Linux*, Third Edition; *Using Multimedia ToolBook 3.0*; and *Client/Server Programming with RPC and DCE*. She has a bachelor's degree in computer science from the University of North Carolina - Asheville. In addition to the Web and the Internet, her interests include working with stained glass, roughhousing with her German shepherd, and traveling.

WINDOWS
NT
Professional
Library

Windows NT & UNIX
Integration Guide

David Gunter
Steven Burnett
Lola Gunter

Osborne **McGraw-Hill**

Berkeley   New York   St. Louis   San Francisco
Auckland   Bogotá   Hamburg   London   Madrid
Mexico City   Milan   Montreal   New Delhi   Panama City
Paris   São Paulo   Singapore   Sydney
Tokyo   Toronto

Osborne / **McGraw-Hill**
2600 Tenth Street
Berkeley, California 94710
U.S.A.

For information on translations or book distributors outside the U.S.A., or to arrange bulk purchase discounts for sales promotions, premiums, or fund-raisers, please contact Osborne / **McGraw-Hill** at the above address.

Windows NT & UNIX Integration Guide

234567890 DOC 9987

ISBN 0-07-882395-1

Publisher	**Copy Editor**
Brandon A. Nordin	Tim Barr
Editor-in-Chief	**Proofreader**
Scott Rogers	Joe Sadusky
Acquisitions Editors	**Indexer**
Wendy Rinaldi	David Heiret
Lisa Lucas	
	Computer Designer
Project Editor	Robert Steele
Claire Splan	
	Illustrator
Editorial Assistant	Leslee Bassin
Ann Sellers	
	Series Design
Technical Editor	Peter Hancik
Peter Auditlore	
	Cover Design
	Adrian Morgan

To Lola, always.
—David

To Merrie: thanks. I love you.
—Steve

To David and my mother, Lola: Thanks for believing in me!
—Lola

WINDOWS NT
Professional Library

AT A GLANCE

WINDOWS NT
Professional Library

CONTENTS

ACKNOWLEDGMENTS

With any book project, there are so many different people involved that it becomes difficult to make a complete list. First off, thanks go to Wendy Rinaldi at Osborne for giving us the opportunity to work on this exciting series. Lisa Lucas did an outstanding job of managing and coordinating all the various pieces of the project. I really do appreciate all your effort, Lisa! Also at Osborne, Claire Splan did an excellent job of coordinating the book's copyediting effort. In addition to these folks, I'd like to thank the other editors, artists, and production people at Osborne who worked hard on this project. Fred Huebner and Jack Tackett provided lots of reference information, checked and rechecked outlines, and were excellent information sources for the project. Nicole German of Hummingbird Communications helped us get permission to include all the Hummingbird demos on the CD-ROM. Kurt McNett from Syntax, Inc. worked with us and our schedules to get demo versions of their software for the CD. In addition, I'd like to thank the authors of the various shareware and freeware packages who gave us permission to include their work on the CD. I'd like to thank Lola and Steve for being so easy to work with! Finally, a word of thanks goes out to all our friends for their support and understanding when Lola and I disappeared for three months to work on yet another book project!

—David Gunter

I'd like to thank Lisa Lucas and Wendy Rinaldi of Osborne, who together provided great assistance in coordinating this project. Mark DeMario and Don Jerman provided early advice on the scope of the work. Stan Briggs of Network Computer Solutions was helpful to me by allowing unlimited access to his firm's network lab environment. Also, Jeff Barker and Julie Stewart of Seagate Software were helpful in preparation of parts of this book. My wife Merrie was tolerant of my work schedules, which helped a great deal. Finally, I'd like to thank Dave and Lola for inviting me along on this project, and for being great to work with. Thanks for everything, you two.

—Steve Burnett

In addition to all the people mentioned by David and Steve, I'd also like to thank David Fugate of Waterside for his efforts on behalf of this book. Thanks to Steve, for being easy to work with, as always. And a special thanks to David Gunter, for developing the initial concept, including me in this project, and giving me just the right phrase when the words were stuck. Thanks guys!

—Lola Gunter

CHAPTER 1

The Role of UNIX and NT in the Modern Network

Microsoft holds the lion's share of the PC operating system market and is rapidly making inroads into the high-end workstation market, the traditional bastion of UNIX. As such, there is an increasing need to integrate Microsoft NT systems with UNIX systems in a heterogeneous environment. Traditionally, administering NT systems has required very different sets of skills from those required for administrating Unix systems, with each camp unaware of the services and software available to the other. This book is a guide to help each side of the UNIX / NT environment understand the other.

NT AND UNIX INTEGRATION

In this book, we'll discuss NT and UNIX integration issues and present "real world" solutions to common problems. In addition, we'll cover a sampling of both commercial and freeware products that can be used to implement integration solutions.

The book deals with more than just the boundary of where UNIX and NT meet. Some sections discuss equivalent tools on UNIX and NT platforms, such as using sendmail on UNIX and Exchange on NT. Other sections address how to share resources or file system services between UNIX and NT. We present real problems and issues that you are likely to encounter.

Every environment is different. You might have an NT network and decide you want to add a UNIX server to handle mail, news, and Internet access for performance or security reasons. You might have a mixed environment of UNIX and NT workstations to meet the varying demands of your users for system performance or software tools. Or, you might be primarily a Microsoft shop that is just getting into UNIX development and integration. Regardless, there are lots of issues where NT and UNIX come together.

Who Is This Book For?

If you are an intermediate or advanced system or network professional who is responsible for creating and managing a mixed network of UNIX and Windows NT systems, this book is for you. It's intended for people who work as an administrator with either UNIX or NT, have user-level knowledge of the other platform, and find themselves needing to integrate the two. This includes the UNIX system administrator who now needs to include NT workstations in the company network, as well as the NT administrator who needs to add UNIX workstations to his or her NT network.

Since we're targeting both types of system administrators, you may see some rudimentary material in some of the chapters. Remember that there are different levels of administrators with different backgrounds. So, if some information is a bit basic for you, just skip over it and head on to the good stuff!

What Is This Book About?

In this book, we'll explore issues you're likely to encounter when integrating UNIX and NT. We'll discuss a variety of topics that are critical in successfully managing an integrated network. These include issues you might encounter on either platform, and some that are unique to either NT or UNIX. We'll cover NT-specific issues, UNIX-specific issues, and integration solutions where we can.

Think of this book as a toolkit containing products, components, and techniques, plus the information you need to help you make Windows NT and UNIX work together in an office environment. In addition to the information within these pages, there is also a CD-ROM containing shareware, freeware, and commercial demo products designed to assist with UNIX/NT integration, tools, and a selection of useful FAQ's. Specific topics that we cover include

▼ **NT File Services on UNIX**   Discussion of the type of file services and browsing ability supported by NT. Emphasis on the Samba product for providing NT file services via UNIX. Includes sections for installing, configuring, and troubleshooting Samba, and a discussion of the TotalNet Advanced Server as a commercial counterpart to Samba.

■ **UNIX File Services on NT**   Introduction to the types of file services supported by UNIX. Discussion of the NFS filesharing protocol, with emphasis on providing UNIX file services via NT. Discussion of both commercial and freeware NFS products, and how to use them to provide UNIX file services from NT computers.

■ **Backup in a Mixed Environment**   Introduction to the various file system types, backup strategies, and tools that are applicable in an integrated network. Discussion of commercial tools such as Legato Networker.

■ **Mail Services with SMTP**   Introduction to electronic mail. Discussion of UNIX sendmail architecture and configuration. Discussion of basic NT Exchange configuration. UNIX-to-Exchange mailbox migration.

■ **Mixed Printing Environments**   Discussion of the various printing environments—NT printing, UNIX printing (*lpd, lpr,* etc.). Integration techniques and issues. Implications for user clients. Discussion of commercial solutions, such as Network Instruments' NIPrint (LPR & LPD client for Windows).

■ **Networking NT and UNIX**   Introduction to problems and protocols that are encountered when networking NT and UNIX. The Windows Internet Name System (WINS). Dynamic TCP/IP configuration using DHCP, including advantages and disadvantages. Specific protocol information, including NetBT.

■ **DNS Configuration**   Discussion of DNS service, its purpose, and its function. Configuration information with examples for both NT and UNIX.

■ **Remote Access Service**   Introduction to Remote Access Service (RAS). Configuration and management. Setting up remote dialing. Using RAS for Internet access. Routing IP via NT. Discussion of PPTP protocol.

■ **Microsoft Internet Information Server**   Introduction to the Microsoft IIS server. Installation and configuration information for IIS under NT.

■ **UNIX Web Servers** Introduction to UNIX-based Web servers. Installation and configuration information for Apache under UNIX.

■ **Other Internet Servers** Discussion of Internet services such as Usenet news and the Web. Platform-specific implementation details for protocols and servers including NNTP and HTTP, as well as Microsoft's FTP server for NT.

■ **Desktop Applications** Introduction to cross-platform desktop applications. Discussion of X Window-based applications for NT and UNIX utilities for NT, such as Hummingbird's eXceed. Windows on UNIX hardware using software such as ExodusTech's NTerprise and WinDD. Other GUI solutions such as Citrix WinFrame and NTerprise.

▲ **System and Network Management** General system management advice. Discussion of Windows NT Server's built-in tools. Discussion of protocols (SNMP, MIBs, JMAPI, WBEM). The Network Computer (NC) and its implications. Web-based interfaces and Java-based management trends in systems and network management tools.

What This Book Is Not About

Integration encompasses a great many topics. Alas, this book doesn't cover them all. While we do cover a great deal of material, there's plenty more to know. Below are a series of topics this book **does not** address. If you need these questions answered, you'll want to look elsewhere:

▼ Developing cross-platform software for UNIX and NT

■ Porting software UNIX to NT or vice-versa

▲ Setting up a UNIX or NT network from scratch

ROLES

UNIX and NT grew up in different ways, and as a result, have played different roles in the modern office network. While UNIX primarily came from the minicomputer and engineering realm, Windows NT has a history rooted in the personal computer world.

These two operating systems have very different histories and legacies. You will find that many system administrators are extremely opinionated about one system or the other. NT administrators will complain that UNIX is old, outdated, and has cryptic commands. UNIX administrators complain that NT is unreliable, doesn't scale well, and is a Microsoft product. The amusing thing is that both sides are at least partially correct.

UNIX history

UNIX was developed in the late 1960s. Since that time, it has evolved into the predominant enterprise operating system, providing a reliable, stable, multitasking, multiprocessing, multiuser environment.

One of the reasons for UNIX's current popularity amongst workstation vendors is its portability. It has a layered architecture and is written in a relatively architecture-neutral language. These features, and relatively cheap source-code availability, made UNIX an excellent choice for many vendors looking for a fast way to get an operating system on their new hardware.

NT History

Microsoft began shipping Windows NT in 1993. Prior to that, Microsoft and IBM were jointly developing OS/2. Microsoft knew that OS/2 would not have long to live if it couldn't keep up with new hardware. So, Microsoft began its own project, independent of IBM, to produce a "portable" version of OS/2 that could be moved quickly between different hardware platforms. This was the NT, or *New Technology*, project. The NT project became Windows NT as Microsoft abandoned the OS/2 effort.

Early releases of Windows NT were buggy. However, with Windows NT 4.0, Microsoft is beginning to make headway into traditional UNIX territory. Microsoft has set out to develop an integrated solution for businesses that includes file and print services, communication services, applications, and intranet and Internet services.

NT provides a wide selection of features typically found in workstation or mainframe operating systems, including

▼ A robust filesystem

■ Multiprotocol networking

■ Distributed filesystem support

■ Distributed system management

▲ Access-control-list based security

UNIX Roles

UNIX grew up in the engineering world. It has been the operating system of choice for businesses who wanted to move mission-critical applications from mainframes because of its performance, robustness, and flexibility. Because most commercial versions of UNIX are produced by companies that also sell workstation hardware, UNIX has traditionally found its place in the high-performance computing market. Table 1-1 lists some of the traditional roles that UNIX has filled in the business arena.

Task	Description
Heavy duty I/O	Applications that require high I/O bandwidth, such as databases, commonly use a UNIX implementation platform. Most versions of UNIX run on custom hardware and are capable of offering higher performance I/O bandwidth.
Multitasking server	UNIX is a multitasking operating system designed to make it easy to work with multiple processes.
Web servers	UNIX has long been the de facto operating system for Internet applications, including Web servers. UNIX is still the most popular platform for Internet Web servers today.
SMTP server	Electronic mail via SMTP has commonly resided on a UNIX system. Many organizations use UNIX as their primary mail server for its robustness and reliability.
News server	As with Web servers, Usenet news is commonly implemented via NNTP servers running on UNIX platforms.
File server	By adding large amounts of disk space to UNIX servers, they can make very effective file servers for both application and user directories.
Database server	Large scale, heavy duty, commercial databases are very common in the UNIX world. Commercial products such as Oracle, Sybase, and Informix all operate under multiple versions of UNIX.
CPU-intensive applications	Desktop UNIX workstations are commonly used in engineering and design for CPU-intensive applications such as CAD/CAM.

Table 1-1.   Common Roles for UNIX in the Corporate Information Systems Arena

NT Roles

Windows NT, unlike UNIX, evolved from the IBM personal computer platform. As a more powerful version of Microsoft Windows, NT's goal in life is to be Microsoft's workstation-quality operating system. Unlike UNIX, Microsoft Windows NT's history comes from the personal computing arena, with much more emphasis on graphical user interfaces and desktop applications.

In today's network, you might find Windows NT working as a BackOffice server, providing SQL Server database support, or providing electronic mail services via

Exchange. Other common uses for NT servers are as file, application, and print servers for PC desktop workstations running some Windows variant. Microsoft is making inroads into the Internet server market with its Internet Information Server, but UNIX still dominates in this area.

More and more companies are adopting Windows NT for both server and client platforms, but they do have concerns. Many information systems managers are concerned with NT's scalability and robustness. Others are hesitant to wholeheartedly adopt "the Microsoft way."

Advantages and Disadvantages

Nowadays, distinctions between the two operating systems are starting to blur as Windows NT begins to mature as a product. Mixed environments are becoming increasingly common. Through integration, businesses can leverage the operating system strengths that best suit their needs. For example, a UNIX server might provide your Internet backbone—serving as the Web server platform and providing a news and email gateway. Some people might run Windows 95 or Windows NT workstations within a Windows NT network. UNIX users in the same network might use applications like Microsoft Word or Microsoft Project (located on a Windows NT server) on their workstation by running Citrix's WinDD and sharing files exported via NFS from an NT workstation or via Samba.

Neither operating system is the perfect solution for all situations. You need to carefully evaluate which operating system, or combination of services from different operating systems, will serve you better. Both UNIX and NT have distinct advantages and disadvantages. Table 1-2 lists some of the advantages and disadvantages of UNIX.

Advantages—UNIX	Disadvantages—UNIX
Stable	Comes in many different varieties, many with subtle differences
Proven reliability	
Scales well	Servers and workstations tend to be expensive
Powerful	
Supported by multiple vendors	UNIX administration is a specialized skill
Provides excellent automation & scripting capabilities	
	Commands tend to be cryptic
Provides backbone for most Internet services, such as NNTP, HTTP, and SMTP	Lacks the same desktop user applications as are available on PC platforms
Is an "open" system	

Table 1-2.   UNIX Has Its Advantages and Disadvantages

Advantages—Windows NT	Disadvantages—Windows NT
Servers and workstations tend to be cheaper than for UNIX , except for free	Provided by a single vendor
	Stability and reliability have yet to be conclusively proven
UNIX versions such as Linux	Owned by Microsoft, and is subject to
Typically easier to administer and use	their design plans—is a "closed"
Wide variety of third-party user applications	system
	Lacks native scripting and process
Backwards compatibility with many 16-bit Windows applications	automation tools, although these are available from third-party developers

Table 1-3.   Windows NT Has Its Advantages and Disadvantages

Just as UNIX works better in some situations than in others, Microsoft Windows NT has its own set of advantages and disadvantages, as shown in Table 1-3.

SUMMARY

So where do you go from here? UNIX and NT both seem to be facts of life in today's office network. Although they evolved from very different backgrounds, both operating systems are overlapping in the services that they now provide.

Your goal, as a system administrator, is to implement effective strategies for maximizing your computing resources. If you are running a mixed network with both NT and UNIX systems, the chances are that you will want to develop some type of interoperability. Also, the chances are that you are much more familiar with one of these two operating systems than you are with the other.

In this book, we attempt to present ideas and solutions to help you succeed at integrating your NT and UNIX environments. This book is by no means complete; new products and strategies are being developed daily. However, in this book, we will address some of the most common problems and concerns that you may encounter, and present workable solutions where possible.

CHAPTER 2

NT File Services
on UNIX

UNIX and Windows NT have taken different routes as they have become common operating systems in today's computing environment. It is now somewhat normal for UNIX system administrators to find themselves handed a few NT workstations to administer, or for the NT and PC support group to have to design networks and support UNIX workstations.

When faced with this type of environment, the creative system administrator will look for ways to get Windows NT and UNIX working together to maximize system resources and user productivity. One way to accomplish this is to provide cross-platform file services and print services from your servers.

CROSS-PLATFORM SERVICES TO THE RESCUE

Cross-platform file services allow you to maximize the use of your file servers by providing access to clients of a different operating system. Cross-platform print services maximize the use of printers that would otherwise be unavailable to non-UNIX clients.

In this chapter, we will look at the issue of cross-platform file services, specifically, providing Windows NT-accessible file services from a UNIX platform. We will look at some of the issues involved when working with different file systems, describe the common network protocols involved, and explore some of the tools that are available to facilitate UNIX-to-NT file system services.

NOTE: In case you are wondering, cross-platform file services work both ways. In addition to UNIX providing file services for Windows NT, an NT server can be used to provide UNIX-accessible file services as well. See Chapter 3 for more information on UNIX file services on Windows NT servers.

INTRODUCTION TO SMB

Let's assume, for the sake of this chapter, that you have a group of UNIX servers that provide file services and application services for desktop UNIX workstations. Then, out of the blue, you find yourself having to support Microsoft clients as well. The reasons why don't particularly matter. In fact, no one probably consulted you at all before installing Windows NT; they just expect you to make it work!

In this situation, an effective solution could be to make your UNIX systems act as servers for the NT systems. In order to do this, you first need make the two systems communicate. To make them communicate, you need to know a little about SMB.

SMB is an abbreviation for the *Server Message Block* protocol, and it is the standard protocol that Windows NT uses for sharing file and print services. It was designed as a protocol for sharing files, printers, and ports between computers. It also supports sharing communications elements, such as mailslots and named pipes. It was first developed by Microsoft and Intel as the Open-NET File Sharing Protocol, released in 1987.

SMB operates in a request-response fashion, wherein the client sends requests, contained in Server Message Blocks (SMBs), to the server. The server receives these SMBs, interprets them, and sends a response back to the client. Whenever a computer shares a resource over the network via SMB, it becomes a server in this scenario. When a computer attaches to a shared resource, it becomes a client. In Windows NT, it is possible to act as both a server and a client simultaneously. SMB communication takes place by using the NetBIOS interface, which can operate over a variety of protocols.

NOTE: In a mixed NT and UNIX environment, the most common use of NetBIOS is called NetBIOS over TCP/IP, also known as NetBT. For more information on NetBIOS and NetBT, see Chapter 7.

Once a client connects to a server and is authenticated, the client can proceed to send commands to the server to open files, read and write files, close files, delete files, search directories, and execute other file and directory commands. These commands are encapsulated in specially formatted SMBs. There are different formats of SMBs to handle the different commands available. In addition, the SMB protocol has evolved into different protocol variants.

The SMB protocol provides two levels of security in its security models. The first security model supported by SMB is *share level security.* Under the share level security model, shared resources, known as *shares,* can be assigned a password. Knowing the password will grant a user access to the share. The second type of SMB security is known as *user level security.* With user level security, access protections are applied to individual files, and access rights are determined on a per-user basis. A user must be authenticated by the share server and assigned a numeric user ID. This user ID is then compared to the access protections assigned to each file.

CIFS—COMMON INTERNET FILE SYSTEM

Microsoft, the original developer of SMB, is busy cranking out a new and improved file and print sharing protocol. The *Common Internet File System (CIFS)* is designed to be a viable alternative to Sun's WebNFS protocol and to support file and printer sharing over the World Wide Web.

CIFS has several advantages over SMB, with support for TCP/IP and DNS being among the most visible. Under CIFS, server names are actually DNS names, complete with host and domain components. This change moves CIFS away from the limited NetBIOS name structure, where no domain information is available. CIFS also supports such developments as Unicode file names for internationalization, as well as the extended file attributes found in most modern file systems.

CIFS has not yet been widely adopted. Microsoft has offered it to the Internet Engineering Task Force as a draft standard, and many vendors have pledged support for this protocol. Currently, however, the two sides of the UNIX-to-NT filesharing coin remain SMB and NFS.

INTRODUCTION TO SAMBA

In order to provide NT-native file system support and print sharing from a UNIX file server to NT workstations, you must find a way to convince UNIX to provide SMB protocol support. One of the easiest ways to provide file and print sharing is with the *Samba* package. Samba, developed in Australia by Andrew Tridgell, is an SMB server package that runs under UNIX. By using Samba, UNIX systems can create shares that can be used by Windows-based computers. In addition, Samba provides tools that allow UNIX users to attach to shares from Windows computers and to transfer files.

NOTE: In addition to running on UNIX servers, Samba also runs under VMS, NetWare, and OS/2.

Samba runs on many different varieties of UNIX. Currently, Samba is available for the following operating systems:

- ▼ SunOS
- SOLARIS 2.2 and above
- Linux, with and without shadow passwords
- SVR4
- ULTRIX
- OSF/1 (DEC Alpha only)
- OSF/1 with NIS and Fast Crypt (DEC Alpha only)
- OSF/1 V2.0 Enhanced Security (DEC Alpha only)
- AIX
- BSDI
- NetBSD
- SEQUENT
- HP-UX
- SGI, including IRIX 4.*x.x* and IRIX 5.*x.x*
- FreeBSD
- NeXT 3.2 and above
- NeXT OS 2.*x*
- NeXT OS 3.0

- ISC SVR3V4 in POSIX mode
- ISC SVR3V4 in iBCS2 mode
- A/UX 3.0
- SCO with shadow passwords
- SCO with shadow passwords, without YP
- SCO with TCB passwords
- SCO 3.2v2 (ODT 1.1) with TCP passwords
- Intergraph
- DGUX
- ▲ Apollo Domain/OS sr10.3 (BSD4.3)

With this many operating systems supported, chances are that there is a version available for your particular type of UNIX. Samba is freely available under the terms of the GNU Public License and can be downloaded from the primary Samba website at **http://lake.canberra.edu.au/pub/samba/samba.html**. This site is an excellent source for Samba related information, documentation, and mailing lists, as well.

Before you dismiss Samba as yet another free software solution and head off in search of "real" software, consider how many people are using Samba. The Samba website has a survey, which lists many of the Samba installations around the world. For example, Bank of America has about 1,200 Samba hosts, providing services to 15,000 clients!

COMPILING AND INSTALLING SAMBA

The first step in setting up a Samba server is to download the Samba software. Fire up your favorite web browser and head down under to the main Samba website, located at **http://lake.canberra.edu.au/pub/samba/samba.html**. From here, you will find links to the source distribution, as well as to the various binary distributions. Samba is available in precompiled binary format for a variety of UNIX systems. However, most system administrators will probably prefer to download the source distribution and custom build Samba to meet their needs. This way, you know that no one did strange things to your code, and you have the source on hand if you need to make modifications, patches, or enhancements.

Put the source distribution in its own directory on your system, preferably wherever you keep source distributions for other packages, and extract it from the archive file that you downloaded. Once you have unarchived the distribution, you should see a directory named something like *samba-1.9.16p11*. Change into this directory and you're ready to start building the distribution.

NOTE: For detailed instructions on how to install Samba, consult the file *INSTALL.txt* that comes with the Samba distribution.

Editing the Makefile

The first step in building the distribution is to configure the file that controls the build process, known as the *Makefile*. Change directory to the *source* directory, make a backup copy of this file, and then edit the original with your favorite UNIX text editor.

At the top of the *Makefile*, you will see some configuration lines like these:

```
# The directories to put things in. If you use multiple
# architectures or share the samba binaries across NFS then
# you will probably want to change this layout.
BASEDIR = /usr/local/samba
BINDIR = $(BASEDIR)/bin
SBINDIR = $(BASEDIR)/bin
LIBDIR = $(BASEDIR)/lib
VARDIR = $(BASEDIR)/var
```

The information in these lines determines where Samba is installed. By default, Samba is installed in the */usr/local/samba* directory. If you need it to be installed somewhere else, change the value of the "BASEDIR" variable. For example, if you wanted to install Samba in */usr/local/utils/samba* instead, you would edit "BASEDIR" to be

```
BASEDIR = /usr/local/utils/samba
```

NOTE: Lines starting with the # character in the Makefile are comments and are ignored during the build process.

In addition to changing the base directory where Samba is installed, there are several additional lines that allow you to change where specific files are installed. Simply read through the first page or so of the *Makefile* to find the appropriate entries. The comments are very helpful.

Once you have decided where to install Samba, you need to configure the *Makefile* so that it compiles for your particular version of UNIX. As you scroll down through the *Makefile*, you will see sections for several different operating systems, all commented out, similar to these:

```
# This is for SUNOS 4. Use the SUNOS5 entry for Solaris 2.
# Note that you cannot use Suns "cc" compiler
# as it's not an Ansi-C compiler. Get gcc or acc.
# Note that if you have adjunct passwords you may need the GETPWANAM
# or PWDAUTH option. There have been reports that using
# PWDAUTH may crash your pwdauthd server so GETPWANAM is preferable
# (and probably faster)
# contributed by Andrew.Tridgell@anu.edu.au
```

```
# FLAGSM = -DSUNOS4
# LIBSM =
# AWK = nawk

# Use this for Linux with shadow passwords
# contributed by Andrew.Tridgell@anu.edu.au
# add -DLINUX_BIGCRYPT if you have shadow passwords
# but don't have the
# right libraries and includes
# FLAGSM = -DLINUX -DSHADOW_PWD
# LIBSM = -lshadow

# Use this for Linux without shadow passwords
# contributed by Andrew.Tridgell@anu.edu.au
# AXPROC defines DEC Alpha Processor
# FLAGSM = -DLINUX -DAXPROC
# FLAGSM = -DLINUX
# LIBSM =

# Use this for Linux with shadow passwords and quota
# contributed by xeno@mix.hive.no
# Tested on the 1.3.57 kernel and ext2fs filesystem.
# Notes:
# /usr/include/sys/quota.h must be a symlink to
# /usr/include/linux/quota.h
# The directory quota here must be a symlink to your quota package.
# I just do 'ln -sf /usr/src/quota-1.50 quota' in this directory to
# get it to work.
# FLAGSM = -O3 -m486 -DLINUX -DSHADOW_PWD -DQUOTAS
# LIBSM = -lshadow

# This is for SUNOS5.4 and later (also known as Solaris 2.4 and
# later)
# contributed by Andrew.Tridgell@anu.edu.au
# FLAGSM = -DSUNOS5 -DSHADOW_PWD -DNETGROUP
# LIBSM = -lsocket -lnsl
# AWK = nawk
```

This is only a sample of the configuration entries in the Samba *Makefile*. There is an entry for each operating system that Samba supports. To configure the Samba installation for your particular version of UNIX, find the appropriate section and uncomment the configuration flags. For example, if we were installing on a Linux system without shadow passwords running on an Intel processor, we would modify the comments in the following section of the *Makefile*:

```
# Use this for Linux without shadow passwords
# contributed by Andrew.Tridgell@anu.edu.au
# AXPROC defines DEC Alpha Processor
# FLAGSM = -DLINUX -DAXPROC
FLAGSM = -DLINUX
LIBSM =
```

Similarly, if we were installing on a Sun, running Solaris 2.4 or later, we would use the following section instead:

```
# This is for SUNOS5.4 and later (also known as Solaris 2.4 and
# later)
# contributed by Andrew.Tridgell@anu.edu.au
FLAGSM = -DSUNOS5 -DSHADOW_PWD -DNETGROUP
LIBSM = -lsocket -lnsl
AWK = nawk
```

CAUTION: Make sure that you only enable one operating system section of the *Makefile*, as Samba will not build correctly if multiple sections are uncommented. If you do uncomment multiple sections, and Samba manages to build, it may behave unpredictably.

Building Samba

After you have modified the *Makefile* so that you can build Samba for your particular version of UNIX, simply issue the *make* command at the UNIX prompt to build the Samba distribution. You will see a lot of messages produced by the compiler during the build process. If you have trouble with the build, or you just want to keep a record of the build messages for reference, you can capture the output to a file with the command

```
# make | tee /usr/local/samba/buildlog.txt
```

After Samba compiles and links, you can install Samba by issuing the *make install* command. You need to be logged in as *root* in order to issue *install* Samba. The *make install* command copies the various pieces of the Samba distribution to their proper locations in your file system, and installs the Samba *man* (short for manual) pages in the appropriate directories.

NOTE: If you are a bit paranoid about running install scripts blindly, most versions of UNIX allow you to see what the *make install* command will do before actually doing it. If your version of *make* supports the -n option, you can type

```
make -n install
```

This will cause *make* to go through the steps of the install process and print out what it is doing, without actually doing anything.

At this point you should have a basic Samba configuration installed. The next step in the process is to configure Samba for your particular environment.

CONFIGURING SAMBA

Before you can use Samba as an NT file service provider, you have to configure it properly. When you configure Samba, you set its operational parameters, create entries for the directories that you want to share, and make network printers available. Samba configuration also allows you to establish user access permissions for shares.

Virtually all parts of the Samba configuration process are managed by a central configuration file called *smb.conf*. If you chose to install Samba in its default location, the file should be located in the */usr/local/samba/lib* directory. The file is in ASCII format and is editable by your favorite UNIX text editor.

The syntax of the *smb.conf* file is pretty straightforward. The file is broken into sections, with the section names in square brackets. Within each section, parameters are set by statements in a "name = value" format. The easiest way to get familiar with the Samba configuration file is to work through the details of one. The following listing shows a sample *smb.conf* file:

```
[global]
    printing = bsd
    printcap name = /etc/printcap
    load printers = yes
    guest account = pcguest
;   This next option sets a separate log file for each client. Remove
;   it if you want a combined log file.
    log file = /usr/local/samba/log.%m
;   You will need a world readable lock directory
;   and "share modes=yes"
```

```
;   if you want to support the file sharing modes for multiple users
;   of the same files
;   lock directory = /usr/local/samba/var/locks
;   share modes = yes

[homes]
    comment = Home Directories
    browseable = no
    read only = no
    create mode = 0750

[printers]
    comment = All Printers
    browseable = no
    printable = yes
    public = no
    writable = no
    create mode = 0700

; you might also want this one, notice that it is
; read only so as not to give
; people without an account write access.
;
; [tmp]
;    comment = Temporary file space
;    path = /tmp
;    read only = yes
;    public = yes
;
; Other examples.
;
; A private printer, usable only by fred. Spool data
; will be placed in fred's
; home directory. Note that fred must have
; write access to the spool directory,
; wherever it is.
[fredsprn]
    comment = Fred's Printer
    valid users = fred
    path = /homes/fred
    printer = freds_printer
    public = no
    writable = no
    printable = yes
```

```
;
; A private directory, usable only by fred.
; Note that fred requires write
; access to the directory.
[fredsdir]
    comment = Fred's Service

    path = /usr/somewhere/private
    valid users = fred
    public = no
    writable = yes
    printable = no
;
; A publicly accessible directory, but read only,
; except for people in the staff group
[public]
    comment = Public Stuff
    path = /usr/somewhere/public
    public = yes
    writable = no
    printable = no
    write list = @staff
;
; a service which has a different directory for each
; machine that connects this allows you to tailor configurations
; to incoming machines. You could also use the %u option to
; tailor it by username. The %m gets replaced with the machine
; name that is connecting.
[pchome]
  comment = PC Directories
  path = /usr/pc/%m
  public = no
  writable = yes
;
;
; A publicly accessible directory, read/write to all users.
; Note that all files created in the directory by users will
; be owned by the default user, so any user with access can
; delete any other user's files. Obviously this
; directory must be writable by the default user. Another user
; could of course be specified, in which case all files would be
; owned by that user instead.
[public]
    path = /usr/somewhere/else/public
```

```
    public = yes
    only guest = yes
    writable = yes
    printable = no
;
;
; The following two entries demonstrate how to share a
; directory so that two users can place files there that
; will be owned by the specific users. In this setup, the
; directory should be writable by both users and should have
; the sticky bit set on it to prevent abuse. Obviously this
; could be extended to as many users as required.
[myshare]
    comment = Mary's and Fred's stuff
    path = /usr/somewhere/shared
    valid users = mary fred
    public = no
    writable = yes
    printable = no
    create mask = 0765
```

Special Sections

In addition to the custom sections that control access to shares, the *smb.conf* file has three special sections, [global], [homes], and [printers]. Let's look at these first.

Global Section

The [global] section is used to configure parameters that apply to the server as a whole, and to provide defaults for other sections. Take a look at the [global] section from the previous sample configuration file:

```
[global]
    printing = bsd
    printcap name = /etc/printcap
    load printers = yes
    guest account = pcguest
;   This next option sets a separate log file for each client. Remove
;   it if you want a combined log file.
    log file = /usr/local/samba/log.%m
```

The first entry tells Samba what type of printing subsystem is available on your UNIX system. Different versions of UNIX handle printing differently. The second line lets

Samba know where the printer characteristics are defined. The "load printers = yes" line tells Samba to go ahead and load all the printers in the *printcap* file so that they are available for browsing. The next line specifies a username for a guest account entry. This username is used to authenticate guests for services that allow guest users to connect. On some systems, this can be set to the username *nobody*; however, on other systems, the *nobody* user will not be able to print. This username typically shows up in the password file as a valid, non-privileged user that is not able to log in. The last line in the [global] section sets access logging with a log file for each client that connects. The "%m" parameter in the log file name will be replaced with the client name, so that there will be a separate log file for each client.

Homes Section

The [homes] section allows clients to connect to a user's home directory, without having a specific entry for the directory in the *smb.conf* file. When a service request is made, the rest of the *smb.conf* file is searched to find the specific service that was requested. If the service is not found, and the [homes] section is present, the password file is searched to find the home directory for the user. Samba then makes the user's home directory available as a share by cloning the [homes] section entry. Here is a sample [homes] entry:

```
[homes]
    comment = Home Directories
    browseable = no
    read only = no
    create mode = 0750
```

The "comment" field is used by a client attempting to see what shares are available on this server. The next parameter controls whether Samba will display home directories in the network browse list. The "read only" parameter controls whether a user will be able to create and change files in their home directory. The "create mode" parameter sets the file permissions for a user's home directory. In this case, permission is set to read/write/execute for the user, and read/execute for group access.

NOTE: UNIX file permissions can be represented in octal format as well as alphabetic format. See the *man* page for the UNIX *chmod* command for more information on permissions.

Printers Section

The [printers] section is used in a manner similar to the [homes] section. If the [printers] section is present, a user can connect to any printer defined in the UNIX host's */etc/printcap* file, even if the printer does not have a service entry in the *smb.conf* file. Take a look at the [printers] section from the previous sample configuration file:

```
[printers]
    comment = All Printers
    browseable = no
    printable = yes
    public = no
    writable = no
    create mode = 0700
```

Some of these parameters will look familiar from the other two special sections we have just discussed. The "comment," "browsable," and "create mode" parameters are the same as you've just seen. The "printable" parameter simply tells Samba that this is a printer resource that you can print to. Setting the "public" parameter to "no" disables guest access and prevents unauthorized users from printing to printers on your system. The "writable" parameter is set to "no" because this is a printer resource, not a file system resource.

Sharing File Systems

Once you've set up your system defaults for general operation, home directories, and printing, you can move on to setting up shared directories. Configuring a share with Samba is very easy: simply add a new section for the share you want to create, and fill in the parameters. There are many different parameter options that you can provide when creating shares, depending on how you wish to limit access, browsing, permissions, etc.

NOTE: For a complete list of all the parameters allowed in the *smb.conf* file, see the man page for *smb.conf*.

Let's look at a couple of examples of creating a share. In the first example, we are going to create a shared directory that is only accessible by one user.

```
[testshare]
    comment = A Sample Test Share
    path = /usr/local/private
    valid users = skippy
    browseable = yes
    public = no
    writable = yes
    printable = no
```

You've seen a lot of these parameters before, from reading about the special sections in the Samba configuration file, so we won't bore you to death going over them again.

The two new lines that are particularly interesting are the "path = /usr/local/private" line and the "valid users = skippy" line. The "path" parameter tells Samba which directory to make available as a network share; in this case, it is the */usr/local/private* directory. The "valid users" parameter is used to restrict access to a particular user on the system.

Let's look at one more share definition, for completeness.

```
[public]
    comment = Public Stuff
    path = /usr/local/public
    public = yes
    writable = no
    printable = no
    write list = @staff
```

This particular share definition creates a share named "public" that is designed to be readable by anyone, with only users in the "staff" group having write access. By setting the "public" parameter to "yes," Samba allows guest access to this account, with no write access. However, the "write list" parameter allows you to create a list of users who can write to this directory, overriding the "writable" parameter.

In the case of this share, the user list who can write to this directory is set to *@staff*. The @ symbol tells Samba to interpret the name that follows as a UNIX group name, defined in the */etc/group* file. Alternatively, you can list usernames separated by commas in this type of list. You can also mix usernames and group names, as long as the group names are preceded by the @ symbol.

NOTE: If you need to restrict access to certain shares, either for read or write access, consider creating UNIX groups and giving those groups access with the "read list" and "write list" Samba parameters.

USER AUTHENTICATION WITH SAMBA

In order to access resources that have been shared with Samba, users need to be authenticated. User authentication allows Samba to restrict access to shares and to control read and write permissions for files and directories. Currently, Samba supports three different mechanisms for authenticating user access to shares, all of which are controlled by the "security" keyword in the *smb.conf* file.

Share Security

The *share* security option tells Samba to restrict access based on share permissions. This is the oldest security model available in Samba and provides the least security.

User Security

The *user* security option tells Samba to use username validation for access to network shares. When a user attempts to connect to a share on a Samba server, Samba attempts to validate the user's username and password in the local password file. If the user is validated, the user is granted or denied access to the share based on its share permissions. This option is very useful if your PC-based accounts have the same usernames as your UNIX-based accounts.

In order to use the user security option, you must create accounts on your UNIX system for all of your PC users that will be connecting to Samba shares. Some system administrators may be reluctant to do this, as this can greatly increase the number of user entries in the system password file and thus make password file management much more difficult.

Server Security

Fortunately, there is a solution to the problem of having to provide UNIX usernames for all your PC-based users. Samba now allows you to redirect all user authentication requests to a separate SMB server. This SMB server does not have to be another UNIX system running Samba; it can be any SMB server capable of authenticating users, such as a Windows NT computer. So, by electing to use the server security model, you can centralize all your PC usernames and passwords on an NT system and use that system for Samba authentication!

In order to set up server-based security, add two lines such as the following to the [global] section of the *smb.conf* file.

```
security=server
password server = NTSRV1
```

The first line, "security=server," tells Samba to use the server security model. The second line tells Samba which computer will act as the authentication server. You must specify the NetBIOS name for the authentication server, not its DNS name. Chances are that you will have to edit your */etc/hosts* file and add an entry for the authentication server's NetBIOS name.

NOTE: By using server authentication, you are trusting another server to accurately verify all users and authenticate them for you. Never rely on a password server that you do not trust completely!

The remote authentication server will authenticate all usernames and passwords automatically. If authentication should fail, Samba will resort to the user security model as a fallback mechanism.

PRINTING WITH SAMBA

Not only does Samba allow you to share file systems with clients, it allows you to share printers as well. When a PC-based client prints to a Samba server, the server receives the request, translates it, and passes it on to the UNIX printing system. Samba does not do the actual printing; it merely acts as the middleman.

Printing to UNIX Printers

Providing a printer configuration with Samba is very similar to sharing a file system. In fact, there are a couple of ways to do it. The easiest way to set up SMB printing is to create the [printers] special section of the *smb.conf* file and use it in conjunction with your UNIX */etc/printcap* file. Remember from earlier in this chapter that the [printers] section provides defaults for all printers in the */etc/printcap* file. If you add the directive "load printers = yes" to this section, Samba will load your */etc/printcap* file and apply all the defaults to the printers it finds there.

In order to print correctly, Samba needs to know what kind of printing subsystem your variety of UNIX supports. Samba supports several different printing subsystems. If your version of UNIX uses the *lpr* command, you should set "printing = bsd" in the [global] section of *smb.conf*. Similarly, if your UNIX uses the *lp* command, you should set "printing = sysv." HP-UX and AIX have their own print settings, "hpux" and "aix," respectively.

Samba uses the printing subsystem specified in the *smb.conf* file to determine what default commands to use for printing and print management. Usually, Samba makes reasonable guesses for the default commands. However, if you want total control, you can adjust the print commands directly within the Samba configuration file. There are several options that allow you to provide new commands for Samba to use. Three of the most common commands to customize are listed in Table 2-1.

In addition to using all the printers in the */etc/printcap* file via the [printers] section of your Samba configuration file, Samba also supports exporting individual printers as shared network printers. This is accomplished in much the same way as exporting individual shared file systems. By sharing individual printers instead of using the system default printers, you can prevent users from seeing all the printers on your system, restrict access to a certain subset of printers, and provide a finer level of control over each different printer.

To create a new shared printer, simply create a section for it in the Samba configuration file. Let's look at an example:

```
[graphicprt]
   comment = Graphics Staff Printer
   valid users = @graphics
   path = /var/spool/graphicsprt
   printer = graphics_prt001
   public = no
   writable = no
   printable = yes
```

Samba Directive	Example	Use
print command	print command = lpr -r -P%p %s	Samba uses this command as the actual command for printing a file. The *%p* macro gets replaced automatically with the name of the printer, and the *%s* macro is replaced with the name of the spool file to be printed.
lpq command	lpq command = lpq -P%p	This command is used to query the printing subsystem and return a list of jobs in a given printer. The *%p* macro is replaced with the name of the printer.
lprm command	lprm command = lprm -P%p %j	Samba uses this command to remove a job from a print spool. The *%j* macro is replaced by the job number returned from the *lpq* command.

Table 2-1. Common Print Command Customizations for Samba

We want to create a new printer share for use by staff in the graphics group. This configuration entry creates a new share with the SMB share name *graphicprt*. By using the "valid users = @graphics" directive, we limit access only to people in the graphics group. The "path" directive is used to direct print jobs to the appropriate spool directory, and the "printer" directive gives the name of the printer so that Samba can find it in */etc/printcap*. In addition, we've set the "public = no" directive to prevent guest users from printing to this printer.

That's all there is to it. As you can see, it is very simple to create and share a new printer definition with Samba. You can, of course, customize more details for individual printers by adding the appropriate configuration directives. For a complete list of the customization directives supported by Samba, see the *man* page for the *smb.conf* file.

Printing to PC Printers

Now that you've seen how easy it is to create new print shares via Samba, you're probably ready for something a bit more difficult. You're probably wondering if you can use Samba to print to PC-based printers in addition to sharing UNIX-based printers. Well, you can, but it's not a particularly easy task. Before attempting to use PC-based printers, you should have some familiarity with configuring UNIX-based printers and editing the */etc/printcap* file.

The first step to sharing a PC-based printer is to create an entry for that printer in the UNIX system's */etc/printcap* file. Here is an example *printcap* entry for a Hewlett-Packard DeskJet 870Cse printer:

```
dj870:\
    :cm= DeskJet 870Cse:\
    :sd=/var/spool/lpd/dj870:\
    :af=/var/spool/lpd/dj870/acct:\
    :if=/usr/local/etc/smbprint:\
    :mx=0:\
    :lp=/dev/null:
```

This syntax looks horribly cryptic, but that is just the way the */etc/printcap* file works. One line in this entry that is particularly interesting is the line

```
:if=/usr/local/etc/smbprint:\
```

which tells the printing system to use the file */usr/local/etc/smbprint* as an input filter. This file is a shell script that actually calls the appropriate Samba program to print to the PC computer.

NOTE: For those UNIX gurus among us, you may have noticed an accounting file line in the /etc/printcap entry, specifically, ":af=/var/spool/lpd/dj870/acct:". This line must be present for printing to work. The *smbprint* script uses the accounting file entry to determine the path to a special configuration file.

The detailed syntax of the *printcap* file is beyond the scope of this chapter. For more information on the inner workings of the *printcap* file, see the *man* page for *printcap*.

Next, you need to provide Samba with some configuration information for this printer. In the */var/spool/lpd/PRINTNAME* directory, where "PRINTNAME" is the name of the actual printer (in this case, dj870), use your favorite UNIX text editor to create a file named *.config*. This file should contain three lines that give the NetBIOS name of the PC with the printer attached, the name of the printer share, and the password required to connect to the shared printer. So, continuing on with our example, the file */var/spool/lpd/dj870/.config* might contain the following lines:

```
server=GRAPHSRV
service=HPDJ_870CSE
password=""
```

These entries tell Samba that the NetBIOS name of the PC server is "GRAPHSRV" and that it is sharing its printer with the share name "HPDJ_870CSE." No password is required to connect to this print service.

So you see, you can get Samba to print to a PC-based print share, but it is just a bit more complicated than printing to a UNIX-based share. If you want to see the ugly details of how this all works, take a look at the *smbprint* shell script that comes with the Samba distribution. This script handles the fine points of printing to PC-based shares and has some detailed examples.

RUNNING SAMBA

Wow! We're almost there. After all that configuration, you are finally ready to fire up Samba and get to work. However, before you actually start Samba, you should verify that your configuration file is correct and error-free. Samba provides the *testparm* program, which does this for you. If *testparm* gives you the OK that your configuration file will work, you can go ahead and start up Samba.

The actual Samba server consists of two UNIX daemons, *smbd* and *nmbd*. The *smbd* process is the daemon that provides SMB file and print service sharing. The *nmbd* daemon is a support process that provides NetBIOS name server support. In fact, *nmbd* can provide most of the functionality of a WINS server on Windows NT.

When starting the Samba daemons, you must decide whether to start them as daemons at boot time or to have them automatically started from *inetd*. Don't try to do both—bad things can happen to Samba if you do. Starting the Samba processes as daemons will cause them to run continuously, which takes up a little CPU time and process space. However, if run directly as daemons, the Samba processes will respond slightly faster to service requests. Starting the Samba processes from *inetd* will ensure that they only start when a request is sent; however, they will be slower to respond to connections, since the processes will have to be created each time a connection request comes in.

Starting Samba as a Daemon

Starting the Samba processes as daemons is very simple. Simply give the following two commands as *root:*

```
/usr/local/samba/bin/smbd -D
/usr/local/samba/bin/nmbd -D
```

Using the "-D" flag causes Samba to start as a daemon that will continue to run after the creating process is terminated. This is not the default behavior. You must use the "-D" flag if you want to run the processes as daemons.

In order to have the Samba processes start automatically, simply put the two preceding commands into your local startup script.

Starting Samba from inetd

The *inetd* process is a UNIX daemon that is charged with automatically starting other processes as requests come in for them. Since the *inetd* daemon starts other processes automatically, processes do not need to be running continuously, consuming CPU time and memory. The Samba processes can be started via *inetd* if necessary, but this can make Samba seem slower, as the processes will have to be started for every service request.

NOTE: The syntax of the *inetd* configuration files is different on different varieties of UNIX. Consult the man page for *inetd.conf* for the exact syntax for your platform.

To enable Samba via *inetd*, first edit the */etc/services* file with your favorite UNIX text editor. Look for entries for TCP port 139 and UDP port 137. If none are found, add the following lines to your */etc/services* file:

```
netbios-ns      137/udp
netbios-ssn     139/tcp
```

If you find service entries on UDP port 137 and TCP port 139, make a note of the service names. You will need them for the next step.

Next, you need to add entries into the *inetd.conf* file, so that *inetd* will be able to start the Samba processes. A typical set of entries would look like

```
netbios-ssn stream tcp nowait root /usr/local/samba/bin/smbd smbd
netbios-ns dgram udp wait root /usr/local/samba/bin/nmbd nmbd
```

Remember that the syntax of *inetd.conf* can differ. Check the *man* pages to be sure.

If you found entries for UDP port 137 and TCP port 139 when you checked the */etc/services* file earlier, compare the service names to the service names in the first column of these two *inetd.conf* entries. The service names must match exactly. Some versions of UNIX use different capitalization or use underscores instead of hyphens in the service names. If the service names on your system are different, change these *inetd.conf* entries to match.

At this point, you can simply restart the *inetd* process so that it will re-read its configuration file. Many versions of UNIX allow you to do *kill -HUP* on the process ID of *inetd*, to cause it to re-read its configuration file without having to stop and start the *inetd* process.

Using *smbclient*

Not only can Samba make UNIX directories and printers available as network shares to Windows computers via SMB, but you can also use Samba to access shared directories on other Windows computers as well. Samba provides a client program, appropriately named *smbclient*, that allows you to attach to other network shares.

The *smbclient* program provides a line mode interface similar to FTP that allows you to transfer files with a network share on another SMB server. It does not allow you to mount an SMB share as a local UNIX directory. You can also use *smbclient* to list the available shares on another server as well.

While there are several command line options available with *smbclient*, most users use the program to either query a server to find out what shares are available, or to connect to a server to transfer files. In order to list the shares available on a particular SMB server, use the "-L" option with *smbclient*, as in the following example:

```
smbclient -L -I ntsrv.mydomain.com
```

The second set of arguments, "-I ntsrv.mydomain.com," specifies the DNS host name or IP address of the server. Since UNIX, by default, doesn't know anything about NetBIOS names, the "-I" argument allows you to give the DNS name of the server instead. Without the "-I" argument, *smbclient* will treat the server name as a NetBIOS name and will attempt to resolve it via the standard NetBIOS name resolution process.

NOTE: For more information on how NetBIOS names are resolved, see "The NetBIOS API" section in Chapter 7.

The second common use for *smbclient* is to connect to a network share and exchange files. Let's assume that you want to connect to the service \\NTSRV\PUBLIC as the user smith. Using *smbclient*, the command would be

```
smbclient '\\NTSRV\PUBLIC' -I ntsrv.mydomain.com -U smith
```

Samba may prompt you for a password if one is required to connect to the service. Note that the NetBIOS name for the server and the share are enclosed in single quotes. This is to keep the UNIX shell from trying to translate the \ characters.

Once you have connected to a share, *smbclient* provides commands that are very similar to FTP. For example, you have *get*, *put*, *cd*, and *dir* available. For a complete list of commands, you can simply type **help** at the command prompt.

TOTALNET ADVANCED SERVER

Samba is by no means the only SMB server for UNIX, although it is one of the most popular. Another very popular alternative is the commercial product TotalNet Advanced

Server (TAS), developed by Syntax, Inc. Sun Microsystems has announced that it is shipping its new Netra™ NFS 150 Version 1.1 servers with a fully functional TAS server installed.

TAS is a robust client/server solution aimed at integrating dissimilar operating systems. It provides SMB-based connectivity to a variety of SMB clients, including Windows NT, LAN Manager, LAN Server, and DEC Pathworks. In addition to the SMB client connectivity, TAS goes a couple of steps further by providing NetWare connectivity via the IPX/SPX protocol suite, and Macintosh connectivity by using Appletalk. Each of these three areas—SMB, NetWare, and Macintosh—is referred to as a *realm* by TAS.

The TotalNet Advanced Server consists of several components. Administrative tasks are handled through a user-friendly HTML interface called *TotalAdmin*. The TotalAdmin interface allows system administrators to manage the TAS configuration from a standard web browser. By using a web browser management scheme, TotalAdmin provides a consistent interface for changing servers, service names, and passwords; viewing error logs; sharing new resources; and modifying security parameters. Since TotalAdmin is web-browser based, administrators can easily manage TAS remotely from any computer equipped with a web browser.

TAS also includes a component known as the *Enterprise Name Server*, which maintains a database of the NetBIOS names and machine addresses used by all computers in the network. This database is automatically updated with NetBIOS names and addresses.

TAS is a robust application server that makes it easier to connect UNIX and NT systems via SMB. Syntax has just released TAS version 5.0, which has a variety of features, including

▼ **Support for Unmodified Clients** There is no need to modify client operating system installations in order to have them work with TAS.

■ **Scalability** TAS is based on a multithreaded architecture that scales well to provide support for large numbers of clients.

■ **Username Mapping** TAS provides username mapping via a set of mapping files. These mapping files are used to map usernames from PCs to UNIX systems transparently.

■ **Unified File Name Mapping** TAS supports log filenames in all three supported realms and will map filenames as readably as possible, subject to the operating system limitations on particular clients.

■ **Security** TAS supports three different methods for authenticating users: proxy authentication, encrypted passwords, and clear text.

■ **Browsing** TAS supports Microsoft's browsing standards and can participate in network browsing.

▲ **Print Services** TAS provides access to print devices, whether they are attached to the TAS server, function as network printers, or are attached to network servers. TAS is also capable of providing print redirection to remote TAS servers and other SMB servers.

TAS Security

TAS is designed to have a flexible security policy that can be configured to suit the needs of the system administrator. Under TAS, user passwords can be transmitted either as clear text or in encrypted form.

Choosing clear text password transmission is less secure, but offers the most flexibility. Clear text passwords are managed with native UNIX tools such as the *passwd* program. By offering the most flexibility, clear text passwords may be stored in any supported UNIX authentication database, including NIS, NIS+, DCE, and the */etc/passwd* file.

Encrypted passwords offer a higher level of security than clear text passwords. When using encrypted passwords, user passwords are stored in a special TAS password file. The client encrypts a password with a one-way encryption algorithm and sends the password to the TAS server. The TAS server then validates the password against the TAS database. Using the encrypted password scheme requires you to use the *tnpasswd* utility program, supplied with TAS, for managing user passwords.

TAS also supports proxy authentication, similar to that found in Samba. With proxy authentication, another server, known as the *proxy server*, is used to authenticate user passwords. Since password authentication is delegated to another server, system administrators rely on the native security measures available on the proxy server. With proxy authentication, TAS has no impact on the password storage or management. When enabling proxy authentication for NetBIOS clients, the proxy server must understand the SMB protocol. Under NetWare, the proxy server must be a NetWare server. Proxy authentication is not supported for Macintosh clients running Appletalk.

Managing Usernames with TAS

Different operating systems support different standards for usernames. Under most versions of UNIX, usernames are limited to eight characters in length. However, under Windows NT, usernames can be up to 32 characters in length. In order to access UNIX services when being authenticated directory by TAS on UNIX, a user's PC username must match their UNIX username.

This issue creates problems when system administrators have already devised a naming convention and would normally have to change all PC usernames to match the more restrictive UNIX usernames. Fortunately, TAS provides a username mapping function.

Username mapping in TAS allows the system administrator to establish a mapping database that translates the PC username into a UNIX username. This mapping is performed on the server's side of the network conversation and is transparent to the user. In order to simplify management of the username mapping database, username mapping is managed via TAS's TotalAdmin web-based interface.

SUMMARY

One of the best ways to maximize a diverse UNIX and Windows NT environment is to implement file and printer sharing. This allows you to maximize your resources, both in terms of file servers and by making network printers available to users.

In this chapter, we looked at a couple of ways to implement file and print sharing. The Server Message Block, or SMB, protocol is commonly used by Microsoft Windows NT and Windows 95 as a filesharing mechanism. We introduced the SMB protocol and discussed how Microsoft uses it for file services. We also introduced the Common Internet File System (CIFS) as an up-and-coming protocol designed to support file and print sharing over the World Wide Web.

Next, we examined two different ways of implementing Windows-compatible file services on UNIX. The first, Samba, is a freely available SMB server implementation that runs under UNIX and provides the ability to create custom file shares. Samba can also be used to share home directories and UNIX printers. With a little creativity, Samba can be used to allow UNIX users to print to PC-based printers as well. Samba is very widely implemented, with some sites having thousands of servers and clients.

The second implementation that we examined is a commercial product from Syntax, Inc. Known as TotalNet Advanced Server, or TAS, this product provides SMB services from UNIX as well. In addition to providing SMB services, TAS also facilitates file and print sharing with NetWare and Appletalk-based computers.

As you can see, there are some very viable solutions available that provide NT file and print services from UNIX. In the next chapter, we will look at the reverse side of the coin, namely, how to provide UNIX-accessible file services from NT systems by using the NFS protocol.

CHAPTER 3

UNIX File Services on NT

Information is critical in business. People need access to many types of information—spreadsheets, reports, business modes, schedules, etc.—and to the applications that manipulate that information. One of the biggest challenges in distributed, heterogeneous networks is giving users access to the files and applications they need, wherever those files exist on the network. Network File Sharing (NFS) allows UNIX and Windows NT users to easily access files on either platform.

WHAT IS NFS?

The Network File System (NFS) was one of the most important technologies to emerge from the Ethernet-TCP/IP-UNIX environment of the 1980s. It was announcemed in 1984, and has become a de facto standard for distributed file services in multivendor internetwork environments. In a nutshell, NFS hides underlying details about where files are physically stored. It allows files that are physically located elsewhere to appear as if they are part of a local file system. NFS is both a standard specification and a set of software products that enable file access across a network.

NFS primarily utilizes two different protocol mechanisms: the External Data Representation (XDR) protocol, which operates at the presentation layer, and Remote Procedure Calls (RPC), which operate at the session layer. These two protocols are the foundation for all NFS interaction. RPC provides the basis for message exchanges between clients and servers. The XDR protocol provides data translation between different types of computers and operating systems.

From a user perspective, NFS is transparent. Depending on how NFS has been set up, users may be able to log onto any workstation in their network and see their files. Files that are physically under a different operating system are just as easily accessed as those under the operating system they're using.

From a system administrator standpoint, NFS is a distributed file system. An NFS server has one or more file systems that are mounted by NFS clients. To NFS clients, remote disks look like local disks. This also means that files on an NFS server can be accessed by many different NFS client computers, centralizing file utilization.

NOTE: A common use for NFS includes creating a common area for people to get files.

While NFS provides a mechanism to share files, it doesn't provide the capability to run applications across platforms. For example, if you're a UNIX user and have an NT directory mounted through NFS, you can change directory to what looks like a fairly normal UNIX directory. However, if there are NT programs in that directory—say, Microsoft Word or Intuit Quicken—you won't be able to run them. To do that, you need desktop application emulator software like Tektronix's WinDD or Sun's WABI. For more information on this topic, see Chapter 13.

NOTE: Although users on different operating systems can't run executables through NFS, those who are on the same operating system can. This is useful, for instance, when you want to set up an area for people to run common software.

A BRIEF HISTORY OF NFS

NFS was originally developed by Sun Microsystems, Inc., in the mid 1980s, to simplify the sharing of files between different types of computers. Sun published the specifications and created a UNIX implementation, which they now also license to other developers.

NOTE: Companies that currently license and resell NFS include IBM, NEC, Pyramid Technology, Digital Equipment Corporation, Hewlett-Packard, Fujitsu, NCR, and Silicon Graphics, to name but a few.

Since its initial development, NFS has grown to support scalable, high-performance global filesharing in environments consisting of UNIX workstations and servers, minicomputers, mainframes, and PCs. Today, NFS is the de facto standard for distributed file access and is usually bundled with UNIX operating systems. Because the specifications are in the public domain, many different hardware and software vendors have implemented NFS on a variety of hardware platforms.

TECHNICAL OVERVIEW

NFS is both scalable and flexible. It supports small to large networks, as well as a wide range of hardware and operating systems. It can effectively support small networks of less than 10 clients or large networks of more than 25,000 clients, physically scattered over the globe.

NFS is built on the RPC protocol and imposes a client-server relationship on the computers that use it. This means that NFS software is installed on the NFS server and on each NFS client. An NFS server is a host that owns one or more file systems and makes them available on a network. NFS clients then mount file systems from one or more servers. In addition, NFS provides file locking services, which control multiple accesses to the same file.

In an NFS environment, a Windows NT system can act either as an NFS client or an NFS server. As an NT NFS client of a UNIX NFS server, Windows NT users could access remote UNIX NFS servers as if they were local file systems. As an NT NFS server with UNIX clients, UNIX users could access remote NT file systems.

FILE PERMISSIONS

One of the key functions NFS software performs when transferring files between NT and UNIX is preserving file permissions. This can be tricky, because NT's NTFS (NT File System) supports a higher degree of access control than is possible under UNIX.

Windows NT Permissions

Under Windows NT NTFS, each file and directory is owned by one account. The owner of this account is the only one who has the right to access, modify, and secure it from outside access. By default, the owner is the user who created the resource.

NOTE: An exception to this is a user who is in the Administrator group. In this case, all users who are in the Administrator group co-own any resource created by any group member.

In addition to permissions, each file and directory has at least one access control list (ACL) entry that defines a user's or group's access to a file or directory. By using multiple ACL's, you have a great deal of control over who has access to what.

Windows NT User Permissions

The owner of a file or directory may grant a user the following types of access:

No Access	directory or file	User cannot access the file or directory by any means.
List	directory only	User can view the contents of a directory, but cannot access those contents.
Read	directory or file	User can read files or execute programs, but cannot modify them in any way.
Add	directory only	User can write files to a directory, but cannot view or read the contents of the directory.
Add and Read	directory or file	User can view, read, and save new files, but cannot modify existing files.
Change	directory or file	User can view, read, execute, or save new files; modify or delete existing files; change file attributes; or delete the directory.
Full Control	directory or file	User can read, execute, modify, delete, change permissions, or take ownership away from the current owner.

Special Access   directory or file   Allows the owner or any user granted "P" permission to custom-build an access control entry for an ACL.

Table 3-1 shows directory permissions required for each type of access.
Table 3-2 shows file permissions required for each type of access.

Windows NT Group Permissions

Windows NT contains two types of groups—local groups and built-in groups. *Local groups* are used to assign rights and permissions to a local system and resources. They are user-defined and are used to assign permissions to files and directories. *Built-in groups* are designed for system management. They are predefined and preassigned specific rights aimed at system management. Both types of groups can contain local users, domain users, and global groups. From trusted domains, each type of group can also contain users and global groups.

Level	Read (r)	Execute (x)	Write (w)	Delete (d)	Change Permissions (p)	Take Ownership (o)
No Access						
List	√	√				
Read	√	√				
Add	√	√				
Add and Read	√	À	À	À		
Change	√	À	À	À		
Full Control	√	À	À	À	À	À
Special Access (any combination)	√	√	À	À	À	À

Table 3-1. Windows NT Directory Permissions

Level	Read (r)	Execute (x)	Write (w)	Delete (d)	Change Permissions (p)	Take Ownership (o)
No Access						
Read	√	√				
Add and Read	√	√				
Change	√	√	À	√		
Full Control	√	√	À	√	√	√
Special Access (any combination)	√	√	À	√	√	√

Table 3-2.   Windows NT File Permissions

UNIX Permissions

In UNIX there are three categories of access permissions: *user, group,* and *other* (also known as *world*) for files and directories. Each category is set to individually enable or disable read (r), write (w), and execute (x) privileges. UNIX systems also store a numeric owner (UID) and group (GID) identifier for each file or directory. Together, access permissions and identifiers determine a user's access to a file or directory.

NOTE: UNIX permissions also determine the file type. For example, even if a file is really an executable, it cannot be run unless the execute (x) flag has been set.

The owner of a file or directory may grant the following types of access to themselves (owner), their group (group), or everyone else (other or world):

Read	directory or file	User can read a file or view contents of a directory.
Write	directory or file	User can modify or delete a file or directory. They can also create a new file or directory.
Execute	directory or file	User can *cd* to a directory, or execute a file.

Owners typically have *rwx* access, while group and world access are limited. However, the file owner can change this to be anything they want.

UNIX File Permissions

User permissions define access for a file's owner. Each user should have a different UID. When a user saves a file in NFS, the UNIX system automatically saves the UID in the file's directory entry, similar to a directory entry for a file under the NTFS or FAT file system. Each user who accesses the file with the same UID receives the owner's access permissions.

UNIX Group Permissions

Group permissions define access for all users who belong to a group. A user may be a member of several groups; however, only one group is "active" at a time. Each group has a unique GID. Similar to user permissions, when a user saves a file in NFS, the UNIX system saves the GID of the user's current group in the file's directory entry. Each user who accesses the file with the same GID receives the group's access permissions.

File Mapping

When you transfer files between UNIX and NT using NFS, file permissions must be mapped to equivalents on each system. The first step is to authenticate the user's identity. NFS software attempts to translate the user login ID to an equivalent login ID on the other system. If NFS can't translate the login ID, the next step is to use a translation table. If there isn't a translation, the NFS software can either assign an ID or end the connection.

NOTE: NT NFS products such as Hummingbird Communication NFS Maestro and NetManage's Chameleon™ NFS/X handle mapping in roughly the same way.

For example, when an NT user accesses a UNIX file system via NFS, the authentication process may use a special daemon on the UNIX system that attempts to translate the NT login ID to a UNIX account name. If the daemon can't translate the login ID, the NFS product uses a UID/GID translation table instead. If no translation is available, the NFS software can either assign an ID or end the connection.

NOTE: Most NT NFS products maintain a translation table. It usually must be set up before using the NFS software.

When a UNIX user creates a file under NTFS, the NFS software often uses NTFS's Special Access permission flags rather than standard NTFS access types (Add, Full Control, etc.). This allows NFS to assign the appropriate access to files. For example, under UNIX, write permission also implies delete. Depending on the NT NFS product you choose, the software may set Special Access flags for both write and delete.

The user, group, and other UNIX access permissions directly map to three Windows NT ACL entries for a file on NTFS. Table 3-3 shows this relationship.

UNIX permission	Windows NT ACL
owner	user permissions
group	group permissions
other (or world)	group Everyone permission

Table 3-3.   Equivalent UNIX and NT File Permissions

File mapping is handled differently among the various NT NFS products. As you look at different NT NFS products, there a few questions you may want to consider:

▼ How does the software handle special file and directory permissions in place of NTFS's default permissions?

■ How does the software handle SID (system ID) mappings between NT users and groups and UID and GIDs on UNIX counterparts?

▲ How does the software handle naming differences between UNIX and NT?

NFS FILE NAMING ISSUES

One problem that you may run into when integrating UNIX and NT file systems with NFS is the way the two platforms handle alphabetic case in filenames. UNIX file systems are completely case sensitive. This means that the files *TEST*, *test*, and *Test* can all exist in the same directory. These names refer to three different, distinct files.

NT, by comparison, preserves filename case, but does not recognize differences in case. Thus, if you stored a file with the name *TEST*, it would be written to disk as *TEST*. However, you could refer to the file in a program as *test*, and NT would open the file *TEST*. This prevents you from having multiple files with the same name, differing only by case, in the same directory. In fact, some NT programs will change the case of the filename when they save the file to disk.

Since UNIX is case sensitive, and NT is not, problems can occur when trying to access files via NFS. UNIX clients will attempt to map the filename exactly as you typed it, so you must get the case correct. NT clients going to UNIX servers may or may not change the case of the filename before sending it to the UNIX system as a request. Different NT NFS programs handle filename case differently.

NFS ON UNIX

Since we're looking at using NFS as a means of sharing file systems between UNIX and NT, let's start off by exploring how NFS works in the UNIX environment. Since NFS is the de facto method of sharing file systems under UNIX, virtually all UNIX systems are already capable of functioning as either an NFS client or NFS server. Sometimes a single UNIX system will perform both client and server roles.

A word of caution is warranted here, however. It is easy to design "bad" NFS configurations. Since the goal of NFS is to mount file systems transparently to the user, it is very tempting for the system administrator to export and mount things all over the place. You should design your NFS setup carefully, taking the time to decide which machines will be servers, which will be clients, and exactly what their roles will be.

A complex, "organic" NFS configuration can be a nightmare to administer. In addition, your users will want things to stay the same as much as possible. When setting up an NFS environment, you should take care to make files available in the same directory structures as much as possible in order to minimize the impact on your users. Your users will thank you for it, or rather, they won't hassle you because things suddenly stop working.

Exporting File Systems

Virtually all versions of UNIX use a text configuration file for specifying the file systems that will be made available via NFS. In most cases, this file is named */etc/exports*. Most versions of UNIX are set up to automatically become an NFS server if they have file systems configured for export. So, when a UNIX system boots, it typically looks for the */etc/exports* file and becomes an NFS server if it finds it.

NOTE: Under Sun Solaris, some of the filenames and commands are different from those listed here. These files and commands are given as examples only, although they work on a wide variety of UNIX systems.

The */etc/exports* file lists the file systems that a UNIX system makes available via NFS. In addition to listing the file systems, it also contains access permissions and restrictions for those file systems. NFS does not advertise its exported file systems the way some other operating systems do. Instead, it maintains a list of currently exported file systems, which it uses to respond to mount requests from NFS clients.

Most UNIX file systems or subdirectories can be exported via NFS, with a couple of exceptions. Only local file systems can be exported; you cannot export a remote file system via NFS. Also, if you try to export a subdirectory or a parent directory of a file system that is already exported, the file system that you are trying to export must be on a different physical partition or device. Thus, if */usr/local* is exported via NFS, you cannot export */usr/local/bin* unless it exists on a different partition or device.

NOTE: You can use the UNIX *df* command to determine which physical device a file system is mounted on. The *df* command will also tell you if a file system is mounted from a remote NFS server.

Exporting file systems via NFS is actually a two-step process. First, you must create the appropriate entries in the */etc/exports* file. Then you must tell UNIX to actually make the file systems available. The syntax of the */etc/exports* file is not very complicated. Let's look at an example:

```
# A sample /etc/exports file
/projects    -access=ivanova:sheridan,rw=ivanova:sheridan
/usr/local/bin    -ro,anon=nobody
/home/biff        -access=wks03,rw=wks03
/home/security_hole
```

In this sample */etc/exports* file, you can see that each line lists a file system to be exported, plus the options, if any, for that file system. Table 3-4 lists some of the most commonly used options in the */etc/exports* file. Note that since multiple options are allowed on one line, the option groups are separated by commas, and the arguments for each option are separated by colons.

Looking back at our example listing, you can see that we are exporting four file systems. The first line

```
/projects    -access=ivanova:sheridan,rw=ivanova:sheridan
```

makes the file system named */projects* available. Its access restrictions limit all access to the workstations "ivanova" and "sheridan." Also, only these two workstations can write to this file system.

The second export line,

```
/usr/local/bin    -ro,anon=nobody
```

makes the */usr/local/bin* directory available. Its options limit its use to be read-only, and map any anonymous users to the *nobody* UID. Since no hosts are listed in an access list, all hosts on the Internet can mount this file system, although the mount will be read-only.

The third entry in the */etc/exports* example file,

```
/home/biff        -access=wks03,rw=wks03
```

is very similar to the first entry. The */home/biff* directory is exported with access and read-write privileges granted only to the host "wks03."

Option	Description
-access=*host:host*: ...	Allows mount access only to the hosts in the access list. All other hosts will not be able to mount this file system.
-anon=*uid*	Map anonymous users, users who do not appear in the server's password database, to this user ID. This option is used to restrict access from anonymous users. Most systems set the anonymous user to be the system user *nobody*.
-ro	Make a file system read-only. No one will be able to write to a file system with the *ro* flag specified.
-rw=*host:host*: ...	Allows read-write access only to the hosts in the access list. All other hosts will not be able to write to this file system. If no host name is specified, all hosts will be given write access to this file system.
-root=*host:host*: ...	Allows the root user on a particular file system to be treated as root on this exported file system. Use with caution.

Table 3-4.   Common Export Options for the */etc/exports* File

The fourth line in our example file

```
/home/security_hole
```

has no access options, and makes the directory */home/security_hole* available to everyone.

NOTE: NFS's default behavior is to grant read-write access and no access restrictions if there are no access options specified. This means that the directory */home/security_hole* can be mounted, and is writable, by anyone on the Internet. This is a bad idea! You should always control access to your exported file systems, especially read-write access. By comparison, the */usr/local/bin* directory is mountable by anyone, but is read-only. If your site uses the Network Information Service (NIS), you can set up netgroups of workstations to limit access to file systems via NFS.

Once you have entered your file systems into the */etc/exports* file, you need to make them available via NFS. Many systems use the *exportfs* command to do this. Other UNIX variants use the *nfsd* daemon to export file systems directly. For the purposes of our example, we will assume that you are using the *exportfs* command.

NOTE: On Solaris, the command is *share* and has a slightly different syntax.

The *exportfs* command can be used to export all file systems in the */etc/exports* file, export only a selected file system, or re-export all the file systems. To export all unexported file systems, simply give the command

```
# exportfs
```

If you want to re-export all the file systems in your */etc/exports* file, use the "-a" option, as in

```
# exportfs -a
```

This causes the *nfsd* daemon to re-export all file systems, including the ones already exported.

Mounting File Systems

Now that you have exported your file systems from your NFS server, you need to mount them at your NFS clients. Since this is the UNIX section of the chapter, let's spend a couple of minutes talking about how to mount these exported file systems to a UNIX client. Remember that the NFS server that has exported these file systems could be either a UNIX or NT system. For the purposes of mounting the file systems, it doesn't make any real difference.

Under UNIX, there are two basic ways to mount an NFS file system. For long-term mounts that you want to remount every time your system boots, you can place an entry in the default file systems file, typically called */etc/fstab*. When your UNIX system boots, the *mount* command will read this file and will then attempt to mount every file system in the file. Here are a couple of lines from a generic */etc/fstab* file that show how you would list NFS file systems for automatic mount. Remember that the syntax of this configuration file will differ slightly among versions of UNIX.

```
server:/home/marcus      /home/marcus     nfs   rw,hard    0 0
zippy:/pub               /pub             nfs   rw,hard    0 0
```

The first entry on each line, such as "server:/home/marcus," lists the name of the NFS server, followed by a colon, then followed by the name of the exported file system. The second entry on the line, "/home/marcus," tells the *mount* command where we want the file system mounted locally. The third entry, "nfs," tells *mount* to treat this as an NFS file system. The fourth entry, "rw,hard," is a list of mount options that tells *mount* to make the file system read-write and to hard mount it. The last entries, "0 0," are numbers used by the UNIX *fsck* utility that automatically checks file systems. NFS mounts should always have this entry set to "0 0."

The second way to mount exported NFS file systems is to mount them directly with the *mount* command. For example, to mount the first file system entry in the previous example, we would give the command

```
# mount -t nfs -o rw,hard server:/home/marcus /home/marcus
```

You can see that most of the information from the "/etc/fstab" line is used in the *mount* command. The "-t nfs" option tells *mount* that this is an NFS file system. The "-o rw,hard" option tells *mount* to mount the file system read-write and hard. The next two things on the line are the server and file system, and the destination mount point, respectively. If you use the *mount* command, the new file system will remain mounted until you either unmount it or reboot the system. If you reboot the system, the new file system will not be remounted unless you place an appropriate entry in the */etc/fstab* file.

Hard Mounts vs. Soft Mounts

You may have been wondering about the "hard" mount option from the previous section. NFS can mount file systems in one of two ways, known as *hard mounts* and *soft mounts*.

In a hard mount, NFS treats the file system like a local device. If the NFS server goes down, or the network link between the server and client becomes unavailable, any processes that try to access the NFS resource will hang, as the NFS client tries repeatedly to access the resource. This is known as *process blocking*. It looks to the client as though a local disk has dropped offline. When the server's exported file system becomes available again, NFS will allow the blocked processes to resume operation, thus guaranteeing the integrity of data written to the hard mounted file system.

Using a soft mount changes the behavior slightly. With a soft mount, the NFS access to the remote file system will eventually fail, and the process will continue automatically. While this will prevent processes from hanging, it does not guarantee that data will be written correctly to file systems that are soft mounted. You should not use a soft mount on any file system that you are writing data to.

HUMMINGBIRD NFS MAESTRO

One of the down sides of using NFS as a filesharing system in NT is the need to install NFS servers and clients on your NT systems. Fortunately, there are several NT-compatible packages available to choose from. The first NFS package that we're going to examine is NFS Maestro for Windows NT Server, available from Hummingbird Communications, Ltd.

NFS Maestro is an NFS server implementation, designed to run under Windows NT. Since NFS Maestro is only the NFS server portion, you will need an NFS client in order to mount NFS-exported NFS partitions on an NT machine. UNIX systems typically have native NFS clients. NFS Maestro provides both an NFS server and NFS client for Windows NT that operate as NT services. These services operate at the ring 0 level of the operating system, as a kernel mode implementation.By installing and using NFS Maestro, users make available any standard disk or CD-ROM that is locally attached.

Installation

One of the nice things about NFS Maestro is its ease of installation. Simply run the *setup* program from the NFS Maestro installation media, and select the destination directory. NFS Maestro tells you when installation is complete. That's all there is to the installation phase!

Configuration

Configuring NFS Maestro is fairly simple as well. NFS Maestro, like UNIX, uses a list of exported file systems, located in a file named EXPORTS. The EXPORTS file must be located in the NFS Maestro install directory.

When NFS Maestro is first installed, a skeleton EXPORTS file is created, which does not contain any valid file systems. NFS Maestro will attempt to automatically start, and will generate an error indicating a bad or missing EXPORTS file. In order to add file systems to the exports file, you must first stop NFS Maestro.

To stop the NFS Maestro service, open the Control Panel and select Services. Highlight the service named HCLNFSServer, and click the Stop button. Once the NFS server service has been stopped, you can edit the EXPORTS file and add your file systems to export.

The EXPORTS file for NFS Maestro uses a syntax that is very similar to the common UNIX syntax, and is documented very well in the skeleton EXPORTS file. The following is the skeleton EXPORTS file from NFS Maestro, with one valid file system added at the end:

```
#Entries in this file are formatted as either of:
#
#        Resource [ host1 [ host2 ... hostn ] ]
#
#        Resource [  Option[,Option...] ]
#
#Note that spaces are important in this file. Export entries are defined
#as follows:
#
#
#        Resource        Print Queue name or pathname of the directory
#                            (e.g., c:\usr\home)
#                            (UNIX- type entries are  also valid, e.g.,
#                                /usr/home=c:\usr\home.)
#
#        host?           Client's machine name (e.g., PC-1)
#
#        Option  Specifies optional characteristics for the directory
#                        being exported. More than one option can be
#                        entered by separating them with commas. The first option
#                        must be preceded with a dash (-). The default
#                        export parameters are access for everyone and
```

```
#                     read-write permission for everyone.
#          Choose from the following options:
#
#       ro
#                           Exports the directory to all users with read only
#permission. If not specified, the directory is exported with read write
#permission.
#
#          rw=Client1[:Client2:Client3...]
#                           Exports the directory with read write permission to
#the machines specified by the Client parameter. All other users have read
#only permission.
#
#          access = Client1[:Client2:Client3...]
#                           Restricts access to client(s) listed. Can be used
#in combination with read-write option to further define permissions.
#
#          root = Client1[:Client2:Client3...]
#                           Allows user root access from the client(s) listed.
#
#          There should be only one line for each resource exported. The first
#entry for a resource will take precedence over any other entries for the
#same resource.
#
# To export your entire C: drive to some clients read-only, some clients
#read-write and allow root access from some hosts, the following would be
#used.
#
#/c ro,access=host1,host2,rw=host3,host4,root=host3
#
# host1 and host2 has read-only access
# host3 and host4 has read/write access
# root on host3 has root permission
# host5 can't access the drive
#
#
#below are the file systems that We are testing with
#Comment:  I don't think we should export directories that don't exist.

#          could we not check for this and not export them.
c:\public -ro,access=marcus
```

Once you have entered your file systems into the EXPORTS file, you can restart the HCLNFSServer service from Services in Control Panel.

Security

While NT supports three different types of file systems, only the NTFS system provides security and access control at both the file and directory level. By exporting NTFS file systems, you gain the ability to control file system access according to the native permissions and access control lists set on the exported NTFS file system. Since NFS Maestro runs as an NT service, it preserves NTFS file permissions on exported NTFS file systems. If you export a file system that is FAT-based, you will have no user level access control for file accesses. You will only be able to say which workstations are allowed to access the file system, and if they are read-only or read-write.

Name Mapping

In order to access an exported NFS file system, a user must be authenticated. UNIX and NT NFS clients automatically authenticate their users locally by having them log into the system. If NFS Maestro is used as a stand-alone server, the user attempting to access an NFS resource must have a valid NT username. If the user has a valid username, the username is compared to an internal list to find the mapping between usernames and UIDs. Some systems, such as UNIX, have static UIDs that are always assigned to a specific user. On other systems, such as PC-based clients, the users do not have static UIDs. NFS Maestro allows the system administrator to build a list of username-to-UID mappings with the control panel for Name Mappings, which is installed with NFS Maestro. Figure 3-1 shows the control panel for NFS Maestro Name Mappings.

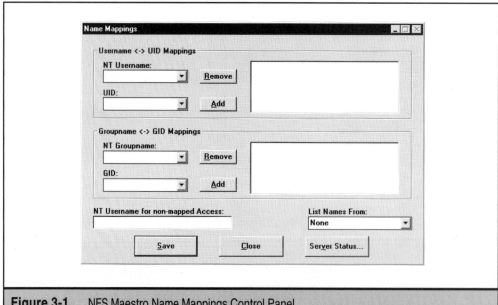

Figure 3-1. NFS Maestro Name Mappings Control Panel

NETMANAGE NFS

Another commercial NFS implementation is available from NetManage. As a component of its Chameleon/ UNIXLink 97 package, NetManage's NFS implementation provides robust NFS client and server software. This new release supports long filenames for more descriptive naming, as well as the ability to refer to file systems via Windows NT UNC names. The UNIXLink 97 package also integrates NFS file access into the Windows Explorer interface, making it easy to access remote drives and directories.

SOSSNT SERVER

Those of you looking for an inexpensive NFS solution shouldn't feel left out. The SOSSNT server, an acronym for Son of Stan's Server for NT, is an NT port of the PC-based SOSS NFS server. The software is freely available under the terms of the GNU Public License.

SOSSNT is started by running the RUNSOSS.BAT file located in the SOSSNT executables directory. SOSSNT uses an exports file named EXPORT.US to export NFS file systems. In addition, SOSSNT provides support for NTFS security and for mapping UNIX and NT user IDs and group IDs.

While SOSSNT is not the most feature-rich NFS server available, it is free, and comes with full source code. It is fairly easy to install and configure. One significant downside, however, is that SOSSNT does not run as a native NT service, but rather as a batch file. This requires that the batch file be started every time the NT server is rebooted.

SUMMARY

In the UNIX world, NFS is the de facto standard for sharing file systems. When integrating with an NT environment, it can provide a viable means of sharing file systems between UNIX and NT. In this chapter, we looked at what NFS does and its history, an introduction to some technical aspects of NFS, and how NFS manages file system permissions. We also examined the effects of alphabetic case in filenames when exporting NFS file systems.

A computer using NFS can function as either an NFS server or an NFS client. UNIX typically provides NFS capability as a native component of the operating system, while NT requires that you purchase third-party add-on products. We examined how to configure UNIX as both an NFS server and client, and looked at some commercial and free solutions for NT.

Properly thought out and implemented, NFS can provide the link that you need to share file systems between your UNIX and NT systems. It does have limitations, including file case mapping, UID and GID mapping, and the requirement that you install software on every NT computer. However, if you have a computing environment with a large number of UNIX systems, NFS could be the solution you are looking for.

WINDOWS
NT
Professional
Library

CHAPTER 4

Backup in a Multiplatform Environment

Backups are a safety precaution and a fact of life. All sorts of things can go wrong that can damage or completely erase your data. Hardware can fail, software can malfunction, and users can accidentally delete files.

With your company's future riding on the integrity of its data, backups are a part of system administration that no administrator can ignore. When you add multiple operating systems, such as UNIX and Windows NT, to the mix, things get even more complicated. In this chapter, we will explore some of the things you need to consider when performing backups in a multiplatform environment.

BACKUPS ARE ESSENTIAL

There can be any number of reasons why your computer data could become lost or damaged. Regardless of the reason, the users of your computer systems expect to be able to retrieve their programs should they become lost or accidentally deleted. The very survival of your company may ride on your having the ability to restore files from backup. Clearly, you need to have a comprehensive backup plan that adequately protects your software and data.

Not only do you need to simply do backups, you need to decide on a whole range of issues. For example, you will need to decide on the backup schedule, the type of media and backup device to use, which file systems to back up, what kind of off-site storage, if any, you will use, and what kind of documentation you will have for your backup process. Depending on the size of your computing environment, you may have some cost issues as well. For example, do you need a robotic tape changer? Do you need to do backups at 2:00 AM to minimize user down time? If you need to do backups in the middle of the night, will you have to pay an operator to come in and monitor the backup process?

Just when you think you've thought of all the problems, the issue of cross-platform backups rears its ugly head. If you have a mixed UNIX and NT shop, which you probably do or you wouldn't be reading this book, you get a whole new set of problems. Do you try to integrate backups of both systems into one common set of backup software? If so, how? If not, how are you going to manage two sets of backups? Do you buy a commercial product, or "roll your own"?

So you see, backups are an essential part of managing any computing environment. However, having a good backup strategy requires some careful planning and attention to detail. Let's look at some solutions to these problems and explore some different backup options for different platforms.

SCHEDULING BACKUPS

How often do you need to back up data? Well, that depends to a large degree on your specific computing needs and how quickly you need to have data restored. In an ideal world, you would like to be able to restore any deleted file at any time. While that's probably not realistic, you should be able to restore any file to a previous state that is within a few hours to a day old.

When you perform backups, you usually have at least a couple of options for the type of backup that you do. *Full backups*, sometimes called *image backups*, are complete backups of every file on the system. *Incremental backups*, by comparison, only back up files that have changed.

Some systems support different types of incremental backups. For example, you may be able to do an incremental backup that only backs up the files that have changed since the last incremental backup. You may have the option to back up only files that have changed since the last full backup. On most UNIX systems, the *dump* program allows you to make incremental backups with different levels. This allows you to have different degrees of backup take place on different days. For example, if you are using different backup levels, a level 2 incremental will back up anything that has changed since the last level 0, level 1, or level 2 backup. A level 1 incremental backup will back up any files that have changed since the last level 0 or level 1 backup.

NOTE: In your computing environment, you will probably have certain files and file systems that are more critical than others. For example, your operating system software probably doesn't change much and can be backed up with less frequency than your databases. Your backup policies should reflect these differences.

Let's look at some sample backup schedules. If you have a very time-sensitive computing environment, you might find it necessary to back up all your data every day. This would mean a daily full backup. While this schedule gives you the most security, it is also the most time consuming. You will have to ensure that you have adequate down time every day to perform the backup, as well as adequate bandwidth on your backup devices to handle the volume of data.

Another option is to perform a full backup once a week, say Saturday night for example, and then perform incremental backups for every other day of the week. When you restore files from this type of backup arrangement, you start by restoring from the full backup, then restore from the most recent backup backwards to the least recent. This way, you are not copying over files that have already been restored. By using the one full backup and daily incremental schedule, your data is protected, even though you might have to go to several tapes to completely restore your system.

If you find yourself without enough resources to perform backups at the level you would like, you may need to use a schedule that has multiple levels of backups. Such a schedule might have a full backup once a month, level 1 incremental backups once per week, and level 2 backups on the other days. By only doing a full backup once per month, you limit your maximum backup device usage to the shortest time possible. As level 1 backups will take less space than a full backup, but more space than a level 2 backup, backup resources are minimized here as well. The disadvantages are that it can take significantly longer to restore files, and you might find yourself in a bind if one of your level 1 tapes or your full backup tape develops a defect.

OFF-SITE STORAGE

Whenever you develop and implement a backup plan, you should include provisions for storing at least some of your backup media offsite. In the event that your offices are damaged by fire, flood, or other natural disaster, off-site backups could save your company from financial disaster.

Ideally, you could store all your backup media in an off-site location. However, if you have a large amount of data that is backed up on a regular basis, this might be prohibitive due to the amount of backup media. Also, if all your backups are in an off-site location, it becomes very inconvenient to easily restore files. After all, you really don't want to hop in your car, drive to an off-site storage facility, find the right tape, drive back to work, restore a file, and take the tape back to off-site storage every time someone deletes a file by accident!

As with all things backup related, off-site storage decisions are a balancing act between safety and security on one hand, and cost and inconvenience on the other. Many sites choose to store only full backups offsite. If your site performs a full backup weekly with daily incrementals, you might opt to keep one week's work of backups on site, and then keep the rest of your backup rotation at an off-site location.

If you have multiple sites that are backed up regularly, each site should have a designated off-site storage location. To minimize cost, you could use a different company location as the off-site storage facility. For example, the Denver branch could send its off-site tapes to the San Francisco office, the San Francisco office could send its off-site tapes to the Atlanta office, and the Atlanta office could send its off-site tapes to the Denver office. This type of plan minimizes cost, but since the off-site backups are not physically close to the office to which they belong, they are not immediately accessible. If Denver had a sudden need for its off-site backup tape from San Francisco, it would have to be sent by courier.

What are your alternatives to using another branch office for off-site storage? There are companies that will provide secure, fire-proof, off-site data storage for a fee. If you have a small company, a very cheap, secure, and effective solution is to rent a safe deposit box or two at a local bank.

DOCUMENTATION

It seems that all system administrators have a "love/hate" relationship with system documentation. On one hand, they love having accurate documentation that reflects their current system configuration, all modifications to hardware and software, and all current policies and procedures. On the other hand, most system administrators are already doing enough work for three or four people, and writing and updating process and configuration documentation just never seems to make it to the top of the list.

Now that we have admitted that documentation is never one of a system administrator's favorite tasks, we have to tell you that you need to document. When you devise a backup strategy for your operation, you should make sure that the backup process is fully documented. By "fully documented," we mean that you need to document not only the actual backup process, but also all the critical information associated with backups.

Your documentation for the current backup process should include lists of the file systems or disks that are backed up, which computers they are located on, and the exact backup schedule for each disk or file system. This backup schedule needs to include dates and times of backups, plus what backup levels are performed when. In addition, you need to document the exact procedures for performing both backups and restores, the details of your tape rotation plan, and the details of your off-site storage arrangements.

This document is always a work in progress. As you make changes to your computing environment, you must make changes to the documentation. Make sure that you keep your process documentation up to date, so that it accurately reflects your current procedures. Also, make sure that other members of your staff, as well as your management, know where your documentation is—just in case you get run over by a bus on your way to work!

BACKUPS ON UNIX

Before we start discussing the specifics of backing up UNIX systems, we need to look at how UNIX handles disks and partitions. UNIX attempts to make virtually everything look like a file or directory to the user. The UNIX file system is constructed in an inverted tree structure, with a single root directory at the top. Directories descend from this root directory, each of which contains other files and directories. Path names in UNIX are a list of directories separated by the / character.

If the path is a complete path name, it will start with a / character, indicating that the path starts at the root directory. Some sample path names might look like */usr/local/bin/perl* and */usr/local/lib*. In the first example, */usr/local/bin/perl*, the leading / character indicates that the path starts at the root directory. The components *usr*, *local*, and *bin* are a list of subdirectories in the path. So, *usr* is a subdirectory of the root directory. The *local* directory is a subdirectory of the *usr* directory, and *bin* is a subdirectory of *local*. The last entry in the path, *perl*, is the name of a file in the */usr/local/bin* directory. In the second example, */usr/local/lib*, *usr* is a subdirectory of the root directory and *local* is a subdirectory of *usr*. The last element, *lib*, is a subdirectory of *local*. Notice that the syntax for directory names and file names in a path statement is identical in UNIX. You can't just look at the path name and know if it refers to a directory or a file. If you aren't that familiar with UNIX, you can get confused fairly easily here.

Did you notice that we did not refer to specific disks or disk partitions anywhere in the path statement? What disk and partition is */usr/local/bin/perl* located on? You can't tell from the file's path. UNIX tries to hide this information from the user, in order to make the file system look like one big logical tree structure.

In reality, different disks and partitions really make up the file system tree. UNIX mounts a specific disk and partition to a particular directory name in the file system tree. So, as you change directories down through the directory tree, you will actually switch to directories that are physically located on different disks.

UNIX automatically mounts these disk partitions into the directory tree at boot time, by reading a particular configuration file. Depending on your version of UNIX, this file could be called */etc/fstab*, */etc/vfstab*, or something similar. This file contains, in typically cryptic UNIX syntax, a list of disks and partitions to mount and the directory names to mount them into.

By now you are probably wanting to know what all this has to do with backups under UNIX. Well, it is important for a couple of reasons. First of all, depending on the way you do your backups, you might need to know what disk and partition a directory structure is located on when you back it up. Second, if you have a catastrophic system failure and you need to restore from backup completely, you definitely will want to know how your disk partitions are laid out, and which file systems correspond to which disks and partitions.

NOTE: It is a very good idea to keep up-to-date paper copies of all your disk partition maps, as well as your file system mount configuration file, */etc/fstab*. This information will be critical if you need to perform a complete restore!

UNIX provides several different utilities that can be used for system backups. These utilities differ in their sophistication. Some are useful for quickly archiving files, while others can manage more detailed backup strategies. We will look at three utilities that are the most commonly used for backups. You will likely find at least two of these utilities on any UNIX system that you encounter. In addition to these native UNIX utilities, there are several third-party software packages for performing backups. A bit later in the chapter, we will look at a couple of these that can handle multiple platforms.

Using tar for Backups

One of the easier UNIX utilities that can be used to perform backups is the *tar* program. With its name coming from the words *tape archive*, you can guess that *tar* was developed to archive files and directories onto tape. In reality, you can use *tar* to back up to almost any backup device, including other disk partitions.

Another common use of *tar* is to create an archive file, commonly called a *tar file*. A tar file allows you to make a copy of a group of programs, or an entire directory tree, and store it in a single file.

NOTE: Most installable UNIX software that you download off the Web is in tar file format.

Using *tar* for backups has both advantages and disadvantages. As for its advantages, *tar* is relatively easy to use, once you master its syntax. It is also widely available on virtually every UNIX platform. Tar files can typically be read by any given UNIX system's version of *tar*. In addition, *tar* has been around a long time and is very reliable.

However, *tar* has some significant disadvantages that may rule it out completely for your backups. Different UNIX operating systems have different versions of *tar*. Some of these versions limit length of the file name that can be backed up. This can prevent you from being able to back up a very deep directory tree, as the total length of the file path names can exceed the capability of your version of *tar*. Also, some versions of *tar* are incapable of making backups that span multiple tapes. Special UNIX files, such as device files located in the */dev* directory, cannot be backed up with *tar*. Finally, *tar* doesn't know anything about a file's backup history, so it has no way to support incremental backups. If you want to perform incremental backups with *tar,* you will need to write some shell scripts to manage the details of incremental backups yourself.

If you look at the *man* (short for *manual*) page for *tar*, its syntax looks pretty complicated. The *tar* utility has a lot of options, many of which you will probably never use. By mastering only a few options, you can use *tar* pretty effectively. Table 4-1 shows some of the most common options for the *tar* command.

These options will get you through most of the situations that you will encounter when using *tar.* In addition to these frequently used options, some versions of *tar* support the "z" option, which tells *tar* that the output file is to be compressed. Some versions also support the "M" option, which tells *tar* to create the output on multiple volumes.

Doing Backups with *tar*

OK, let's look at how we actually can use *tar* to back up files and directories. In this first example, we are going to back up a user's directory to a tar file.

```
tar cvf /tmp/smith.tar /home/smith
```

The "c" option tells *tar* that we are creating a tar archive. The "v" option tells *tar* to be verbose in its output. The "f /tmp/smith.tar" option tells *tar* that the tar archive being created is going to be named *smith.tar.*

Option	Description
c	Creates a tar archive or tar file.
t	Prints the table of contents for a tar archive.
x	Extracts a file from a tar archive and restores it to disk.
v	Verbose output. Gives a detailed description of what *tar* is doing.
p	Preserves ownership, group, and permission information when restoring files.
f *filename*	Tells *tar* to operate on the tar archive named *filename*. The *filename* argument can either be an actual file name or a device name.

Table 4-1.   Common Command Options for the *tar* Command

Now, instead of making a tar archive file, what if we want to back up Mr. Smith's directory to a tape? We can use the exact same syntax, except the tar archive file name changes to be the name of the tape device. Let's say you have a tape device on your UNIX system, and the tape drive is named */dev/rmt3*. In order to back up Mr. Smith's home directory to the tape drive, we change the command to be

```
tar cvf /dev/rmt3 /home/smith
```

> **NOTE:** Physical device names are different under virtually every vendor's version of UNIX. We will use the */dev/rmt3* format in our examples, but be aware that the device names associated with your UNIX system may well be very different.

Restoring From Backup

Restoring files from a tar archive is very similar to backing them up. Let's say, for example, that you have just downloaded a nifty new UNIX utility, and you want to extract the tar archive. For the purposes of this example, let's assume that you've downloaded the file to the */tmp* directory and named it *newstuff.tar*, and you want to expand the archive into the */usr/local/src* directory. You would then use the command

```
tar xvf /tmp/newstuff.tar /usr/local/src
```

As you can see, the command to expand the tar file looks almost identical to the command used to create the archive in the first place.

> **NOTE:** Before restoring files from an archive, it is usually a good idea to look at the table of contents for the archive just to make sure that everything is where you think it is. To look at the table of contents for a tar archive, use the command
>
> ```
> tar tvf filename
> ```
>
> where "filename" is the name of the archive file.

Directories in Archive Files

When creating a tar archive, either directly to a backup device or to an archive file, *tar* allows you to specify which files can go into that archive. Since you can either give a list of files, possibly with a wildcard, or you can give a directory name, how your tar file is structured depends on the way you specify the files.

If you choose to create a tar file giving the name of a directory, *tar* will add the directory entry to the tar file first, then recursively descend into the directory, adding the files and directories that it encounters. The net result of this is that when you extract the files from the tar file, *tar* will recreate the top directory entry first.

On the other hand, if you simply give a list of files, *tar* will add them to the archive without creating a directory entry at the top. When you extract the files from the archive, you will end up with a bunch of files in your current directory.

It is usually preferable to use a directory name as the top level entry in a tar archive, if possible. This way, when the tar file is expanded, the only thing that will be created in the target directory is a new directory entry. All the files from the tar archive will be expanded in this new directory.

Let's look at an example to help clarify this a bit. Assume that you have written a new piece of UNIX utility software that you want to turn into a tar file and put out on the Net for everyone to use. You have all the source code for your new utility software in a directory called *niftyutil*. With all the source and header files for your utility software, the *niftyutil* directory contains somewhere over 100 files. How do you make the tar file?

Your first option is to change directory to the *niftyutil* directory and create the tar file there. For example, you could type

```
$ cd niftyutil
$ tar cvf ../niftyutil.tar *
```

The first command changes directory to the *niftyutil* directory, and the second command creates the tar file. The tar file is created one directory level up, with the name *niftyutil.tar*.

What happens when a user downloads this software and puts it in his */usr/local/src* directory and then expands it? Well, the unlucky user gets over 100 files in his */usr/local/src* directory! Why? Because when you created the tar file, you did not add a directory entry as the first item.

> **NOTE:** If you look carefully at this example, you will see that we create the tar file up one directory. We can't create it in the current directory because we have used a wildcard to tell *tar* to add all files in the directory to the tar file. If we create the tar file in the same directory, *tar* will try to add the tar file to the tar file, and will probably get very confused!

Instead of changing into the *niftyutil* directory as we did in the previous example, you could create the tar file as follows:

```
$ tar cvf niftyutil.tar niftyutil
```

Using the *tar* command this way adds the *niftyutil* directory as the first entry in the tar file. So, when a user expands this version of the tar file, only the *niftyutil* directory will be created in the target directory.

Using *cpio* for Backups

The next step up from *tar* is the *cpio* utility. The name *cpio* comes from *copy archives in and out*. Like *tar*, *cpio* creates archive files; however, it overcomes some of the limitations of *tar.* With *cpio*, you can back up special files such as device files, and *cpio* has a bit more intelligence when it encounters bad blocks or bad sectors while restoring files.

However, *cpio* still has some disadvantages. *cpio* still has length limitations on path names (though the length limitations are longer than those required by *tar*), and some users find its syntax to be cryptic. As with *tar*, *cpio* does not provide intrinsic support for incremental backups.

You'll find that *cpio* is a bit strange in the way that it processes file names and creates archives. You see, *cpio* reads the names of the files to archive from the standard input stream and writes the result of the archive to the standard output stream. This means that you will virtually always see the output of some command that generates a list of files redirected as input to *cpio*. Also, you will virtually always see the output of a *cpio* command redirected into another file. We'll see an example of this in just a moment.

As with *tar*, *cpio* has a lot of command options, but you can usually get by with only a few. Table 4-2 lists some of the most common command options for *cpio*.

OK, let's look at how to create cpio archive files. Logically, the process is very similar to using *tar*. As with *tar*, *cpio* allows you to either use a file name or a device name as the output. In our first example, we're going to revisit Mr. Smith's home directory from a few examples ago. If we want to create a cpio archive of Mr. Smith's directory, we could do it as follows:

```
# cd /home
# ls -R smith | cpio -o > smithdir.cpio
```

We do a recursive listing of the directory *smith* and pipe the output of the *ls* command to *cpio*. The *cpio* command uses the "-o" option to create an output file and redirects the

Option	Description
i	Reads in a cpio file from the standard input. Copy in mode.
O	Creates an output cpio file from the standard input. Copy out mode.
B	Causes *cpio* to read and write with a block size of 5120 bytes per record. This option is used to cause data to be written more efficiently to tape.
V	Verbose mode. Tells *cpio* to give verbose output about what it is doing.
d	Creates directories as needed.

Table 4-2.   Commonly Used Options for the *cpio* Command

output file into the file *smithdir.cpio*. We could have used other commands, such as *find* or *cat*, to generate the list of file names to archive.

> **NOTE:**   Just like with *tar*, it is a good idea to use a directory name as the first entry in the cpio output file. Also, make sure to create the cpio output file in a different directory than the one you are archiving.

Now that we have archived Mr. Smith's home directory, let's restore it to a new location, */home/visitors/smith*. We do this as follows:

```
# cd /home
# mkdir visitors
# cd visitors
# cat /home/smithdir.cpio | cpio -id
```

Note that we use the *cat* command to send the cpio file into *cpio* via the standard input. The "-i" option tells *cpio* that we are sending it a cpio file. The "-d" option tells *cpio* to create any subdirectories as needed.

Using *dump* for Backups

The most powerful backup utilities that are native to most versions of UNIX are the *dump* and *restore* commands. The *dump* command provides real backups (including all special and device files), handles multiple volumes, provides support for incremental backups, and does not have a file name path length limitation.

In order to support incremental backups, *dump* writes information to a special file, typically called */etc/dumpdates*. The */etc/dumpdates* file contains information about which file systems were backed up, when they were backed up, and what level dump was performed.

When you use *dump* to perform a backup of your system, especially a level 0 or level 1 backup, the file systems need to be in an inactive state. This prevents changes from being made to files as they are being backed up. If a file system is actively having changes made to as it is being backed up, *dump* may not record an accurate copy of some files, and they may be impossible to restore.

You have a couple of options here. The safest way to guarantee that there is no file system activity is to bring the system down to single-user mode. Once in single-user mode, only the system administrator can log in, and no *cron* jobs are started automatically. However, UNIX requires operator intervention in order to bring the system to single-user mode, do backups, and then bring the system back up to multiuser mode. Your other option is to perform backups at a period of very low system usage, typically in the middle of the night or on weekends. When scheduling backups for the middle of the night, take care not to run backups during a time when *cron* might be starting other jobs that will modify the file system. Even if there are no interactive users on your system, having the accounting program write to the file system during a level 0 dump can completely corrupt the dump so that it cannot be restored!

As with the other backup and archive utilities, there are several commonly used options for the *dump* command. Table 4-3 lists the most common options for *dump*.

As with all UNIX utilities, the version of *dump* for your system may have different options. Check the system documentation for your particular flavor of UNIX for more in-depth information on *dump*'s parameters.

Unlike *tar* and *cpio, dump* usually operates at the disk-partition level. Therefore, you need to known which disk partitions and file systems you have, and where they are mounted in your file system tree. This way, all your backups correspond directly to a specific disk partition. This makes it a lot easier to rebuild a disk after it has had a complete crash. Alternatively, you can specify a directory name to back up instead.

Let's look at an example of the *dump* command. Assume that you want to back up your */home* file system, and */home* is located on disk partition */dev/sda4*. To do a level 0 dump of */dev/sda3*, to a tape that is 1,600 feet long at 1,200 bytes per inch, and store the dump on tape drive */dev/rmt0*, you would use the command

```
dump 0usdf 1600 1200 /dev/rmt0 /dev/sda3
```

This does look pretty cryptic, but you can figure it out easily. The "0" indicates a level 0 dump. The "u" tells dump to update the dump record file. The next three options, "s,"

Option	Description
0-9	The dump level. A dump level of 0 backs up everything. A dump level of 1 backs up everything that has changed since the last level 0 dump. A dump level of 2 backups up everything that has changed since the last level 1 or level 0, whichever is more recent. Dump levels 3 to 9 work the same way.
u	Causes *dump* to update the dump record file, typically */etc/dumpdates*. Most versions of *dump* are not smart enough to update this file unless you explicitly tell it to do so.
s	The size of the backup tape in feet.
d	The density of the backup tape in bytes per inch.
f	The file name to dump to. This file name is typically a system device name, such as the tape drive */dev/rmt3*.
v	Verifies the integrity of the backup against the original files.

Table 4-3.   Commonly Used Options for the *dump* Command

"d," and "f," specify the tape size, density, and dump device, respectively. Notice that all three of these options take parameters. *dump* allows you to group the options and then follow them by the parameters in the correct order. So, we see "sdf" grouped together, with "1600" being the parameter for the "s" option, "1200" being the parameter for the "d" option, and "/dev/rmt0" being the parameter for the "f" option.

NOTE: It is very important that the parameters for the options to be listed in the same sequence as the options that they correspond to.

Most versions of UNIX support a variant of the *dump* command that allows you to do dumps over the network. This allows you to back up computers that do not have backup devices directly attached to them. This variant of *dump* is typically called *rdump*, with the corresponding variant of *restore*, called *rrestore*.

BACKUPS ON NT

Unlike the UNIX world, Windows NT is still deeply attached to its DOS heritage. While still supporting the DOS FAT file system, NT also provides the NTFS file system as a native mode option. Under Windows NT, file systems are structured with a particular disk or disk partition as the top-level component, as opposed to the root directory in a UNIX environment. One consequence of this is that you can have several logical drives in an NT environment, each with complete file systems, whereas UNIX provides a single logical file system that attempts to conceal the hardware details as much as possible.

Working With NT Backup

Like UNIX, Windows NT ships with an integrated backup system that, while not extremely full-featured, is adequate for general use. This backup utility, cleverly named Windows NT Backup, is started from the Administrative Tools group under Programs in the Start menu.

When you first start Windows NT Backup, its main screen is displayed, as shown in Figure 4-1. As you can see, there are two windows visible. One lists all drives available for backup, including any shared folders on other computers that you have mapped as network drives. The other window shows the current tape drive status.

To select a drive to back up, simply click the checkbox next to the drive in the main Windows NT Backup screen. If you want to back up specific files and directories, double-click the drive icon in the main Windows NT Backup screen, and click the checkbox next to the directories and files that you want to back up. You can also use the Check and Uncheck options from the Select menu to make your files selections. Basically, the file selection mechanism in Windows NT Backup is very similar to the Windows NT Explorer interface; simply browse through the directories and select the ones that you want to back up.

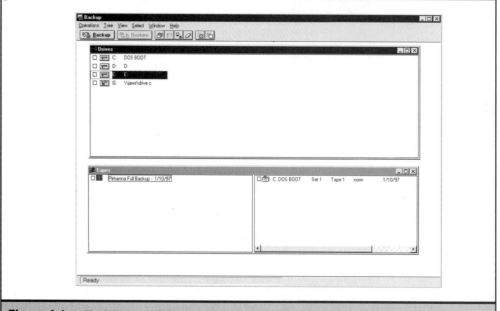

Figure 4-1.   The Windows NT Backup main program screen

NOTE: Regardless of which files you select, Windows NT Backup will only back up the files that you have access to. NT file permissions and share permissions are still in effect.

When you have selected the files or drives to back up to tape, insert a tape in your tape drive and select Backup from the Operations menu. This action displays the Backup Information dialog box, as shown in Figure 4-2.

The Backup Information dialog box is where you fill in all the information about your current backup. It lists the current tape name, creation date, and owner at the top of the dialog box, so that you don't overwrite a tape by accident. Below the tape information are several fields that let you control how this tape will be treated. You can enter a new tape name, and you can choose to append this backup to the end of the previous one on the tape, or to replace all backups on the tape entirely. In addition, you can choose to verify the tape to try to detect any errors during backup, and you can restrict access to the tape's owner or an administrator for security purposes.

There are two additional options in this portion of the Backup Information dialog box, which may or may not be greyed out. The "Backup Local Registry" option allows you to make a backup of your local registry to tape. This option is available if you have selected the local drive that contains your registry. The Hardware Compression option tells your tape drive to use its built-in hardware compression algorithm to try to compress

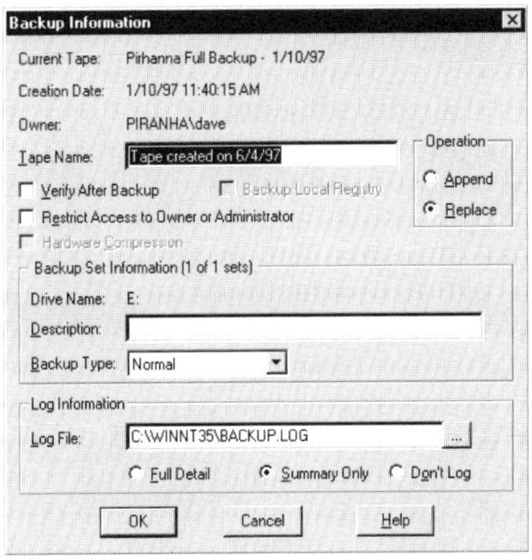

Figure 4-2. The Backup Information dialog box

the backup into the smallest space. This option is available if your tape drive supports compression.

After you have entered the correct information in the tape information section, you can move on to the backup set information section. This section tells you the name of the drives that you have selected for backup. You can enter a descriptive comment as well if you wish. Below the comment section is a drop-down list box that allows you to select the type of backup operation you wish to perform. Table 4-4 lists the options that are available.

After you set your backup options, you can choose to log information about this backup by entering a log file name at the bottom of the Backup Information dialog box and selecting the appropriate radio button.

When you have finished entering all the information about your backup, click the OK button to start the backup.

NT Backup Limitations

While Windows NT Backup is bundled as a component of the Windows NT operating system, it is not as full-featured and robust as other commercial tools. Windows NT Backup has some serious limitations that may cause you to look for another commercial tool, depending on your needs.

Windows NT Backup does not support any type of remote or client/server operation. The Windows NT Backup program must be run from a computer with an attached tape drive and cannot be managed remotely. There is no way for a backup server to poll clients over the network and back them up. This means that in order to back up drives on a

Backup Type	Description
Normal	Backs up all selected files, whether they have changed since the last backup or not. Marks files as backed up.
Copy	Makes a tape copy of the selected files without marking them as being backed up.
Differential	Backs up the selected files that have changed since the last backup. Does not mark files as being backed up. Since the differential backup option does not mark files as being backed up, when two consecutive differential backups are performed, files backed up in the first backup will be backed up again in the second backup.
Incremental	Backs up the selected files that have changed since the last backup. Marks the files as having been backed up.
Daily	Backs up files that have changed that day, without marking them as backed up.

Table 4-4. Types of Backup Operations Supported by Windows NT Backup

remote computer, you must share them so that they are accessible from an NT computer with an attached tape drive. This may be undesirable, or not even possible, depending on how your network is set up.

Windows NT Backup is designed to work only with tape drives. At this time, there is no way to use another type of media, such as optical, WORM, or Iomega JAZ disks. Nor does Windows NT Backup support backups to another disk partition.

Windows NT Backup is designed as a file backup utility. As such, it cannot perform mirror backups that produce a disk image identical to the one being backed up.

Also, there is no facility in Windows NT Backup for scheduling unattended backups at a different time. If you want to run scheduled, unattended backups, you must write a batch file that uses the *ntbackup* command. When run from a batch file, the *ntbackup* command does not support backing up individual files; only directories can be backed up. To schedule a backup at a particular time, use the *at* command.

NOTE: To use the *at* command, you must have the Windows NT Scheduler service running.

As you can see, there are some serious limitations to the Windows NT Backup program. However, if you are in a small computing environment with only a few servers and clients, it can be a very easy-to-use solution.

CROSS-PLATFORM ISSUES

As you have seen, there are tools available for performing backups under both UNIX and Windows NT, although both have their limitations. When it comes time to address backup issues in a multiplatform environment, it becomes even more challenging. None of the native backup tools represent a truly effective solution. UNIX and NT have different types of file systems with very different structures, as well as different file permission mechanisms. They also have different commonly used ways of exporting or sharing file systems.

The type of backup solution that you choose for your network depends, to a large degree, on your network environment itself. What are your primary operating systems? Are you primarily a UNIX shop with a few NT clients? Or, are you a large NT shop that uses NT for file and application servers, with only a few UNIX workstations? In the first case, you might want to consider a cross-platform backup system that uses one of your UNIX servers as your primary backup server. In the second case, you might want to use an NT system as your primary backup server. If you choose to use a commercial client/server solution, you will need to know which packages support which operating systems as clients and servers.

Backing up Exported File Systems

One way to back up file systems in a multiplatform environment is to export the file system, via some server protocol, and have a backup server attach to it and back it up. To export a file system, the client essentially becomes a file server for a brief period of time.

The client, depending on the type of system being used as the backup server, would make its file systems available to the server via a protocol such as NFS or Microsoft Networking (NetBT). The server then attaches to the exported file system by mounting it, if the server is a UNIX system, or mapping it to a network drive, in the case of Windows NT. The server then proceeds with the backup, detaching itself from the exported file system at the appropriate time.

This sounds quite simple, but in reality, performing backups using exported file systems in a multiplatform environment can be very difficult. First of all, the NTFS file system has an extensive file permission structure that includes Access Control Lists (ACLs). If you are using a Windows NT-based NFS server to export file systems to a UNIX system for backup, file permissions and ACLs may not be retained correctly if the file system is restored. Different implementations of NFS for Windows NT handle ACLs in different ways.

Secondly, NFS, unlike NT, does not convert a file name to upper case when searching for a file. NT preserves file name case when writing the file to disk, but when you retrieve the file, it treats *TheFile.txt*, *THEFILE.TXT*, and *thefile.txt* as the same file. Under UNIX, these would be three different files since UNIX completely implements case-sensitive directory and file names.

Third, support for transparently attaching to SMB-shared file systems, such as with Microsoft Networking or Samba, is very limited. On the UNIX side, many SMB clients such as Samba operate within the context of a command-line program, which is unsuitable for backups. On the NT side, most UNIX systems do not support SMB shares without third-party software. Even then, the areas to be shared are usually required to be special directories set aside for that purpose.

Fourth, if none of the above reasons stops you from trying to do backups with exported file systems, consider that you must actually export or share these file systems in order to back them up. Depending on your environment, this can pose a great security risk. Are your network and NFS setup secure enough that, when you share the root partition of your primary server, you can guarantee that no one can break in and steal your passwords and configuration files? How secure will your registry be when you share your NT boot drive?

If you can work around all these issues involved with cross-platform file system sharing, it can be an inexpensive solution. However, the smart system administrator should be prepared for problems.

Client/Server Backup Systems

In order to solve the multiplatform backup problem, several companies have developed backup software that runs in a client/server mode. One primary computer, typically the server with the backup device attached, serves as the backup server. This computer will have a special server package installed that sets backup times, parameters, and computers and file systems to back up.

Each client that is to be backed up will run a special client program. Depending on the operating system, the client software can be run as a background process in UNIX, a Windows NT service, or a foreground interactive program. At certain predetermined times, the server polls the client computers and initiates a backup over the network.

Since the client sends the data directly to the server without relying on an intermediate process, client/server backup circumvents the problems associated with using exported or shared file systems as a backup source. There is no need for the server to mount the shared file systems from the client. All that the server and client need is a clear network communications path between them.

Commercial Multiplatform Tools

OK, you've decided that you really do need to install a commercial, cross-platform, network backup tool. What are your options? There are several companies that produce this type of product, although they will support different types of clients and servers. Backup tools from different manufacturers will have different limitations as well. The following sections give some examples of popular multiplatform backup software packages, as well as where you can go for more information.

Legato Networker

Networker is a high-powered, very effective, enterprise-wide tool for distributed systems backup. It operates effectively as a client/server solution in networks with multiple operating systems. Networker supports Windows NT, NetWare, and a variety of UNIX systems. In addition, Networker provides support for a wide variety of backup devices, including robotic tape changers. It also provides an easy-to-use graphical interface that greatly simplifies backup and restore procedures. For more information on Legato Networker, see Legato's website at **http://www.legato.com**.

Cheyenne ARCserve

Cheyenne Software produces ARCserve, another top-quality tool for distributed backup. The ARCserve server is available for both Windows NT and UNIX, with client software available for a wide variety of platforms, including Windows NT, multiple types of UNIX, Windows 95, OS/2, NetWare, and Macintosh. ARCserve also provides backup and restore modules for databases such as Oracle, Sybase, and Informix, and workgroup applications such as Lotus Notes. For more information about Cheyenne's ARCserve line of products, see the storage management section of their website at **http://www.cheyenne.com**.

Seagate Backup Exec

Seagate Backup Exec, formerly Arcada Backup Exec, is a 32-bit native backup solution designed to operate on a Windows NT platform. It provides extensive client support for UNIX, Windows NT, Windows 95, Windows for Workgroups, OS/2, and Macintosh. In addition, Backup Exec provides integrated support for all Microsoft Back Office servers and is compatible with the Microsoft Tape Format (MTF) used by Windows NT Backup. For more information on Seagate's Backup Exec, you can check out their website at **http://www.smg.seagatesoftware.com**.

HIBACK

HIBACK from HICOMP provides yet another multiplatform backup tool. In addition to providing clients for a large number of operating systems, HIBACK's server component also runs on Windows NT, NetWare, and a large variety of different types of UNIX systems. In addition, HIBACK has been awarded the *Complementary Software with Certified Interface* certification for SAP R/3 on UNIX and Windows NT. HIBACK provides demo versions of some of their products, available for download from their website at **http://www.hicomp.com/hicomp/**.

SUMMARY

Multiplatform backups are a difficult task, no matter what your computing environment looks like. In this chapter, we examined the different backup utilities available under

UNIX and Windows NT and looked at how to establish a secure, reliable backup schedule. We then looked at the problems surrounding multiplatform backups and explored solutions. We discussed the details of client/server backup tools and examined the issues surrounding backing up exported and shared file systems. Finally, we discussed some commercially available products that can help solve some of the problems that you will encounter when doing multiplatform backups.

Backups are an essential component of systems management. At some point, a disk drive will fail, a server will crash, or a user will delete files. Only by having a consistent, thorough backup plan will you be able to recover the data. The very survival of your company, and your job, may very well depend upon having a good backup policy in place.

WINDOWS
NT
Professional
Library

CHAPTER 5

Mail Services with SMTP

Electronic mail was one of the earliest capabilities to evolve when computer networks were first being developed. As networks have grown, so have many different standards and formats for file transfer, electronic mail, and other functions of networks. Over time, more general formats for cross-networked communication have evolved. One of these formats is *Simple Mail Transfer Protocol,* or SMTP. In addition to a more standardized format for electronic mail messages, techniques were needed that could route mail between the different networks. One almost ubiquitous answer to the problem of mail routing is found in Eric Allman's sendmail. Of course, sendmail has not been the only answer to electronic mail transfer.

This chapter will first discuss some of the general issues of electronic mail across multiple heterogeneous networks and the Internet in general. Concepts and definitions will be presented, along with the mail standards as defined in the RFCs (Request for Comment) that sendmail and other applications have tried to address, and several of the protocols defined for use in electronic messaging. The next section of this chapter will cover sendmail: the UNIX-based subsystem in widest use on the Internet. The final section of this chapter will discuss Microsoft's Exchange Server for Windows NT as a mail and groupware tool.

ELECTRONIC MAIL: AN OVERVIEW

This section will present a broad overview of electronic messaging. The first part will discuss some of the general concepts of electronic mail, including two basic kinds of mail software and where sendmail belongs in the division. The next part of this section will present the RFCs (Request for Comment), where the protocols used to communicate within and across networks are defined. The last part of this section explains some of the protocols used to define electronic messages.

History and General Concepts

IBM's PROFS was one of the first widely used office mail systems. Mainframe-based, PROFS had features similar to modern email systems such as Exchange and Notes: strong administration and management tools, security customization, and scheduling capabilities. PROFS and other messaging systems of the time shared several similarities: whether mainframe or UNIX-based, they were text-based and were host-based centralized messaging systems.

As personal computers grew in acceptance and spread through corporations, people started to take advantage of the shift in computing power from the glass-wall mainframe system to the more distributed desktop systems. An early application of personal computer LANs was file sharing, using a central file server and a shared, universally accessible network drive. Messaging systems were one of the first areas to take advantage of the new power on users' desktops, and so host-based messaging shifted (in some cases) to LAN-based messaging.

Shared-File Messaging

LAN-based messaging, also called shared-file messaging, is exemplified by such products as cc:Mail. In shared-file messaging, the desktop client has all the power and all the control. Clients send messages to a mailbox, which is simply a server directory, and poll the server to retrieve mail from their specified mailbox directory. The server is passive and only stores messages: it does no processing or sorting and has no provisions to set rules to control message flow. Shared-file messaging provided the following gains over host-based messaging:

▼   Added attachments to text-only messages

■   Required lower-cost servers

■   A simplified setup

▲   Improved performance for some actions

However, shared-file messaging systems introduced new problems. Because each user needed full access to the file system, including others' mailboxes, security was an issue. Also, since each client polls a mailserver to see if there's new mail, network traffic went up. While server or workstation performance may be a bottleneck at times, more often than not, a limiting factor is network bandwidth.

Client/Server Messaging

Client/server messaging systems broke up the tasks of message processing between the desktop workstations and the servers. By using a push model for messages, mail clients no longer clog the network by constant polling for new messages. Client/server messaging also improved on shared-file messaging by improving security so that users have a more difficult time reading others' mail. Finally, by providing a more intelligent server, sorting and processing of messages can occur before messages are transferred across the network to a client.

Mail User Agents and Mail Transport Agents

Three major concepts of electronic mail transport an administrator should know about are the *Mail User Agent* (MUA), the *Mail Transport Agent* (MTA), and the *Mail Delivery Agent* (MDA). An MUA is the user interface—the software that the user uses to read his mail, organize mail into directories or folders, and send mail. People prefer different features in MUAs, and not all MUAs are available on all platforms. Many MUAs can coexist on the same machine. For example, a UNIX workstation may have installed and usable, by anyone logged in, the following MUAs: mailx, elm, pine, mailtool (if running Solaris), and dtmail (if the Common Desktop Environment is present). A given user may use any one of the several MUAs present to write and address mail. Other MUAs are included in multipurpose software, such as the mail capabilities built into Lotus Notes and Netscape Mail.

sendmail, however, is a Mail Transport Agent. MTAs aren't used to write a mail message; they're used to route the mail from one MUA on a machine to another MTA. sendmail is not intended as a user interface routine, and is used only to deliver preformatted messages. Mail routing may occur either locally on the same machine, or remotely on another machine or network. In a local mail transfer, where both the sender and destination have accounts on the same machine, the MTA is responsible for transporting mail from itself to a local MDA, and in the process possibly transforming protocols, addresses, and routing the mail. For example, a message created on a UUCP network will require some transformation before that message can be received by a person on a TCP/IP network. The MTA acts as a gateway, a mechanism for getting a message from one network to another network that uses different protocols. In the vast majority of cases, there will be only a single MTA on a given machine.

While sendmail handles SMTP mail transfer between MTAs directly, sendmail relies on Mail Delivery Agents (MDAs) to handle local delivery from the sendmail queue to a queue used by an MUA. Two common MDAs that sendmail is often configured to use are */bin/mail* and *procmail*. While /bin/mail is almost universally available on UNIX systems, procmail is also widely available, and is both faster and much more capable than the standard /bin/mail, providing strong capabilities for advance sorting and processing of mail. The relationship between these three components of electronic mail are shown in Figure 5-1.

An analogy for the MUA/MTA/MDA relationship is that an MUA does what a person does when they want to send a letter in the physical world—they write a letter, wrap it in an envelope, put an address and stamp on it, then deliver the letter to a post office. MTAs are like the post office, accepting the letter and examining the address, reformatting the address if necessary, and routing the letter either to a mailbox in the same post office (if the letter is local), or to another post office (for a remote destination).

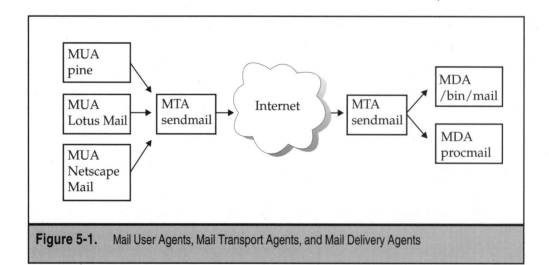

Figure 5-1.   Mail User Agents, Mail Transport Agents, and Mail Delivery Agents

An MDA is the postal worker who delivers the mail from the post office to your location. In the case of a gateway, as was just mentioned, the analogy could be extended. An MTA that receives a letter for a destination in another country has to transfer that message to another MTA that knows how to deliver letters in the destination country.

RFCs

An *RFC* is a formal description of protocol formats used on the Internet. These protocols are also adhered to by many non-Internet systems. The Requests for Comment (RFC) are issued by the Internet Engineering Task Force (IETF). The RFCs are identified and referred to by number for brevity—it's easier to refer to RFC822 than "Standard for the Format of ARPA Internet Text Messages." There are over two thousand RFCs as of this writing, some made obsolete by later RFCs. To find a given RFC, look for the IETF on the World Wide Web at **http://www.ietf.org/**.

Many of the RFCs set standards for mail exchange. sendmail and other MTAs address the needs and definitions of many of these protocols. However, attempting to describe in detail all of the RFCs relevant to mail transport and format could take years. This section will confine its scope to presenting the reference number, title, and a short definition of some of the RFCs most important to mail transfer over the Internet.

In chronological (and thus numeric) order, the RFCs relevant to sendmail are presented in Table 5-1.

Protocols

sendmail uses the *Simple Mail Transfer Protocol* (SMTP) to move messages between two mailservers. Acting only as a server-to-server protocol, SMTP requires another protocol, such as POP3, to collect and process messages locally and deliver the messages to a particular user. SMTP is the communications protocol used most commonly in UNIX-based networks for mail over TCP/IP (Transmission Control Protocol/Internet Protocol) links. Unlike the UUCP (UNIX-to-UNIX Copy Program) protocol, which has to have a "map" of which machines are between the sender and the destination, TCP/IP allows one system on a network to talk "directly" to another by passing packets of information back and forth between the two. Protocols used over the Internet are also presented in a format called Request for Comment (RFC), issued by the Internet Engineering Task Force. For example, the SMTP protocol just mentioned is defined in RFC821, appropriately titled "Simple Mail Transfer Protocol." This section will present some of the relevant protocols.

SMTP and ESMTP

SMTP is a TCP-based client-server protocol, originally defined in the IETF's RFC821. SMTP is complex in details, but it is fundamentally simple. After a reliable connection is established, the mail client (MUA) initiates a brief handshaking sequence with the mailserver (MTA). The client then sends one or more messages to the MTA for delivery. Before each message is sent, the mail client sends a list of the message's local recipients

Number	Title	Comment
RFC819	Domain Naming Convention for Internet User Applications	
RFC821	Simple Mail Transfer Protocol	Defines SMTP
RFC822	Standard for the Format of ARPA Internet Text Messages	Defines the format (headers, body, and how to separate the two) for Internet text mail messages
RFC976	UUCP Mail Interchange Format Standard	Defines the UNIX-to-UNIX-Copy-Protocol (UUCP) format of mail messages between two UNIX systems
RFC1123	Requirements for Internet Hosts—Application and Support	Extends and updates RFC822, mostly by clarifying ambiguous issues in the original document
RFC1327	Mapping between X.400(1988) / ISO 10021 and RFC 822	Updates RFC822
RFC1521 and RFC1522	MIME (Multipurpose Internet Mail Extensions) Parts One and Two	Provide another extension to the mail format defined in RFC822 by defining Multipurpose Internet Mail Extensions (MIME), which, among other things, allows insertion of binary files such as graphics and sound to mail messages. These two are now obsolete due to RFC2045-2049

Table 5-1.   RFCs Relevant to Electronic Mail Messaging

Number	Title	Comment
RFC1651	SMTP Service Extensions	Introduced ESTMP (Extended Simple Mail Transfer Protocol)
RFC1652	SMTP Service Extension for 8-bit MIME Transport	
RFC1653	MTP Service Extension for Message Size Declaration	
RFC1869	SMTP Service Extensions	Makes obsolete RFC1651
RFC1870	SMTP Service Extension for Message Size Declaration	Makes obsolete RFC1653
RFC1891	SMTP Service Extension for Delivery Status Notifications	
RFC1892	The Multipart/Report Content Type for the Reporting of Mail System Administrative Messages	
RFC1893	Enhanced Mail System Status Codes	
RFC1894	An Extensible Message Format for Delivery Status Notifications	
RFC2045-2049	MIME (Multipurpose Internet Mail Extensions) Part One through Five	Made RFC1521 and RFC1522 obsolete

Table 5-1.   RFCs Relevant to Electronic Mail Messaging (*continued*)

and the sender's address. In an obvious paper mail parallel, this information is referred to as the message's envelope.

The handshaking sequence and message content exchange takes place in a formal language made up of four-character commands and three-digit reply codes. For example, an ESMTP mail exchange log might look like this:

```
$ /usr/sbin/sendmail -v philip@testbox.org < message
philip@testbox.org... Connecting to blackbox.testbox.org. via smtp...
220 blackbox.testbox.org ESMTP Sendmail 8.8.5/8.8.5/; Sat, 18 Feb 1998
17:32:24 -0700
>>> EHLO malkuth.hesod.org
250 blackbox.testbox.org Hello richard@malkuth.hesod.org
[168.9.100.13], pleased to meet you
>>> MAIL From:<richard@malkuth.hesod.org>
250 <richard@malkuth.hesod.org>... Sender ok
>>> RCPT To:<philip@testbox.org>
250 Recipient ok
>>> DATA
354 Enter mail, end with "." on a line by itself
>>> .
250 WAA11745 Message accepted for delivery
philip@testbox.org... Sent (WAA11745 Message accepted for delivery)
Closing connection to blackbox.testbox.org.
>>> QUIT
221 blackbox.testbox.org closing connection
```

A framework for additional features in electronic mail is called *Extended Simple Mail Transport Protocol* (ESMTP). ESMTP is a mechanism by which extensions to traditional SMTP can be negotiated between the client and server. The mechanism as described in RFC1651 is open-ended: two of the possible extensions have been defined in RFC1652 and RFC1653.

RFC1652 defines 8-bit MIME transport, which enables sending 8-bit data in mail messages without having to use base64, quoted-printable, or another encoding method. Furthermore, this is accomplished without the breakage that can result from sending 8-bit data to an RFC821-compliant SMTP server that doesn't know what to do with the received components.

Message size declaration, as defined in RFC1653, offers a graceful way for servers to limit the size of message they are prepared to accept. With RFC821 SMTP, the only possibility is for the server to discard the message after it has been sent in its entirety, after the message has crossed the network onto the server. There is no way for the mail client to be told that the discarding was caused by the size of the message.

Other extensions possible with ESMTP include requesting a delivery status notification on outgoing messages, so senders can be notified when messages arrive at their destination, and also negotiating encryption between secure mailservers for more secure mail.

Mail Message Format

SMTP defined how to transfer a mail message across the Internet, but did not define how to recognize a mail message. RFC822 defines the format of Internet electronic mail messages. The format is simple, as befits a standard:

▼ A header containing various required and optional message attributes

■ A blank line

▲ The message contents

The header fields predominate in the short example message shown here:

```
Return-Path: philip@testbox.org
Received: from blackbox.testbox.org (blackbox.testbox.org
[168.9.100.10]) by malkuth.hesod.org (8.8.5/8.8.5) with ESMTP id
WAA01322 for <robert@hesod.org>; Sat, 18 Feb 1998 18:17:06 -0500
Received: from beta.testbox.org (beta.testbox.org [207.266.47.2]) by
blackbox.testbox.org (8.8.5/8.8.5) with  SMTP id WAA13732 for
<robert@hesod.org>; Sat, 18 Feb 1998 18:22:06 -0500
Message-Id: <199802180506.WAA13732@blackbox.testbox.org>
X-Sender: pete@blackbox.testbox.org
X-Mailer: Macintosh Eudora Lite Version 2.1.2
Mime-Version: 1.0
Content-Type: text/plain; charset="us-ascii"
Date: Sat, 18 Feb 1998 18:22:08 -0500
To: robert@hesod.org
From: Philip Wylie <philip@testbox.org>
Subject: Test message
This is a test message.
Philip
```

The blank line after the "Subject" line divides the header from the message body that follows. Any subsequent blank line is part of the message body and has no structural significance. Most header fields are brief and have a fairly obvious meaning (such as "Subject"), while some others are lengthy and not readily understood (such as "Received ..."). For a good explanation of the many standard and less-standard header fields, see Chapter 35 of *sendmail, Second Edition* by Bryan Costales and Eric Allman (O'Reilly and Associates, Inc., 1997).

Each header line consists of a "keyword-value" pair that defines a single characteristic for that message. A required characteristic of a mail message is the recipient of the message. This characteristic is defined by the keyword "To:", one or more spacebar or tab characters, then the value that specifies the mailing address of the recipient. In the message above, this characteristic is defined by the line

```
To: robert@hesod.org
```

POP and IMAP

POP (*Post Office Protocol*) and IMAP (*Internet Message Access Protocol*) are both Internet-based message protocols. Of the two, POP is the older protocol. IMAP was designed to include POP capabilities, and adds support for offline, online, and disconnected modes of remote mailbox access. POP and IMAP are both defined in IETF RFCs: POP3 is defined in RFC1939, and IMAP4 is defined in RFC1730.

POP was designed to support *offline* mail processing. In the offline paradigm, mail is delivered to a mailserver, and a user operates a mail client program that connects to the server and downloads all of the pending mail to the user's local machine. All mail processing of those messages is local to the mail client machine. Offline mode functions as a "store-and-forward" service, intended to move mail when requested from the mail-server or drop point to a single destination mail client machine, usually a personal computer. Once the mail has been delivered to the mail client, the messages are then deleted from the mailserver.

IMAP can also do offline mail processing, but IMAP's main functionality is in online and disconnected modes of operation. In online mode, mail is also delivered to a mail-server, but the mail client does not download all of the mail at once and then delete it from the server. Acting in a client-server style, the client can ask the server for only the headers of messages, or the bodies of selected messages, or to search for messages meeting certain criteria. Messages in the mail repository on the server can be marked with various status flags, such as "read" or "deleted," and they stay in the server repository until they are explicitly removed by the user's actions, which may not occur until a later session. Essentially, IMAP is designed to permit manipulation of remote mailboxes as if they were local to the user. Depending on the mail client's implementation of IMAP, and the mail behavior defined by the mail administrator, the user may either save messages directly onto the client machine, or save them on the server, as they desire.

Offline and online mailers both allow access to new incoming messages on the mail server from a variety of different mail clients. However, offline and online modes suit different requirements and styles of use. Offline mode is best suited for users who use a single client machine routinely, but offline mode is ill-suited for the users who wish to access their recent messages or stored-message folders from different machines at different times. Since offline mode is equivalent to downloading and deleting the mail from the server, using offline mail access from different computers at different times causes mail to become scattered across different desktops. This is not entirely true if you are working in a distributed environment such as the OSF's DCE (Distributed Computing Environment) and are using a common network file system. Such a common network file system may introduce network performance and file locking problems, depending on the implementation. In such a case, the access mode is more online than offline—it just appears offline to you. However, offline access does minimize the use of server resources and connect time when used via dial-up.

The differences between online and offline access modes can be summarized in a few sentences. Offline mode is user-initiated retrieval to a single client machine with the following characteristics:

▼ Minimal use of connection time

▲ Minimal use of server resources

Online mode has these characteristics:

▼ Interactive access to multiple mailboxes from multiple clients

■ Ability to use different computers at different times

■ Ability to use "data-less" client machines

■ Platform-independent access to multiple mailboxes

▲ Possibility of concurrent access to shared mailboxes

The ability to access one's incoming and message archive folders from different computers, at different times, may be an unimportant advantage to those who always use the same desktop to access their mail, but such an ability is a significant advantage for those who use multiple computers.

POP and IMAP do share several common characteristics:

▼ Both can support offline operation

■ Mail needs to be delivered to a shared, "always up" mailserver

■ New mail is accessible from a variety of client platform types, and also accessible from anywhere in network

■ Both are defined by Internet RFCs as open protocols

■ Clients are available for multiple platforms, both freeware and commercial

▲ Protocols deal only with accessing mail—both rely on SMTP to send mail

POP's primary advantage is that it is a simpler protocol than IMAP and is therefore easier to implement. IMAP has several advantages over POP: IMAP can manipulate persistent message status flags, and can store messages in addition to fetching them, so you can append a message from an incoming message folder to an archive folder. IMAP can access and manage multiple mailboxes on the same or on different servers at the same time. IMAP's ability to allow concurrent updates and access to shared mailboxes is useful if multiple individuals are processing messages coming into a common inbox—a change made by one is presented to other active mail clients in real-time.

IMAP is also suitable for accessing non-mail format data such as Usenet or documents. Finally, IMAP can also operate in offline mode for minimum connection time and/or server impact. Consider a low-bandwidth connection, typically a dial-up connection. If a message arrives with a several megabyte video file attached to a one-line text message that reads, "Take a look at this demo," POP will send the entire message.

Using an IMAP client allows you to just transfer the header or body of the text without the attached video file, letting you decide if you want to wait for the video to download.

X.400

X.400 is an older mail standard supported by several MTAs. X.400 is a non-IETF standard, having been originally defined by the International Telecommunications Union (ITU) and the International Standards Organization (ISO). The X.400 standards are published in cooperation by ISO and ITU.

X.400 and Internet mail have several things in common:

▼ Both are primarily hierarchical, with administrators at a "higher level" assigning names at the "level below"

■ Both use a restricted character set for naming

■ Both can be separated into components that are important to the mail network

■ Both claim to be globally unique addressing schemes

▲ Neither maps cleanly into the other

Contrast the following two strings:

```
G=Allan; S=Meyers; O=testbox; OU=mailserver; PRMD=admin; ADMD=admin; C=org
Allan.Meyers@mailserver.testbox.org
```

There are several apparent differences:

▼ The second line is shorter

■ The first line has labels for pieces of the address

■ One element (admin) occurs twice in the first, but not at all in the second

■ The order of the elements "mailserver" and "testbox" is reversed

▲ Typing the first requires more keys to be used

There are also differences that aren't apparent at first, but become clearer when you investigate the underlying technology. While Internet mailers route on "mailserver.testbox.org" as an unit, ADMDs and PRMDs often expect to route on the "C,ADMD,PRMD" triple only; ADMDs route primarily on the "C,ADMD" portion. "mailserver.testbox.org" is resolvable from a unique root using DNS from any node on the Internet. There is no process executable in real time that determines whether "PRMD=admin; ADMD=admin; C=org" is a valid triple from any X.400 node. Details of attempting to map an Internet email address to an X.400 address format may be found in the IETF's RFC1327. RFC 1506 acts as a tutorial on RFC1327. Also, RFC1494, RFC1495, and RFC1496 specify mappings between X.400 and Internet mail when MIME is considered.

X.500 and LDAP

Sending a message requires that you define the following:

▼ The content of the message

■ The sender (you)

▲ The recipient

Two of these components are addresses. If you do not know a person's address, you need a way to find it. Directory services attempt to assist people in finding the address of a recipient (hopefully the user knows what his own address is). X.500 was one attempt to define a global directory service, and LDAP (Lightweight Directory Access Protocol) tried to make X.500 easier to implement (that's why the word lightweight was included in the protocol's name). This section will discuss the concepts and structure of X.500 and LDAP.

A directory service depends on a namespace—a method of referencing and retrieving a group of related information, such as a person's name, organization, physical address, and email address. In X.500, the namespace is hierarchical and explicitly defined, requiring a somewhat complicated management strategy. X.500's naming model defines the structure of the entries in the namespace, but it does not specify the presentation format of that information to the user. Each entry in a X.500 DIT (Directory Information Tree) is a collection of attributes. Similar to the RFC822 mail message header definitions, each attribute is defined as containing a type element and a corresponding value attribute element.

The X.500 standard defines several object classes for directories, with the capacity for locally-defined extensions. The basic object classes include such categories as alias, country, locality, organization, and person (name). Objects are defined by their attributes. There are approximately forty basic attribute types, including Common Name (CN), Organization Name (ON), Street Address (SA), and country (C).

Users access a directory through a DUA (*Directory User Agent*). A DUA transfers the directory request to a DSA (*Directory System Agent*) through DAP (*Directory Access Protocol*). A directory is composed of at least one DSA. Multiple DSAs may share directory information between themselves. If they cannot share information (usually for business or security-related reasons), a DSA may refer the DUA's request to a specific DSA.

X.500 is an application-level protocol using the OSI stack to communicate over the network, which can require a great deal of processing overhead. LDAP, as defined in RFC1777, was created to allow access to X.500 without the same overhead as a full X.500 DAP implementation. The basic model of LDAP is a client using the TCP/IP protocol, interacting with a single LDAP server. That LDAP server uses OSI protocols to communicate with other X.500 servers on behalf of the client.

Like X.500, LDAP bases its directory model on entries, where the distinguished name is used to precisely refer to an address. But where X.500 uses a structured approach to the data, LDAP uses a simpler string-based approach for representing directory entries, described in RFC 1779. LDAP supports simple authentication (use of a clear text password) and Kerberos 4 for security purposes. Future versions of LDAP will support the use of public-key cryptography.

However, using LDAP has some limitations. First, X.500 allowed a server to query other servers or refer the request to other servers. Currently LDAP does not include this ability—if a search fails, it fails. Also, since more of the work is conducted on the server than the client, this requires a more powerful server.

LDAP has been evolving from a lightweight gateway, to an X.500 directory, to a more robust, middleweight stand-alone directory service. Netscape Corporation, for example, has been driving efforts to integrate Web access to LDAP, as defined in the LDAP URL format in RFC1959. Netscape was also involved in extending LDAP to use the SSL (Secure Sockets Layer) protocol, which would add user authentication, data encryption, and data integrity protection, and would also support access control lists and define a format for directory interchange.

sendmail

This section will discuss sendmail, one of the most universally reviled subsystems in all of UNIX. sendmail installation, configuration, and maintenance has long been considered one of the few true nightmares of UNIX system administration.

In general, this assessment is largely true. sendmail is difficult to configure, and can be approached in much the same way that novices approach UNIX. When one person complained in a Usenet newsgroup (**comp.unix.admin**) that UNIX made it easy to shoot himself in the foot, another person replied that if UNIX prevented the first person (a comparative novice) from doing something stupid, it would also prevent the second person (a comparative expert) from doing something clever. In response to charges that sendmail administration is complicated, Eric Allman, the creator of sendmail, said, "Configuring sendmail is complex because the world is complex." sendmail administration follows the guideline set by Spider-Man—"With great power comes great responsibility." The good news about sendmail is that it can do just about anything you can think of. The bad news about sendmail is that it can do just about anything you can think of. Telling it how to do what you want it to can be a chore.

On the positive side, while sendmail is difficult to work with, recent versions have improved the task of sendmail configuration and administration substantially. The addition of a large set of m4 macros, and using intelligible names for options in addition to the single-character switches in the configuration file, has made sendmail configuration an easier task than previously. sendmail is also a reasonably mature product. While flaws are still found almost monthly, sendmail is used in enterprise networks for mail delivery across a wide set of networks and in high-volume environments.

This first part of this section will discuss the history of sendmail. The next part will cover a broad overview of the architecture of sendmail: what sendmail's pieces look like, and how they fit together. The third part will cover configuration and installation issues and advice, followed by a section covering some general sendmail survival advice, some troubleshooting tips, and pointers for further information. The fifth part of this section will examine some of the other UNIX-based MTAs (mail transport agents) that fill the same role as sendmail, such as Qmail, Smail, and Zmailer. The final part of this section will return to sendmail by examining a commercial port of sendmail for Windows NT, and how a prior investment in UNIX sendmail skills can carry over into a Windows NT environment.

History of sendmail

In order to understand why sendmail is what it is, you should know some of what happened, and how sendmail grew to fit a particular role. This section will provide a short overview of how sendmail came to be.

In the late 1970s, Eric Allman was studying and working at the University of California at Berkeley. The predecessor to sendmail, called delivermail, was released in 1979, and addressed the problem of transferring mail between the three current networks on campus: ARPANET, which was using NCP (Network Control Protocol); a UUCP mail system; and an internal network called BerkNet.

The following year, ARPANET started to convert from NCP to TCP (Transmission Control Protocol). Previously, mail was delivered using FTP (File Transfer Protocol), but the SMTP (Simple Mail Transfer Protocol) was developed to handle the new mail requirements for the possible growth of the network by several orders of magnitude.

In response to these changes in the networks, Allman adopted an inclusive approach to formats of electronic mail messages. If a message didn't match the formats, sendmail attempted to make the message's format fit, rather than immediately rejecting the message. Allman also chose to limit the functional goal of sendmail to routing mail, rather than write an end-user mailtool such as elm or pine. The first public release of sendmail was released with the 4.1c version of BSD (Berkeley Software Distribution) UNIX. Like most UNIX software, sendmail is available in raw uncompiled form, with users expected to compile their own versions before installation.

Meanwhile, others were extending sendmail's capabilities. In the late 1980s, a Swedish developer, Lennart Lovstrand, created a version of sendmail with significant enhancements, which was dubbed IDA sendmail. IDA sendmail development was taken over by Neil Rickert and Paul Pomes of Illinois, who continued to extend and improve it. About the time Rickert and Pomes started work on IDA sendmail, Paul Vixie started work on a variant of sendmail he dubbed KJ (King James) sendmail. In addition to these freeware efforts, several commercial vendors, including Sun and Hewlett-Packard, developed their own versions of sendmail as they saw needs for improvements not included in the current versions. The result of all this parallel development was the existence of several versions of sendmail with varying feature sets and incompatible configuration files.

Therefore, Allman started a major rewrite of sendmail in the mid-1990s. Significant improvements were made, many of the features from the various versions were incorporated into the rewrite, and security was improved. Allman continues at this time to improve and update sendmail, adding new features and fixing security flaws as they are discovered. At some point, a long-term goal of Allman's is a complete rewrite of sendmail aimed to meeting future anticipated needs. However, the sequel to sendmail is not here today.

Architecture

This section will not address detailed issues of installing sendmail. In general, compilation and installation of the sendmail distribution is often uncomplicated. The source package includes make-description files tailored for many different systems, as well as a "build" script that chooses the correct one for the local environment. (See the section "Pointers and Further Information" later in this chapter for information to find sendmail on the Internet.) Occasionally you will need to make some minor changes to the closest make-description file to match the specific local system. Of course, be sure to read the README files before proceeding with compiling sendmail from the source.

See sendmail Run

sendmail itself typically runs on UNIX systems as a *daemon* in order to listen for incoming mail. A daemon is a UNIX system program that runs in the background without a controlling terminal window. When run as a daemon, sendmail will fork (unless instructed not to on startup) and run in the background, listening on socket 25 for incoming SMTP connections. The command to run sendmail as a daemon on a Berkeley UNIX-based system may look something like this:

```
/usr/lib/sendmail -bd -q30m
```

This command is often included as part of the startup commands executed when the UNIX system boots. Here is a sample of a command, taken from a startup script named *sendmail.init* on a Linux system, found in the */etc/rc.d/init.d* directory:

```
# Start daemons.
echo -n "Starting sendmail: "
daemon sendmail -bd -q1h
echo
touch /var/lock/subsys/sendmail
;;
```

You can see the *-bd* command that launches sendmail as a daemon and the *-q1h* switch that instructs it to check the queue once per hour. In contrast, the sample command preceding this has the *-q* switch instructing sendmail to check the queue every thirty minutes.

TIP: Several of the sendmail commands with specific options have aliases (not to be confused with mail address aliases). For example, another name for the *sendmail -bd* command is *smtpd.*

The first action sendmail takes when started is to read the */etc/sendmail.cf* configuration file. The *sendmail.cf* and dependent configuration files are presented in the next section.

Configuration: the sendmail.cf File

One reason sendmail is considered to be extremely powerful is the full access provided to the underlying configuration files. As mail messages are funneled through sendmail's configuration files, sendmail performs all message routing functions, including parsing, forwarding, delivering, returning, and queuing. This section describes the major configuration options available within sendmail.

The *sendmail.cf* file is the core of sendmail. A complex configuration file read only once at run time, *sendmail.cf* contains three important types of information:

▼ Options such as operational control switches, mailer definitions, and the locations of other sendmail sub-configuration files

■ Macros for use in rulesets

▲ Rulesets for rewriting addresses on incoming and outgoing messages

NOTE: No one (repeat that: no one) writes a *sendmail.cf* file starting with a blank page in a text editor. If you are creating a new central mailserver for a network, by examining the available resources on the Internet, you can almost certainly find a *sendmail.cf* file that requires only minimal editing to get your mailserver started. After you have a functioning mailserver, make a backup of the working configuration and put it somewhere safe.

For those people who don't want to write a *sendmail.cf* file from a blank page, but can't seem to find a template that fits their needs, V8 sendmail added the use of m4. m4 is a macro preprocessor that is used to generate *sendmail.cf* files containing the features you select. A sendmail m4 creation file typically should be given a *.mc* (macro configuration) file suffix, but this is not required for the process to work. Many sample *.mc* scripts are supplied with the standard sendmail distributions.

For example, a minimum *.mc* file for a Solaris workstation (without appropriate comments) could be something like this:

```
OSTYPE(solaris2)dnl
MAILER(local)dnl
```

These two are the only two required macros in a *.mc* file. You are likely to want more features, but this file named *smallest_solaris.mc* could be run with the following command (assuming you are in the */usr/lib/sendmail/cf/cf* directory, which is where the standard sendmail distribution places m4 files):

```
m4 ../m4/cf.m4 smallest_solaris.mc > sendmail.cf
```

The *m4* calls the m4 preprocessor, the *../m4/cf.m4* identifies m4's default configuration file, *smallest_solaris.mc* is the two-line macro configuration file, and the output is placed in the *sendmail.cf* file. Now that you have used m4 to generate a *sendmail.cf* file containing exactly the features you requested, you will still need to customize the *sendmail.cf* file for use at your site. Using m4 for *sendmail.cf* generation, however, is fast and accurate. In addition to the many m4 macros that ship with the sendmail distribution, you can also write your own as you feel necessary, and include them for use.

For a quick jumpstart on sendmail configuration, there is a World Wide Web form interface to the m4 configuration tool for V8 sendmail at **http://www. completeis.com/ sendmail/sendmail.cgi**.

Select your desired options with the web form, and a *sendmail.cf* file with the chosen options is returned. If nothing else, this allows a look at the complexity of a *sendmail.cf* file.

File Locations   *sendmail.cf* is the first file that sendmail reads on startup, and contains the locations of all other sub-configuration files sendmail uses. These files and their default locations are presented in Table 5-2.

These are only the default locations of the files. Since their location is defined within *sendmail.cf*, they may be set to whatever name and directory path you like.

Options   There are far too many options in sendmail to list them all. The syntax for options comes in two types: cryptic and less cryptic. In the cryptic version of option syntax, the *O* (capital *o*, not zero) command starts an option command in the *sendmail.cf* file. To illustrate, here are two sample commands from a *sendmail.cf* file, as shown:

```
OA/etc/aliases
```

File Name and Location	Description
/etc/aliases	ASCII text list of defined aliases to names
/etc/aliases.db	Database of aliases complied from */etc/aliases*
/etc/sendmail.hf	Help file
/var/log/sendmail.st	Collected statistics
/var/spool/mqueue/*	Temporary files for mail queue
/var/run/sendmail.pid	The process ID of the daemon

Table 5-2.   Sendmail Configuration Files

and

```
O AliasFile=/etc/aliases
```

Both perform the same thing—they tell sendmail to look in */etc/aliases* for the *aliases* file. Notice the syntax change: the single character version (*OA*) does not contain a space between the *O* and the letter signifying which option is being set, while the name version (*O AliasFile*) must contain a space between the *O* command and the name of the option. Like all other sendmail commands, the *O* must be in the left-most position on the line, which is also column 1.

This restriction prevents misinterpretation of commands, such as this next line which may also be found in a *sendmail.cf* file:

```
DMMOON
```

This command defines (*D*) a macro (*M*) to have the value (*MOON*), so $M may be used in the rewriting rules instead of typing "MOON." Without the restriction that commands are identified by the left-hand column, the *O* in MOON might be interpreted as a command.

The options just presented illustrate the form of the option command for use within a configuration file. However, options may be defined either in an m4 macro file or on the command line. The command line versions of the above options would use a dash before the option, a lower-case *o* to indicate a single-character option command, and an upper-case *O* to indicate a named option command, like so:

```
-oA/etc/aliases
```

and

```
-O AliasFile=/etc/aliases or -OAliasFile=/etc/aliases
```

NOTE: Some UNIX vendors ship sendmail with the operating system, but do not necessarily ship the latest version. In most cases (like for V8 sendmail), the vendor-supplied version will include a pre-compiled binary and a predefined *sendmail.cf* file, but little else of the full V8 sendmail package. Often, the default setup is designed for a desktop workstation forwarding all its mail to a central mail exchanger, but the default configuration is unlikely to be suited for use as a central mail exchanger. This area is where sendmail's large installation base is helpful: there is probably a sample configuration file similar enough to your needs so as to require only minor modification.

Rulesets

sendmail uses rules to rewrite addresses on incoming and outgoing mail. These rules are the center of sendmail's capability, as well as its complexity. sendmail rewriting rules are a specialized text-oriented programming language. Eric Allman designed sendmail so that rules perform two core tasks:

▼ Examine each recipient's address to determine which of one or several MDAs should be used to send the message to (or nearer to) the recipient; and

▲ Transform addresses in both the envelope and the message header to facilitate delivery or reply.

By generalizing the tasks to use rewriting rules, instead of coding the tasks directly, Allman made sendmail flexible enough to be adapted and extended as mail protocols were updated, replaced, or added. Adding a rule to transform an address is easier for most people than hacking the source code, which is what would be required if Allman hadn't designed rulesets.

Rewriting rules are organized into rulesets. A ruleset is a subroutine or module consisting of a sequence of rules. When an address is passed to a ruleset, the subroutine passes the address to each of its rules in order. If the matching clause matches the investigated address, the rule is applied, the address is transformed, and the result is passed to the next rule. If the address does not match the current rule, the address is not transformed and the next rule in the set is tried.

Ruleset Syntax   Rulesets are identified by numbers: each new ruleset begins with an *S* in the left-hand column, followed by its identifying number. Each rule in the set follows. Rules begin with the letter *R* and are not numbered. The ruleset is terminated when a non-*R* command is encountered. For example:

```
######################################
###    Ruleset 0 -- Parse Address    ###
######################################
S0
R$*          $: $>98 $1          handle local hacks
```

Rule syntax is cryptic, but fairly simple. Each rule has a left-hand side and a right-hand side. A comment portion is optional. The two sides and the optional comment are separated by tabs (not spaces). The left-hand side is compared to the address as a pattern. If the pattern matches the left-hand side, the address is transformed by the rule's right-hand side and is passed on to the next rule.

In *sendmail.cf,* an octothorp (#) begins a comment line. Empty lines are ignored. The *S0* defines the beginning of Ruleset 0. The *R* on the next line defines the beginning of a rule. The *$** accepts every address that is passed to it, and the *$: $>98 $1* passes the address to Ruleset 98 for further processing. The "handle local hacks" is a comment. Since rules are tab-delimited, the comment portion does not require a comment marker (#) at its beginning.

The Main Rulesets   There are several standard rulesets. These rulesets may appear in any order in *sendmail.cf*—when sendmail reads the configuration file, it sorts the rules appropriately. A ruleset that is expected but not present does not cause an error when the configuration file is read: it is treated as if it were present, but containing no rules. The following are the main rulesets:

▼ Ruleset 0 resolves an MDA by reading the address

■ Ruleset 1 processes the sender's address

■ Ruleset 2 processes the recipient's address

■ Ruleset 3 preprocesses all addresses

■ Ruleset 4 post-processes all addresses

▲ Ruleset 5 rewrites unaliased local users

Aliases An alias is a convenient abbreviation for one or more full mailing addresses. While an alias may be merely a nickname for a longer address you don't want to type every time, such as "fred" for "frederick.smith@somecompany.com," an alias may also be the name of a list of several recipients. Many MUAs maintain their own alias lists, but these alias lists are normally in formats that aren't shareable with other MUAs. For example, if you typically use Sun's mailtool on a Solaris platform, its *alias* file will not be available to Netscape Mail when you write a letter with that tool. In contrast, the many possible alias lists contained in aliases maintained in sendmail's *alias* file will be recognized and expanded when a message is processed by sendmail, regardless of the MUA used to create that message. sendmail allows for multiple *alias* files, up to twelve (and that number is also configurable).

Survival Tips

sendmail administration is, as previously mentioned, highly complex. Just as you should look to others who have successfully built mailservers, and their *sendmail.cf* files in particular, you should also listen to other advice they might have. This section presents some of the more important tips on working with sendmail.

Debugging Mode

The *sendmail -d* command-line switch starts sendmail in debugging mode. Debugging mode can produce a great deal of output, too detailed to go into specifics in this book. To see the debugging mode in operation, enter the following command in a UNIX terminal window:

sendmail -d <your_local_name_here> < /dev/null

This command will mail a message of */dev/null* (nothing) to yourself, and display the resulting actions as sendmail processes the message. The output will typically be several screens worth of information. For a more concise example of debugging, enter this next command using the *-d0.1* command-line switch to return a minimum of information:

sendmail -d0.1 -bp

The response should resemble the following:

```
Version 8.8.5
Compiled with: LOG MATCHGECOS MIME7TO8 MIME8TO7 NAMED_BIND NETINET
NETUNIX NEWDB QUEUE SCANF SMTP USERDB
=========== SYSTEM IDENTITY (after readcf) ============
      (short domain name) $w = homebase
  (canonical domain name) $j = homebase.testbox.org
         (subdomain name) $m = testbox.org
              (node name) $k = homebase.testbox.org
==============================================================
Mail queue is empty
```

You can see useful information in this response, all of which would have been included in the first example, but buried with the other details of a general debugging output. This command shows the following:

▼ (in line 1) the version number of sendmail running—This is good to help determine if you need to apply the latest security patch

■ (in lines 2 and 3) compiled options—Helpful to see what options were selected when this version of sendmail was compiled

■ (in lines 4 through 9) system identity—How sendmail processed the host name

▲ (in line 10) mail queue status—Whether the mail queue for the user running the command (you) is empty or full. This line is the minimal amount of response when using the mail queue *-bp* command-line switch

The options available in debugging mode are many and varied: sendmail may be instructed to return only the types of information you want. For example, if you want to watch the daemon in operation, you need to include the *-d99.100* command-line switch as part of the selected debugging options. Otherwise the daemon will not include its own output.

Rule-Testing Mode

Use of the *-bt* command-line switch with the *sendmail* command runs sendmail in rule-testing mode. The rule-testing mode allows you to test the result of changes you've made to the sendmail configuration files. Enter this command in a UNIX terminal window,

sendmail -bt

and you should see a response similar to this next listing:

```
ADDRESS TEST MODE (ruleset 3 NOT automatically invoked)
Enter <ruleset> <address>
>
```

You should notice the prompt is now >, indicating you are in sendmail's interactive rule-testing mode. Enter a ruleset number as a starting point for address processing and an address for testing. For example, entering

> **> 3 testuser@testbox.org**

returns the following response:

```
rewrite: ruleset    3    input: testuser @ testbox . org
rewrite: ruleset   96    input: testuser < @ testbox . org >
rewrite: ruleset   96 returns: testuser < @ testbox . org >
rewrite: ruleset    3 returns: testuser < @ testbox . org >
```

You can see that the address is broken into pieces in ruleset 3, passed to ruleset 96, then back to ruleset 3.

NOTE: running sendmail in rule-testing mode starts a new sendmail process, which reads the *sendmail.cf* file after you've made changes. At this point, a sendmail daemon running on the same system hasn't noticed the changes to the configuration file, and won't notice the new rules until the daemon is stopped and restarted. Of course, you should always have a copy of the working *sendmail.cf* file safely stored elsewhere while you are editing the configuration file.

Even without editing the configuration file, the *-bt* switch is an excellent way to learn the workings of sendmail on a current system. As the *-bt* switch doesn't change any of sendmail's configuration, using *-bt* can serve as a self-paced tutorial to a functioning sendmail configuration.

Restart the Daemon After Editing Configuration

sendmail only reads the *sendmail.cf* file once on startup. Whenever you change the *sendmail.cf* file, you must restart sendmail in order to have the sendmail daemon reread the *sendmail.cf*. This advice sounds almost as basic as asking, "Is the system still plugged in?" It can, however, be forgotten after too long a session spent staring at *sendmail.cf* rulesets in a text editor.

Rebuild the Aliases Database

Also, if you add aliases to the */etc/alias* file, remember to rebuild the *aliases.db* alias database by running sendmail with the *-bi* command-line flag. Another name for the *sendmail -bi* command is *newaliases*. A word of caution: sendmail may take several minutes to rebuild a large aliases database, and mail delivery is suspended while the aliases database is rebuilding.

Keep Backups

Similarly basic advice: always keep a version of the old (as in working) *sendmail.cf* file, especially when changing the active version. Being able to return to a working configuration by copying the old file back into place, then killing and restarting the sendmail daemon, can take only a minute or two, and you can debug what went wrong with the edited file at your leisure.

Upgrade sendmail Quickly

Often, the latest version of any given software is distrusted, on the theory that while fixing old bugs or adding new features, another bug was introduced. Therefore, a general rule of thumb is to wait a while after a new version of software appears, and let some other person's network meltdown. However, sendmail is an exception to this general rule. New versions of sendmail are sometimes released because a flaw has been found that "allows non-local users to issue arbitrary commands as root." sendmail is a rare case in the software world where early adoption is a good idea. Keep up with sendmail upgrades, or acknowledge that you are probably leaving an exploitable security breach. As should be your usual practice, remember to copy the old working version of sendmail and configuration files elsewhere for fast restoration if a problem occurs during the upgrade. The problem of security flaws in older versions of sendmail is exacerbated by the fact that some UNIX vendors ship sendmail with the operating system, but do not necessarily ship the latest version. Solaris 2.5.1, for example, included sendmail V8.7, when V8.8 had been available for months. Given the security flaws in earlier versions, if a system is accessible from the Internet, either upgrade or remove the older sendmail from that system.

Look Elsewhere to Solve the Problem

Finally, sendmail is not always the source of the problem. sendmail uses the Domain Name System (DNS) to help it deliver mail to remote users. Proper handling of mail requires that both sendmail and DNS be accurately configured. For example, sendmail queries the local DNS daemon to find any recorded "Mail Exchange" MX records for the recipient's domain. If no MX records are listed for a domain, sendmail will query DNS for CNAME (Canonical Name) or A (Address) records to determine a possible mail exchanger. If your local DNS server configuration contains an erroneous MX record, even a correctly configured sendmail daemon may never see incoming messages. Remote MTAs (other sendmails on remote mailservers, for example) may never see mail intended for users in their domains because the local DNS directs the messages incorrectly.

Pointers and Further Information

As this chapter has repeatedly stressed, sendmail administration is not for everyone. If you are interested in or required to deal with sendmail, there are some excellent resources for further information.

Seek Help

The first reference to examine is Bryan Costales and Eric Allman's book *sendmail, Second Edition*, mentioned earlier in this chapter. This book, at over a thousand pages, is the definitive reference on the topic of sendmail, and should be considered mandatory if you are working with sendmail at all. Nicknamed the "bat book," because the cover illustration features a fruit bat (the rumor that the illustration is of a vampire bat is a minor myth), *sendmail, Second Edition* covers the latest major version of sendmail (V8.8) as of this writing. Other books exist that address sendmail issues, but this book is the one resource you must have.

The website devoted to the sendmail subsystem is, unsurprisingly, **http://www.sendmail.org**. From this website, you can find the ftp source to use in compiling sendmail for your system, as well as several other resources. The README files distributed with the source code, of course, contain much specific information, and should be read before proceeding with compiling and installing sendmail on a system. The Usenet newsgroup **comp.mail.sendmail** is a high-volume newsgroup devoted to sendmail administration. An extensive FAQ (Frequently Asked Questions) file on sendmail is edited and maintained by Brad Knowles, with monthly updates. The **comp.mail.sendmail** FAQ may be found on the Internet at **ftp://rtfm.mit.edu/ pub/usenet/news.answers/mail/sendmail-faq/**. As per usual with Usenet newsgroups, new readers of a newsgroup are requested to please read the FAQ files compiled from the newsgroup, then read the newsgroup before posting a question that's been answered weekly for the last two years. This newsgroup is an excellent resource for the latest news or configuration advice. Finally, procmail was mentioned earlier as a powerful replacement for the standard mail delivery agents because of its preprocessing abilities. The latest version of procmail can be found at **ftp://ftp.informatik.rwth-aachen.de/ pub/packages/procmail/**.

CERT and CIAC Advisories

The U.S. Department of Energy's Computer Incident Advisory Capability (CIAC) was established in 1989 to provide computer security services to employees and contractors of the United States Department of Energy. The CIAC manages mailing lists for the following two electronic publications:

▼ CIAC-Bulletin—CIAC Information Bulletins and Advisory Notices containing important, time-critical computer security information

▲ CIAC-Notes—A periodic collection of less urgent computer security information

To subscribe to one of these lists, send mail to: **majordomo@tholia.llnl.gov.**
In the BODY (not subject) of the message type (either or both)

subscribe ciac-bulletin
subscribe ciac-notes

Why are these mailing lists described in a chapter about sendmail? Because sendmail has been the source of several security violations for UNIX-based systems over the years. If a security flaw is discovered in sendmail, a fix or patch will likely be rapidly developed, and severe sendmail security flaws will be the focus of a CIAC Bulletin or Advisory.

Other Mail Transport Agents

sendmail's cryptic commands and confusing configuration have caused some people to renounce sendmail altogether. However, these people still need an MTA. This section discusses a few of the alternatives to sendmail available for the UNIX world, such as Qmail, Smail, and Zmailer.

Qmail

Qmail is written by Dan Bernstein of Australia and is intended as a complete replacement for the entire sendmail subsystem on UNIX hosts operating as mailservers. Bernstein was motivated to write Qmail with goals of security, simplicity, reliability, and efficiency in mind. Since security was considered paramount, Bernstein designed Qmail to minimize the use of setuid and root, which have been areas of attack in sendmail, along with a five-way trust partitioning that provides multiple security checks.

A significant strength of Qmail is its support for mailing lists. Qmail makes it very easy for local users to set up their own mailing lists via a generalizable forwarding mechanism. An additional module allows simplified management of subscription requests for mailing lists. Since Qmail tracks mail messages until it reaches a "finally delivered to" address, Qmail examines the result and compares the destination to the originator, preventing endless mail-forwarding loops.

Qmail is also simplified in comparison to other MTAs. Qmail's forwarding mechanism that allows users individual mailing list control substitutes for other MTAs' separate mechanisms for forwarding, mailing lists, and aliasing. This reduces Qmail's overall size, which reduces the lines of code that need to be bug-checked, and also reduces the load on the mailserver.

Qmail is designed to be a feature-rich replacement for sendmail. Qmail supports RFC821 and RFC822, RFC974, RFC1123, RFC1651, RFC1652, RFC1854, and RFC1939 (for POP3 services), as well as a long list of features. A wrapper for Qmail allows it to masquerade as sendmail to MUAs, so the thousands of users of the (for example) pine MUA don't have to change their configuration when sendmail is replaced by Qmail.

For reliability, Qmail was designed with a straight-paper-path philosophy that was intended to ensure that a message, once accepted into the system, will never be lost. Qmail supports a user mailbox design called maildir, in addition to the older mbox format. The maildir user format is designed to survive if the mailserver crashes during delivery. The maildir format is also designed to work well for mail delivery under NFS (Network File System) networks.

When speaking with administrators using Qmail, efficiency is a word that continues to come up in the conversation. Partially as a result of Qmail's simplicity, several reported instances exist of networks switching to Qmail on a smaller fileserver than was used for sendmail, and seeing improved mail handling throughput.

On the other hand, there are some possible concerns when comparing sendmail to Qmail. sendmail, however clunky, can do almost everything asked of it. At least one administrator out there has likely faced and solved a problem using sendmail, similar to the one confronting you right now, or the one you'll eventually face. Qmail users haven't had enough time yet to solve the world's problems. While Qmail is simple to administer, the simplicity may limit the product's flexibility. Finally, sendmail has been in constant use worldwide since 1979, whereas Qmail achieved 1.0 release in January 1997. With these caveats in mind, Qmail may still be a strong contender as a replacement for sendmail at some sites, especially if a mailserver is serving many high-volume mailing lists. Qmail's design specifications and its supporters are enough evidence that it is worth exploring the option of testing Qmail for use as your network's MTA.

Smail

Smail (currently in version 3—Smail3) was written by Ronald S. Karr and Landon Curt Noll. Smail3 is a mail router and delivery program that works for UUCP and TCP networks, and is capable of acting as a mail gateway between the two. Smail3 supports many of the Internet protocols for email, focusing on UUCP and SMTP. Other features common to MTAs included in Smail are support for *alias* files, *.forward* files, and mail list directories. For use with UUCP networks, Smail supports *pathalias* files. Smail supports use of the Domain Naming System (DNS) for mail routing, and can automatically query UUCP for neighboring sites.

NOTE: Pathalias is an application that reads UUCP Map Project maps and constructs a database containing the minimum cost route to any machine in the maps.

Mailing list performance is enhanced by passing many addresses with a single message transfer. Where sendmail uses *sendmail.cf* and other configuration files to resolve addresses based on their syntax, Smail3 uses a database model to resolve an address based on its content. The set of methods that Smail3 uses for resolving local addresses and hosts is configurable and extensible, but Smail3's methods for parsing addresses are not configurable.

For more information on Smail3, see the Usenet newsgroup **comp.mail.smail**. A mailing list is also available. To subscribe, send mail to **smail3-users-request @cs.athabascau.ca**.

Zmailer

ZMailer is intended for gateways, mail servers or other large site environments that have extreme demands on the abilities of the mailer. Zmailer was intended to handle some of the higher-volume mailserver requirements where sendmail begins to have difficulty. As with every MTA since (and including) sendmail, security was a primary goal. Like sendmail, Zmailer was designed to have a high amount of flexibility, with extensive configuration options and a generalized database interface. The database interface allows Zmailer to draw routing information from

- ▼ Sorted files
- ■ Unsorted files
- ■ dbm, ndbm, and gdbm databases

■ nis (yellow pages)

▲ DNS through a BIND resolver (Berkeley Internet Name Domain, a widely popular implementation of DNS)

Zmailer supports the MIME facilities for message transport, as initially defined in RFC1521 and RFC1522. Zmailer also provides a mail-to-Usenet-news gateway and has support for mailing lists. Zmailer is supplied with a default configuration file that is designed to work for most sites. This configuration file is likely to require at least some customization to work for your site. More information on Zmailer is available through the Usenet newsgroup **comp.mail.zmail**.

Sendmail for Windows NT

Ports of sendmail for almost every UNIX platform in existence have been available for some time now. sendmail is freeware, and Eric Allman has made the source code available since the beginning (when you were expected to compile your own software for your particular systems). Allman also provided advice for people needing to port sendmail to an unsupported system. With the release of Windows NT and Microsoft's positioning of Windows NT as a server platform, it is only natural that someone would have taken the sendmail source code and ported sendmail for use on Windows NT.

sendmail: Welcome to Windows NT

MetaInfo, Inc. has ported a current release of sendmail (V8.8) to Windows NT, and added a graphical user interface (GUI) for managing the configuration files. As with several vendor-shipped versions of UNIX sendmail, Sendmail for Windows NT ships with a pre-configured *sendmail.cf* file that is intended to address the needs of many networks. Since Sendmail for Windows NT is a port of the sendmail source code, MetaInfo claims that the sendmail configuration and data files are transferable between UNIX and NT mailservers. Since distributed and remote management is an important issue, Sendmail for Windows NT also includes a Web-based administration and configuration tool.

Supported Protocols

As a port of UNIX sendmail, Sendmail for Windows NT is an SMTP-compliant MTA. Like Qmail, this product includes integration of POP3 account administration as defined in RFC1939, as well as full support of MIME attachments. Sendmail for Windows NT also supports the finger protocol as described in RFC 1288, which allows remote clients to discover basic information about users on the local system.

One important caveat is that, as part of the requirements of porting, Sendmail for Windows NT is not based on the absolute latest version of UNIX sendmail. As of this writing, the current release of UNIX sendmail is 8.8.6, where Sendmail for Windows NT 2.0 is based on V8.8.4. UNIX sendmail V8.8.5 was released due to a security flaw discovered in V8.8.4, wherein a buffer overflow was identified that could allowed a remote attacker to gain root access. This problem was described in CERT Advisory CA-97.05 (available through the CERT Coordination Center's website at http://www.cert.org). While MetaInfo's porting efforts are expected to continue, it is possible that their commercial version may continue to lag behind the UNIX development of sendmail. If you choose to use Sendmail for Windows NT, you may want to be mindful of any identified vulnerabilities in the version of sendmail you are currently using, and if those vulnerabilities are potentially harmful to your mailserver.

Installation

Installation is a straightforward process. Like most Windows programs, Sendmail for Windows NT uses an Installation Wizard to aid setup. During the installation, the wizard checks system requirements, folder permissions, and current domain information, as well as initializing the system Registry. The Registry is updated with several new values in the HKEY_LOCAL_MACHINE hive, in the directory \Software\MetaInfo\Sendmail\Parameters.

Configuration

There are two ways of "configuring" Sendmail for Windows NT:

▼ Configuring sendmail either through manual editing of the configuration files, or through a Web-based Administrator tool; and

▲ Configuring sendmail to operate as an application under Windows NT.

Manual editing of the configuration files has already received coverage in the Architecture section of this chapter, and will not be repeated here. First, the Web-based Administrator tool will be presented, with its positive and negative aspects, followed by a look at the OS-to-application relationship in the Windows Control Panel.

The Web Administrator The Web Administrator is a web forms-based application that allows the use of a web browser such as Netscape Navigator or Microsoft Internet Explorer to edit the sendmail configuration files, including *sendmail.cf, sendmail.cw,* and the *aliases* files. Since Sendmail for Windows NT is a port of UNIX sendmail, administrators who are already experienced with UNIX sendmail may prefer to directly edit the files as they have done previously. One detail that provides evidence of the UNIX port is that filenames in the *sendmail.cf* file must use / (forward slash—the UNIX syntax), rather than \ (back slash—the Windows/DOS syntax), as the directory separator character.

By default, the Web Administrator tool uses port 5000 instead of the standard HTTP (Hypertext Transfer Protocol) port of 80. Accessing a non-standard port for a protocol is accomplished by specifying the port after the machine name. For example, you can launch the Web Administrator by starting your preferred web browser and entering the following URL (Uniform Resource Locator):

http://MAILSERVER:5000

where MAILSERVER is the name of the Windows NT machine where Sendmail was installed. After you log in to the Web Administrator tool, the main menu window is displayed as shown in Figure 5-2.

NOTE: The release notes warn that using the Web Administrator for configuration essentially precludes manual editing from that point on. For example, in all of the sub-configuration files (every file listed in Table 5-2 except *sendmail.cf*) the Web Administrator is used on, all comments are stripped out. The absence of comments could make returning to a manual editing strategy very difficult, whether sendmail remained on Windows NT or you moved the mailserver back to a UNIX workstation.

The Windows NT Sendmail Control Panel   The Control Panel provides the ability to read and edit values and settings related to how Sendmail works with Windows NT. To examine the Control Panel, open the My Computer folder, then the Control Panel folder, then start the Sendmail Control Panel by double-clicking on the Sendmail icon. One view of the Control Panel is shown in Figure 5-3.

You can configure the Web Administrator to allow access only from networks or machines you specify, and change the Web Administrator's port address to some value other than 5000 on the Config Security page of the Sendmail Control Panel. Once you

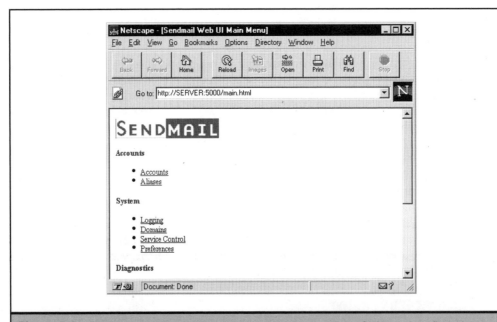

Figure 5-2.   The Sendmail for Windows NT Web Administrator allows GUI-based configuration

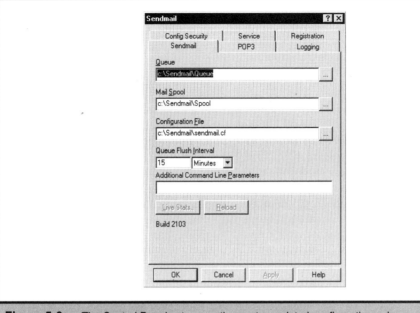

Figure 5-3.   The Control Panel sets operating system-related configuration values

change the value, you must then stop and restart the Web service before this change takes effect.

MICROSOFT EXCHANGE SERVER

Microsoft Exchange Server is a Windows NT-based product offering a wide array of message and data capabilities. Some of these capabilities include several features designed to improve group information sharing and work flow, customizable extensions through MAPI, support for a wide variety of protocols, and tight integration with the operating system. First, this section will examine some of Exchange Server's features, then its components and architecture. The next section will discuss the close integration between Exchange Server and Windows NT, followed by some strategic advice to consider when planning an Exchange Server implementation. The last section will provide two tools designed to aid migration of UNIX mailboxes to Windows Exchange sites.

Overview of Features

Administration of Exchange Server is conducted primarily through an Administrator graphical user interface. The Administrator GUI resembles the Windows File Manager and allows you to select any object within the Exchange hierarchy and view its properties.

Exchange Server is designed to allow backing up of messaging stores without shutting down the mailserver, a feature that is more important as electronic mail becomes vital to more organizations. Multiple routes between sites may be defined so that when one path goes down, a secondary path is available immediately.

Forms

Forms allow you to define workflow of electronic documents through your organization. Using the Forms Designer, you can create many of the common documents used in your organization online and place the information in a database-accessible format without having to scan or re-key the data. Does anyone remember when a promise of business computing was a "paperless office?" Electronic forms are a step closer toward reducing the clutter of paper on most computer professionals' desks.

The Forms Designer is actually a simplified version of a Visual Basic programming environment. While you can use the Forms Designer without any knowledge of Visual Basic, experienced Visual Basic developers can apply their knowledge to create extremely robust forms. A form is a (usually small) Visual Basic application.

NOTE: Using forms in an organization requires the use of Exchange clients that are capable of supporting Visual Basic. As of this writing, the Macintosh Exchange client cannot use forms because Visual Basic has not been ported to the Macintosh OS.

MAPI

The Messaging Application Programming Interface (MAPI) is a group of functions allowing integration of add-ons into the Exchange environment. The MAPI functions may be called by C, C++, or Visual Basic programs, through an OLE-messaging component, to directly manipulate Exchange objects. The Microsoft Exchange mail client and Microsoft Outlook are both built on MAPI. As a result of the MAPI specification being easily available, many third-party developers have released several products intended to work with and extend Exchange. Some of these third-party extensions to the Exchange environment include fax, logon, and message retrieval capabilities, as well as security enhancements, such as the integration of PGP public-key cryptography into the Exchange mail client.

Protocols

Exchange Server 5.0 supports ESMTP, allowing many of the features mentioned in the second half of the "SMTP and ESMTP" section of this chapter, such as delivery status notification and server-defined maximum size limits on incoming messages.

Exchange 5.0 includes full support for Lightweight Directory Access Protocol (LDAP) built into both its clients and the server. As of this writing, Microsoft has announced its ADS (Active Directory Services) will support LDAP3 and work with X.500, using subsets of the Directory Access Protocol and Directory Systems Protocol components of X.500. Exchange Server may also act as a POP3 server, if desired.

Webmail

The web browser-client feature of Microsoft Exchange Server allows you to read your Exchange mail and view folders, both public and private, over the World Wide Web via HTTP (Hypertext Transfer Protocol). The requirements for the client-end web browser are the following:

▼ Frames

■ Java

▲ Javascript

As of this writing, the latest versions of both Netscape Navigator and Microsoft Internet Explorer meet these requirements.

NOTE: Java and Javascript must be enabled, as well as present, in the browser. Some corporations require users of Java-equipped browsers to turn off Java, considering it a security violation.

In addition to a browser as described above and the URL (Uniform Resource Locator) for the Exchange Server, you will need the username for the Exchange mailbox in order to read your mail. You will not need a login name to view public folders, documents, files, and newsgroups designated as world-accessible.

NNTP

Network News Transfer Protocol, as defined in RFC977, is a simple text-based protocol similar to SMTP that allows the following:

▼ The reading of news articles by clients from a server

■ The posting of news articles from clients to servers

▲ The transfer of news messages between servers

RFC1036 defined the format of news messages similar to the format defined for mail messages in RFC822, but with the addition of a few header formats required for news usage that were not necessary for mail transfer (such as the newsgroup header).

Exchange treats Usenet newsgroups as public folders: newsgroups served through the Exchange Server are placed in public folders. Administrators may control access to the public folders on an action (read/write/delete) level for each user or group of users. This newsgroup-public folder relationship is bi-directional: any public folder may be published as a newsgroup via NNTP to any newsreader application that can reach that particular Exchange Server.

Components and Architecture

Exchange Server consists of four major components and some optional components that interact to provide Exchange's set of services. This section will present descriptions of these four components and their interactions. These four components are as follows:

▼ System Attendant

■ Message Transfer Agent

■ Information Store

▲ Directory Service

Core Exchange Server Components

The System Attendant is the central intelligence for an Exchange Server. Acting as a maintenance service, the System Attendant monitors connections between Exchange servers, and also collects other information about each Exchange server for use by monitoring tools. The System Attendant is responsible for creating destination addresses for new mail recipients, and is also responsible for compiling routing tables, verifying directory replication, and logging information about mail messages for tracking purposes.

The Message Transfer Agent acts just as sendmail does in the UNIX world. The Exchange MTA maps addresses, routes messages, and (where necessary) provides message format conversion to the destination system's format standard, if known. The MTA also replicates the Directory Service between Exchange servers in a site.

The Information Store is a server-based storage facility, holding all data received by an Exchange server. The Information Store is comprised of these two separate databases:

▼ **Private** Holding messages in all users' mailboxes. Users may store messages in personal folders on their local workstations, but Exchange, by default, uses the server to store messages

▲ **Public** Holding all the public folders

The Information Store allows administrators the ability to set maximum size limits and access permissions on every mailbox or public folder it contains. The Directory Service contains information on every defined Exchange user, mailbox, and distribution list for that Exchange site. In addition, Exchange can also incorporate organizational information as part of the address: a person's entry in the Exchange Server's Global Address Book can include that person's manager as well as their staff. Having such information as part of that person's address properties eases the task of getting messages sent to the correct group of people. The Directory Store also holds the routing tables compiled by the System Attendant. This mass of information is shared between every Exchange server in the site.

Optional Exchange Server Components

One of the optional Exchange components is the Key Management Server, providing the ability to digitally sign and encrypt messages. Within this chapter, a discussion of the Key Management Server is found in the "Exchange Server Security Extensions" section. Other optional components of Exchange are several connectors. A connector links a Microsoft Exchange server with other servers. For example, a site connector links an Exchange Server into another Exchange server to form a multiserver Exchange site. For linking to non-Exchange mailservers, Microsoft provides connectors for X.400, Microsoft Mail, Lotus cc:Mail, and SMTP, as well as to a PROFS gateway.

Exchange and NT Integration

Exchange is closely integrated with the Windows NT operating system in several areas. This section will first discuss the logical layout of sites and domains, then some of the integrated security features, and close with the Exchange-related extensions to the Windows NT administrative toolset.

Sites and Domains

Exchange architecture relies on the central concepts of sites and organizations. An Organization is the top level of the Exchange installation. Within an organization, there may be many sites. A site consists of one or more Exchange servers with a reliable, high-speed connection between the servers. Windows NT domain boundaries do not necessarily have any relationship to Exchange site boundaries: all Exchange servers in a site must have a reliable network connection to all other site members, but may be in other trusted Windows NT domains. More about the relationship of sites and domains is presented in the "Planning a Microsoft Exchange Implementation" section of this chapter.

Exchange Security

Microsoft Exchange is tightly integrated with Windows NT. One of the areas in which this integration is pronounced is in security. Exchange uses several of the security capabilities within Windows NT. This section provides a brief overview of Windows NT security, then discusses some of the advanced security specific to Exchange, such as key management.

Windows NT Security   Windows NT security relies on four concepts:

- ▼ Authentication
- ■ Domain architecture
- ■ Account type
- ▲ Access controls

In order to gain access to Windows NT system resources, every user, process, or service must log in to the system. Authentication is the process of requesting a username and password from every user, process, or service, and verifying the match of the two. Once the identity (the username) and validation (password) are confirmed as matching, Windows NT assigns that user, process, or service the appropriate security context. The security context defines the access allowed to that identity. Microsoft Exchange uses Windows NT's authentication process—once a user logs in, the operating system determines if that user is allowed to access Exchange.

A Windows NT domain is one or more Windows NT Server or servers using the same security scheme and user account registry set. Within a domain, there are three kinds of servers: Primary Domain Controllers (PDC), Backup Domain Controllers (BDC), and Stand-Alone Servers.

Every domain must have at least one PDC. PDCs replicate the security database to all BDCs. A PDC must have Windows NT Server reinstalled to change to a BDC or a Stand-Alone Server.

BDCs maintain a backup of the security database for the domain and provide load balancing by answering authentication requests if the PDC is busy. A BDC may be promoted to a PDC, but must have Windows NT Server reinstalled to change to a Stand-Alone Server.

Stand-Alone Servers have no responsibilities for authenticating logins. It is recommended that servers dedicated as Exchange servers, SQL servers, or for other client/server applications be configured as Stand-Alone Servers. Stand-Alone Servers cannot be converted to either PDCs or BDCs. Windows NT Server must be reinstalled in order to change the role of a Stand-Alone Server within the domain.

With a single login, a user can access every Windows NT server and all attached resources within that domain. Two domains may have no trust relationship, a one-way trust relationship—where a user in Domain A may access any resource in Domain B, but a user in Domain B cannot reach any resource in Domain A—or a two-way trust relationship, where all users in both domains may reach all resources in both domains. (Trust relationships are actually one-way: a two-way trust relationship is simply two one-way trust relationships, but the two are separate issues.) In Windows NT 4.0, trust relationships are not transitive: if Domain A and Domain B trust each other, and Domain B and Domain C trust each other, Domain A does not necessarily trust Domain C. Windows NT 5.0 is expected to include a transitive trust relationship. Trust relationships are defined from within both domains using a password chosen for the occasion, and severable from either side.

NOTE: Don't bother remembering the trust password. About fifteen minutes after defining the trust relationship, Windows NT changes the password to something else and doesn't reveal it, then changes the password approximately weekly thereafter.

There are two main kinds of Windows NT accounts: user accounts and service accounts. User accounts may be assigned to a Microsoft Exchange mailbox, either in single or multiple. A user must be defined in the same domain that the Exchange server is a member of, or in a domain trusted by the Exchange server's domain. When Windows NT Server starts, several services launch and log into the system automatically.

Windows NT provides access controls by defining each user or service as having specific permissions to access network resources. The following are the network resources for which NT provides access controls:

▼ **Mailbox** Each mailbox may have one or more user accounts set as the mailbox's user public folder. The owner of a public folder may allow mailboxes, distribution lists, and other public folders the rights to read, create, edit, or delete the public folder's contents

■ **Directory** Directory permissions are set as part of the user's account database, allowing actions within those directories

▲ **Group** Windows NT has local groups and global groups. By grouping together accounts with similar needs, less time needs to be spent on administration. Local groups may contain users (both from the same or from trusted domains) and global groups, but may not contain other local groups

Exchange Server Security Extensions Microsoft Exchange Server provides additional security features beyond those in Windows NT. An optional component of Exchange Server, the Key Management Server provides for digital signatures and encryption of messages through the use of public-key cryptography. Both CAST and DES encryption algorithms are supported.

NOTE: Only one Exchange Server may be used as a Key Management Server; having multiple advanced security databases can lead to errors in authentication as well as encryption.

Administrative Tools

Since Exchange runs as a service within the Windows NT operating system, it acts in the same way as a background process under UNIX. An Exchange service is normally configured to run at boot time, and it runs without requiring a user to log in and launch the application. Its activity is monitored by the Windows NT Event Viewer, and the NT Server Manager stops and starts the Exchange process. As a 32-bit application, Exchange supports NT's threading capability, allowing extra processes to be created in response to an increased load, up to the hardware limits of the server.

When Exchange Server is installed on Windows NT, new functionality is added to the User Manager for Domains administrative tool. The User Manager can then administer user mailboxes, assigning and removing Exchange mailbox access permissions to user accounts. The Windows NT Performance Monitor is also extended to allow measurement of Exchange-specific parameters, such as RPC packet transmission speed, I/O performance, and so on.

Planning a Microsoft Exchange Implementation

Advance planning is important to reduce unexpected costs. Microsoft has defined a planning strategy for implementing Exchange in many situations. Although this is a very general set of guidelines, many of these steps will be applicable to many situations. Admittedly, several of these steps may look like common sense to you, but unfortunately, common sense isn't common. (A much richer and detailed guide to planning an Exchange implementation is available on the World Wide Web at **http://www.microsoft.com/exchange/plan/plan15.htm**.)

1. **Assess the users' needs.**

   What do the users need to be able to do? Are they heavy users of electronic mail? (In Microsoft's own implementation of Exchange, they discovered their employees averaged 38 messages per person per day.) If users are expecting to make strong use of Exchange's public folders for sharing information, you may want to define some Exchange servers specifically as public folder servers, allowing mail service to be isolated from the shared folders when backups must be performed.

2. **Identify your company's geographic spread.**

   The company's geographical profile can assist in answering several questions, such as what connectors are best suited to link parts of your organization. Since network costs tend to closely parallel the geographic spread of a company, your company's geographic distribution may provide a visual key to connection speeds between sites.

3. **Choose a naming strategy.**

   What naming scheme will you use for your organization, sites, servers, mailboxes, distribution lists, public folders, and custom recipients? Good naming strategies allow simple addition and identification of sites, servers, gateways, connectors, users, and all other required objects. Exchange Server uses three levels in its directory-naming scheme. The first level, Organization, is equivalent to the X.500 Organization [O] and the X.400 PRMD address element. The second level, Site Name, is equivalent to the X.500 Organizational Unit [OU] and the X.400 Organization address element. The third level of Exchange objects are X.500 Common Names.

4. **Assess the network.**

   Network topology should be a major factor in planning an Exchange installation. In addition to examining the cable type, connection bandwidth, network traffic patterns, and reliability of the connections between portions of the network, this planning phase also considers the protocols and operating systems in use on the network.

5. **Choose or discover a Windows NT domain topology.**

Since Exchange Server relies on Windows NT security to authenticate users and permit Microsoft Exchange Server services, you will need to carefully understand the existing NT domain model for the organization. If you're just beginning to implement Windows NT in your organization, congratulations! You have a chance to do it right! A domain is a group of servers that share common security policy and user account databases. Changing a domain structure once it is implemented is extremely difficult. Site boundaries depend on the domain structure in place, and sites spanning domain boundaries require the domains to trust each other. Allowing a trust relationship between two Windows NT domains may be prohibited at "OSI layer 8"—the company politics layer.

6. **Determine the number of sites and site boundaries.**

   Based on the previous questions, what is the appropriate number of sites and appropriate size for each site in your organization? Here are some additional points to consider:

   ▼ All Microsoft Exchange Server computers within a site must be able to communicate through synchronous RPCs (Remote Procedure Calls)

   ■ Windows NT security must be set up in a way that allows the Microsoft Exchange Servers within a site to authenticate each other

   ▲ Permanent connections must exist between Exchange Server computers in a site

7. **Link sites.**

   Microsoft Exchange provides several connectors for linking sites together. The site connector, for example, uses RPCs for communications and provides load balancing and fault tolerance between servers, but at the expense of increased network traffic (the default setting for synchronizing between two connected Exchange servers is five minutes). The RAS dial-up connector is limited to the speed of the modems involved, but can be defined as a backup connector in case someone with a backhoe accidentally cuts the physical cable your site connector travels over. Exchange also provides an X.400 connector, an Internet Mail Service connector for SMTP mailservers, and Microsoft Mail and Lotus cc:Mail connectors.

8. **Plan sites.**

   Each site will have at least one server, but how many? Will different Exchange servers be tasked to perform separate functions? Who will administer the servers in the organization?

9. **Plan servers within a site.**

   This step identifies the hardware and software requirements of each server.

10. **Plan connections to other systems.**

Exchange Server includes a wide array of gateways for use with SMTP mail systems, Microsoft Mail and Lotus cc:Mail, and several others. The information you discovered in Steps 1 and 4 should be useful here.

11. **Validate and optimize the design.**

In simple English, go back, look at the requirements, examine the anticipated load, then review (for example) the domain models and see if an alternate plan meets the requirements better.

12. **Execute the plan.**

Now you identify what you need to do to implement the design you created in the previous eleven steps. What hardware do you need to order and when, what happens to users' current mailboxes, how will implementing the plan affect current network support, and so on.

UNIX Mail to Exchange Migration Tools

As an example of how to migrate a UNIX-format mailbox into Microsoft Exchange, here is a perl script that can remail entire mailboxes. When run by a sendmail-trusted entity such as root, the script should deliver the mail without rewriting the "From:" lines. Admittedly, this only avoids the "manually" part of "without manually resending each message." The script either edits or inserts a "Subject:" header line to indicate the folder from which the message came.

```perl
#!/usr/local/bin/perl5
$debug=0;
usage() if ($#ARGV < 1);
$smopen = 0;
$user = shift @ARGV;
foreach (@ARGV) {
        forwardmail( $user, $_ );
}
# End of Main Program ------------------------------------------------
sub forwardmail {
        local($user, $folder) = @_;
        local($smopen, $needsubj);
        #
        # open the old mailbox and pipe the messages found within through
        # 'sendmail' for delivery.
        #
        if ( open(MBOX, "$folder") ) {
                $smopen = 0;
                while (<MBOX>) {
                        if (/^From (\S+)\s/) {
```

```
                        $from = $1;
                        close(SENDMAIL) if ($smopen);
                        printf "From: $from\n";
                        open(SENDMAIL, "| /usr/lib/sendmail
                          -f${from} $user");
                        $smopen = 1;
                        $needsubj = 1;
            } else {
                        if (/^Subject: /) {
                            s/^Subject: /Subject: [fwd: $folder] /;
                              print;
                                $needsubj = 0;
                        } elsif ((/^$/) && ($needsubj)) {
                                print SENDMAIL "Subject: [fwd:
                                    $folder] (no subject)\n";
                                $needsubj = 0;
                        }
                        print(SENDMAIL);
                }
            }
            close(SENDMAIL) if ($smopen && (! $debug));
        }
        $smopen = 0;
close(MBOX);
}
sub usage { die "usage: pkgfolders user_name folder [...]\n"; }
```

Another shareware tool that transfers SMTP mailboxes into an Exchange Server private mail store is too long to display, but may be found on the World Wide Web at **http://samantha.ccc.ox.ac.uk**, and is also included on the CD-ROM accompanying this book. This tool transfers SMTP mailboxes into an Exchange Server private mail store. It scans a mailbox and migrates files suitable for transfer into Exchange by using the Exchange Migration Wizard supplied with Exchange Server.

SUMMARY

This chapter has attempted to present some of the background and development of standards for transferring mail across heterogeneous networks and some of the likelier candidates for use as mail hubs or MTAs. If your work environment uses sendmail, you should now have a better understanding of the tasks facing the person or persons responsible for working with sendmail. If your environment uses or will be using Microsoft Exchange, you should now have an understanding of the capabilities of Exchange Server for messaging and sharing of information.

As mail services develop in complexity, capability, and extent, mail will continue to grow as a component of network traffic, and is likely to grow faster than the network bandwidth growth. In UNIX-based email environments with Mail User Agents such as pine and elm, users could be castigated for quoting an entire message just to add "Me too!" at the bottom, or for using a signature block longer than four or so lines. With the addition of multimedia components to mail user agents, it is increasingly common to see users sending mail messages in HTML format that arrive in another user's mailbox as raw HTML, complete with visible tags obscuring the message content; using a company logo as part of their signature file in every message they send; or casually deciding to forward the latest version of Netscape Navigator (at several megabytes) as a file attachment to an email message. Mail administrators should observe the usage of their users and provide guidance, recommendations, and rules for correct use of the mail system.

CHAPTER 6

Mixed Printing Environments

Although computers are not typewriters, many computers are used primarily for word processing. Eventually, a majority of computer professionals are going to need a paper or other physical representation of what they see on a monitor screen. Since you and everyone else are likely still waiting for "the paperless office" to become a reality, any network near you probably has at least one printer somewhere on it, and users of the network will want to access the printers.

Printing components of operating systems tend to include the same major features: spooling directories to hold uncompleted print jobs; print queues to define the order of uncompleted print jobs; print server processes or daemons to transfer print jobs from a spooling directory to a physical printer; user commands to create print jobs; and administrator commands to view, modify, and manage print jobs and queues. Windows NT and UNIX systems have all of these components, but printing is implemented differently on the two operating systems. UNIX itself is hardly monolithic: the various flavors of UNIX implement printing in two major, and not very compatible, methods.

This chapter will discuss printing terms in the Windows NT and UNIX worlds, address the architecture and configuration of printing services on Windows NT as well as UNIX, and present advice and strategies for providing print services to network users. The first major section will discuss Windows NT printing issues, the second will discuss UNIX printing information, and the third will discuss print service strategies.

WINDOWS NT PRINTING

Windows NT printing is primarily defined and controlled through use of the graphical user interface. This section will first present the terminology Microsoft uses to describe printing in Windows NT, then cover several topics relating to TCP/IP Printing, and close with a description of the Windows NT printing sequence.

Glossary of Terms

Windows NT uses a set of precisely-defined terms for the world of printing. The following are some of those terms:

PRINTING DEVICE   A physical object that prints hard copy output. Printing devices may be local (using a workstation as a print server) or networked (connected directly to the network).

PRINTER   A software interface (on an NT desktop) that a user uses to control a printing device. "Printer" is short for "logical printer." A printer can send to several printing devices, and several printers can target the same printing device.

PRINTER DRIVER   The software that allows an application to send a print job in an intelligible format to a printing device. Printer drivers consist of three components: a printer graphics driver, a printer interface driver, and a characterization data file. Printer drivers are typically not binary-compatible between platforms, so a printer driver for Windows NT on an Intel processor will not function for Windows NT installed on an Alpha processor.

PHYSICAL PORT   A port with a cable connecting a print server to a printing device.

LOGICAL PORT   A logical network connection to a remote printing device.

PRINTER POOL   A group of multiple printing devices that appear as a single printer to the user. The printing devices must use the same printer driver, and are driven by a common print server.

PRINT SPOOLER   Software that accepts, orders, and dispatches print jobs to a printing device or printer pool.

PRINT MONITOR   The print monitor communicates with the printing device, sending data and receiving status messages.

TCP/IP Printing Services in Windows NT

TCP/IP printing services in Windows NT provide two important services:

▼ The ability to use networked printing devices

▲ The ability for UNIX and other TCP/IP-speaking operating systems to print to a printing device directly attached to a Windows NT computer

Networked printing devices have their own network adapter cards and are not attached to a Windows or UNIX print server. A networked printing device acts as its own print server and must be able to accept, reject, and queue print jobs directly. Windows NT communicates to networked printing devices using NetBEUI by default, and also can use TCP/IP printing services such as *lpr* and *lpd*, which may be installed separately. Other workstations on the network can use whatever other protocol the printing device will accept, such as NetWare's IPX protocol.

Installing TCP/IP Printing on Windows NT

By default, Windows NT Server does not install with TCP/IP or TCP/IP printing services. Obviously, installing TCP/IP Printing on a Windows NT workstation requires TCP/IP to be installed first. Other information you will need to know before installing TCP/IP Printing on Windows NT includes the following:

▼ The IP address or the DNS name of the host where the printing device is connected

■ The printer name of the UNIX host, if the printing device is attached to a UNIX host

▲ An IP address for each networked printing device ("networked" meaning attached directly to the network)

To install TCP/IP printing services on Windows NT, follow these steps:

1. Open the Control Panel folder, then open the Network applet.

2. Select the Services tab, then click the Add button to display the Select Network Service menu.

3. Select Microsoft TCP/IP Printing in the listbox, then click the OK button.

4. The next window will have a text entry field. You will be prompted to enter the path to the Windows NT distribution files. Enter the path in the field, then click the Continue button.

5. A progress bar will appear, showing the progress of downloading the files to the folder. When the file download is finished, click the Close button.

6. If the installation process discovers a problem, it will display a diagnostic message. If you see a message indicating the installation was successful, reboot the machine.

Printer Configuration Locations in the Registry

To administer Windows NT effectively, you need to understand what the Registry is and how to access and edit the Registry settings. The Windows NT Registry is a binary database that stores parameters about the local workstation, the users and their customized desktops, installed applications, and so on. You view and edit the Registry through the Registry Editor. If Windows NT is installed on the C drive of a workstation, the Registry Editor is typically installed in the C:\WINNT\ directory and is named REGEDT32.EXE.

In Windows NT Server 4.0, the Registry Editor printing parameters are stored in the Registry in the following location: HKEY_LOCAL_MACHINE\System\ CurrentControlSet\Control\Print, shown in Figure 6-1.

An administrator can define this subkey as read-only on a workstation to restrict users from adding new printers, whether the printer is attached locally to the Windows NT workstation or remotely across the network. HKEY_CURRENT_USER\ Software\Microsoft\Windows NT\CurrentVersion\PrinterPorts stores information about printers available to the current user.

If a printing device breaks down, the Windows NT print server local to that printer can still accept print jobs into a print queue. Print job forwarding is turned off by default, but you can turn on print job forwarding if necessary. Editing the NullSessionShares value in the HKEY_LOCAL_MACHINE\System\CurrentControlSet\Services\ LanmanServer\Parameters will allow the print server to forward print jobs to another server. Add a remote printer share name in the NullSessionShares value to enable print job forwarding.

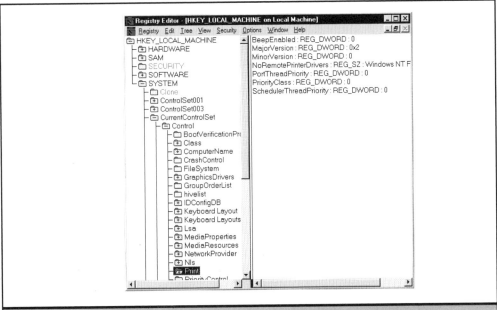

Figure 6-1.   The Registry Editor provides direct access to Windows NT printing parameters

Automatic Printer Driver Updates

The download of the printer driver happens automatically, with no user intervention. Printer drivers communicate directly with the hardware and do not use the Windows NT Hardware Abstraction Layer. In the right environment, auto-downloading of printer drivers can simplify an administrator's work. Since Microsoft has changed printer drivers with every version of Windows, Windows NT 3.51 clients will need Windows NT 3.51 printer drivers. Automatically downloading a Windows NT 4 printer driver will stop printing from an NT 3.51 workstation. Similarly, downloading a Windows NT 4 printer driver for Intel processors will stop printing if your workstation is NT 4, but on an Alpha processor.

If you want to disable automatic updating of the client printer driver, you can do it in one of two ways. First, you can select the C:\WINNT\SYSTEM32\SPOOL\DRIVERS folder that the printer drivers are stored in, and then unshare it. Alternatively, the auto-download feature on each client may be disabled by editing the appropriate entry in the HKEY_LOCAL_MACHINE hive of the Registry. The solution you choose will probably be motivated by the numbers of affected clients.

Microsoft has had several sets of printer driver releases for Windows NT 3.5x and 4.0. A good source of information can be found in articles from the Microsoft Knowledge Base. Some of the more interesting Knowledge Base articles are presented in Table 6-1.

Article Number	Article Title
Q121786	LPR and LPD Registry Entries for TCP/IP Printing
Q132460	Troubleshooting Windows NT Print Server Alteration of Print Jobs
Q124734	Text of RFC1179 Standard for Windows NT TCP/IP Printing
Q154291	Installing Cross Platform Print Drivers in Windows NT 4.0
Q154612	Installing Windows NT 4.0 Printer Drivers on a 3.5x Server

Table 6-1.   Selected Microsoft Knowledge Base Printing Articles

Peer Level Printing Within a Windows NT Network

So, how does printing happen under Windows NT? This section presents the sequence of events a print job goes through after a print command is issued in an application by a user. The first four steps describe a Windows NT client that is using a local printing device attached directly to the workstation.

1. The client workstation checks the print server to see if the version of the printer driver on the print server is newer than the version resident on the client. If the print server has a newer printer driver than the client, the client first downloads the printer driver, then continues.

2. The Win32 application generates GDI (Graphical Device Interface) commands and creates a file describing the print job in EMF (Windows Enhanced MetaFile) format. EMF format is the default data type for print jobs for PCL printers, while RAW format is the default data type for print jobs destined for PostScript printers. EMF files are device-independent, while RAW files are already prepared for a single kind of physical printer.

3. The EMF file is passed to the printer (remember the glossary—"printer" means the software interface on the client desktop).

4. The spooler directs the print job to a print router. If the printing device is local (attached directly to the workstation), the print router passes the job to the local printing device.

If the printing device is remote and attached to a Windows NT print server (either Workstation or Server), the sequence is a little longer. For example, think of two Windows NT workstations: the first is used by a user who wishes to print a page, and a second is a workstation with a printing device attached to the physical port LPT1. Steps 1, 2, and 3 occur as previously described, but in step 4, the print router routes the print job to a remote print spooler. Printing then continues with the following additional steps:

5. The print spooler sends the print job (still in EMF format) to the print processor for rendering. The print processor renders the print job into a format the printing device can accept and returns the job to the print spooler.

6. The print monitor sends the file to the printing device through a physical port. As status messages are sent back from the printing device, the print monitor updates the print job's status.

7. The printing device produces hard copy output from the print job. By default, the print monitor sends a completion message to the user when the printing device is done. The confirmation message may be disabled, if desired.

NOTE: On the server, the print job is queued by the print spooler in the sequence received. Although an administrator can alter the order of selected jobs in a print queue, there is no control in Windows NT to assign a higher or lower priority to a specific user or workstation's print jobs.

Windows NT User and Administrator Printing Privileges

For this discussion, "administrator" will refer to any user account with membership in any of the following groups: the Administrator, Print Operator, or Server Operator groups in Windows NT Server; or Administrator or Power User groups in Windows NT Workstation. "User" will refer to a user account without membership in any of these groups.

User Privileges

Users in Windows NT have the following abilities:

- ▼ Set the default printer
- ■ View a local or remote print queue (double-click on a printer)
- ■ Pause and restart, or delete their own print jobs, but not others' (select the print job in the print queue)
- ■ Display details about a document (right-click on the document and select Properties)
- ■ Display details about a printer (right-click on the printer and select Properties)
- ▲ Connect to remote printers

Administrator Privileges

Administrators, in addition to having the preceding user's abilities, have the following abilities:

▼ Install or remove printers

■ Change printer configuration settings

■ Administer print servers remotely

■ Set permissions for local or remote printers

■ Establish or disable auditing

■ Delete any print job in the queue

■ Reorder any print job in the queue

■ Install printer drivers locally or remotely

▲ Redirect print jobs

Installing a Printer on Windows NT

Users use printers to send print jobs to printing devices. Ordinary users cannot add a printer, but users with Power User group membership for their workstation can (remember, a printer in Windows NT means the software interface to a physical printing device). This section will demonstrate how to add a printer for a printing device attached to the local computer.

To add a printer to the local computer, follow these steps:

1. Open the Printers Folder (found in the Control Panel) and double-click the Add Printers icon to start the Add Printer Wizard. The first window will prompt to choose the manager of the printer. The two choices are My Computer and Network printer server. Select the radio button next to My Computer and click the Next button on the window.

2. The second window displays choices for the physical port connecting the printing device to the computer. Choose an appropriate port, such as LPT1, and click the Next button to go to the third window.

3. The third window displays choices for the manufacturer and model of the printer. In a nice graphical user interface (GUI) design, shown in Figure 6-2, selecting a manufacturer in the left listbox indexes the right listbox to that manufacturer's set of printers. When you have selected a printer, click the Next button to see the next window.

4. The fourth window prompts you to enter a name for the new printer. Enter a name and click the Next button.

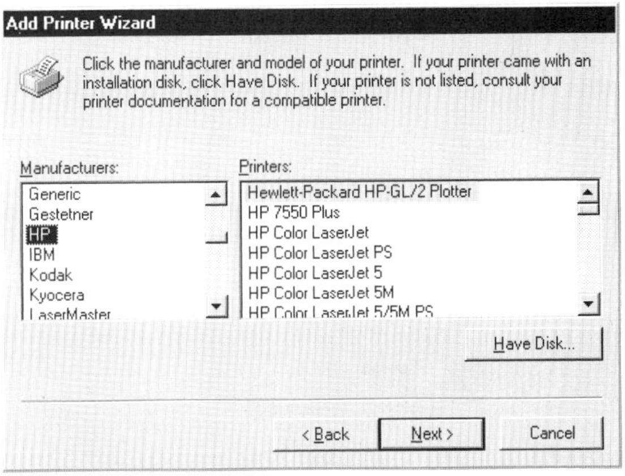

Figure 6-2.   The Add Printer Wizard aids fast selection of your printing device

5. The fifth window, shown in Figure 6-3, asks you to decide if you will share this printer with other network users. Select the Shared option and enter a name for the printer. This name does not have to be the same name you entered in the previous window. When you choose to share the printer, the listbox at the bottom of the window becomes usable. Choose the operating systems of all clients that will be accessing this printer. When you are done, click the Next button to go to the last window.

6. The final window asks if you want to print a test page to test the configuration. Make your choice and click the Finish button to complete adding a printer.

In contrast to adding a local printer, adding a remote printer is a comparatively simple operation. The printer is already configured with a printer server elsewhere. Selecting Network printer server on the window, described earlier in Step 1, displays a second window, which displays all shared printers on the network. Choose a printer from the Shared Printers listbox, then click the OK button. Alternatively, you could use the Windows NT Explorer to browse the Network Neighborhood. Once you have found a shared printer on the network, right-click on the printer and choose Install from the pop-up menu to install that printer to your desktop.

Since Windows NT printers are software interfaces to physical printing devices, you can create multiple printers on the same desktop that point to the same printing device.

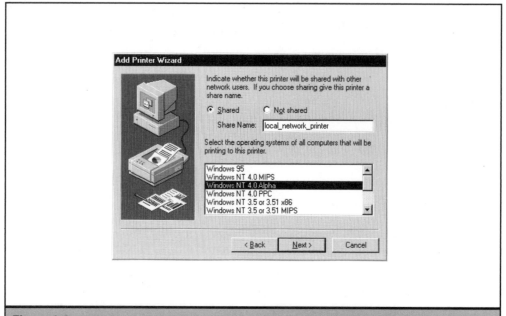

Figure 6-3.   The Sharing configuration window defines who has access to the printer

For example, you may have a printing device attached to your workstation. You decide you want to share the printer with others in your immediate area, but you still want to have priority on your printer. You can create two printers on your desktop: the first one is unshared with high priority, and the second printer is shared for everyone's use, but with lower priority.

Configuring Printer Properties

You access the printer properties by right-clicking on the printer icon and choosing Properties from the pop-up menu. The Printer Properties window will appear. The Properties window has six tabs: General, Ports, Scheduling, Sharing, Security, and Device Settings. Figure 6-4 shows a sample Printer Properties window for the HP LaserJet 4P/4MP PS printer.

GENERAL   The General tab displays information and comments about the printer. You can change the printer driver by selecting a driver from the Driver drop-down listbox. The Separator Page button allows for the choice of a standard page to be printed between print jobs, allowing multiple users of a networked printer to more easily find their documents. The Print Processor button allows you to choose the print processor the EMF file should be sent to. Although the *winprint* print processor is installed by default in Windows NT, a print processor for a fax machine could be chosen here.

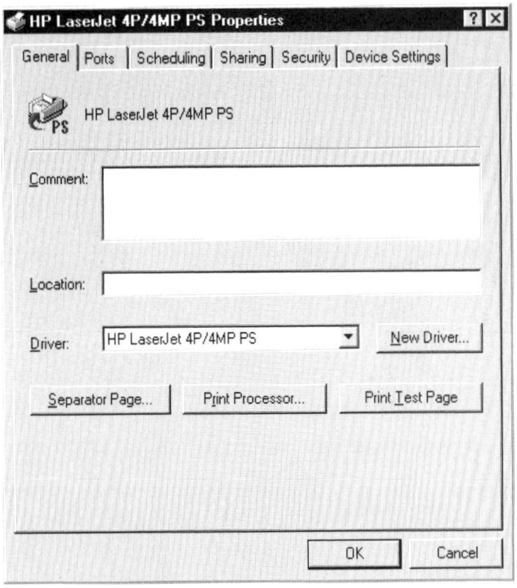

Figure 6-4. The General Printer Properties window displays basic information

PORTS The Ports tab displays the ports, both physical and logical, available to your workstation. You define printer pooling from this window. If you select multiple ports and check the checkbox at the bottom of the window labeled "Enable printer pooling," print jobs sent to the printer will print to the first available printing device. Each printing device must be able to use the same print driver.

SCHEDULING The Scheduling tab, shown in detail in Figure 6-5, allows you to define priorities and to manage the print spooler. The Priority slidebar allows you to change the priority for the print spooler from between 1 (lowest) and 99 (highest). Some of the other options available on this window allow you to turn off the print spooler and print directly to the printing device, hold mismatched documents instead of rejecting them, and hold printed documents in the spool after printing.

SHARING The Sharing tab allows you to change whether the printer is shared, as well as the operating systems you want to include printer drivers for. This window is where you would go when you need to modify a printer to support the first Windows NT Alpha workstation to be added to the network.

SECURITY The Security tab allows you to set permissions, enable or disable auditing, and view or change ownership of print jobs. The four permission levels are:

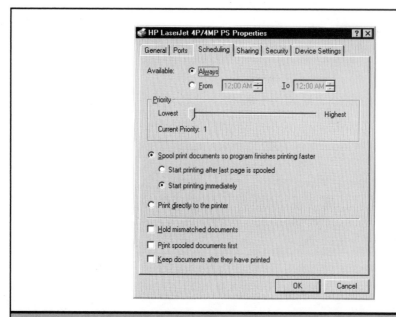

Figure 6-5. The Printer Properties—Scheduling window controls printer priority and spooling

▼ **Print** The spooler will accept print jobs from this user or group. This is the default access level for the Everyone group.

■ **Manage Documents** The user or group can pause, resume, restart, or delete documents from the print queue. A user who is not an administrator can always perform the above actions on his own print jobs; Manage Documents allows the user to act on other users' documents. This is the default access level for the Owner-Creator of a print job.

■ **Full Control** In addition to the permissions granted by Manage Documents, the user or group can change printer properties, create or delete printers, change printer permissions, and take ownership of a printer. This is the default access level for the Administrator group.

▲ **No Access** The user or group is not allowed to use the printer at all. No Access overrides any other permissions a user or group might have. For example, you could deny a Server Operator the ability to print to a particular printer.

DEVICE SETTINGS The Device Settings tab, shown in Figure 6-6, displays specific information about the printing device. A useful feature available in this window is the ability to map form names and types to trays in printing devices holding multiple trays. By allowing meaningful associations between trays and form types, this feature

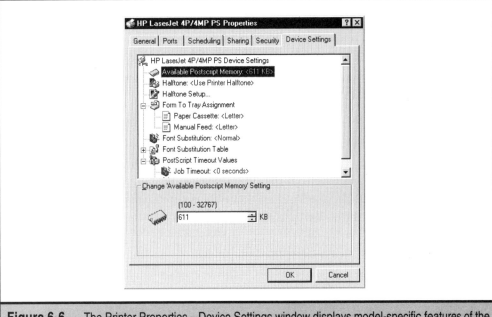

Figure 6-6. The Printer Properties—Device Settings window displays model-specific features of the printer

reduces the number of users who would otherwise select tray 2 and print their document onto 11" by 17" paper when they thought they'd chosen 8 1/2" by 14", or onto A4 paper when they thought they'd selected the envelope tray.

UNIX PRINTING

UNIX printing commands have been part of the operating system since its beginning, when ASCII line printers were the standard hard copy production method. Over the years, the printing subsystems of UNIX have been extended, enhanced, and simply hacked in order to work with dot-matrix printers, plotters, laser printers, and almost any other hard copy output device that can be imagined.

UNIX, of course, is not one-of-a-kind operating system: there are many flavors of UNIX. The two major families of these many flavors of UNIX are BSD (Berkeley Software Distribution) and System V. Proper coverage of the history of the UNIX lineages is beyond the scope of this book, but the various flavors of UNIX are either more like BSD UNIX, more like System V UNIX, or some mix of the two. One of the widest areas of variation between the two families is in the printing subsystem. A quick way to identify the family of the particular flavor of UNIX you are looking at is to look for the *lpsched* print queue daemon or the */etc/printcap* file. If *lpsched* is present, the UNIX you are looking at is a System V family relation. If */etc/printcap* is present, the UNIX you are looking at is a BSD derivation.

UNIX Glossary

UNIX has its own set of terms used for printing issues. If you're unfamiliar with them, here are a few of the ones you'll need to know:

SPOOLER   The print spooler receives, stores, prioritizes, and dispatches print jobs to a printer.

PRINTER   In the UNIX world, a printer is the same as a Windows NT printing device: a physical object that produces hard copy output.

RIP   A Raster Image Processor accepts a document in a PDL (Page Description Language) and converts the file to a bitmap format from which a printer can produce hard copy output. The RIP processing can occur either on the host computer sending the print job or on the printer itself. For example, many modern printers can accept files in Adobe's popular PostScript RIP format. Processing to convert the PostScript file to bitmap format occurs on the printer.

PDL   A Page Description Language describes how to print images on a page. While a bitmap image also does this, PDL files are more abstracted, making them easier to move between platforms. Some of the better-known PDLs are Adobe's PostScript, Hewlett-Packard's HPGL (Hewlett-Packard Graphics Language) and PCL (Printer Command Language), and Microsoft's EMF (Enhanced MetaFile, formerly known as Windows MetaFile).

BSD Printing

Operating systems in the BSD UNIX family include SunOS, Digital UNIX, and Linux, as well as AIX. (AIX has its own print queue system that is a specific instance of a general job queue system, but it accepts BSD as well as System V print commands as alternatives to its native command set.) This section will first examine BSD UNIX printing subsystem components, then discuss the procedure for adding a local printer to a BSD UNIX workstation.

BSD Printing Subsystem Components

Since BSD UNIX printing architecture is supported by Windows NT print servers, whereas System V printing is not, this section will be more detailed than the following section on System V printing. BSD-derived UNIX printing uses the following files and executables as major components:

lpd   *lpd* is the printer daemon responsible for moving a print job from the spooling directory to the physical printer.

lpr   *lpr* accepts a print job from either the local workstation or a remote client and places the print job into the spooling directory.

lpq   *lpq* displays or lists the print jobs currently in the print queue.

lprm   This deletes a print job from the spooling directory. Due to the permissions that should be defined on the printer spool directory, *lprm* is restricted to deleting a user's own jobs.

lpc   An administrative interface to printing, *lpc* originally was an acronym for line printer control. It is used to view and change the status of the printer and to alter the order of print jobs waiting in the print queue.

/etc/printcap   The */etc/printcap* file describes all printing devices for which the local print spooler is configured to send print jobs. A sample *printcap* entry for a standard design line printer would look like this:

```
# lineprinter - system default printer
lp|line printer:\
    :sd=/var/spool/lp:if=/usr/lib/lpf:lf=/var/adm/lpd-errors:\
    :lo=lp0LOCK:lp=/dev/lp:pl=66:pw=132:af=/var/adm/lpaf
```

Comment lines begin with an octothorp (#), also known as a number sign. The first line in a printcap entry has the printer name (*lp*). The printer given the name *lp* in the */etc/printcap* file is the system default printer. The other entries in this sample indicate the error logfile pathname (*lf*), the lock filename (*lo*), the device specific file (*lp*), the page length (*pl*), the page width (*pw*), and the accounting file pathname (*af*).

PRINT JOB   A print job is a file that has been generated and sent to a print queue to await actual printing. "Print job" is the BSD UNIX term; System V calls the same concept a "print request."

Installing a New Printer Under BSD UNIX

Adding a new printer locally to a BSD UNIX workstation is a reasonably simple task. The following are the steps required to configure a BSD UNIX workstation as a print server. Since the various flavors of UNIX do differ, a check of the specific operating system documentation for precise steps is recommended.

1. Physically attach the printer to the computer. Printers are commonly attached through the parallel port, the serial port, or the SCSI (Small Computer Systems Interface) port. If the printer is a serial line, disable the line by creating or editing a line for that serial port in the appropriate UNIX configuration file, such as */etc/ttytab*.

2. Confirm that the *lpd* daemon is started at system boot time. If this is the first printer added to the UNIX workstation, you may have to edit the system startup files to start *lpd*. UNIX system startup files are often in the */etc/rc* or */etc/rc.d* directory—check your operating system documentation.

3. Edit the */etc/printcap* file to add or un-comment an entry for your printer. Many UNIXes provide an extensive */etc/printcap* file with all entries commented out and inactive, so look to see if your printer is already listed. If the printer is not in the */etc/printcap* file, check the printer documentation—many printer manufacturers can provide */etc/printcap* entries for their printers.

4. Create a spooling directory for the printer, which often is located in the */var/spool* directory. Each physical printer will require a separate spooling directory. Under BSD UNIX printing, the print job is copied to the spooling directory; therefore, plan carefully and select a size for the spooling directory appropriate for the expected users. The spooling directory should be owned by the same group and user that the *lpd* daemon runs as. The spooling directory should also have access mode 755. Mode 755 means only the user has write-access to the directory, but everyone (including the user) has read and execute permission to the directory. This security precaution prevents users from inserting a print job at the top of a busy print queue, deleting print jobs from the queue, or otherwise acting in an inappropriate manner.

5. Create the printer accounting file, as defined in the printer's */etc/printcap* file, and assign it the same ownership and permission as the printer's spooling directory.

6. Start and enable the printer queue with the command **lpc up <printer_name>**.

7. Test the setup by attempting to print a file.

System V Printing

We will not address System V printing in as much detail as BSD printing, because the Windows NT print server does not support the System V print architecture. Operating systems in the System V family include Solaris, HP-UX, IRIX, and SCO UNIX, as well as AIX (as alternates to its native command set). System V printing consists of four major components: *lpsched*, spooling directories, user commands, and administrative commands.

lpsched   The *lpsched* executable lives in */usr/lib/lp* directory. The *lpsched* daemon is started when the system boots and controls when and where print jobs are passed to which physical printers.

SPOOLING DIRECTORIES   Under System V printing, a spooling directory typically is created as */var/spool/lp/request/<printer_name>*. Unlike BSD UNIX, System V spooling directories only hold print request information, but the actual print job is not copied to the System V spooling directory unless the *-c* command line parameter is used with the *lp* command.

USER COMMANDS   User commands under System V include the following: *lp* to create a print request, *cancel* to cancel a print request (by that user only, unless the user is an administrator), and *lpstat* to display a print queue's contents and available printers.

The *lp* command can also be used to modify the order of print requests within a print queue.

ADMINISTRATIVE COMMANDS System V administrative commands include *lpadmin, lpuser, lpmove, lpshut,* and the *accept, reject, enable,* and *disable* commands.

The *lpadmin* command is used to define a new physical printer, or to edit existing printers to a UNIX System V workstation. The *lpusers* command is used to define print priority as a system-wide variable for that printer, or to define priority values for specific users. Print requests may be transferred from one print queue to another with the *lpmove* command. The *lpshut* command shuts down the printing service on the workstation (which is recommended before editing the printer configuration with *lpadmin*). The *reject* and *accept* commands stop and start transferal of print requests to a spooling directory, while the *enable* and *disable* commands stop and start transferal of print requests from the spooling directory to the printer.

Samba and Printing

Samba is a freeware suite of programs written by Andrew Tridgell. The Samba suite works together to allow clients access to a server's filespace and printers via the SMB (Server Message Block) protocol. Written for several flavors of UNIX, Samba also runs on NetWare, OS/2, and VMS. In practice, this means that you can redirect disks and printers to UNIX disks and printers from Windows and Windows NT clients, Linux clients, and OS/2 clients. A generic UNIX client program allows UNIX users to use an ftp-like interface to access filespace and printers on any other SMB server. The Samba suite is discussed in more detail in Chapter 2.

One problem has been reported with using Samba and networked printers. Consider the situation where a Windows NT client workstation's printer (the software interface) is defined as pointing to a networked printer. If the networked printer is connected to the Windows NT client via a Samba server, and this printer is switched off, disconnected, or otherwise not connected to the network, then this user's connection to filesystems mounted via Samba will be slow, because the Windows NT printer (the software interface) repeatedly queries the network, looking for the missing physical printer. If the printer is connected to the network and active, there is no problem.

GENERAL ADVICE AND PRINTER STRATEGIES

In this chapter, many of the technical printing issues in Windows NT and UNIX environments have been covered. Terminology has been provided so you can use the right vocabulary in the appropriate camps. Additionally, some of the underlying architecture has been presented, so you know what happens when a user drops a Word document onto a printer icon, on a Windows NT desktop, destined for a remote printer on a UNIX print server across the network. There are, however, issues outside the network. The following section will address some of the physical issues.

General Printing Advice

Much of this section's advice originates from the fact that printing uses physical resources. One signature file seen on the Internet reads, "This message printed from 100% recycled electrons." Unlike electronic mail, printing uses up paper and laser toner or ink. With this distinction in mind, here are some tips mostly aimed at conserving usage.

PRINTER ACCOUNTING IS USEFUL AS A MONITORING TOOL   A general rule is, "If you can't measure it, you can't tell how well you're doing." For example, monitoring assisted recently at a university, where the use of the printers at a student computer lab increased from two thousand pages a week to over twelve thousand pages a week. Using the printer accounting tools, the administrators were able to determine that students were editing term papers and reprinting the entire document, often with only a single page changed.

TURN OFF THE USE OF BANNER PAGES IF THEY ARE UNNECESSARY   In many cases, where a large number of users access a shared printer, this advice is not practical. However, in other cases, such as a smaller office area with a printer shared by a few people, or a non-shared printer used by a single person, the printing of banner pages can be a significant use of resources. If a non-shared printer is used by a single person for short letters, banner pages (in this extreme case) can approach fifty percent of the total page count.

ALWAYS PROVIDE RECYCLING BINS   Users go through an astonishing amount of paper per day. The paperless office will probably become a reality for the general information technology workforce about the same time the personal helicopter for commuting to work comes into general usage. Opinions vary on the cost-effectiveness of refurbishing used laser toner cartridges. While the dollar-cost of a refurbished cartridge is less than a new one, refurbished cartridges do not always last as long as new ones. Examine what the options are in your area before deciding, but consider the idea before rejecting it.

PROVIDE PRINTING PREVIEWERS, AND EDUCATE THE USERS   The first part of this advice is often simple to implement: print preview is a common option in almost all of the word processing and page layout programs on the market. Encouraging users to use print preview before using hard copy is an administrative policy decision; it is not a policy that can be automated into the network. Although WYSIWYG (What You See Is What You Get) printing is another myth similar in attainability to the paperless office, print previews can be used to determine whether the hard copy output is at least fairly close to the desired result.

KEEP EXTRA MATERIALS ON HAND   Has it been mentioned that users go through paper and toner cartridges at an astonishing rate? If Napoleon was correct when he said, "An army marches on its stomach," imagine (or remember) what happens when the printers run out of supplies. When a software development firm misses a due date to a client because the documentation couldn't be printed because the laser toner cartridge ran empty, and there were none available locally, senior management tends to come looking for an explanation.

Strategies

So now that you've seen how to add a printer to a network, what choice do you make? A printer may reside as a local printer for a Windows NT server, a UNIX server, or in many cases may attach directly to the network. This section will compare some of the pros and cons of each of the three options.

ATTACHING A PRINTER TO A WINDOWS NT PRINT SERVER   Attaching a printer directly to a Windows NT workstation as a print server gives some benefits. One primary benefit is that Windows NT peer-to-peer networking is fairly stable and requires minimal configuration. Using Windows NT as a print server gives reliable access to the attached printer by the other Windows workstations on the local network and gives the use of the print server's hard disk as a print spooler. Installing TCP/IP Printing on the print server also grants access to the printer from any other platform on the network that supports TCP/IP, which, most likely, is every platform present.

If you choose to use Windows NT as a print server, remember the relative limitations and performance optimizations of Windows NT Workstation versus Windows NT Server. Windows NT Workstation is limited by license to only ten simultaneous TCP/IP connections. Also, Windows NT Server has its performance optimized for background applications performance. In other words, someone may be logged into a Windows NT Server console, and their word processing application will get secondary preference from the CPU in favor of the (name/file/print/RAS/whatever) server functions the server is providing to remote users.

However, the Windows NT print server does not support UNIX systems which use *lpsched*—this includes such operating systems as Solaris and IRIX. UNIX clients using a Windows NT print server must use *lpd*. UNIX systems that use *lpsched* must either have a printer available on a UNIX print server or install the *lpd* print system (available over the Internet in source code, and in various third-party commercial offerings) on each client. While adding *lpd* will allow use of Windows NT print servers, doing so is yet another task in an administrator's list and introduces another chance for problems to appear.

ATTACHING A PRINTER TO A UNIX PRINT SERVER   Attaching a printer to a UNIX print server provides many of the advantages of attaching a printer to a Windows NT print server: reliable access to the printer by other similar systems on the network, and use of the local workstation as a print spooler. Windows NT clients with TCP/IP Printing installed may also access the printer.

A NETWORKED STAND-ALONE PRINTER   Many printers today, including some in the small/home office categories, are manufactured with network cards, and even smaller laser printers that don't ship with networking built in can be inexpensively equipped with networking capability. For instance, Hewlett-Packard printers lacking networking capability can use JetDirect or Farallon attachments to add an Ethernet interface for about the cost of a laser toner cartridge. Such printers are attached directly to the network, are as much of an individual node on the network as any file server, and do not require you to dedicate any part of a workstation's activity as a print server. As long as the network itself is functioning, the printer is accessible.

On the other hand, no one can use a network printer on a congested Ethernet network. In addition, since workstations of either UNIX or Windows NT tend to have larger storage devices than printers, a stand-alone printer will be limited to a comparatively small print queue. Client workstations attempting to send to the remote print queue on the stand-alone printer may overload the print queue sooner than if the print queue was resident on a workstation.

However, even if the printing device itself can stand alone, you may want to still configure the printing device as a printer attached to either a UNIX host or a Windows NT host. A local workstation/printer arrangement provides a diagnostic checkpoint for printing troubles—a heterogeneous UNIX/NT environment may contain multiple flavors of UNIX, as well as multiple versions of Windows NT, Windows 3.1 or 3.11, Windows 95, NetWare, Macintosh, and so on. If a local print job from the print server succeeds when a print job from over the network is rejected, you know at least a portion of the printing system is still working and configured properly. If part of the network experiences difficulty, at least one person can use the printer while the network is being repaired.

SUMMARY

As shown, TCP/IP printing services in Windows NT provide both better accessibility for non-Windows workstations in the network and better control over access to the printing devices. When laser printing devices were new, they were the high-end printers whose use had to be jealously guarded because they consumed expensive resources. Now that laser printers are common, color laser and dye-sublimation printers as well as large plotters are protected devices. Microsoft's TCP/IP printing services provide better control over which users may access specific printing devices than what the NetBEUI networking protocol provides.

When adding printing resources to a network, you should be guided by the strengths of the information technology support staff and the needs and distributions of the users. If the network primarily consists of Windows workstations with only a few UNIX file servers, it would make little sense to attach printers to the UNIX servers. Similarly, if a majority of the printers on the network are already set up on the UNIX portion of the network, simply extend the current configuration. Networked printers are popular options now. Large and fast printers are commonly installed directly onto the network for the same reason early laser printers were networked: they are expensive to install everywhere, and it is reasonable to share a rare resource.

CHAPTER 7

Networking NT and UNIX

When integrating UNIX and NT systems, knowledge of networking and network protocols becomes essential. UNIX systems typically provide networking via the TCP/IP protocol, while NT can implement several different protocols. If the administrator who has been tasked with making a network integration function properly comes from a UNIX environment, he or she will most likely not be familiar with NT's use of NetBEUI, NetBIOS names, WINS, or DHCP. On the other hand, if the administrator comes from an NT environment, he or she may have had no exposure to TCP/IP at all, possibly having run their NT environment using NetBEUI or IPX.

It is impossible to cover all the networking theory that you would need to know in one chapter. In this chapter, we are going to look at some of the significant details that you should know if you are going to network NT and UNIX systems.

NETWORKING AND THE OSI MODEL

In order to connect various computing resources on a network, we have to be able to discuss the details of the network architecture. For computers to be able to communicate with each other, they must speak the same language or *protocol*. Most protocols have several different functions and operate in a layered fashion. In addition to the protocols, computers must use compatible hardware in order to communicate.

In 1978, an organization known as the International Standards Organization (ISO) developed a model for describing network architectures. In 1984, the ISO revised this model and named it the Open Systems Interconnection (OSI) reference model. The OSI model is widely used as a framework for describing networks and how network components interact at different levels.

The OSI Model Architecture

The OSI model contends that networks operate in a layered fashion, with a specific set of responsibilities located at each layer. Each particular layer in the OSI model covers the responsibilities of network function, hardware, and protocols. Figure 7-1 shows the OSI layered network model.

By dividing the network into seven layers, different services and functions can be specified at each layer. Each layer in the network communicates with its adjoining layers above and below it through a set of boundaries called *interfaces*.

The primary role of each layer is to provide a set of services to the layer above it, and to hide the details of how those services are implemented from the higher layer. This allows for each layer to act as if it is communicating directly with its corresponding layer on another computer, when in reality data is being passed down through the OSI layers, out on to the network, and back up through the OSI model on the receiving computer. The appearance of communicating directly with a corresponding layer on another computer is known as *virtual communication*. Let's look at the services provided by the various layers of the OSI model.

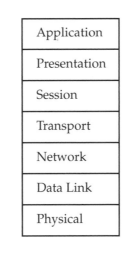

Figure 7-1.   The OSI layered network model

Physical Layer

The bottom layer in the OSI model is the Physical layer. The Physical layer is responsible for transmitting the data stream over some type of physical media, such as Ethernet or fiber optic cable. The Physical layer defines the details of the transmission media, the details of the computer interface to the transmission media, and the hardware data encoding scheme that is used. The data encoding scheme defines how the media sends a 1 or a 0 and ensures that the data sent is received as a 1 or 0 at the other end. It also defines how bits are translated into electrical or optical signals.

Data Link Layer

The second layer from the bottom is the Data Link layer. This layer is responsible for taking data from the Network layer and transmitting it over the network. It takes data chunks, known as *frames,* from the Network layer, adds some control information, and passes the frames on to the Physical layer for actual transmission.

In addition to the actual data, a Data Link layer frame may contain information such as the source and destination IDs, as well as some error detection codes, so that the Data Link layer on the other end can verify that the data frame is error-free. Since the Data Link layer is responsible for error-free transmission, it will resend any frames that were damaged or have errors.

Network Layer

The next layer up from the Data Link layer is the Network layer. The Network layer is responsible for addressing network data, translating logical addresses and names into physical addresses, and determining the best route from the source computer to the destination computer. In addition, if the Transport layer sends a block of data, known as a *packet*, that is too large for the lower levels of the network to handle, the Network layer segments the packet into smaller pieces. The corresponding Network layer on the receiving end reassembles the pieces into the original packet. This process is known as *segmentation and reassembly*.

Transport Layer

The Transport layer lives above the Network layer. The Transport layer's goal in life is to ensure that packets are delivered error-free, in sequence, with no duplication or loss. This layer takes long messages in the data stream and breaks them into packets. Since the Transport layer is responsible for ensuring packet delivery, it will request retransmission of packets that have errors or that it did not receive.

Session Layer

The Session layer allows two applications to maintain a dialog called a *session*. The Session layer manages name recognition functions and security between the two sides of the conversation. It also manages the dialog interaction between the two computers.

Presentation Layer

The Presentation layer provides translation functions for the data stream. It translates formats, protocols, character sets, etc. It may translate data into a widely implemented, intermediate format before it is sent onto the network. The Presentation layer is also responsible for data encryption and data compression.

Application Layer

The Application layer lives at the top of the OSI seven-layer model. This layer provides the services that directly interact with client applications. Its services provide network support for applications such as electronic mail and file transfers.

THE TCP/IP PROTOCOL SUITE

Protocols are the languages that computers use to speak to each other. The TCP/IP protocol suite is one of the most widely used sets of network communication protocols in existence. In the mid-1970s, the United States Department of Defense's Advanced Research Projects Agency (ARPA) undertook the task of figuring out how to make different networks interoperate. ARPA began working with universities and computer firms in order to develop new communications standards. Out of this alliance came a new set of protocols that formed the basis for TCP/IP.

Today, the TCP/IP protocol suite provides the backbone for the Internet. Virtually all UNIX systems implement TCP/IP as their primary networking protocol. Microsoft has adopted TCP/IP as the protocol of choice for NT, as well. If you are going to use Windows NT and UNIX in a network environment where they will interoperate and share services, you will be required to understand and manage a TCP/IP network.

TCP/IP has been widely adopted and implemented on a variety of platforms. However, it remains complex and fairly difficult to configure. The next few sections look at some of the key issues involved with understanding the TCP/IP protocol suite and managing a TCP/IP network.

The Protocol Stack

We refer to TCP/IP as the *TCP/IP protocol suite* because it really is composed of several different protocols. Since TCP/IP was around before the OSI model was developed, it doesn't fit nicely into the OSI seven-layer model. However, we can use the OSI model to help get a feel for how the different protocols that make up the TCP/IP protocol suite interact.

At the top portion of the TCP/IP protocol suite, we have the user application interface protocols, such as *Telnet* for remote login, the *File Transfer Protocol (FTP)* for transferring data files, and the *Simple Mail Transport Protocol (SMTP)*. We also have some other high-level TCP/IP protocols that support complex network functions, such as the *Network File System (NFS)* and the *Domain Name Service (DNS)*. These protocols roughly map to the Presentation and Application layers in the OSI model. Some of these protocols also incorporate features defined in the Session layer.

At the middle level of the TCP/IP protocol suite, we find two protocols that support functions defined in the Transport layer of the OSI model. These protocols are the *Transmission Control Protocol (TCP)* and the *User Datagram Protocol (UDP)*. TCP is a connection-oriented protocol that is responsible for providing reliable, sequenced, error-free packet delivery over the network. When a TCP protocol session is established, the two computers form a logical connection, transmit a sequence of data, and then dissolve the connection.

UDP is similar in function to TCP, except that it is not connection-oriented and does not guarantee reliable delivery. UDP is a *connectionless* protocol. With UDP, there is no need to have the overhead of setting up and dissolving a network connection. It simply transmits a packet, known as a *datagram*, to its destination host. UDP does not check to see if the packet was received successfully or not.

At the bottom level of the TCP/IP protocol suite we find the *Internet Protocol (IP)*. IP provides a connectionless Network layer protocol that addresses and routes packets. It also provides support for packet fragmentation and reassembly. Since IP is a connectionless protocol, it does not guarantee reliable delivery of network packets.

Addressing

The Internet Protocol (IP) is the Network layer component of the TCP/IP protocol suite and is, therefore, responsible for handling network addresses. IP requires that each computer or network device have a unique address assigned to it.

IP addresses are composed of four 8-bit numbers separated by decimals. Each of the four numbers that make up an IP address is referred to as an *octet*, and may have a value in the range from 0 to 255. Depending on the type of IP address, some portion will designate a particular network or subnetwork, and the remainder of the address will indicate the particular host on that network. An example of an IP address is

207.68.156.49

Certain values used in an IP address have special meanings. The numbers 0, 127, and 255 are reserved: The number 0 refers to the current network or host. The number 127 indicates a lookback to the current host. The number 255 indicates that the message should be broadcast to all hosts on the network.

Types of IP Addresses

Networks can be of vastly different sizes. As a result, there are different categories of IP addresses designed to be used in different size networks. These different categories are called *address classes*. There are three address classes in common use today: Class A, Class B, and Class C.

A class A IP address is designed for very large networks. In a class A address, the first octet of the address indicates the network, and can have a range from 1 to 126. The last three octets indicate the particular host on the network. Since only the first octet is used, and the numbers 0 and 127 are reserved, there can only be 126 class A networks in existence. However, a class A network can have over 16 million different addresses!

Class B networks are designed for midsize networks, such as those used by corporations and universities. A class B network uses the first two octets for identifying the network, and the last two octets for indicating the host. There can be 16,384 class B networks, each with 65,534 host addresses.

Class C networks are used for small networks. Only the last octet is used for the host ID portion, giving 254 hosts per network. However, there can be over 2 million class C networks. Table 7-1 summarizes the different characteristics of the network address classes.

In addition to class A, B, and C addresses, there are class D and E addresses as well. Class D is reserved for specialized network traffic known as multicast addressing. Class E is reserved for experimentation and research.

Common Problems With IP Addresses

You've configured TCP/IP and assigned your IP addresses, but things don't appear to be working correctly. What could be wrong? While there are any number of things that

Class	Number of Networks	Number of Hosts per Network	Valid Network IDs
A	126	16,721,214	001–126
B	16,384	65,534	128.0–191.255
C	2,097,152	254	192.0.0–223.255.255

Table 7-1. IP Address Class Characteristics

can be wrong with a TCP/IP network configuration, for IP addresses, there are only a couple of common mistakes.

First of all, your network address could be set incorrectly. This will cause all network traffic to be routed to the wrong network. Second, you could have the same IP address assigned to multiple computers. This is a very common mistake and can be hard to troubleshoot. Duplicate IP addresses can cause some very strange behavior, which can appear and disappear. Windows NT will not initialize its network connection if it detects a duplicate IP address and will indicate the error with a message in the error log. However, you can still have duplicate IP addresses with UNIX systems, or by configuring a UNIX system to have a duplicate address of an existing NT workstation. Your network administrator should assign IP addresses in a very controlled manner to prevent duplicate addresses. Never, ever, allow a user to "make up" an address for their computer!

ROUTING

The Internet Protocol is responsible for routing packets of data, known as datagrams, to their destination over a group of connected networks, known as an internetwork. Routing destinations can be local, on another network with a known route to that network, or completely remote. In this section, we'll look at some of the details of routing and help you understand the difference between and the significance of logical and physical addresses.

Physical Addresses vs. Logical Addresses

Under IP, every host connected to the network must have an IP address. This address is a *logical* address. Logical addresses have no relationship to the physical hardware used or the physical media that the host is connected to. Logical addresses are assigned to an organization, and are then assigned by that organization to network devices as needed. Recall that an IP address contains both a network portion and a host portion. The network portion is logically assigned based on a criteria assigned by the network administrator.

Physical addresses, by comparison, are assigned to a particular piece of hardware. When you buy an Ethernet card from some manufacturer, the card has a specific Ethernet address burned into the hardware of that card. This address cannot be changed, thus the term "physical" address. If you move the card from one computer to another, the physical address of the card will not change.

Routing deals with the logical address rather than the physical address. Since you can assign logical addresses yourself based on your own criteria, routing allows you to segment your network along logical, organization-specific lines.

Bridges vs. Routers

A bridge is a network device that manages traffic based on its physical address. Bridges function at the Data Link layer in the OSI model. Bridges allow you to separate your network into different physical segments in order to manage network traffic. When you install a bridge in a network, you create two physical segments. The bridge monitors network traffic and builds a table of physical addresses. This table keeps track of which side of the bridge a particular physical address is on. If network traffic is sent from one host to another, and they are both on the same side of the bridge, the bridge will not forward the traffic to the other side. Since bridges operate at the Data Link layer, they do not know anything about routing and logical addresses. They can only manage network traffic by keeping track of the physical addresses.

Routers, on the other hand, operate at the Network level in the OSI model. Routers are used to separate a network into multiple logical networks. Traffic is controlled and manipulated based on logical addresses, such as the IP address.

Let's look at an example of why you would use a router. Say you have two groups in your company, sales and research and development (R&D), and you want to have them on separate networks. By installing a router, you can separate the sales network from the R&D network, based on the corporate function of the two departments involved. You would simply assign different IP addresses with a different network component to sales and R&D, and configure a router to route between the two. That way, all sales traffic would stay on the sales network, and all R&D traffic on the R&D network. Only traffic specifically sent from one network to the other would pass through the router. In fact, even broadcast packets would not be sent, as routers do not forward broadcasts.

Routable vs. Non-Routable Protocols

As you can probably gather, IP is a *routable* protocol. A routable protocol is one that can be managed with a router rather than a bridge. For a protocol to be routable, it must have some method of encoding a network address into its logical address. IP is a routable protocol because its addresses are broken down into separate network and host portions.

A non-routable protocol does not have a network address component. Most non-routable protocols were developed to operate in a local LAN environment and were never meant to travel outside the local LAN.

Why is the distinction between routable and non-routable an issue? Because many Microsoft networks still use NetBEUI, which is a non-routable protocol. If your network relies on routers for traffic routing and management, you will not be able to use NetBEUI as an NT protocol without enabling the Windows Internet Name System (WINS), which we will discuss later in the chapter.

Local Routes

OK, we've seen how routers and bridges can manage network traffic based on logical or physical addresses, respectively. So how do the mechanics of routing work? There are a couple of scenarios. Let's start with the simplest.

Let's assume that you are sending an IP datagram to a host on your local network. The IP layer on the sending computer will request the physical address of the destination computer via something known as the *Address Resolution Protocol* (ARP). If the destination computer is on the same network, ARP will return the physical address of the destination to the sender. IP then adds the source and destination addresses to the datagram, and drops the datagram down through the OSI stack until it goes out on the network.

Once the datagram, know called a frame, hits the network, it passes through all the network interfaces on its network segment. Each network interface examines the destination physical address of the frame and compares it to its own. When the frame lands in the network interface of its intended destination, it is passed up the OSI stack to the IP layer. All other hosts will ignore the frame, once they figure out it wasn't intended for them.

Think about this for a moment. Every network interface has to examine every frame on the local segment to see if it belongs to them. So, if we add more network devices to the segment, we add more traffic in the form of frames. Eventually, performance will start to suffer as network interfaces spend more and more time examining frames that were not meant for them in the first place. This is why most large networks are really several small network joined by routers. By using this strategy, only the network interfaces on the destination network segment have to examine the frame that gets sent.

Remote Routes

Instead of being on the local network, the destination for an IP address might be on a remote network. IP figures this out by matching the network portion of the address with the network portion of the address of the sender. If they are on different networks, IP forwards the datagram to a router. This router then compares the network addresses again. If the destination is still remote, it forwards the datagram on to another router, and the whole process repeats.

Eventually, one of two things will happen. First of all, the IP datagram could make its way to a router with a network address that matches the network portion of the destination address. If this happens, the router treats the IP datagram as though it were a local route, calls ARP, and fills in the physical address of the destination. Second, the datagram may just die in the network. Each datagram has a data field known as the Time-To-Live (TTL) field. Each time a datagram passes through a router, the TTL field is decremented. If it reaches zero before the datagram reaches its destination, the datagram is thrown out, and an error message is sent back to the sender. This mechanism keeps packets from being trapped in a network "twilight zone" forever.

Default Gateway

So, where does the network send a datagram when it doesn't know the route to its final destination? The IP protocol routes the datagram to the *default gateway* on the network. The default gateway is a router that you designate to receive traffic when no local route can be found on your network. Typically, this is the router that connects your organization to the outside world and the Internet. The default gateway is specified in each computer's network configuration.

Static and Dynamic Routes

By this time, you're probably wondering how routers know where to send datagrams if they cannot be delivered locally. Sure, we can send them to the default gateway, but how does the default gateway know where to send them?

Basically, there are two answers. Routers can be configured with *static routes* or can implement *dynamic routing*. Static routes are routing tables that map network destinations to a specific router. When a datagram arrives at a router that uses static routing, it will look up the destination network in its routing table and send the datagram to the corresponding router. Since static route tables must be manually maintained, they can get to be very time-consuming in a large network.

Dynamic routing is the solution to the shortcomings of manually maintained routing tables. When routers are able to use dynamic routing, the routers communicate with each other and exchange routing information via protocols such as RIP or OSPF. The routing tables are generated automatically and are passed back and forth between routers.

HOST NAMES

Host names are text names that act as aliases for network addresses. Within a UNIX environment, the term *host name* refers to the name of a particular network device that is mapped to an IP address. In the Microsoft world, host name can refer to a name mapped to either an IP address or a NetBIOS name. We'll talk about NetBIOS names in a second.

Why would we want to complicate things by using host names in addition to network addresses? Simple: because they're easier to remember. It is easier for us to remember a name associated with an organization than it is to remember a string of numbers. Also, by using host names, we can hide the address details from the end user. This way, if we want to change the network address of some computer, we can do so without changing its name.

DNS Names

In TCP/IP, a host name is an alias that is mapped to an IP address. Host names are stored in a distributed database known as the *Domain Name Service (DNS)*. The DNS database is queried by systems that are trying to resolve a host name into an IP address.

NOTE: For more information on DNS, see Chapter 8.

DNS uses a name space that is organized in a tree structure. At the top of the tree are the general subdivisions that determine the type of organization the name belongs to. For example, "com" refers to a commercial organization, and "edu" refers to an educational organization. DNS divides its name space into logical domains. Each domain is a logical collection of TCP/IP hosts. Typically, there will be one top-level domain in an organization, with additional subdomains under it. For example, **ncsu.edu** is the domain that refers to North Carolina State University, and **cs.ncsu.edu** is a subdomain for the Computer Science department. To specify a particular host within a domain, simply concatenate its host name and domain name, separated by a period character. For example, **www.ncsu.edu** is the NCSU web server. The host **sun1.cs.ncsu.edu** might be a UNIX system in the Computer Science department.

NetBIOS Names

Windows NT is capable of supporting multiple networking protocols. The *Network Basic Input/Output System* (NetBIOS) is a network application programming interface (API) that is used with the Microsoft Networking architecture and has shaped a significant portion of NT's network name space. Microsoft uses NetBIOS names for NT domain names, share names, printer names, and computer names.

When you give a command to map a remote directory, such as

```
net use G: \\FILESRV\PUBLIC
```

you are using a couple of different NetBIOS names. The name FILESRV is the NetBIOS name of the server that has the directory that we are mapping. The name PUBLIC is the actual directory located on the server FILESRV. NetBIOS names can be a maximum of 15 characters long. NetBIOS names are not case sensitive, and are typically written in all uppercase.

As we mentioned earlier in this section, NetBIOS is an API that provides access to network services. It is commonly, though by no means always, used in conjunction with the NetBEUI protocol. NetBIOS can be bound to several different protocols, including TCP/IP, so that systems may honor NetBIOS requests or Server Message Block (SMB) messages from other systems.

DNS NAME RESOLUTION

Recall that DNS maps host names to IP addresses. When someone uses a DNS host name, the name must be *resolved*, or mapped to an IP address. This process usually takes a couple of steps, as there are multiple locations where IP address mappings are stored.

NOTE: Where we provide a directory path into the Windows NT system directories in the examples in this chapter, we assume that your Windows NT root directory is WINNT. If you have named the Windows NT root directory something else, change the directory path names to reflect where NT is installed on your system

When a computer needs to resolve a DNS host name, it first checks its own name to see if the request is local. If its own name doesn't match, it typically looks in a static file on the computer first. This file, known as a *hosts* file, is a static mapping of host names and IP address pairs. Since this file is static, it is never automatically updated by DNS. You either manually edit the file or use a local tool to add and delete entries. On UNIX systems, the *hosts* file is typically located in */etc/hosts*. On Windows NT, the file is located in *\WINNT\system32\drivers\etc\HOSTS*.

NOTE: Notice that the NT version of the hosts file is named HOSTS. and has only a period at the end with no extension. If you edit the file with a text editor, make sure that the editor does not rename the file HOSTS.txt, or with some other extension.

If the system fails to find a match in the local hosts file, it then contacts one or more DNS servers, provided that it has been configured to do so. On UNIX systems, the information for locating DNS servers is typically located in the file */etc/resolv.conf*. Under Windows NT, the DNS server information is specified in the DNS Configuration Dialog box.

If no match is made after querying a DNS server, UNIX will return an error. NT will then try to resolve the name as a NetBIOS name. We will discuss NetBIOS name resolution later in the chapter.

Hosts File

The hosts file, whether HOSTS. in NT or */etc/hosts* in UNIX, is a flat text file that contains DNS name and IP address mapping pairs. In some ways, the hosts file is a holdover from the old days of the Internet. Originally, the Internet was a fairly small place. Host additions, deletions, and address changes were propagated by a flat hosts file that was distributed over the Net. As the Internet grew, this solution became unwieldy, and the DNS system was developed.

You may wonder why we would want to have this file, since DNS will resolve things for us. Most UNIX systems require a hosts file in order to map the local host name to an IP address, so that the local computer knows its address. Under NT, the hosts file is not required. By using a local hosts file, you can provide local address mappings that will be used if the DNS system is not available. If you include your common servers and destinations in your hosts file, and DNS goes down, you can still resolve addresses for the entries in your hosts file.

There is something that you should be aware of, however. NT checks the hosts file first and uses the address that it finds there, if it finds one. This means that if the hosts file has an address that is out of date, NT will use the incorrect address. On some UNIX systems, it is possible to change the order of how UNIX will check the hosts file and DNS. These changes are made by special configuration options in the */etc/resolv.conf* file. For more information on changing the DNS resolution order on your UNIX system, look in the online help with the following commands:

```
man resolver
man resolv.conf
```

SUBNETTING A NETWORK

As you know, a network provides a means for computers and other devices to communicate. The word *subnet* refers to subdividing a network into sections. Different physical network segments can be joined into an internetwork by interconnecting them with routers. Each physical network segment requires a separate means of identifying that particular segment.

Remember that IP addresses, such as 192.168.1.1, are divided into a network IP portion and a host ID portion. The different classes of addresses use different parts of the IP address to represent the host ID and network ID. In the above example, the default network portion consists of the first three octets, 192.168.1, and the default host portion consists of the last octet, 1 (i.e., it is a class C network). Sometimes you will find it necessary to divide the network portion up in such a way that it now can represent multiple networks. This dividing of the network ID is known as *subnetting* and is accomplished by using a custom *subnet mask*.

Subnet Masks

Why would we want to divide the network portion of our IP address up to create subnets? Let's look at an example:

Assume that you've got a small company network with less than 100 users, and you have been assigned a class C network address, 192.168.1.0, by your ISP. You, being a network savvy administrator, know that a class C address uses three octets for the network portion and one octet for the host ID. You also know that you can't use the numbers 0 or 255 to represent hosts, so you can have up to 253 different addresses in your class C office network. In fact, their addresses would be in the range from 192.168.1.1 to 192.168.1.253.

Now, what happens if you need to break your network into two physical segments, say, one for development and one for marketing? Sure, you can stick a router in between and make them separate segments, but, in order for the router to work, they have to be different subnets. What do you do? You could go back to your ISP and pay for another class C address for the other segment, but you've already got plenty of room in your existing class C network. The smart thing to do is to subnet your class C network and break it into two networks. You can do this by applying a custom subnet mask, which we will cover later in the chapter. By picking the right subnet mask, you can cause your network to have a small number of network IDs with a larger number of host IDs, or you can have a large number of smaller subnetworks. It all depends on your organization and how many subnets you need.

Networks and Default Masks

So what is this crazy thing called a subnet mask, and what does it do? A subnet mask is a four-octet number sequence that looks similar to an IP address. Its job in life is to determine which part of an IP address is the network ID, and which part is the host ID.

When you set up TCP/IP on a system, whether NT or UNIX, you have to supply a subnet mask. This lets TCP/IP figure out how to divide up IP addresses into their network and host parts. In fact, the system may offer you a default subnet mask when you configure it. How can the system know what subnet mask you need? Well, it can't really, but it makes an educated guess. You see, each of the different classes of IP addresses has a default subnet mask that comes with it for free. If you don't want to change the default manner in which the network and host portions are broken up in a particular address, you can simply use the default masks. Table 7-2 shows the address classes and their default masks.

The default subnet masks allow the different address classes to divide up their IP addresses in different ratios. The default subnet mask for a class A network reserves the first octet for the network ID portion, and the last three octets for the host portion. For a class B address, the first two octets make up the network portion by default, and the last

IP Address Class	Default Subnet Mask
Class A	255.0.0.0
Class B	255.255.0.0
Class C	255.255.255.0

Table 7-2.   The Different Classes of IP Addresses and Their Default Subnet Masks

two octets are reserved for the host portion. In a class C network, the default mask reserves the first three octets for the network portion, leaving only the last octet for the host ID.

How Subnet Masks Work

OK, so subnet masks look sort of like IP addresses, and they are used to divide up IP addresses into network IDs and host IDs. Exactly how do they do this? First of all, realize that we can write IP addresses in a binary form. To do this, we just translate each octet into its binary equivalent. For example, the IP address 192.168.16.1 would be written in binary as

```
11000000 10101000 00010000 00000001
```

We can do the same thing with subnet masks. Since 192.168.16.1 is a class C address, its default subnet mask is 255.255.255.0. Writing the subnet mask in binary, we get

```
11111111 11111111 11111111 00000000
```

Now, if we place the binary subnet mask under the binary IP address, we can use it to figure out the host and network portions of the IP address. The bits of the IP address that correspond to 1's in the subnet mask make up the network portion of the address. The 0's in the subnet mask correspond to the bits in the IP address that make up the host portion of the address. To figure out the network ID portion, look for the 1's in the subnet mask and copy down the corresponding bit of the IP address. When you find a 0 in the subnet mask, just fill in a 0. So, for example,

```
11000000 10101000 00010000 00000001    IP Address
11111111 11111111 11111111 00000000    Subnet Mask
11000000 10101000 00010000 00000000    Network ID
```

Translating our network ID back to dotted decimal, we get 192.168.1.0, which gives us a network ID that corresponds exactly to the first three octets in the address. Now, let's use the subnet mask to get the host ID portion. It's just like what we did for the network portion, except we look for 0's in the subnet mask instead of 1's.

```
11000000 10101000 00010000 00000001    IP Address
11111111 11111111 11111111 00000000    Subnet Mask
00000000 00000000 00000000 00000001    Host ID
```

Translating the host ID back to dotted decimal, we get 0.0.0.1, which gives us a host ID that corresponds exactly to the last octet in the address.

In this example, there are 24 bits in the non-zero network ID portion of the address, as is the default in a class C network with the default subnet mask. There are 8 bits in the non-zero host ID portion of the address, which are available for us to assign to hosts. Since, we can't use all zeros or all ones for a host number, this gives us a maximum of $2^8 - 2$ or 254 hosts on this class C network. If we need more host addresses, we will have to go to a bigger network class or get another Class C address space.

This process works with any class of network. Let's look at another example. What happens if we take the address 172.21.192.7 and apply the default subnet mask? Since the first octet is between 128 and 191, this is a class B address. The default subnet mask for a class B address is 255.255.0.0. Translating the address into binary, we get

```
10101100 00010101 11000000 00000111
```

If we translate the class B default subnet mask into binary, we get

```
11111111 11111111 00000000 00000000
```

Putting the binary IP address over the subnet mask and solving for the network ID, we get

```
10101100 00010101 11000000 00000111          IP Address
11111111 11111111 00000000 00000000          Subnet Mask
10101100 00010101 00000000 00000000          Network ID
```

This results in a decimal network ID of 172.21.0.0. Doing the same operation to solve for the host ID gives us

```
10101100 00010101 11000000 00000111          IP Address
11111111 11111111 00000000 00000000          Subnet Mask
00000000 00000000 11000000 00000111          Network ID
```

From this, we see that the decimal host ID portion of the address is 0.0.192.7.

Since the default class B subnet mask splits the address right down the middle, the network ID portion consists of 16 bits, and the host ID portion consists of 16 bits. So, with a class B address and the default subnet mask, we get one network with up to $2^{16} - 2$ or 65,534 possible host addresses.

Custom Subnetting

Now that you have seen the mechanics of how subnets separate an IP address into a network and host ID portion, you can see that you get a fixed number of bits to assign to hosts for addressing purposes. The network portion of your address space is fixed; you can't change it. You only have flexibility to deal with the address portion. So, no matter what class of network you have, by default you have one network segment address with multiple host addresses.

What if you need to divide your network into multiple segments? You might have some remote segments that you need to connect, or you might want to reduce broadcasts and local traffic by using routers. There are lots of reasons why you might need to create multiple network segments in your network.

Since each network segment connected by a router is its own subnet, each network segment requires its own unique network ID. If you already have an address assigned to you, then you will have to create a custom subnet mask to divide your network properly.

Before you start creating a custom subnet mask, you need to figure out how many subnets you are going to need. You also need to take into account the maximum number of hosts per subnet that you will need. When we start figuring out the custom subnet, you will see that there is a tradeoff between the number of subnets and the number of hosts per subnet. You should plan for future expansion as best you can, because figuring out the subnet mask and changing the subnet mask and addresses on all your systems is a time-consuming process. You don't want to repeat it any more often than necessary!

OK, it's example time. Let's say that you have a software development company with a class C address space, 192.168.183.0. You want to divide your network into five subnets, one each for development, sales, marketing, quality assurance and testing, and company administration. You figure that your company will be less than 100 people for quite a while, and you won't need more than 20 addresses in any subnet for the foreseeable future.

To subnet your class C network into five subnets, you are going to take some bits from the host ID portion of your network and reassign them to the network ID. To do this, you need to create a custom subnet mask. The first thing to do is figure out how many bits you need in order to create your custom subnet mask. Since the math for this is in binary, subnets are allocated on a power of two basis. Also, remember that we can't have a subnet whose address is all zeros or all ones. By using three extra bits, we can get $2^3 - 2$ or 6 subnets. Since we can't get exactly five subnets, we can reserve one for future use.

By moving three bits from the host ID portion to the network ID, we leave five bits for the actual host ID. This gives us $2^5 - 2$ or 30 valid host IDs per subnet. Since we only need 20 host IDs per subnet, it looks like that three extra bits will work for us. Our default subnet mask for a class C network is 255.255.255.0, which, in binary, looks like

```
11111111 11111111 11111111 00000000
```

Let's go ahead and add the three bits from the host portion to the right-hand side of the network portion of the subnet mask. This gives us

```
11111111 11111111 11111111 11100000
```

which translates back into decimal as 255.255.255.224. This is our new subnet mask!

Before you can plug the new subnet mask in and make your new subnets, we've got to figure out what our new network IDs and host IDs will be. This can get a bit complicated, so we'll go slowly.

Our original class C address is 192.168.183.0, which translates into binary as

```
11000000 10101000 10110111 0000000
```

Since we're adding three bits to the network ID, the network address will expand just like the subnet mask. To get our new network IDs, we add all the possible permutations of the three-bit value, excluding 000 and 111. This gives us six new network IDs, as shown in Table 7-3.

These new network addresses may look a bit confusing, because they don't end in 0 like all the other network addresses that you have seen. Just remember, there are five bits at the end of each of these subnet addresses that are reserved for your host IDs. So how do we assign host IDs? We just start filling in the host ID bits on the end. (Remember, we can't use all 0's or all 1's for the host ID; all 1's is reserved for broadcast.) Table 7-4 shows some of the host addresses for the 192.168.183.32 subnet. There are 30 possible addresses in each subnet.

The host addresses simply count upwards from subnet number to one less than the next subnet number. So, in the .32 subnet, the first host address is .33, and the last is .63, because the next subnet number is .64.

Subnet Tables

While you can calculate all the details of custom subnets by hand, it is a time-consuming task. To make life easier, you can use the following tables, which give the general subnet information for each class of networks. Each table gives the number of subnets and number of hosts per subnet available for each possible subnet mask. It also shows how many bits must be shifted from the host ID portion to the network ID portion. You will still have to calculate the network IDs by hand. However, just remember that the host IDs

Subnet Number	Subnet in Binary	Subnet in Dotted Decimal
Subnet 1	11000000 10101000 10110111 00100000	192.168.183.32
Subnet 2	11000000 10101000 10110111 01000000	192.168.183.64
Subnet 3	11000000 10101000 10110111 01100000	192.168.183.96
Subnet 4	11000000 10101000 10110111 10000000	192.168.183.128
Subnet 5	11000000 10101000 10110111 10100000	192.168.183.160
Subnet 6	11000000 10101000 10110111 11000000	192.168.183.192

Table 7-3.   Six New Subnets of 192.168.183.0

Host Address Number	Host Address in Binary	Host Address in Dotted Decimal
Host 1	11000000 10101000 10110111 00100001	192.168.183.33
Host 2	11000000 10101000 10110111 00100010	192.168.183.34
Host 3	11000000 10101000 10110111 00100011	192.168.183.35
Host 4	11000000 10101000 10110111 00100100	192.168.183.36
…	…	…
Host 28	11000000 10101000 10110111 00111101	192.168.183.61
Host 28	11000000 10101000 10110111 00111110	192.168.183.62
Host 30	11000000 10101000 10110111 00111111	192.168.183.63

Table 7-4.   Host Addresses for the Subnet 192.168.183.32

count upwards from the starting subnet network ID and stop at one less than the next subnet network ID. Table 7-5 shows the subnet information for class A networks.

Table 7-6 shows the subnet information for class B networks.

Table 7-7 shows the subnet information for class C networks.

Number of Subnets	Hosts per Subnet	Bits Required	Subnet Mask
2	4,194,302	2	255.192.0.0
6	2,097,150	3	255.224.0.0
14	1,048,574	4	255.240.0.0
30	524,286	5	255.248.0.0
62	262,142	6	255.252.0.0
126	131,070	7	255.254.0.0
254	65,534	8	255.255.0.0

Table 7-5.   Subnet Information for Class A Networks

Number of Subnets	Hosts per Subnet	Bits Required	Subnet Mask
2	16,382	2	255.255.192.0
6	8,190	3	255.255.224.0
14	4,094	4	255.255.240.0
30	2,046	5	255.255.248.0
62	1,022	6	255.255.252.0
126	510	7	255.255.254.0
254	254	8	255.255.255.0

Table 7-6. Subnet Information for Class B Networks

DYNAMIC HOST CONFIGURATION PROTOCOL

As anyone who has ever had to manage a TCP/IP network knows, keeping track of IP address assignments and configuring workstations can be a time-consuming task. TCP/IP requires each device to have a separate unique address that cannot conflict with any other network device. You must, therefore, take care when assigning or reassigning addresses to make sure that you do not duplicate addresses between systems. Also,

Number of Subnets	Hosts per Subnet	Bits Required	Subnet Mask
2	62	2	255.255.255.192
6	30	3	255.255.255.224
14	14	4	255.255.255.240
30	6	5	255.255.255.248
62	2	6	255.255.255.252
invalid	invalid	7	255.255.255.254
invalid	invalid	8	255.255.255.255

Table 7-7. Subnet Information for Class C Networks

TCP/IP has several configuration parameters, which makes it even easier to cause errors when configuring a workstation.

Microsoft has developed a system known as the *Dynamic Host Configuration Protocol* (DHCP) in an attempt to solve these problems. Their solution, depending on your point of view, is at least partially successful. DHCP is a system that automatically configures a TCP/IP client when it boots up, providing it with a unique IP address, plus other configuration information such as its default gateway, DNS servers, WINS servers, etc. So, in theory, all you have to do is set up a DHCP server, tell your clients to use it for configuration, and all your TCP/IP configuration headaches are a thing of the past.

To DHCP or Not to DHCP?

Unfortunately, there is a slight difference between theory and practice. You see, no matter how much Microsoft would like you to believe that DHCP is a magic cure-all, DHCP has some serious limitations. For example, only a Windows NT server can act as a DHCP server, and DHCP clients must be running Windows NT Server or Workstation 3.5 or greater, Windows 95, certain versions of the MS Networking Client or LAN Manager server for MS-DOS, or Windows for Workgroups with a particular version of TCP/IP software. Note that UNIX doesn't get to play in the DHCP world. UNIX cannot currently function as either a DHCP client or server.

In addition to the current requirement that clients and servers be Microsoft products, there are a few other limitations to DCHP that you need to know about before you go down that road.

▼ DHCP servers do not talk to each other. This means that if two DHCP servers are configured to give out the same range of IP addresses, there is no way for one to know what the other has assigned.

■ Unless configured otherwise, DHCP will not provide a specific IP address to a client. It will instead pick an address out of the range of valid addresses. If you have a workstation that needs to be assigned a specific address upon boot, you must manually customize the DHCP profile for that workstation.

■ The IP address and subnet mask provided by the DHCP server is guaranteed to be used by a DHCP client. However, any other options that you enter into the Network Control Panel will override information provided by DHCP. Any modifications that you make to the NT Registry also override DHCP information.

■ DHCP will not detect any IP addresses already in use by non-DHCP clients. This means that you will have to have an accurate list of all IP addresses in use by all UNIX systems, OS/2 systems, Macs, etc., before installing DHCP, and you will have to manually exclude them from DHCP server configuration.

▲ Unless you have routers that are configured for BOOTP forwarding, DHCP servers are confined to their local subnet and will not work across routers.

So, with all these problems, who would want to use DHCP? If you have a very Microsoft-oriented network, with NT servers and lots of Microsoft clients, and you want to centrally manage TCP/IP configuration for your clients, and you don't mind the clients getting a different IP address each time they boot, then DHCP could be a good solution. On the other hand, if you have a lot of UNIX systems or other non-DHCP-capable computers, and only a few Microsoft systems, you should probably steer clear of DHCP, as it will be more trouble than it is worth.

How DHCP Works

OK, if you've decided that DHCP could work in your environment, let's look at how it actually works. DHCP provides IP addresses to clients for a specified period of time. This is known as an *IP lease*.

When a DHCP client boots up, it sends a broadcast message to any DHCP servers on the network requesting an IP lease. Every DHCP server that gets the request, both on local and remote networks, will respond with an offer to lease the client an IP address. The DHCP client will accept the first offer that it gets, and sends out another broadcast message that contains the IP address that it has decided to use. The server that leased the IP address to the DHCP client then sends back an acknowledgment to the client. This process occurs whenever a DHCP client needs a new IP lease.

By default, IP leases expire in three days. The expiration interval can be configured by the system administrator, and can be set so that leases never expire. When its IP lease expires, the DHCP client sends a message to the DHCP server that gave it the lease, requesting that the lease be renewed. If the DHCP server is up and running, and the IP address is still available in the server's list of addresses, it automatically renews the lease. If the address is not available, possibly because the address has been manually assigned to a non-DHCP client and removed from availability, the client has to go through the whole DHCP lease process again.

NOTE: You can configure DHCP so that IP leases do not expire.

The DHCP Server

In order to run a DHCP server, you must have a computer running Windows NT Server 3.5 or later with Microsoft TCP/IP installed. The DHCP server software is installed as a network service in the Network Control Panel.

DHCP is configured with a set of ranges of IP addresses, known as *scopes*. The DHCP server requires a scope be defined for each subnet that the DHCP server will manage. This includes the local subnet and any other subnets that are connected via routers.

Before creating a scope, you will need to know a valid range of IP addresses to include in the scope and all the current non-DHCP-capable IP addresses that are in the range. You will also have to know the details of the specific options that you want to configure, such as netmasks, default gateway addresses, and WINS server addresses. If you have DHCP clients that require static IP addresses, you will need to know the name of the client, its specific IP address, and its specific hardware address, such as its Ethernet address.

Scopes are created and managed, along with general DHCP server configuration and options, in the DHCP Manager Tool. The details for using the DHCP Manager Tool are beyond the scope of this chapter, no pun intended.

THE NETBIOS API

You will recall from the earlier section on NetBIOS names that NetBIOS is a programming API that Microsoft uses to bind to a variety of protocols. While NetBIOS is commonly thought of as being associated with the non-routable NetBEUI protocol, it can be bound to TCP/IP and IPX/SPX as well. NetBIOS is supported by several different networking systems, including

▼ Microsoft's implementation of TCP/IP, IPX, and NetBEUI

■ Microsoft LAN Manager for MS-DOS, UNIX, and OS/2

■ DEC Pathworks from Digital Equipment Corporation

▲ IBM LAN Server

Thus, NetBIOS provides a common programming interface over a variety of networking schemes. For example, a computer running LAN Manager for OS/2 can make a NetBIOS request to a Windows NT system, provided that both are running compatible network protocols.

NetBT

While it is possible to run NetBIOS over a variety of protocols, you will probably be using TCP/IP, especially if you have other UNIX systems. As we said previously, NetBIOS requests are commonly sent via the NetBEUI protocol. NetBEUI has less overhead than TCP/IP, and is, therefore, slightly faster. It is also very simple to install and configure. However, NetBEUI is not a routable protocol. NetBEUI was designed to be used in a LAN environment and will not work with hosts that are separated by routers.

Fortunately, NetBIOS also binds to TCP/IP. This combination is commonly referred to as *NetBT* or *NBT*. Remember that NetBIOS uses different names than UNIX DNS names. So, in order for NetBIOS to function over TCP/IP, there must be some way to map a NetBIOS name to an IP address.

NOTE: NetBIOS is a programmatic API. All requests to NetBIOS use NetBIOS names. NetBIOS does not understand numeric IP addresses directly.

NetBT Name Resolution Process

When a computer using NetBT joins a network, it sends a out registration request. This registration request is either sent to a NetBIOS server or broadcast to the local network via a UDP datagram, depending on the NetBT computer's configuration. The purpose of the NetBIOS registration request is to notify other computers using NetBIOS that a new NetBIOS computer has joined the network, and to register with a NetBIOS name server, such as a WINS server. We will discuss WINS in more detail later in the chapter.

If there is a WINS server on the network, and it receives the registration request from a new host, it checks to see if another computer is already using the NetBIOS name. If so, it sends a notification back to the source computer indicating that the name is already in use.

When an NetBT computer, referred to as the resolving computer, needs to resolve a NetBIOS name to an IP address, it first looks in its local NetBT name cache. This name cache contains all the NetBIOS names that have been resolved since TCP/IP was initialized on the system. Entries in the NetBIOS name cache typically expire after a period of time, to ensure that the cache doesn't grow unbounded and that the entries stay reasonably current.

If the resolving computer doesn't find the name in the NetBIOS name cache, it sends a request to a WINS server, provided that one exists on the network. In order for a computer to access a WINS server for NetBIOS information, the address of the WINS server must be entered in the computer's TCP/IP Configuration dialog box. The computer requesting the NetBIOS resolution will send up to three requests to the WINS server before deciding that the WINS server is not responding. If the WINS server does not respond, the resolving computer will then try a secondary WINS server, if available.

After giving up on the WINS servers, the computer attempting to resolve the name will use something called a *B-node broadcast*. A B-node broadcast is a message broadcast onto the network, requesting the host who has the particular NetBIOS name in question to respond with its NetBIOS name and IP address. B-node broadcasts are limited to the local network, plus any networks connected by routers configured to forward B-node broadcasts. A computer attempting to resolve a NetBIOS name will send up to three B-node broadcasts.

If the resolving computer has come up empty on all its other attempts, it will look in a local static file called the LMHOSTS file. This file is similar to the TCP/IP hosts file in that it is a list of static mappings. However, the LMHOSTS file contains mappings for NetBIOS names to IP addresses.

However, you may not have the LMHOSTS file, and many organizations choose not to configure one, as it can require significant maintenance. In order for a resolving computer to use an LMHOSTS file, you must configure the system to enable it. Click the Start Button, choose Settings, then choose Control Panel and run the Network applet. Select the Protocols tab, and you should see a dialog box similar to the one in Figure 7-2.

Select the TCP/IP protocol and click the Properties ... button. This brings up the Microsoft TCP/IP Properties dialog box. Select the WINS Address tab. You should see a dialog box similar to the one in Figure 7-3.

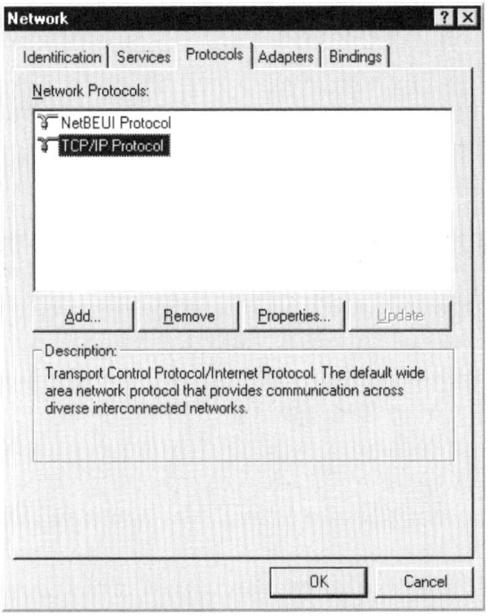

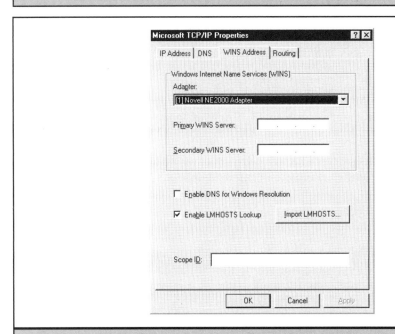

Figure 7-2. The Protocols tab in the Network Control Panel applet

Figure 7-3. The WINS Address tab in the Microsoft TCP/IP Properties dialog box

To allow the computer to use the LMHOSTS file, click the "Enable LMHOSTS Lookup" checkbox. When you enable LMHOSTS lookup, your NT system must have a valid LMHOSTS file in the \ *WINNT* \ *system32* \ *drivers* \ *etc* directory. You can also opt to copy an LMHOSTS file from another computer. To do so, click the "Import LMHOSTS ..." button and select the computer and path to the file to import.

THE WINDOWS INTERNET NAME SERVICE

As you saw earlier in the chapter, NetBIOS clients go through several steps when trying to map NetBIOS names to IP addresses. One of the first steps in this mapping process is to send a query to a WINS server.

In spite of its name, the Windows Internet Name Service (WINS) has nothing to do with the Internet. WINS servers act as a registration point for NetBT clients, so that they can register their NetBIOS name to IP address mapping information. By using a WINS server, NetBIOS clients do not have to broadcast their name queries onto the network. This is beneficial for a couple of reasons. First, each broadcast consumes network bandwith. By sending the name queries directly to a WINS server, there is no need to broadcast a query to everyone on the network. Second, routers are typically not set up to forward NetBIOS broadcasts, so any broadcast queries are limited to the local network.

When a WINS client using NetBT starts up, it sends a registration request to its WINS server. If the address is available, the WINS server sends a response back to the client confirming its IP address and NetBIOS name, and telling it how long its registration is valid for before it must be renewed. When the renewal time expires, the NetBIOS name is deleted from the WINS server. To prevent its name from being deleted when the renewal time expires, the WINS client must send a renewal request to the WINS server before the expire time arrives.

NOTE: By limiting the amount of time that NetBIOS name registration is valid, WINS servers prevent their name database from containing old, out-of-date information.

When a WINS client using NetBT shuts down, it sends a message to its WINS server telling it to remove the client's information from its database.

WINS Servers

The WINS server software is installed as a TCP/IP installation and configuration option in the Network applet of the Control Panel. Once the WINS software is installed, it must be configured. Configuration takes place within the WINS Manager program. A variety of options is available when configuring a WINS server. The details of WINS configuration are beyond the scope of this chapter.

How many WINS servers should you install? In general, you can usually get away with one or two for your entire organization, unless you have a very large number of

WINS clients and the server traffic load becomes prohibitively high. It is good practice to have both a primary and secondary WINS server, in case the primary server should fail.

There is no need to have a WINS server on each subnet. Since each client knows the address of the WINS server, either by manual configuration or via DHCP, requests that go to the WINS servers are sent in normal IP datagrams. This means that WINS server requests are routed normally by all routers on your TCP/IP internetwork.

SUMMARY

The area where Windows NT and UNIX networking meet makes for an interesting mix of topics. If you, as the administrator, come from a UNIX background, you are probably unfamiliar with common NT topics such as NetBIOS, DHCP, and WINS. On the other hand, if you come from an NT background, the TCP/IP protocol suite, especially subnets, may seem to be an obscure art.

In this chapter, we have tried to cover most of the areas where NT and UNIX collide in the networking world. We have discussed the OSI model of networking and how it applies to the TCP/IP protocol suite. We looked at routing and DNS name resolution. Subnets play an important role in creating TCP/IP internetworks, so we explored the steps involved in creating custom subnets.

From the NT side, we examined the issues surrounding NetBIOS, including NetBIOS over TCP/IP, NetBIOS name resolution, and WINS. We also looked at how DHCP can be used in some circumstances to help reduce the management load for a network administrator.

WINDOWS
NT
Professional
Library

CHAPTER 8

DNS Configuration

The Domain Name System, simply referred to as DNS, provides a mechanism for associating hierarchical names with IP addresses. In other words, it provides the mechanism for translating a request for the host name **www.microsoft.com** into its corresponding IP address.

The DNS service is available on both UNIX and NT platforms. In this chapter, we will look at the history of DNS, the various files and data components that make up a DNS system, and the installation and configuration of DNS on both NT and UNIX.

WHAT IS DNS?

When the Internet was first formed, there were very few computers attached to it. It was a straightforward matter to maintain the name/address mapping by having a complete list of all host names and addresses in a local file on each host computer. As more and more computers connected to the Internet, it became clear that this system could not keep up with the growth. When a new host was added, it was necessary to update every host file on every computer. It was evident that a new solution had to be devised.

Domains and Zones

The Domain Name System consists of a *domain name space,* which is constructed in a tree structure. Conceptually, each node in the tree, known as a *domain,* has a database of information about the hosts under its authority. Domains are assigned by the Internet Network Information Center, also known as the Internic (more information on the Internic can be found on the Web at **http://www.internic.net**). Typically, there will be one domain assigned for a single large entity, such as a company or a university. For example, **microsoft.com** is the domain assigned to Microsoft, and **ncsu.edu** is the domain name assigned to North Carolina State University. Figure 8-1 shows the domain name space tree structures of both the Internic and of the fictitious company that owns the domain **fakecompany.com**.

Domains can be divided into logical elements known as *subdomains.* For example, suppose the network folks at The Fake Company wanted to group their sales computers in a separate component of the domain name space. They could create a subdomain like **sales.fakecompany.com** and assign host names to computers within this subdomain. This provides for a logical grouping of hosts and further organizes the domain name space.

The actual information for a domain or subdomain is contained in files known as *zone files.* It is important to note that domains and subdomains refer to logical divisions of the domain name space, while zones refer to the actual files that contain the information. There can be multiple zones for one domain, which can be used for distributing domain management responsibility and redundancy. Figure 8-2 shows examples of zone structure.

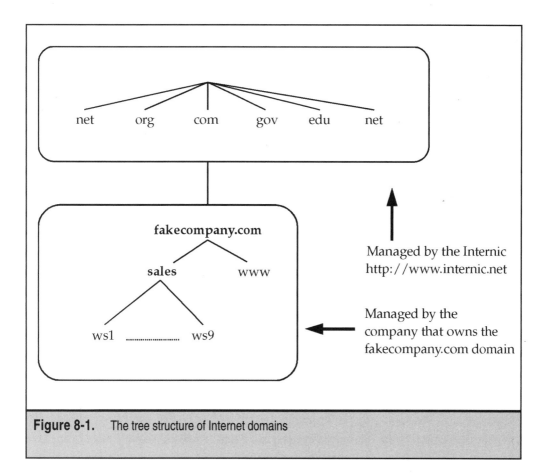

Figure 8-1.   The tree structure of Internet domains

Name Servers

Name servers are programs that contain, maintain, and answer queries regarding the data in the domain name space. Each name server has complete information about a subset of the domain name space. In addition, the server may have cached information about other domains and subdomains as well.

Primary Name Servers

Primary name servers are servers that have their data in local zone files. When an administrator updates or adds host information to a domain, the update is performed at a primary name server. Primary name servers are considered the "last word" in authority for the host information that they serve out to clients.

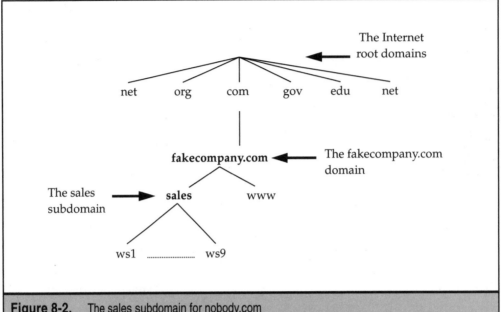

Figure 8-2.   The sales subdomain for nobody.com

Secondary Name Servers

A secondary name server functions similarly to a primary name server in that it answers DNS queries from clients. However, it does not keep its host information in local zone files. Instead, a secondary name server obtains its information via a *zone transfer* from a specific primary name server, known as its *master name server*.

You should consider having multiple name servers, including servers at remote locations, in your DNS configuration. By using multiple secondary servers, you can add redundancy in the event that your primary server fails. In addition, you can use secondary name servers to reduce the load on your primary name server.

Caching-Only Servers

A caching-only server does not have any authority in the domain name space. Nor does it perform zone transfers with a master name server. A caching-only server exists to make queries and cache the results locally. Caching-only servers start with no zone information locally, then build up their cache of domain name space information over time by caching the results of queries. This type of server is useful when you have a slow network link between you and your primary DNS server.

UNIX DNS

In this section, we will examine the process for configuring a DNS server to run under UNIX. Please remember that there are several different varieties of the UNIX operating system commonly used today. As a result, the examples that we give in this section may not be exactly correct for the particular version and release of UNIX that you are using. However, since virtually all UNIX implementations of DNS are based on the same original source, these examples should be very close to the actual details for most versions of UNIX.

The *named* Process

Under UNIX, the DNS name server duties are typically provided by the *named* daemon process. The *named* daemon starts when the computer is booted and reads its initial configuration information from a configuration file. Typically, this file is called *named.boot* and is located in the */etc* directory. Once *named* has started and is initialized with its configuration information, it begins listening for DNS requests on the default network port specified in the */etc/services* file.

NOTE: In the *named.boot* file, as in the other DNS configuration files under UNIX, comments are indicated by the semicolon character and continue to the end of the line.

The *named.boot* file is the roadmap that the *named* daemon uses to find all its other configuration files. There are several options that can be listed in the *named.boot* file. Table 8-1 lists the most common options. Depending on your version of UNIX, these options may be slightly different or you may have additional options.

NOTE: The domain names and IP addresses used in these examples are not valid names and addresses. They are used as examples only.

The following is a sample *named.boot* file:

```
; An example named.boot file
directory /etc/named
cache . named.ca
primary fakecompany.com named.hosts
primary 1.169.192.in-addr.arpa named.rev
```

This boot file sets up the local name server to act as a primary name server for the **fakecompany.com** domain. By using a "directory" option, we have told *named* that it can

Option	Function
Directory	Specifies the directory where the DNS zone files are located
Primary	Tells *named* to be a primary server for the specified domain
Secondary	Tells *named* to be a secondary server for the specified domain
Cache	Tells *named* to cache the results of queries
Forwarders	Causes the local name server to try to contact other servers if it cannot resolve the query locally
Slave	Tells *named* to be a slave server and forward the request to one of the forwarder name servers

Table 8-1.   Common Configuration Options for the */etc/named.boot* File

expect to find its files in the */etc/named* directory. Another common place to put configuration files is in the */var/named* directory.

The next line contains the "cache" option and tells *named* to cache information that it receives and to pre-load its cache from the *named.ca* file.

The "primary" option on the next line directs *named* to become a primary name server for the domain **fakecompany.com**. As the primary name server needs to read its zone information locally, the name of the zone file, *named.hosts*, is specified on the line as well.

Don't be confused by the second "primary" line in the *named.boot* file. According to the second "primary" line, this name server is also a primary server for **1.168.192.in-addr.arpa**, with *named.rev* as the name of the zone file. DNS was originally designed to map names to IP addresses, without the ability to map the other way. By using a second "primary" entry, *named* can be configured to map IP addresses back to DNS names as well.

Zone Files

As we said before, primary name servers load their host information from zone files. These zone files contain all the information for hosts in the particular zone of authority that a given name server has responsibility for. All information in these database files is stored in a format known as a *resource record*. Each resource record has a type associated with it, which is used to indicate the function of that particular resource record.

CAUTION: The file formats used by DNS are fairly complicated and obscure. In fact, most DNS configuration problems can be traced to errors in the configuration files.

There are several different types of resource records available, each serving a different function. Table 8-2 lists the most common types of resource records that you are likely to encounter.

Resource Record Syntax

When describing the details of a resource record in one of the zone files, we use a syntax that is common to all types of resource records. The basic format of a resource record is shown below, with the optional components listed in square brackets:

```
[record owner] [time-to-live] [class] type data
```

The "record owner" field of the resource record indicates the particular thing that the resource record refers to. It can indicate either a domain name or a host name. If no record owner field is given, the domain name of the previous resource record is used.

Resource Record Type	Description
A	An address record that maps a name to an address. The address is specified in the data field in dotted decimal format
CNAME	A canonical name record that is used to assign an additional name to a host. Since there can only be one address record for each host, any additional host name mappings must be given via canonical name records
HINFO	A host information record that provides general information such as hardware type and operating system version
MX	A mail exchanger record that is used to indicate that another computer handles mail delivery for the host listed in the record
NS	A name server record that points to the authoritative server for another zone
PTR	A pointer record that is used to map addresses back to host names
SOA	A Start of Authority record that informs the name server that it has final authority for a list of resource records

Table 8-2.   Common Resource Record Types

The "time-to-live" field indicates how long, in seconds, this particular resource record is valid as an answer to a query. This field is used to specify how long a particular record may be cached after it is retrieved from a server. If you do not specify a time-to-live value, the minimum time-to-live value of the last *Start of Authority* (SOA) resource record is used.

The "class" field is used to indicate that this resource record uses a particular type of networking addresses. The value *IN* is used to indicate a TCP/IP network. As with the "record owner" field, the class of the previous resource record is used if you do not specify a class.

The "type" field, which is required, is used to indicate which type of resource record we're working with. The various resource record types are listed earlier in the chapter.

The "data" field, which is also required, is the actual value that is contained within this resource record. Since there are several different types of resource records, the format of the "data" field is dependent on the particular type of resource record being defined.

The Start of Authority Record

The *Start of Authority*, or SOA, record is used to indicate that the records that follow are authoritative for a particular zone. This means that the name server that contains the SOA record has the final word on the data contained in these records. The data in the authoritative records overrides any cached data on other name servers and any currently held data on secondary name servers.

The SOA record has one of the most complicated data formats of all the resource records. While it uses the same general syntax format described earlier in this chapter, the "data" field is surrounded by parentheses and usually contains more than one line.

Let's look at the fields that make up the complicated data format in the SOA record. The "origin" field gives the canonical name of the primary name server for this domain, which is typically given as a *Fully Qualified Domain Name* (FQDN). An FQDN is a host name that has the entire domain and subdomain information appended, such as **www.fakecompany.com**. If the host name is provided as an FQDN, it will need to end with a period character. This tells the *name server* daemon not to append the current domain name to it by default.

The SOA record also contains information regarding how to contact the domain administrator. This information is contained in the "contact" field. It is specified typically as an Internet electronic mailing address, with one exception: the "at" character (@), typically found in the email address, is replaced by a period. This is due to the fact that, within a resource record, the @ character expands to the value of the *origin* field.

When the domain administrator updates information in the zone files, there must be some mechanism to let the various name servers know that the file has changed and that their zone-transferred and cached copies are no longer current. Since date and time stamps vary with the clock settings on various computers, they are unreliable as a means to indicate change. The SOA record uses an incremented serial number instead. The "serial" field contains an integer serial number that is used to indicate the version number of the zone file.

NOTE: You must increment the SOA serial number every time you change information in one of the zone files. If you forget, secondary servers will not know that the file has been updated and your DNS servers will behave strangely. Forgetting to increment the SOA serial number is one of the most common problems when managing a DNS system.

There are several parameters in the SOA record that relate to time-out and retry options. The "refresh" field indicates how long, in seconds, a secondary server should wait before refreshing and checking the SOA record of the primary name server. Typically, SOA records are not updated that frequently. A typical value for the "refresh" field is about 24 hours.

NOTE: On most UNIX systems, you can force the *named* daemon to reload its configuration, either by rereading its zone files or by initiating a zone transfer. This is typically accomplished by sending a SIGHUP signal to the *named* process. First use the *ps* command to locate the process ID (PID) of the *named* process, and then use the command:

```
kill -HUP named-PID
```

Two fields in the SOA record control how a secondary name server functions when it is unable to contact the primary name server. The "expire" field is used to control how long a secondary name server should wait before it invalidates its zone information, assuming that it hasn't been able to contact the primary name server. The "retry" field tells a secondary name server how long it should wait, in seconds, to retry a request if the primary name server is not available.

You will recall that resource records have a time-to-live value that determines how long a resource record is valid. If you do not specify a time-to-live value in an individual resource record, the record inherits the time-to-live value from the SOA record. The "minimum" field in the SOA record indicates the default resource record time to live, in seconds.

The Primary Zone File

When we configured the *named.boot* file earlier in the chapter, the "primary" line indicated that the primary zone file was *named.hosts*. This file contains the authoritative information for the **fakecompany.com** zone. Here is a sample *named.hosts* file for **fakecompany.com**:

```
; A sample named.hosts file for the
; domain fakecompany.com
;
@ IN SOA nameserver.fakecompany.com. root.fakecompany.com. (
  19            ; The SOA serial number - remember to increment it!
  43200         ; Refresh field - Refresh every 12 hours
  120           ; Retry field -   Retry every 2 minutes
```

```
2592000        ; Expire field -  Expire after 30 days
43200          ; Time-to-live  - Default time-to-live is 12 hours)

IN NS nameserver.fakecompany.com.
;
; Set up an entry for the domain itself fakecompany.com
;
IN A 192.168.1.1
;
; Our nameserver             .
;
nameserver A 192.168.1.1
;
; Our mail server
;
mailer IN A 192.168.1.2
;
; Several client workstations
;

ws1 IN A 192.168.1.3
IN MX 100 mailer.fakecompany.com
ws2 IN A 192.168.1.4
IN MX 100 mailer.fakecompany.com
ws3 IN A 192.168.1.5
IN MX 100 mailer.fakecompany.com
ws4 IN A 192.168.1.6
IN MX 100 mailer.fakecompany.com
ws5 IN A 192.168.1.7
IN MX 100 mailer.fakecompany.com
```

Let's look at this file in detail. The first resource record in the file is the *Start of Authority* (SOA) record for **fakecompany.com**. Recall that the @ character in a resource record translates to be the current origin, **fakecompany.com**. The origin is defined in the main *named* configuration file, *named.boot*. It is listed on the "primary" line in *named.boot*.

Following the @ symbol, we see the "class" and "type" fields, which are listed as

```
IN SOA
```

The "class" field is *IN*, which indicates that this resource record uses TCP/IP addressing. The "type" field, *SOA*, indicates that this is a Start of Authority record. The next entries make up the "data" portion of the SOA record. As we've just seen, this part of an SOA resource record is pretty complicated.

The first element in the "data" field is the canonical name of the primary name server for this domain, **nameserver.fakecompany.com**. Following the name of the name server is the contact email address, **root.fakecompany.com**.

> **NOTE:**   Remember that in the contact email address, we have to replace the normal "at" character (@) with a period character (.) because the @ is translated to be the current value for the domain origin.

The next five fields in the SOA resource record are the numeric parameters that control refreshing and expiration. The first of these numbers is the serial number of the SOA record. Remember to increment this number when you update your zone files so that changes can take place! The next four fields are the "refresh," "retry," "expire," and "time-to-live" fields, respectively. These fields are discussed in detail in the section, "The Start of Authority Record," earlier in the chapter.

Following the SOA record is a name-server resource record, which lists **nameserver.fakecompany.com** as the name server for the **fakecompany.com** domain. Remember that the first field in a resource record is the optional "record owner" field. Since we did not list a value for this field, *named* assumes that we're using the last domain that we specified. Because no domain is listed in the "domain" field, it is assumed to be the last domain specified. What was that last domain that we specified? Look back at the beginning of the SOA record and you will see the @ character. The @ character is the domain; remember that it expands to be the domain from the *named.boot* file, **fakecompany.com**.

The next thing we do is set up an address for the domain itself, in case anyone should try to use **fakecompany.com** as a host name. We do this via an address (*A*) resource record. Normally we would list a host name at the beginning of the *A* record, but since the last thing we referenced was the domain itself, via the @ character, we can just leave the host name portion blank.

> **CAUTION:**   We let *named* figure out the default domain or host name in several examples in this chapter so that you can get practice reading this type of syntax. In reality, you must be careful if you implement zone files this way. If you add an entry in the middle of a file, and that entry has a domain name specified, you will cause problems if other entries use the previously referenced domain in their resource record.

Since **fakecompany.com** is not a real computer, we assigned it the IP address of **192.168.1.1**, which is really the IP address of our name server.

If you look back toward the beginning of the *named.hosts* file, you will see that we listed **nameserver.fakecompany.com** in an *NS* resource record. This tells *named* that **nameserver.fakecompany.com** is the name server for our domain. However, we need to give an IP address for **nameserver.fakecompany.com**. We do this via another *A* record, which looks like

```
nameserver A 192.168.1.1
```

After setting up the address for our name server, we assign an address to our mail server as well. The last several lines in the file assign IP addresses to a series of workstations. You will notice that after each *A* record for a workstation address, there is a line that looks like this:

```
IN MX 100 mailer.fakecompany.com
```

This line contains a mail exchanger (*MX*) record and tells *named* that when mail is received for this workstation, it should be forwarded to the host **mailer.fakecompany.com** instead.

The Cache Configuration File

The DNS process caches results from its queries in order to speed up the resolution of frequently requested name translations. In the *named.boot* configuration file, we entered a line that looked like this:

```
cache . named.ca
```

This line tells *named* to cache queries and to preload its caching information from the file *named.ca.* Unlike the other DNS configuration files, this file is pretty simple. As stated earlier in this chapter, the caching operation of *named* is very important. Fortunately, the *named.ca* file that sets up caching is also usually the simplest of the various DNS configuration files. It lists the root name servers for the various domains along with their IP addresses, so that your DNS server will already have the addresses of the root servers. The following is a sample caching configuration file:

```
; A sample caching configuration file
;
; NS record configuration
;
99999999 IN NS KAVA.NISC.SRI.COM.
99999999 IN NS TERP.UMD.EDU.
99999999 IN NS NS.NIC.DDN.MIL.
99999999 IN NS NS.NASA.GOV.
99999999 IN NS NS.INTERNIC.NET.
;
; Address record configuration
;
NS.NIC.DDN.MIL. 99999999 IN A 192.112.36.4
NS.NASA.GOV. 99999999 IN A 128.102.16.10
KAVA.NISC.SRI.COM. 99999999 IN A 192.33.33.24
TERP.UMD.EDU. 99999999 IN A 128.8.10.90
NS.INTERNIC.NET. 99999999 IN A 198.41.0.4
```

The Reverse Resolution Configuration File

DNS was designed to map names to addresses. However, we also need to be able to map addresses back to names. Recall that we had a line in the *named.boot* configuration file that looked like this:

```
primary 1.168.192.in-addr.arpa named.rev
```

This line tells *named* that we are also the primary server for a domain called **1.168.192.in-addr.arpa**. What is this strange looking domain? The "in-addr.arpa" component tells *named* that this domain does reverse lookups that match IP addresses to host names. The "1.168.192" component is the network portion of our IP address in reverse. The last argument on the "primary" line, *named.rev*, is the zone file that contains the reverse resolution information. This file is very similar in format to the *named.hosts* file, except that it is used to map addresses to host names. Here is a sample *named.rev* file:

```
@ IN SOA nameserver.fakecompany.com. root.fakecompany.com. (
  19              ; The SOA serial number - remember to increment it!
  43200           ; Refresh field - Refresh every 12 hours
  120             ; Retry field -   Retry every 2 minutes
  2592000         ; Expire field -  Expire after 30 days
  43200           ; Time-to-live  - Default time-to-live is 12 hours)
;
; Our nameserver
;
nameserver A 192.168.1.1
;
; Here are the reverse address mappings
;

1 IN PTR nameserver.fakecompany.com.
2 IN PTR mailhost.fakecompany.com.
3 IN PTR ws1.fakecompany.com.
4 IN PTR ws2.fakecompany.com.
5 IN PTR ws3.fakecompany.com.
6 IN PTR ws4.fakecompany.com.
```

As you can see, the *named.rev* file has the same SOA record as the *named.hosts* file. The SOA record sets up authority for the reverse resolution domain. Remember all the discussion about the @ character expanding to be the value of the origin? Well, here it is set to **1.168.192.in-addr.arpa** from the "primary" line in the *named.boot* file.

The first resource record is an *NS* record that indicates the name server. The rest of the records in the file are *PTR* records that map IP addresses to host names. The host names in the *PTR* resource records must be the full canonical name of the host, ending with a period character.

NT DNS

Under Windows NT Server, DNS is not installed by default. Rather, it is an optional service that you install from the Network applet in Control Panel. Prior to installing DNS, you need to check your current TCP/IP configuration, including your DNS client configuration information. When the DNS service is installed, it uses the DNS client configuration information for some of its default settings.

The DNS client configuration information is found by going to the Control Panel and then selecting the Network applet icon. Select the Protocols tab and highlight the TCP/IP protocol line, as shown in Figure 8-3.

Now press the Properties button to set up your TCP/IP properties. From the TCP/IP Properties window, select the DNS tab, as shown in Figure 8-4, and verify that the host name and domain name are correct.

Installing Microsoft DNS is very straightforward. You install it as you would any other network service. Go to the Control Panel, and select the Network applet icon. Select the

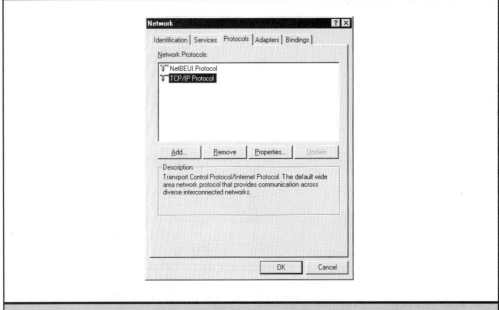

Figure 8-3.   The Protocols tab in the Network Control Panel applet

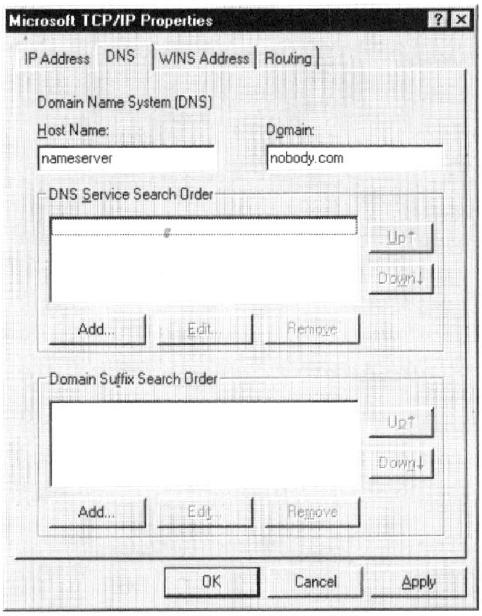

Figure 8-4.   The DNS configuration view in the Network Control Panel applet

Services tab, and click the Add button. From the list of services, select Microsoft DNS Server, and click the OK button.

At this point, you have completed the default installation of the Microsoft DNS server. However, you will have to restart your computer for the DNS service to be available.

Configuring Microsoft DNS

The Microsoft DNS server is configured via the DNS Manager tool, which is available under Administrative Tools from the Start button. Figure 8-5 shows the DNS Manager tool. Since the installation of DNS only installs a basic configuration, no DNS servers will show up in the server list. By selecting New Server from the DNS menu, you can add a local DNS server. Once you add a local DNS server, you can double-click on the server in the Server List to see the zone definitions for that server. By default, Microsoft DNS is installed as a caching-only server, so if you want to use it as a primary or secondary server instead, you have a bit more configuration to do.

Assuming that you want to use your DNS server for something more than a caching server, the first thing you need to do is create zones in the DNS Manager tool. Microsoft's DNS server groups everything by zone, so a zone must be created first.

Once the domain and zone information has been determined, this information must be entered into the DNS configuration using the DNS Manager. To create a zone, right-

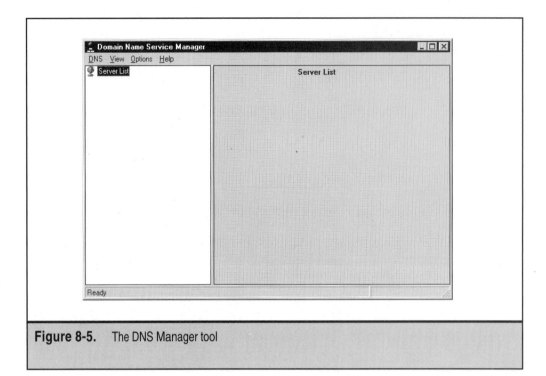

Figure 8-5. The DNS Manager tool

click on the server name, and select New Zone from the menu. If you choose to create a secondary zone, you will need to enter the zone name and the name of the master server.

If you have opted to create a primary server, you'll need to tell DNS the name of the zone and zone files to be stored on your local server. If you give a zone name that already exists in your DNS directory, Microsoft DNS will import the resource records from this zone file automatically. DNS will add the zone into your DNS tree when you have entered all the information. Following the creation of zones, you should use the DNS Manager tool to create subdomains and resource records.

DNS AND WINS

Microsoft Windows NT also provides a service known as the Windows Internet Naming Service (WINS). WINS provides a NetBIOS naming layer above the TCP/IP addressing layer in the network protocol stack. This layer maps Microsoft NetBIOS names to TCP/IP addresses. This mapping allows communications via the NetBIOS name and the Microsoft Universal Naming Convention (UNC) when the target computer is using TCP/IP as its network protocol. Since NetBIOS is not a routable protocol, it uses a flat name space and has no concept of hierarchical name space as found in DNS host and domain names.

The Microsoft DNS and WINS servers are designed to work together to resolve names. Under WINS, hosts are allowed to dynamically register their names with the WINS database, and so may or may not appear as static IP addresses in the regular DNS database.

Microsoft has defined a new resource record of type *WINS* that is attached to the root zone in the domain. This record tells Microsoft's DNS server how to contact the WINS server to resolve name queries for hosts that do not have static DNS entries. For example, a *WINS* resource record might look like

```
@ IN WINS 192.168.1.100
```

NOTE: You should be aware that this resource record is not standard and can adversely affect non-Windows NT DNS servers attempting to perform a zone transfer from an NT primary server.

To enable DNS and WINS cooperation, select the Properties entry of the zone that you want to enable, and enable WINS resolution from the WINS Lookup tab. You will have to enter the IP address of your WINS server at this point.

Adding WINS Lookup to Existing DNS Configurations

If you have an existing DNS architecture and decide to add WINS lookup, you will need to use Microsoft's DNS server on an NT server. The easiest way to provide this functionality is to add a new subdomain to support WINS lookup. For example, if your domain is **fakecompany.com**, you might want to add the subdomain **wins. fakecompany.com** to support WINS lookup. Set up an NT primary DNS server for this zone, and enable WINS lookup, pointing the DNS server to the WINS server.

UNIX OR NT?

As you have seen, there are versions of DNS for both Windows NT and most flavors of UNIX. So, which should you use? Let's look at a few pros and cons.

The DNS implementation under UNIX is very robust and has been extensively tested and is widely deployed. It is based on the Internet Request for Comments (RFC) standards documentation. The vast majority of DNS traffic on the Internet today is served by UNIX-based computers. However, UNIX systems can be difficult to administer, and DNS configuration under UNIX is notoriously difficult. As you have seen earlier in the chapter, UNIX DNS configuration is based on manually edited text files that have a very complicated syntax.

Microsoft shipped their first release version of DNS with Windows NT 3.51. It was shipped as an add-on component with the NT 3.51 resource kit. This release had several major shortcomings and was not robust enough for production use. With Windows NT 4.0, Microsoft has released an updated version of DNS as an NT service. While this release appears much more stable and robust, it has yet to be widely adopted and tested. The current NT 4.0 DNS release does contain graphical management tools that make it much easier to maintain and update zone information, and it does include integration with the WINS protocol to add support for computers that rely on the NetBIOS protocol. However, the DNS-WINS integration component of Microsoft DNS uses non-standard resource record types that are not supported by most other DNS servers. If a non-Microsoft DNS computer attempts a zone transfer from a Microsoft DNS server with DNS-WINS resource records, it may encounter problems. Some users on Internet-support mailing lists have reported unusual behavior from the NT DNS service as well.

In addition to Microsoft's DNS implementation, there are several other versions of DNS that run under Windows NT 4.0. These versions include both commercial implementations and freeware versions. In addition, there is a Windows NT port of the UNIX BIND name server software. A review of some of the most popular NT DNS servers can be found on the Web at **http://guide.sbanetweb.com/net1212.htm**.

NOTE: For extensive information on DNS, including a download link to the NT BIND port, see **http://www.is.co.za/dnsrd/**.

Given the robustness of the UNIX DNS offerings, we would recommend that you implement a UNIX-based DNS if it is feasible in your environment. If you do not have UNIX expertise or are primarily an NT-based organization, you should probably review some of the alternative commercial NT DNS offerings before making a final decision.

DESIGNING A DNS ARCHITECTURE

Now that we have explored the various options available in both NT and UNIX DNS servers, what is the best way to set up your DNS architecture? One of the most important points, from both a management and performance point of view, is deciding how you will structure your domains and subdomains. There are two common approaches to this decision. You can either have one large domain for your whole organization, with hosts addressed directly from the domain name, or you can opt to create subdomains.

Single Domain Model

If you have a fairly small organization, especially if your organization is located in the same geographical area, you might want to consider having one domain, such as **fakecompany.com**. You would then address your hosts directly off the domain name, for example, **ws1.fakecompany.com**. The advantage to this approach is that all domain management is centralized in one location. You don't have to worry about separate subdomains, multiple master servers, different zone files, etc. However, you can suffer some performance problems. If you use multiple secondary name servers, your primary

DNS server can suffer load problems answering refresh queries from the secondary servers. In addition, lots of users making queries against your primary server can reduce its performance.

Subdomain Model

If your organization is geographically dispersed or you have lots of users, it may be to your advantage to create subdomains and manage your DNS entries accordingly. In this model, you would have a single root domain server with an appropriate number of secondary servers supporting it. The root server is responsible for answering requests for hosts that directly connect to the root domain, and for directing querying hosts to the appropriate subdomain servers. These subdomain servers can be organized according to geographic region, departmental function, corporate structure, or whatever makes sense for your organization. For example, if your root domain is **fakecompany.com**, you could create subdomains **sales.fakecompany.com**, **marketing.fakecompany.com**, **development.fakecompany.com**, and **support.fakecompany.com**. By separating the DNS structure into subdomains, you increase the number of systems for which administration will be required; however, you can delegate this responsibility to the appropriate departments or regions. You also reduce the load on the primary DNS servers by separating information into multiple servers.

TROUBLESHOOTING DNS

As you have probably figured out by now, DNS, whether UNIX or NT-based, is a complex system. It is easy to make mistakes that are very difficult to locate. Most of the problems result from syntax errors in your configuration files, or from assigning the wrong address to the wrong computer. Try to remember the following guidelines when implementing and troubleshooting your DNS:

▼ For all entries, check and verify the spelling of host names. Also remember that absolute host names end with a period. Absolute host names are names that are complete as written; they do not need to have a domain name appended to them.

■ Remember to update the serial number in your *SOA* records in your zone files if you make a modification. This will ensure that secondary servers reload the files correctly.

■ Verify that the DNS name and IP address entered in the primary zone file match the corresponding reverse resolution information in the reverse resolution zone file.

■ *SOA* and *CNAME* records can cause all sorts of problems if you are not careful. Misspelling a name or getting a host address wrong here can redirect queries to computers that don't exist.

▲ Microsoft's DNS server uses some non-standard resource records, which can cause problems for UNIX-based secondary DNS servers that zone transfer from the NT DNS server. These records occur primarily when WINS resolution is enabled on the NT server.

The best practice is to thoroughly test your DNS configuration. The *nslookup* utility, available on both NT and UNIX, is an excellent tool for examining your DNS database.

SUMMARY

In this chapter we have looked at many aspects of DNS, including its history and use. We have explored the configuration of DNS zone files in detail and have examined the differences between Microsoft's DNS server for Windows NT 4.0 and the various UNIX DNS servers that are available. In addition, we've looked at several potential pitfalls when setting up and configuring a DNS system, as well as some design principles for choosing the best DNS architecture for your organization. Remember that regardless of your DNS architecture, testing your DNS database thoroughly is one of your best defenses against problems.

DNS is a very complex system and can cause problems that are difficult to locate. However, with a bit of research, planning, and forethought, DNS management is a very manageable task.

WINDOWS
NT
Professional
Library

CHAPTER 9

Remote Access Service

onnecting a computer to a remote network is a very common task. With the wide variety of networking protocols available, network interoperability issues can become very complicated in short order. Microsoft Windows NT provides a mechanism known as the *Remote Access Service* (RAS) that is used to provide remote network connections.

When integrating Windows NT and UNIX environments, it is typically more common to have a Windows NT computer acting as the client, dialing in to a UNIX- or TCP/IP-based network. In this chapter, we will look at RAS in detail, including its installation, configuration, and troubleshooting.

INTRODUCTION TO RAS

The Windows NT Remote Access Service, or RAS, is a robust network application that provides networking services for remote client computers. The RAS server component acts as a remote dial-in point for client computers, and the Dial-Up Networking Application provides client computer network connection services. Figure 9-1 shows an example of how a Windows NT client using RAS can interact with various network services.

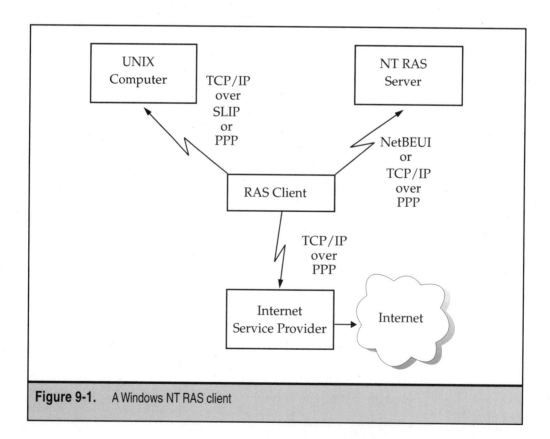

Figure 9-1.   A Windows NT RAS client

RAS supports a wide variety of network programming interfaces and networking protocols, allowing it to work in diverse environments. By using the Point-to-Point Protocol, many different networking protocols can be routed via RAS. RAS also supports a variety of hardware networking media, as described in Table 9-1.

RAS is available on both Windows NT 4.0 Workstation and Windows NT 4.0 Server; however, there are a couple of differences between versions. Under Windows NT Workstation, RAS supports one inbound network connection. If you use RAS under Windows NT Server, up to 256 inbound network connections are available.

LINE PROTOCOLS

A line protocol is the network protocol that provides the underlying connection over an asynchronous data connection. The RAS service supports three different line protocols: the Serial Line Internet Protocol, known as SLIP; the Point-to-Point Protocol, known as PPP; and the Point-to-Point Tunneling Protocol, known as PPTP.

Name	Description
Public Switched Telephone Network (PSTN)	The PSTN is the standard analog telephone service provided by your local telephone company. RAS can connect via the PSTN by using an analog modem
ISDN	The *Integrated Services Digital Network*, or ISDN, is a digital communications network service available from most telephone companies. ISDN provides a higher bandwidth connection than a standard analog phone line, and requires special hardware, which is referred to as an *ISDN Terminal Adapter* or *ISDN Modem*
X.25	The X.25 network is a packet-switched data network. Access to an X.25 network is made via a Packet Assembler Disassembler or PAD device. X.25 supports direct connection via a PAD or analog dial-up connections
Null Modem Cable	A special cable that allows two computers to be connected via their serial ports

Table 9-1.   The Network Media Supported by RAS

Serial Line Internet Protocol

The Serial Line Internet Protocol, or SLIP, is a standard networking line protocol that supports serial line connections via TCP/IP. Today, SLIP is primarily used with older versions of UNIX.

SLIP differs from its younger cousin, PPP, in several important ways. SLIP does not allow any type of negotiation of network configuration, nor does SLIP support any type of encryption. Additionally, SLIP only functions with TCP/IP, and all computers using SLIP must have static IP addresses. The requirement for using static IP addresses prevents central IP address management using Windows NT's Dynamic Host Configuration Protocol (DHCP). While Windows NT supports using SLIP for client computers, RAS does not have a SLIP server component, and therefore cannot be used as a SLIP server.

Point-to-Point Protocol

The Point-to-Point Protocol, or PPP, is the successor to SLIP. It has become the industry standard for asynchronous network communications. PPP offers several features not available in SLIP, including the ability to use multiple network protocols and encrypted passwords. PPP supports negotiation of network configuration between host and client computers, and does not require clients to use static IP addresses. In addition to TCP/IP, PPP supports IPX, NetBEUI, AppleTalk, DECnet, and other protocols.

Since PPP supports a variety of protocols, it is a very flexible network line protocol. When RAS is installed, Windows NT automatically binds it to TCP/IP, IPX, and NetBEUI if these protocols are installed.

Point-to-Point Tunneling Protocol

The Point-to-Point Tunneling Protocol, or PPTP, is an extension of PPP with some interesting features. All traffic over PPTP is encrypted, thus, PPTP allows you to transmit PPP packets over TCP/IP in a secure fashion. Since your network traffic is encrypted, it is extremely difficult to eavesdrop on your network data. By using PPTP as a line protocol, sites can create their own Virtual Private Network, or VPN, over the Internet. A VPN allows a company to use the Internet as a means to join sites in different locations, while maintaining a high level of security and protection for its network traffic.

In addition to its security features, PPTP allows multiple protocols to be sent over a PPP connection. PPTP relies on PPP packets for its network transmission. As such, PPTP can act as a translation layer between a non-TCP/IP protocol, such as IPX, and the PPP-line protocol layer. This allows you to route non-TCP/IP protocols, such as IPX or NetBEUI, over the Internet.

INSTALLING RAS

Like all applications, RAS needs some specific configuration information in order to function properly. Before installing RAS, you need to know which communications port you are going to use, the type of modem that you are installing, the settings for the modem, and the various network protocols that you will want to configure. In addition, assuming that you are configuring TCP/IP, you will need specific address and routing information for your TCP/IP network configuration. RAS installation takes several steps and uses several dialog boxes to complete. In this section, we will walk you through a typical RAS installation.

RAS is a Windows NT network service and is installed through the Network applet of the Control Panel. In order to install RAS, start the Control Panel and double-click on the Network icon. The Network Control Panel dialog box appears, as shown in Figure 9-2.

Select the Services tab in this dialog box, and click the Add… button. This brings up the Select Network Service dialog box, as shown in Figure 9-3. This dialog box allows you to choose a network service to install.

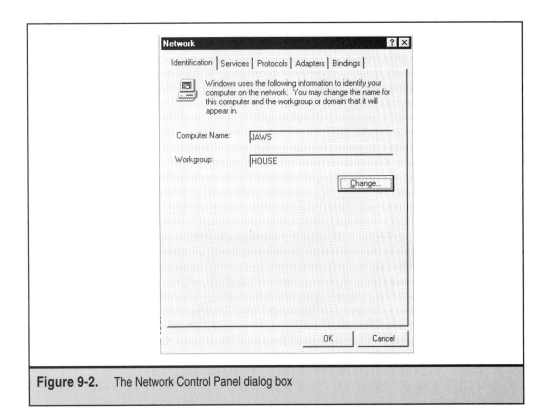

Figure 9-2. The Network Control Panel dialog box

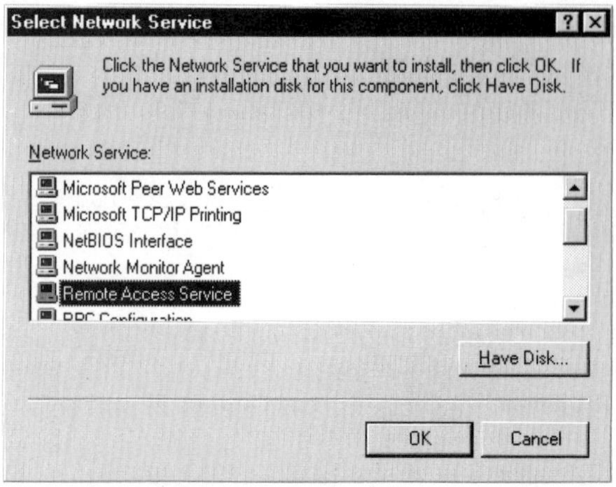

Figure 9-3.   The Select Network Service dialog box

Within the Select Network Service dialog box, select the Remote Access Service entry and click the OK button. Windows NT will prompt you for the path for the Windows NT installation CD-ROM. Windows NT will then display the Add RAS Device dialog box, as shown in Figure 9-4. This dialog prompts you for the communications device that you are going to use with RAS. You can install a new modem by selecting the "Install Modem…" button in the Add RAS Device dialog.

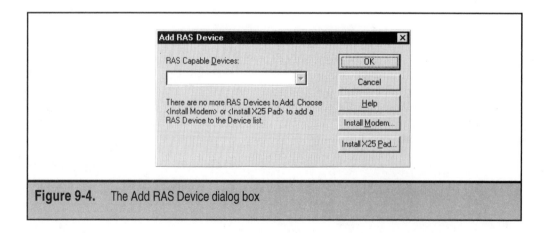

Figure 9-4.   The Add RAS Device dialog box

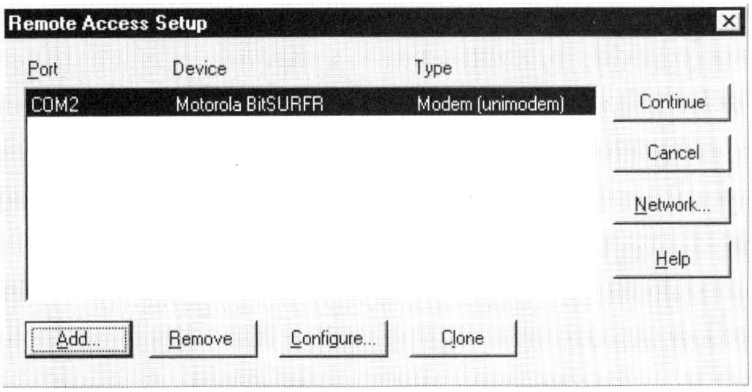

Figure 9-5. The Remote Access Setup dialog box

Once you have selected a RAS device from the Add RAS Device dialog box and clicked the OK button, the Remote Access Setup dialog box appears, as shown in Figure 9-5.

The Remote Access Setup dialog allows you to configure how RAS functions on your Windows NT computer. You should see a listing in this dialog box for the RAS device that you have selected. The first step in configuring the RAS service is to select the Configure... button, which brings up the Configure Port Usage dialog box, as shown in Figure 9-6.

The Configure Port Usage dialog box is used to determine if RAS will function as a client, as a server, or both. First, verify that the port and device information displayed in the dialog box is correct. Second, you must decide if you want RAS to be a client only, a server only, or both. If you want RAS to function as a client only, select the "Dial out only" radio button. To have RAS function as a server only, select the "Receive calls only" radio

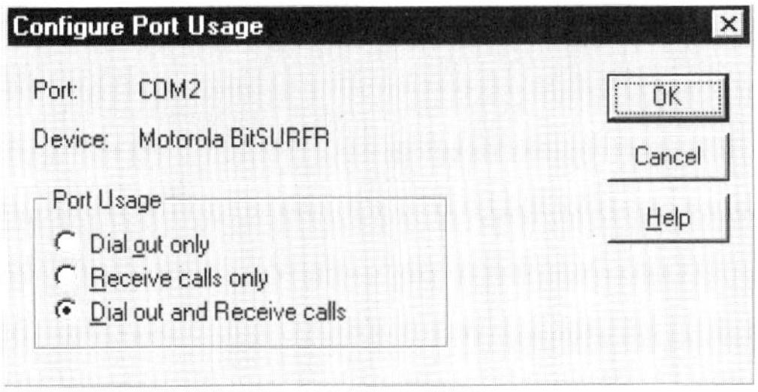

Figure 9-6. The Configure Port Usage dialog box

button. To have RAS operate in both client and server roles, select the "Dial out and Receive calls" radio button. The configuration dialog boxes that appear later are determined by the entry you choose. For this example, we will have our RAS server function as both a client and a server by selecting the "Dial out and Receive calls" radio button and clicking the OK button.

CONFIGURING RAS PROTOCOLS

Clicking the OK button in the Configure Port Usage dialog box dismisses the dialog and returns us to the Remote Access Setup dialog box. To continue with RAS configuration, select the Network... button. This action causes Network Configuration dialog box to appear, as shown in Figure 9-7.

As discussed earlier in the chapter, RAS is capable of using several different network protocols. By default, if TCP/IP, NetBEUI, and IPX are installed on the RAS server, they will be enabled automatically for RAS to use. This offers the most flexibility for remote clients making network connections to the RAS server. The Network Configuration dialog box is used to select the dial-out protocols for clients, the dial-in protocols, and the encryption settings.

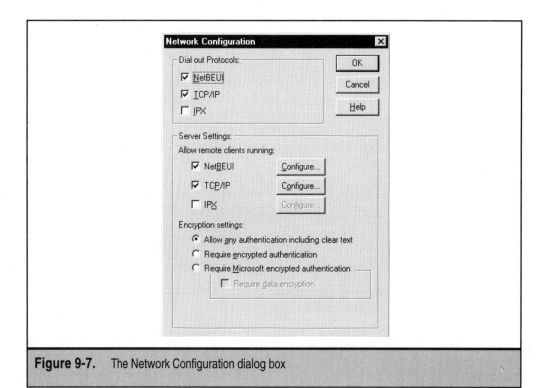

Figure 9-7.   The Network Configuration dialog box

Dial-out Protocols

The "Dial out Protocols" section of the Network Configuration dialog box is used to select the protocols that RAS can use when initiating a dial-out connection as a client. While it is tempting to just select all the protocols available in this section, you should only select the ones that you need. Selecting additional protocols that are not used by the remote host can delay your connection setup time and affect performance.

> **NOTE:**   From a Windows NT and UNIX integration point of view, the most common protocol that you are likely to use is TCP/IP.

Dial-in Protocols

If you have configured RAS to accept incoming calls, you can configure the dial-in protocols that RAS will support. The "Server Settings" section of the Network Configuration dialog box allows you to configure these protocols. As in the "Dial out Protocols" section, RAS dial-in supports TCP/IP, NetBEUI, and IPX. For integrating with a UNIX environment, TCP/IP will be required. If you have other NT workstations dialing in to your RAS server, you might choose to enable NetBEUI as well.

NetBEUI Configuration

NetBEUI is a non-routable protocol used by Windows NT. Configuration of NetBEUI as a dial-in protocol is a very simple process. Just select the NetBEUI checkbox in the Network Configuration dialog box, and click the Configure... button to the right of the checkbox. The RAS Server NetBEUI Configuration dialog box appears, as shown in Figure 9-8.

This dialog box allows you to decide if incoming NetBEUI protocol users can access other computers on your network. You can either decide to allow NetBEUI access to your RAS server only, or you can allow NetBEUI access to all NetBEUI-enabled computers on your network.

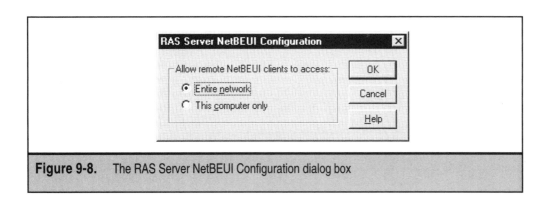

Figure 9-8.   The RAS Server NetBEUI Configuration dialog box

NOTE: You cannot specify particular computers that can be accessed by a dial-up NetBEUI session. It is "all or nothing." Also, since NetBEUI is not a routable protocol, a dial-up user can only access computers on the same network segment as the RAS server. If your network is separated by routers instead of bridges, the NetBEUI traffic will only work on the first segment.

TCP/IP Configuration

TCP/IP is a more complex protocol than NetBEUI, and therefore requires more configuration. To configure TCP/IP as a dial-in protocol, select the TCP/IP checkbox in the Network Configuration dialog box and click the Configure… button. This brings up the RAS Server TCP/IP Configuration dialog box, as shown in Figure 9-9.

At the top of the TCP/IP Configuration dialog box is a section that controls access for TCP/IP clients. Like NetBEUI, you can allow TCP/IP access to your entire network, or you can restrict it to the RAS server.

NOTE: Unlike NetBEUI, TCP/IP is a routable protocol. This means that the protocol will not be blocked by routers on your network.

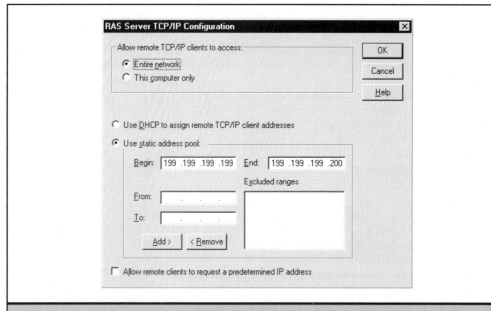

Figure 9-9.   The RAS Server TCP/IP Configuration dialog box

The next section in the TCP/IP Configuration dialog box determines how TCP/IP addresses are assigned to a dial-in connection. You can either provide a set of static addresses for dial-in clients, or you can allow a DHCP server to assign the addresses for you.

> **NOTE:**   DHCP stands for Dynamic Host Configuration Protocol. It is a means for Windows NT to automatically assign IP addresses to computers with minimal administrator intervention. DHCP is covered in more detail in Chapter 7.

If you choose not to use DHCP to configure your incoming TCP/IP addresses, you can enter a series of static addresses for RAS to use. To enable static addresses, click the "Use static address pool:" radio button. This radio button enables several data entry fields that allow you to enter address information.

To enter a range of addresses, type the first address in the range in the Begin address box, and the last address in the range in the End address box. RAS requires that the range encompass at least two TCP/IP addresses.

You can also exclude addresses within the range. To exclude a range of addresses, enter the start of the range in the From address box and the end of the range in the To address box, and click the Add button. The range of addresses will show up in the "Excluded ranges" list box. If you want to remove a range of excluded addresses, simply click the range in the "Excluded ranges" list box and click the Remove button. This enables the range of addresses.

> **NOTE:**   This is a bit confusing and counterintuitive. The Add button adds address ranges to the exclusion list, preventing them from being assigned by RAS. The Remove button removes addresses from the exclusion list, enabling their use by RAS.

The last item in the TCP/IP Configuration dialog box is a checkbox that allows a client to request a specific IP address. If you have assigned a specific TCP/IP address to a client, and you want that client to be able to request that same TCP/IP address each time it connects, then you should check the "Allow remote client to request a predetermined IP address" checkbox.

Encryption Settings

RAS supports various means of encryption for its login authentication process. As with the other major aspects of RAS, encryption is configured from the Network Configuration dialog box. There are three radio buttons that allow you to choose various encryption options.

The first encryption option is to allow any authentication mechanism, including clear text. This option supports several authentication schemes, including MS-CHAP, SPAP, and PAP. It is useful if you have several different types of client software that connect to your RAS server, or if your client software does not support encryption.

NOTE: Although you can use clear text authentication with this option, it is not recommended. Clear text authentication sends usernames and passwords over the network in unencrypted form. Anyone who intercepts the data stream will be able to read your username and password.

The second encryption option is to require encrypted authentication. This option supports any authentication mechanism except PAP, and requests encrypted passwords from all clients.

The third encryption option is to require Microsoft-encrypted authentication. This option supports the MS-CHAP authentication protocol only, and is typically only used between Microsoft clients and servers. With this option, you can enable data encryption as well, ensuring that all data sent over the wire is encrypted.

DIAL-UP NETWORKING

Microsoft Windows NT provides a client application that allows you to establish remote connections with other computers or networks. This application is known as the *Dial-Up Networking* program.

Dial-Up Networking is typically used either to connect to the Internet via an Internet Service Provider (ISP) or to connect to an NT system or domain via a RAS server. To start Dial-Up Networking, click the Start button, choose Programs, then Accessories from the Programs list, and then select Dial-Up Networking. Dial-Up Networking is also typically available by double-clicking the My Computer icon on your desktop. When you start Dial-Up Networking, its main screen is displayed, as shown in Figure 9-10.

Dial-Up Networking maintains information for connections as a list of phonebook entries. Each phonebook entry provides all the information needed to connect to a specific server or network. You create a separate phonebook entry for each service that you connect to. When you wish to initiate a connection to a particular service, simply select the appropriate phonebook entry in the drop-down list box at the top of the Dial-Up Networking screen, then click the Dial button.

Adding a New Dial-Up Networking Phonebook Entry

Each entry in the Dial-Up Networking phonebook list corresponds to a particular service, be it an NT computer, an NT domain, or another service such as an ISP. For each service that you use, you must create a phonebook entry.

To start the process of creating a phonebook entry, click the New button in the Dial-Up Networking program's main screen. This displays the New Phonebook Entry dialog box, as shown in Figure 9-11.

At the top of the New Phonebook Entry dialog box, you will see several tabs labeled Basic, Server, Script, Security, and X.25. Click on the Basic tab to make sure it is to the front.

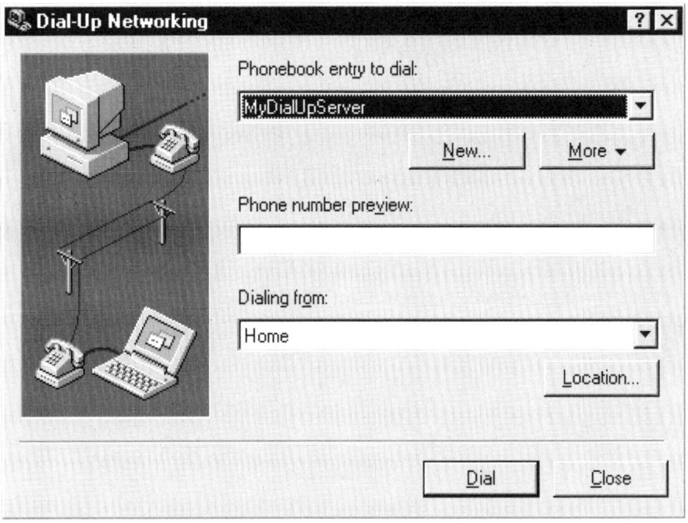

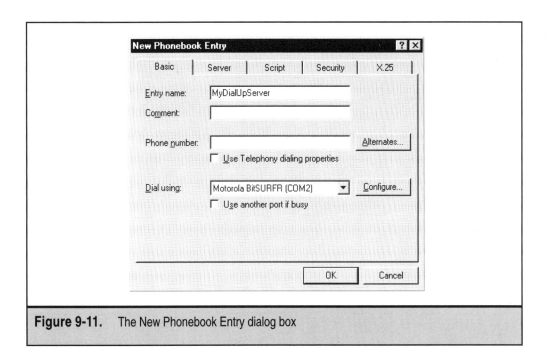

Figure 9-10.   The Dial-Up Networking main program screen

Figure 9-11.   The New Phonebook Entry dialog box

Basic Tab

The first thing you need to do is give a name for this phonebook entry. The name can be anything you want; it only serves to label this particular entry in the Dial-Up Networking phonebook. Following the Entry name field is a Comment field. The Comment field allows you to specify an optional comment about this entry.

The next item to enter is the phone number. If you want to use Windows NT's telephony dialing features, you can select the "Use Telephony dialing properties" checkbox. If you select this checkbox, the telephone dialing page is displayed when you click the Location… button in the Dial-Up Networking main window.

NOTE: NT's telephony dialing properties are useful if you travel to different locations or have special dialing requirements, such as when using a telephone credit card.

The Alternates…button next to the phone number box allows you enter a list of alternate phone numbers to dial if the first one is busy.

At the bottom of the Basic panel is the "Dial using" box. This is a drop-down list box that allows you to pick the particular modem or communications device that you want to use. If you click on the Configure… button, the Modem Configuration dialog box appears, as shown in Figure 9-12. This dialog box allows you to configure your modem settings, including speed, flow control, error control, and compression.

Server Tab

Once you have finished filling out the information in the Basic tab, click the Server tab at the top of the New Phonebook Entry dialog box. From this tab, you specify the type of network server, the protocols to use, and additional options.

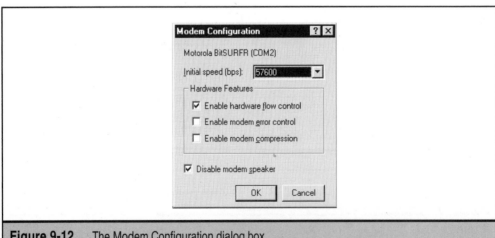

Figure 9-12.   The Modem Configuration dialog box

First, select the type of dial-up server that you will be connecting to from the "Dial-up server type" drop-down list box. For most Windows NT and UNIX applications, you will want to choose the "PPP: Windows NT, Windows 95 Plus, Internet" option.

The second section in the Server tab allows you to select the network protocols that you will use. If you are connecting to the Internet or to a UNIX system, you will want to select TCP/IP. If you are connecting to an NT RAS server or domain, you should select the protocols that your target server supports. For our example, we will select TCP/IP alone.

Before we proceed to configure the TCP/IP settings for our connection, let's look at the last two entries on the Server tab. Two checkboxes are provided. The first is labeled "Enable software compression." RAS supports software compression of data in addition to modem compression. Many users find they get better performance by disabling modem compression and enabling software compression instead. The second checkbox is labeled "Enable PPP LCP extensions." Checking this box causes NT to enable some of the newer features of PPP. As a general rule, you should keep this box checked unless you experience consistent problems dialing in to an older PPP server.

TCP/IP SETTINGS Since we selected TCP/IP as our protocol in the Server tab, we need to configure it. To do this, click the "TCP/IP Settings..." button located to the right of the TCP/IP checkbox. This brings up the PPP TCP/IP Settings dialog box, as shown in Figure 9-13.

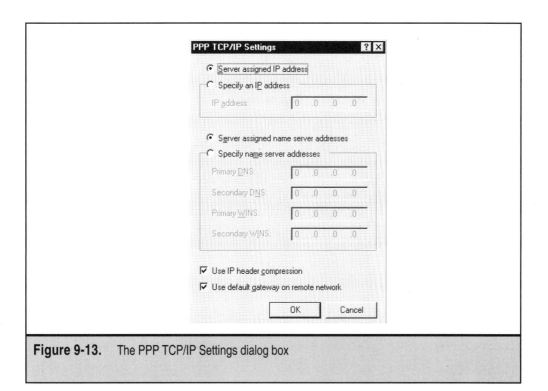

Figure 9-13. The PPP TCP/IP Settings dialog box

NOTE: This dialog box is different from the one we discussed earlier in the chapter. The earlier TCP/IP Configuration dialog was for setting up TCP/IP properties for a RAS server. The PPP TCP/IP Settings dialog box specifies settings for a particular client configuration when dialing in to a server.

The first set of options in the PPP TCP/IP Settings dialog box determines how your IP address is configured. You can opt to have the server give you an IP address, or you can specify an IP address directly. Most ISPs support dynamic IP addressing, which means that they will automatically assign you an address when you connect. In addition, if you are using DHCP and RAS as your server on the other end of your connection, you will need to allow the server to assign an address.

NOTE: You should only use a specific static IP address if you have been assigned one by your network administrator.

The second set of options in this dialog determines how your name server and WINS server addresses are configured.

NOTE: Name servers and WINS are discussed in more detail in Chapter 7. For extensive details on name servers and the Domain Name Service, see Chapter 8.

If the server or service provider that you are connecting to automatically provides your DNS name server addresses and WINS address information, all you have to do is select the radio button labeled "Server assigned name server addresses." If you need to provide the addresses yourself, select the radio button labeled "Specify name server addresses," and enter the address information in the boxes provided.

At the bottom of the Server tab display, there are two more checkboxes. The first one is labeled "Use IP header compression." If this box is checked, Dial-Up Networking will attempt to use Van Jacobson IP header compression when connecting to the remote server. As a general rule, you should select this option unless you have consistent problems making and keeping a connection.

The second checkbox is labeled "Use default gateway on remote network" and is only useful for computers that are using both a local network card and Dial-Up Networking. If this checkbox is selected, any packets that cannot be delivered to the local network via the network card are routed to the default gateway on the remote network, via Dial-Up Networking.

Script Tab

In some cases, especially when connecting to UNIX servers, you may need to have Dial-Up Networking perform a series of specific tasks when establishing a remote connection. Fortunately, Dial-Up Networking provides some scripting capabilities to help you. You enter the Script Configuration section of Dial-Up Networking setup by selecting the Script tab at the top of the New Phonebook Entry dialog box. This action brings up the Script tab display, as shown in Figure 9-14.

By selecting the appropriate option in the Script tab display, you can choose either not to execute a script, to run a particular script after a connection has been made, or to display a terminal window so that you can enter information manually. In order to make modifications to a script, select the "Run this script" radio button, select the script to run, and click the "Edit Script..." button. There are several scripts available, and they are extensively commented to show you how to make custom modifications.

You can also elect to perform actions before Dial-Up Networking dials the phone for a remote connection. To do this, select the "Before dialing..." button. It provides you with a dialog box that allows you the same options as the Script tab display, except the actions take place before the remote system is called.

Security Tab

Clicking the Security tab brings up the Security tab display, as shown in Figure 9-15. From this display, you can configure how Dial-Up Networking encrypts data that it sends to a remote host.

The encryption options are similar to those offered in the RAS server setup section, discussed earlier in the chapter. You can opt to use any authentication method (including clear text); you can use encrypted authentication; or you can specify Microsoft MS-CHAP encrypted authentication. If you are connecting to a non-Microsoft system such as UNIX,

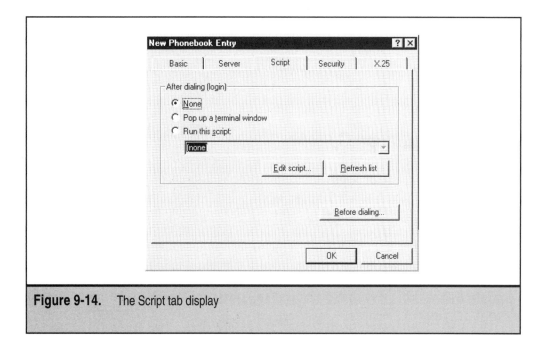

Figure 9-14.   The Script tab display

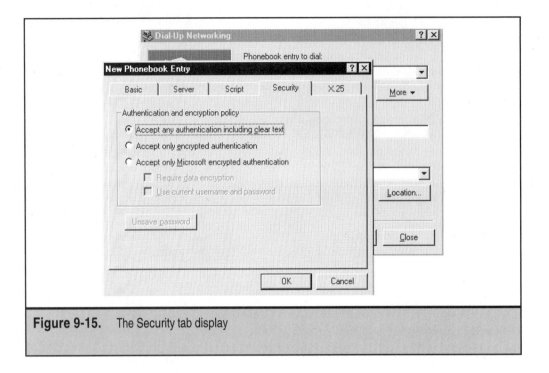

Figure 9-15. The Security tab display

you will probably have to select the option to use any authentication method, including clear text.

X.25 Tab

The X.25 tab is only used to configure information for an X.25 network connection. If you have such a connection, select this tab and enter the information supplied by your network provider.

Additional Configuration Options

Now that you have successfully added a new system to your phonebook, there are some additional customization options that are available within Dial-Up Networking. To see these options, click the More button on the Dial-Up Networking main screen, and a pop-up menu of options will appear, as shown in Figure 9-16.

User Preferences

While we're not going to go over every option in this list, two of the options deserve a closer look. The User Preferences option brings up the User Preferences dialog box, as shown in Figure 9-17. This dialog box allows you to configure several facets of how Dial-Up Networking operates.

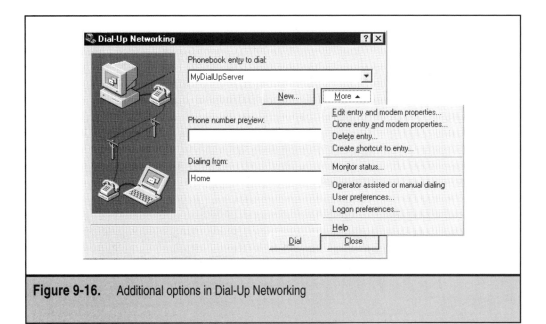

Figure 9-16. Additional options in Dial-Up Networking

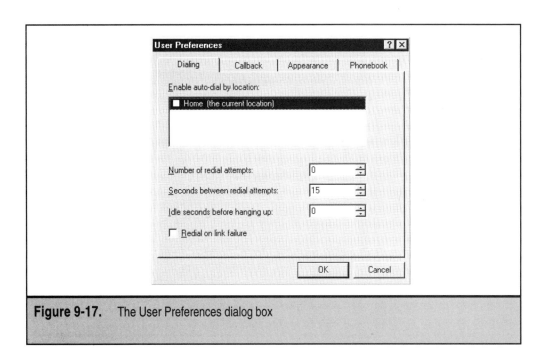

Figure 9-17. The User Preferences dialog box

When initially displayed, the User Preferences dialog box has the Dialing tab in the front. This tab allows you to configure options such as the number of retries allowed, the delay between retries, the idle time before hanging up, and whether or not NT should automatically dial out when you request a service on the remote server.

Selecting the Callback tab, as shown in Figure 9-18, allows you to determine how Dial-Up Networking will behave if the remote server offers to call you back. You can decline callback, enable it, or decide when the server offers.

The Appearance tab, as shown in Figure 9-19, allows you to configure several aspects of how Dial-Up Networking looks and behaves.

Finally, the Phonebook tab, as shown in Figure 9-20, allows you to choose different phonebooks to use when dialing remote connections.

Logon Preferences

The Logon Preferences option is the other entry from the pop-up menu that we need to discuss. It has virtually the same options as the User Preferences option, however, it applies to users that have not logged on to NT and wish to log on to a domain via Dial-Up Networking. This dialog box appears unless you are logged in with administrator privileges.

NOTE: The User Preferences option applies to a user who is already logged in. The Logon Preferences option applies to a user who is logging on via Dial-Up Networking.

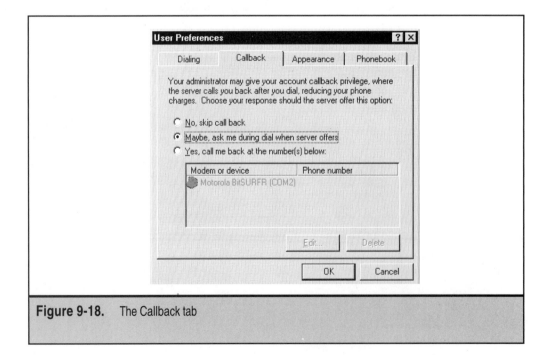

Figure 9-18. The Callback tab

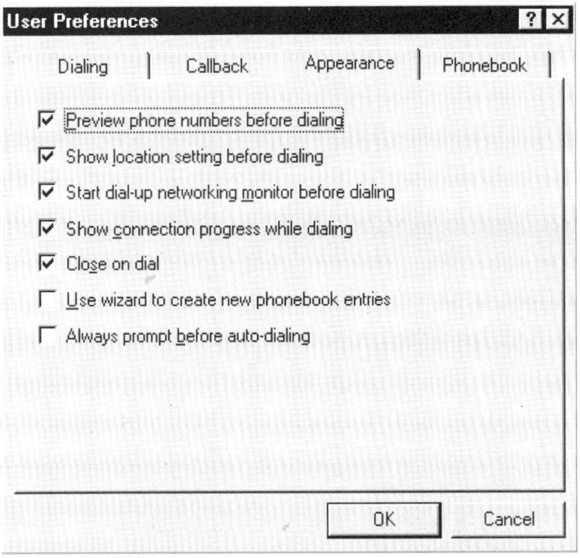

Figure 9-19. The Appearance tab

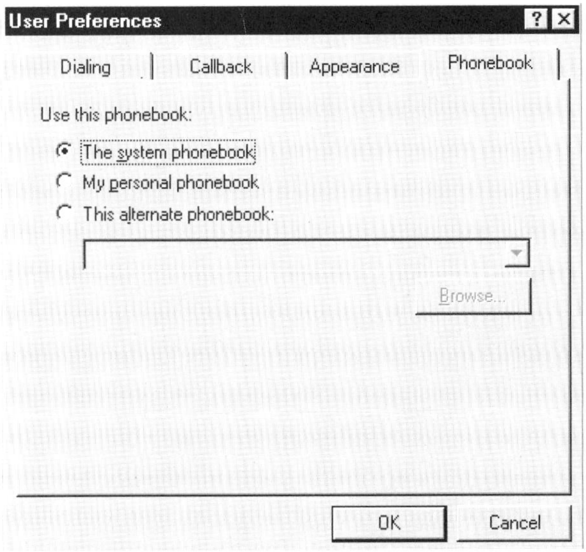

Figure 9-20. The Phonebook tab

MANAGING A RAS SERVER

Now that we've looked at the details of installing a RAS server and using Dial-Up Networking to connect to remote systems, we're going to explore the details of administering a RAS server. RAS is administered via the Remote Access Admin tool. To start this tool, click the Start button, select Programs, then select Administrative Tools (Common) from the Programs list, and choose Remote Access Admin.

When you start Remote Access Admin, the main program screen is displayed, as shown in Figure 9-21.

From the Remote Access Admin tool, you can perform a variety of administrative tasks, including managing the RAS services, granting user dial-in permissions, sending messages to users, and monitoring server status.

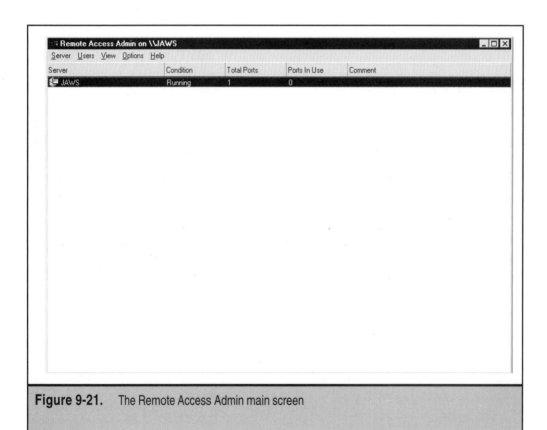

Figure 9-21. The Remote Access Admin main screen

Monitoring Server Status

The main display window of the Remote Access Admin tool displays a list of RAS servers. Each server that you are administering will have an entry in the list. For each server in the list, Remote Access Admin displays the server status, the number of ports available for connections, the number of ports currently in use, and any comments that have been entered.

To see the available ports on a given server, highlight the server in the main Remote Access Admin window and choose Communication Ports from the Server menu. The Communication Ports dialog box is displayed, as shown in Figure 9-22.

This dialog box lists all the valid communication ports on a server, and tells which user is connected to it and when the connection was started.

To examine a particular port in detail, highlight the port in the Communication Ports dialog box and click the "Port Status..." button. This displays the Port Status dialog box, as shown in Figure 9-23.

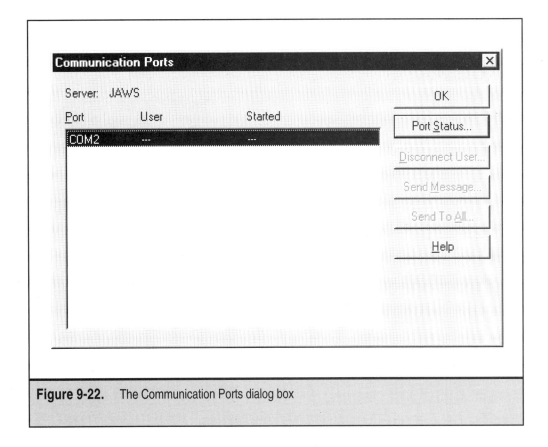

Figure 9-22.   The Communication Ports dialog box

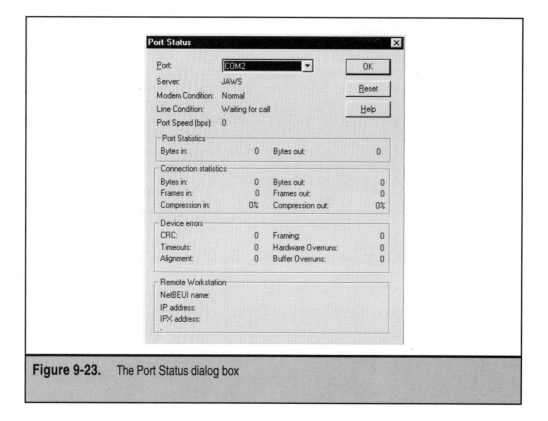

Figure 9-23. The Port Status dialog box

This dialog box shows detailed statistics about the port, including modem status, line condition, connection status and statistics, number of bytes transferred, connection error information, and name and address information for the remote workstation.

User Dial-in Permission

In order for a user to be allowed to dial in to a RAS server, the user must be granted dial-in permission.

NOTE: In order to grant dial-in permission, you must be logged in as an administrator.

Dial-in permission is granted through the Remote Access Admin tool. There is no way to grant dial-in permission through the User Manager for Domains tool. The administrator may opt to grant dial-in permission to all users in the user accounts database, or to grant it only to certain users.

To grant dial-in permission to a user, start the Remote Access Admin tool and select Permissions... from the Users menu. This action displays the Remote Access Permissions dialog box, as shown in Figure 9-24.

In the Remote Access Permissions dialog box, select the user to grant or revoke permission, then check or clear the "Grant dialin permission to user" checkbox, depending on if you wish to grant or revoke permission. You can also grant permission to all users or revoke permission from all users by clicking the appropriate button.

At the bottom of the Remote Access Permissions dialog box is a set of radio buttons that configure how RAS callback is implemented for a user. You can elect to have callback disabled, preset to a certain number, or determined by the user when he or she calls in.

Sending Messages

The administrator can use the Remote Access Admin tool to send messages to a particular user, or to all users that have established remote connections. In order to send a message, select the "Active Users..." menu item from the Users menu, highlight the user that you want to send a message to, and click the "Send Message..." button. To send a message to all remotely connected users, click the "Send to All..." button instead.

Service Management

RAS consists of two Windows NT services: the Remote Access Service and the Remote Access Connection Manager. These two services control RAS's ability to accept connections from remote clients and must be running for RAS to operate as a server. The

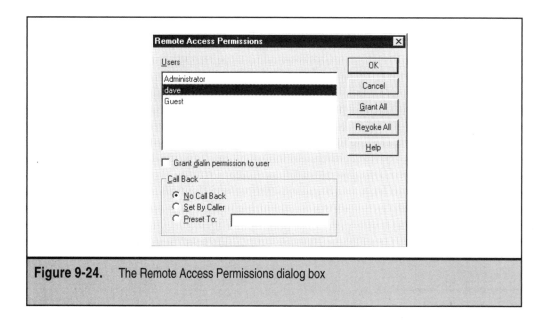

Figure 9-24. The Remote Access Permissions dialog box

Remote Access Admin tool allows you to start, stop, and pause these services. Pausing the RAS services will block any new incoming connections, but will keep current connections intact. Stopping the RAS services will forcibly disconnect any connected remote users.

To start, stop, pause, or continue the Remote Access Services, choose the appropriate menu item from the Server menu. The Services tool in the Windows NT Control Panel can also be used to configure, start, and stop the RAS services.

RAS SECURITY

When making remote network connections, proper authentication and data security are always issues to be concerned with. RAS provides several different methods of authentication to maximize its interoperability with other systems.

Authentication Methods

RAS provides several different authentication methods in order to be accessible from a wide variety of client systems. However, not all of these authentication methods are supported by every possible operating system.

Password Authentication Protocol (PAP)

The Password Authentication Protocol is the least sophisticated method of authenticating a RAS session. It uses clear text data transmission instead of any type of encryption. This means that usernames and passwords are sent unencrypted over the network. If someone were to capture your data stream with a network analyzer, they could see both your username and password!

While this is obviously not the recommended method of authentication, there are plenty of systems that require this method. For example, many SLIP and PPP servers do not support encrypted authentication, and will therefore require using PAP instead.

Challenge Handshake Authentication Protocol (CHAP)

The Challenge Handshake Authentication Protocol, or CHAP, algorithm allows RAS clients to connect to virtually all third-party PPP servers. When a client attempts to connect to a PPP server that supports CHAP, the CHAP server sends a random challenge to the client. The client, using a special non-reversible encryption algorithm, encrypts the challenge with the user's password and sends it back to the server. Since the challenge sent by CHAP is random, it is not possible to record the session and play it back to gain access.

NOTE: Windows NT only supports CHAP for RAS clients dialing in to a non-RAS server. Since the encryption algorithm used by CHAP requires that the password be available to the server in unencrypted form, NT RAS does not support CHAP for incoming connections.

Microsoft Challenge Handshake Authentication Protocol (MS-CHAP)

The Microsoft Challenge Handshake Authentication Protocol, or MS-CHAP, is the most secure authentication protocol supported by the Windows NT RAS server. It uses a Microsoft version of the MD4 algorithm, developed by RSA Inc. By using MS-CHAP, users can also elect to have all data encrypted as it travels over the network. Since MS-CHAP is a Microsoft-specific protocol, it is primarily used for communication and authentication between Microsoft clients and Microsoft servers.

Shiva Password Authentication Protocol (SPAP)

The Shiva Password Authentication Protocol is a special version of PAP that is implemented by Shiva clients and servers. SPAP is implemented as a reversible encryption algorithm that sends passwords in encrypted form. While more secure than PAP, it is not as secure as CHAP.

Callback

When using RAS as a server, it is possible to configure the server to call back a user's modem when the user requests a connection. While many companies use callback to save long-distance toll charges by having RAS call the user back at a remote number, it can also be used to guarantee that the user is calling from a specific location.

Callback is configured in the Remote Access Admin tool, where it is possible to set up RAS to call back a user at a previously specified number. This mechanism provides the highest level of callback security. For example, if someone stole the username and password of a user with preset callback security enabled, RAS would attempt to call the user at the number specified in its configuration database. However, since it would be very unlikely that the password thief would be at this number (typically the user's residence), the attempted login would not succeed.

TROUBLESHOOTING

Configuring RAS can be tricky, and configuration problems can be difficult to spot. Fortunately, RAS can be configured to provide log files for certain processes that are difficult to monitor.

> **NOTE:** Where we provide a directory path into the Windows NT system directories in the examples in this chapter, we assume that your Windows NT root directory is WINNT. If you have named the Windows NT root directory something else, change the directory path names to reflect where NT is installed on your system

Enabling these log files requires editing certain Windows NT Registry parameters with the REGEDT32.EXE program, which is typically located in the \WINNT\ SYSTEM32 directory.

> **CAUTION:** You must exercise extreme caution when editing the Windows NT Registry. If you make a mistake and change the wrong entry, you can make Windows NT unusable and impossible to boot up!

Modem Problems

A common problem that occurs when trying to configure either a remote server or client is troubleshooting configuration problems with the computer's modem. To help you track down modem problems, you can configure RAS to create a log file that captures the initialization data that is exchanged between computer and modem when the modem is initialized.

To enable modem initialization logging, edit the Registry and set the following key to a value of 1:

\HKEY_LOCAL_MACHINE\SYSTEM\CurrentControlSet\Services\RasMan\ Parameters\Logging

The log file created when modem initialization logging is enabled is named DEVICE.LOG and is typically located in the \WINNT\SYSTEM32\RAS directory. After you have enabled logging, you must restart the Remote Access Server service for the change to take effect.

Authentication Problems

Another area that commonly causes problems is authentication. Since different clients and servers will support different authentication protocols, sometimes you will have to experiment to find the most secure protocol supported in your current configuration. If you have a problem with a client authenticating with RAS, try setting your authentication protocol to allow any authentication protocol, including clear text. If this solves your authentication problems, try increasing the level of authentication to reach the highest level that is supported by both systems.

PPP Problems

PPP connections can be difficult to troubleshoot, even on a good day. Fortunately, like modem initialization, RAS provides logging of PPP sessions to help you solve the problem.

To enable PPP logging, edit the Registry by setting the following entry to a value of 1:

\HKEY_LOCAL_MACHINE\SYSTEM\CurrentControlSet\Services\RasMan\ PPP\Logging

The log file created when PPP logging is enabled is named PPP.LOG and is typically located in the \WINNT\SYSTEM32\RAS directory. Examine the PPP.LOG file and look for problems. Typical PPP connection problems can be traced to incorrect authentication protocols, or to the server requiring additional information to be sent. It the latter case, you will probably have to create a login script to automate the PPP login process.

Monitoring Dial-Up Networking Connections

The Dial-Up Networking program provides a monitoring tool that will allow you to monitor network sessions when using RAS in client mode. To start the Dial-Up Networking Monitor, start Dial-Up Networking and choose "Monitor status…" from the More menu. This brings up the Dial-Up Networking Monitors, as shown in Figure 9-25.

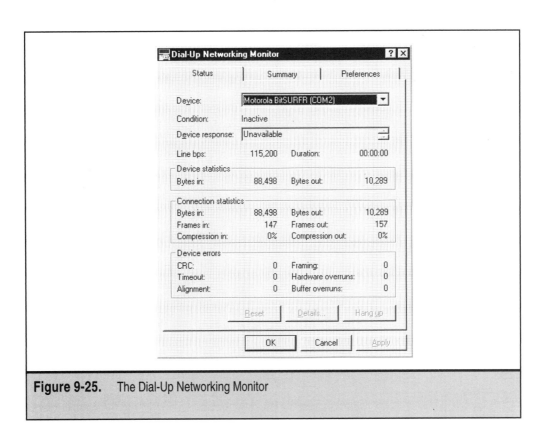

Figure 9-25. The Dial-Up Networking Monitor

The Status tab provides statistics on the current connection, including bytes and frames transferred and device errors. The Summary tab shows which devices are currently used as part of a network connection. The Preferences tab allows you to configure Dial-Up Networking to play an alert sound when certain conditions occur, as well as provide status lights to monitor the status of the connection.

SUMMARY

Windows NT provides extensive capabilities for remote network connections in the form of its Remote Access Service, or RAS. RAS can operate as a dial-in server, providing connections to both NT- and non-NT-based computers. It can also operate as a network client via the Dial-Up Networking program.

In this chapter, we examined the processes for installing and configuring RAS in both its client and server roles. We examined the various security protocols that are provided under RAS and looked at the procedures for managing a RAS server. We also discussed how to troubleshoot problems that might arise when using RAS to make remote connections either to Windows NT systems or to non-NT systems such as UNIX. By using RAS and Dial-Up Networking, you can easily integrate Windows NT into your existing environment either in the role of a remote network client or as a network dial-in server.

CHAPTER 10

Microsoft Internet Information Server

Microsoft Internet Information Server (IIS) provides a range of servers—web (HTTP), FTP, and Gopher—for use with Windows NT. It comes with, and is tightly integrated with, Windows NT Server 4.0 software. IIS works well with Microsoft BackOffice and comes with open database connectivity (ODBC) drivers for Microsoft SQL Server 6.0.

This chapter focuses on the web server (HTTP) portion of IIS, providing installation and configuration information. Services available with the IIS 3.0 update for the web server, such as Index Server and Crystal Reports, are also discussed. While this chapter isn't intended to provide exhaustive coverage of the IIS web server and its configuration options, it will give you a feel for some of the issues involved.

NOTE: IIS administration is a big topic. A single chapter certainly doesn't cover everything you may need—or want—to know. There are a number of books devoted to the subject: you may want to pick up an IIS reference such as the *Internet Information Server 3 Administrator's Guide* by Allen Wyatt (Prima, 1997) or *Windows NT Web Server Handbook* by Tom Sheldon (Osborne/McGraw-Hill, 1996).

OTHER NT SERVERS

IIS isn't the only NT web server available. However, it is, like Apache under UNIX, one of the most widely used Windows NT web servers. See NetCraft's web server survey at **http://www.netcraft.com/survey/** for current statistics.

Like UNIX, there are a number of commercial and free web servers available. WebCompare at **http://webcompare.internet.com/compare/chart.html** provides comparison information for a number of commercial and non-commercial web servers. Want more? Yahoo lists a number of Windows NT HTTP servers at **http://www.yahoo.com/Computers_and_Internet/Software/Internet/World_Wide_Web/ Servers/Windows_NT/**.

For example, Netscape's Enterprise web server provides a document-sharing system to control who edits files and when. Enterprise also includes a feature called AutoCatalog, which lists HTML documents by author, modification date, and popularity. Enterprise comes with some powerful web tools, including Verity's topicSearch search engine and a server configuration saving feature that gets your site running again if modifications make it crash. Enterprise also provides ODBC links via Netscape LiveWire engines.

Netscape's FastTrack is nearly as fast as IIS; maybe even faster with fewer than 12 clients. It takes a broad approach by including ODBC, web authoring tools such as Navigator Gold, and extremely simple remote site management via any frame and Java-compliant browser. However, while it's easy to use, FastTrack might not have everything you're looking for. For example, it lacks Enterprise's configuration and document-management tools.

SETTING UP IIS

IIS can be installed during your Windows NT Server 4.0 installation, or at any point after NT's installation. If you need to install IIS, make sure you are logged on with Administrator privileges and you have your Windows NT Server 4.0 CD-ROM available.

TIP: To see if IIS is already installed, select Programs from the Start menu. If you see an Internet Information Server menu item, it's installed.

Before you install IIS 3.0, make sure the following are already installed:

▼ Windows NT Server 4.0

■ Windows NT 4.0 Service Pack #1 or greater. Service Packs are available on Microsoft's website at **http://www.microsoft.com/NTServerSupport/Content/ ServicePacks/Default.htm**.

NOTE: You will want to install at least Service Pack #3; it fixes some known problems with IIS. For example, the known security problem of Internet users being able to execute programs and retrieve files outside the *wwwroot* tree.

▲ IIS 2.0

Setting Up Windows NT

Windows NT Server must be configured to support IIS. This involves setting up the TCP/IP protocol, and, depending on your site, the DHCP service.

Installing IIS

Installing IIS 3.0 requires that IIS 2.0 is already installed. Both procedures are covered in this section for your convenience.

Installing IIS 2.0

If you did not install IIS 2.0 during your Windows NT Server 4.0 installation, there should be a shortcut to install it on your desktop.

1. From the Start menu, select Programs | Microsoft Internet Server (Common) | Internet Information Server Setup. If you want to add or remove services, use this Setup program.

2. Enter the path where you want IIS installed.

NOTE: It's a good idea to install IIS in an NTFS directory.

3. Select the services you want to install. Table 10-1 lists installation options. The Internet Service Manager is the administration tool for all the services. At a minimum, you will want to install it and the World Wide Web Service.

4. Enter the location of the publishing directories.

NOTE: The World Wide Web Publishing Directory is equivalent to the DocumentRoot in Apache's *srm.conf* file.

5. If you selected ODBC Drivers & Administration, a dialog to install drivers will also appear.

6. When setup is complete, select OK.

7. You're now ready to install IIS 3.0 components.

Installing IIS 3.0

IIS 3.0 consists of several new components that can enhance your web server functionality. Add any or all of the new IIS 3.0 features you want. The two most useful

Option	Description
Internet Service Manager	Administration tool that allows you to control and configure IIS within your local network
World Wide Web Service	WWW (HTTP) server
WWW Service Examples	Sample web pages
Internet Service Manger (HTML)	HTML version of the Internet Service Manager. Remote administration tool used outside of your local network
Gopher Service	Gopher server
FTP Service	FTP server
ODBC Drivers & Administration	Drivers to enable ODBC access from the WWW server Note: You will need to set up the drivers and data sources using the ODBC program in the Control Panel

Table 10-1.   IIS 2.0 Options

from a webmaster standpoint are probably the Index Server and Crystal Reports, which add search and web reporting capabilities to IIS.

1. Get IIS 3.0 files (shown in Table 10-2). You can order IIS 3.0 on CD-ROM from Microsoft at **http://www.microsoft.com/iis/GetIIS/OrderCD/servcd.htm** for a small fee or download files from Microsoft's website at **http://www.microsoft.com/iis/GetIIS/DownloadIIS3/default.htm** for free.

2. Install the new service(s). Each file has its own installation. In general:

   ▼ Execute each file to decompress it.

   ▲ For some files, Setup is automatically executed; for others, you will need to run Setup manually.

NOTE: For updates to components such as ODBC and FrontPage, check out Microsoft's "Help Files, Service Packs & Other Files" page at **http://www.microsoft.com/kb/softlib/chooseproduct.htm**.

Component	Filename/Size	Size (Compressed)	Description
Microsoft Index Server	is11enu.exe	~1.8MB	Website search engine
Active Server Pages	asp.exe	~9MB	Server side web applications (combine ActiveX, HTML, and scripts)
FrontPage 97 Server Extensions	fp9ext_x86_enu.exe	~3MB	Web publishing and graphical site management
Microsoft NetShow	nlssevr.exe (Live Server) nsosrv.exe (On-Demand Server)	~1MB each	Multimedia server (audio and video)
Crystal Reports for Internet Information Server	crystal.exe	~6MB	Tool for report generation from web server logs

Table 10-2. IIS 3.0 Components

Configuration

IIS is primarily configured using the Internet Service Manger. Some services, such as the Index Server, also have HTML-based administration interfaces as well.

Internet Service Manager

The Internet Service Manager is your administration tool for IIS. With it, you can control and configure almost any part of IIS.

To start the Internet Service Manager:

1. From the Start menu, select Programs | Microsoft Index Server (Common) | Internet
   Service Manager.

2. The Internet Service Manager window will display, as shown in Figure 10-1.

3. Select the service you want to manage by double-clicking on it.

NOTE: There is also an HTML version of the Internet Service Manager. See the next section for more details.

To configure various IIS functions, you use property sheets. There are up to four property sheets per service, as shown in Table 10-3. Each IIS service uses a similar set of property sheets. Figure 10-2 shows default web server settings.

Remote Administration

Remote administration means controlling IIS on a machine other than the one you're sitting at. You must have Administrator privileges on the IIS machine to make changes.

Figure 10-1.   Internet Service Manager

Property Sheet Type	Description
Service	Controls how the service can be accessed
Directories	Specifies which directories on your system should be used for published information. This is where you define your directory structure, including virtual directories
Logging	Controls how log files are created by a service
Advanced	Controls site access. For example, you can allow or deny access by IP address

Table 10-3.   General Property Sheets

This can be broken down into two types:

▼   local network (LAN)

▲   Internet

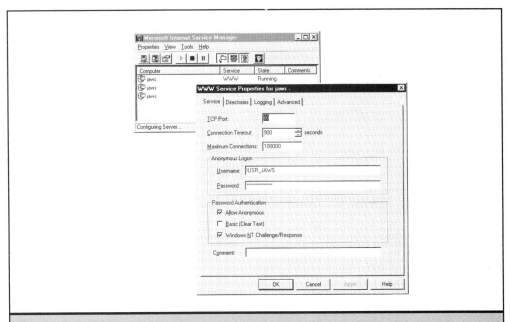

Figure 10-2.   Internet Service Manager property sheets for the web server

LOCAL NETWORK   You can use the Internet Service Manager to control IIS over a network. This type of administration is the same as administration on your local machine.

INTERNET   What if you need to administer IIS from outside your local network? The Internet Service Manager won't let you do this. However, IIS 3.0 gives you the option of administering IIS from a web browser.

Before connecting via your web browser, keep the following in mind:

▼ To use remote administration, you must have Administrator privileges on the server you're connected to.

▲ The web server authentication must include *at least one* of the following: Basic, Windows NT Challenge/Response.

NOTE: Not all web browsers support Windows NT Challenge/Response.

For example, you would connect with the following URL:

http://*www.imanexample.com*/iisadmin

where *www.imanexample.com* would be replaced with the name of your server, as shown in Figure 10-3.

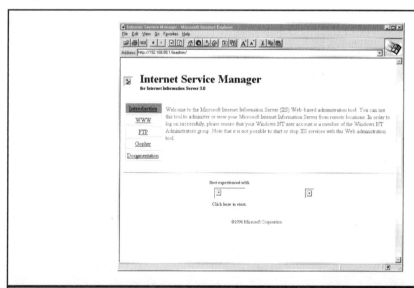

Figure 10-3.   HTML version of the Internet Service Manager

NOTE: The *iisadmin* directory was automatically created when you installed the Internet Service Manager (HTML version).

Using the HTML version is similar to the Internet Service Manager. However, the HTML version has several limitations:

▼ Only web, FTP, and Gopher servers can be administered.

▲ You cannot stop or start servers.

This type of remote administration also relies on the password authentication setting of your web server. Because remote administration is always done through a secure communications channel, you must have Basic, Challenge/Response, or both selected. Otherwise, you won't be able to connect.

NOTE: Password authentication is set in the Internet Service Manager Service tab.

Registry Entries

When IIS 3.0 is installed, a number of keys and entries are added to the Registry. For the most part, you'll make changes to the registry via a GUI, such as the Internet Service Manager or one of the HTML interface tools. However, there are times—such as when you need to add a new MIME type—when you will need to edit the Registry directly.

NOTE: In Apache, IIS Registry entries are roughly analogous to the configuration files. However, unlike Apache, most configuration of these values takes place through a GUI.

To edit the Registry, you can run the Registry editor. Once started, you can select the appropriate hive and view/edit the contents. Most IIS services are in the HKEY_LOCAL_MACHINE hive. Table 10-4 shows the location of major IIS service entries. To start the Registry editor:

1. Select Start | Run | Open.

2. Type **regedt32** and click OK.

3. The Registry editor will start.

CAUTION: Editing the registry incorrectly can cause serious problems, including corruption, which may make it necessary to reinstall Windows NT or other software on which you're making Registry changes. If you make mistakes, your computer's configuration could be damaged. Edit registry entries only for settings that you cannot adjust through the user interface, and be very careful whenever you edit the registry directly. Before editing, it's wise to make a complete system backup or at least a Registry backup before making changes.

Registry Entry Type	Registry Location
Global (Affects all portions of IIS)	HKEY_LOCAL_MACHINE\SYSTEM\ CurrentControlSet\Services\InetInfo\Parameters
Web Server	HKEY_LOCAL_MACHINE\SYSTEM\ CurrentControlSet\Services\W3SVC\Parameters
FTP Service	HKEY_LOCAL_MACHINE\SYSTEM\ CurrentControlSet\Services\FTPSVC\Parameters
Gopher Service	HKEY_LOCAL_MACHINE\SYSTEM\ CurrentControlSet\ServicesGOPERSVC\ Parameters
ASP Server	HKEY_LOCAL_MACHINE\SYSTEM\ CurrentControlSet\Services\W3SVC\ASP\Parameters
Index Server	HKEY_LOCAL_MACHINE\SYSTEM\ CurrentControlSet\Control\contentindex

Table 10-4. Location of IIS Registry Keys

CONFIGURATION OPTIONS

This section discusses a selection of server configurations you may elect to make to your server. While it is not intended to be comprehensive, it does give you an idea of the types of configurations you can make.

IIS Add-ins

The following are some of the IIS 3.0 components you can install for use with your IIS web server. Because each component is independent of the other pieces and has its own installation, you can install any or all of them.

Active Server Pages (ASP)

Active Server Pages (ASP) allow HTML authors to create server-side programs that are translated into HTML before they are served to a browser. They are based on ActiveX, and rely on VBScript or Jscript as the scripting language. Other scripting languages (such as PERL, REXX, and Python) can be added by modifying the Registry key *HKEY_ LOCAL_MACHINE\SYSTEM\CurrentControlSet\Services\W3SVC\ASP* key.

The primary language used (VBScript by default) can be changed by setting the *HKEY_LOCAL_MACHINE\SYSTEM\CurrentControlSet\Services\W3SVC\ASP\Parameters* key (DefaultScriptLanguage value) to the name of the language you want to use.

> *CAUTION:*   Editing the registry incorrectly can cause serious problems, including corruption, which
> may make it necessary to reinstall Windows NT or ASP.

For more information, see Microsoft's ASP FAQ at **http://www.microsoft.com/Support/ActiveServer/content/faq/**.

Index Server

Index Server is a component of IIS 3.0 that provides full-text indexing and a search engine. It will index HTML, plain text, Word, and Excel documents. To index other types of files, you can install additional filters. To add new filters, see the instructions provided with the filter DLL.

After it is installed, Index Server really doesn't require any configuration. It comes with an administration tool called the Administration Page that allows you to manage some Index Server functions, such as determining which directories are indexed and running index statistics.

To get to the Administration Page:

1. Select Start | Programs | Microsoft Index Server (Common) | Index Server Administration.

2. This will start your browser and display the Administration Page, as shown in Figure 10-4.

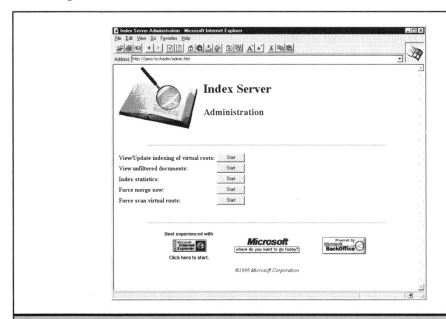

Figure 10-4.   Index Server Administration page

The Index Server only indexes files stored in virtual directories or subdirectories of virtual directories. Virtual directories are discussed later in this chapter. By default, the Index Server will index your entire website. This means all existing virtual directories are automatically included for indexing. If there are directories you don't want indexed, use the Administration Page to limit indexing.

For more information, see the Microsoft Index Server page at **http://www.netraveler.com/Searchhelp/default.htm#Top**.

NetShow

NetShow is designed to deliver multimedia materials over an intranet or the Internet. To allow people to download multimedia information, install NetShow On-Demand. To broadcast to an audience, install NetShow Live. You can install either or both servers.

If you install NetShow On-Demand, you will need add two new MIME types. These MIME types are:

    video/x-ms-asf,asf,,5
    video/x-ms-asf,as,,5

NOTE: See the MIME types section later in this chapter for instructions on adding a new MIME type.

For more information, see Microsoft's NetShow FAQ at **http://www.microsoft.com/InfoServSupport/content/faq/netshow/default.htm**.

Crystal Reports

Seagate Crystal Reports is a tool for producing custom reports from your IIS logs. You can download the free component for use with the IIS web server.

To start Crystal Reports:

1. Select Start | Crystal Reports 4.5 | Crystal Reports 4.5.

2. The Crystal Reports window will display, as shown in Figure 10-5.

If you install the Web Engine, you can also generate reports from a web browser, as shown in Figure 10-6. To bring up the administration page, enter the URL for the *logrpts* directory. For example:

    http://*www.imanexample.com*/**logrpts**

where *www.imanexample.com* would be name of your web server. In Figure 10-6, the name of the server is the same as the name of the workstation.

Use of the reporting feature can put a strain on your web server. If your website is available from the Internet—or services a large number of internal users—you may want

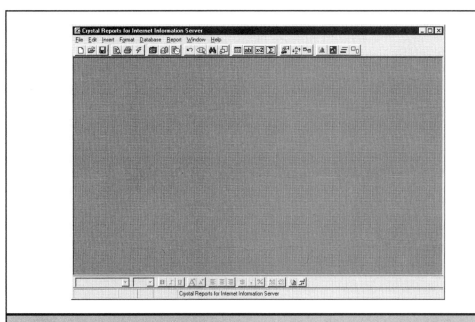

Figure 10-5. Crystal Reports application window

Figure 10-6. Crystal Reports HTML administration page

to limit the number of people who can run reports via the HTML interface. An easy way to restrict access is to change the name of the virtual directory where the administration page is located. Just use the Internet Service Manager to specify a new virtual directory name (from *logrpts* to something else), and only give the new URL out to people who need to generate reports.

Internet Server Application Programming Interface (ISAPI)

The Internet Server Application Programming Interface (ISAPI) is a Microsoft specification for writing applications and tools for an IIS environment. The API enables programmers to create two types of programs: extension DLLs and ISAPI filters.

▼ Extension DLLs are designed to extend the capabilities of the base IIS web server. They are roughly equivalent to regular CGI scripts. No special configuration is needed to run them; just put the files in the */Scripts* or similar directory.

▲ ISAPI filters are also DLLs. However, unlike extension DLLs (or CGIs), filters are called for every URL, regardless of the contents. They allow programmers to create programs that sit between the web server and the Internet/intranet connection. When a filter is loaded, it tells the web server what type of events it wants to process. This is useful for such activities such as logging, compression, custom authentication schemes, and encryption.

NOTE: To add new ISAPI filters, you will need to add them to the *HKEY_LOCAL_MACHINE/ SYSTEM/CurrentControlSet/Services/W3SVC/Parameters* Registry key (Filter DLLs value) and restart your system.

ISAPI (and a similar API for Netscape, NSAPI) is an alternative to CGI programs and offers its own set of advantages and disadvantages. ISAPI tends to be faster than CGI. However, disadvantages include that ISAPI isn't widely supported outside of Microsoft, and if the ISAPI DLL crashes, it could also crash the web server.

Common Gateway Interface (CGI)

The Common Gateway Interface (CGI) is a specification that determines how servers communicate to a script or program and how a script or program formats its reply for use by the server. CGI itself is not a language; it describes a protocol that can be used to write programs for use with a web server. CGI scripts allow people to write simple applications in any number of languages. Scripts run on a web server and can produce output in a user's web browser. User input is passed in through Environment Variables or Standard-In, the program does whatever it was designed to do, and it sends HTML back through Standard-Out. This simple design, combined with languages like Perl and TCL, make CGIs very easy to develop.

As far as server configuration issues are concerned, CGI scripts can be executed out of a server root directory specified as the /*Scripts* directory without any special configuration. However, access to this directory is usually restricted.

CAUTION: All CGI programs, both scripted and compiled, are potentially insecure. The level of security required for a site varies widely. Some sites require users to submit their script or program to a webmaster, who checks that the code doesn't contain security holes before it can be used. Other sites restrict CGI access to trusted users, who are responsible for checking their own code.

NOTE: An alternative to CGI is ISAPI or NSAPI.

Script Directories

IIS expects script to be in the /*Scripts* directory by default. This name is an alias for a physical directory you specify with the Internet Services Manger. The physical directory must be on an NTFS disk.

NOTE: For security purposes, the only permission granted on /*Scripts* is execute-only.

CONFIGURING IIS FOR SCRIPTS   Before scripts can be run, you'll need to configure the permissions for the /*Scripts* directory. This needs to be done in two places: IIS and the Windows NT file system.

In IIS:

1. Start the Internet Service Manager and double-click the computer name of your web server.
2. In the WWW Service Properties dialog, click the Directories tab.
3. In the directory list, double-click the /*Scripts* directory.
4. This brings up the Directory Properties dialog. In the Access portion of this dialog, make sure only the "Execute" checkbox is selected. Note the path used for the /*Scripts* alias: you'll need to know this path for the Windows NT configuration portion.
5. Save your changes and exit out through the dialogs.

In Windows NT:

1. In Windows Explorer, navigate to the physical location of the /*Scripts* directory.
2. Right-click the directory, and choose Properties from the Context menu.
3. In the Properties dialog, click the Security tab.

4. In the Security tab dialog, click Permissions.

5. In the Directory Permissions dialog, set the permissions for this directory and its subdirectories. The Everyone group should only have Read and Execute permissions. You may also want to add the Administrators group and give them Full Control permission.

6. Save your changes and exit out through the dialogs.

Script Languages

A CGI can be written in pretty much any language, as shown in Table 10-5. Capabilities needed for CGIs include

▼ Ability to create 32-bit programs. (The IIS web server only works with 32-bit CGIs because of Windows NT memory usage.)

■ Ability to access environment information variables.

▲ Ability to access command line parameters.

NOTE: If you are porting UNIX CGIs to Windows NT, there are a number of function similarities. Functions like open(), fopen(), read(), write(), etc. are available in the C runtime library of most Win32 C compilers. Also, there is a one-to-one mapping of several UNIX APIs to Win32 APIs, for example, read() to ReadFile(), write() to WriteFile(), open() to CreateFile(), close() to CloseFile().

Many CGI applications are written in PERL (Practical Extraction and Report Language) or C. In addition to the standalone version of PERL, there is also a PERL ISAPI DLL for use with web servers such as IIS.

Language	Possible Download Site(s)
PERL	http://www.perl.hip.com/ (PERL 5.0 DLLs for IIS)
Python	http://www.python.org/
Object REXX	http://www2.hursley.ibm.com/orexx/
TCL/TK	http://www.sunlabs.com/research/tcl/

Table 10-5. Example CGI Languages

NOTE: IIS doesn't support WinCGI. WinCGI is an interface specification for running CGI on Windows platforms. WinCGI is supported other Windows NT web servers, such as Netscape.

Server Side Includes (SSI)

Server Side Includes (SSIs) allow HTML authors to direct the web server to perform some type of processing on the HTML file before it is returned to a browser. HTML files that use the #include statement must use the STM filename extension instead of HTML, for example, *report.STM* instead of *report.HTML*.

NOTE: IIS currently only supports #include.

To change the default extension, *.STM*, change the value of the Registry key *HKEY_LOCAL_MACHINE/SYSTEM/CurrentControlSet/Services/W3SVC/Parameters/ServerSideIncludesExtension*.

NOTE: Using SSIs can reduce website performance. Each file is scanned by the web server for SSI directives before it is sent to the browser.

Imagemaps

Image maps are pictures that allow users to access different documents by clicking on different areas of an image. IIS uses standard CERN or NCSA map file formats.

There are two distinct types of imagemaps: server-side and client-side. Server-side imagemaps are processed by the web server and require some web server processing. Client-side imagemaps are processed by the user's browser and don't require any web server configuration or processing. However, client-side imagemaps are not supported by older browsers, which will simply ignore the coordinates.

NOTE: MapEdit (**http://www.boutell.com/mapedit/**) is a good shareware program for creating map files.

Virtual Servers

A virtual server allows you to have multiple domain names on a single computer. This is also known as Multi-Homing or Multi-Homed Servers. For example, say you wanted to have your internal intranet and your external Internet websites on the same physical workstation. To do this, you could set up a regular server for one site, and a virtual server for the other site. Although they are on the same machine, the URLs for these sites would be different. For example:

http://www.imanexample.com
http://web.imanexample.com

NOTE: Windows NT will only let you set five IP addresses for any given network card. This means, in effect, you are limited to five virtual servers under IIS. You can get around this limitation, but it involves editing the Registry.

To set up a virtual server:

▼ Assign a static IP address for each web server.

■ Bind each IP address to your server's network card.

■ Change your DNS server so it can route the addresses of the virtual server(s).

▲ Set up IIS to handle the virtual server directories.

Virtual Directories

When you set up a server, you specify a home directory. For the server to access files, they must be in subdirectories of the home directory. Virtual directories give you a way to get around this. They essentially allow you to specify an alias for a path, which appears to users to be on your server.

NOTE: IIS provides virtual directory support for web, Gopher, and FTP servers.

To add or edit virtual directories:

1. Start the Internet Service Manager and double-click the appropriate web server.

2. In the WWW Service Properties dialog, click the Directories tab.

3. Add, view, or edit directories as appropriate.

Virtual directories don't show up if directory browsing is turned on; this means users won't see virtual directories or any directory listings. Users must enter the full URL to see the contents of the directory.

For example, when the IIS web server is installed, a number of default virtual directories with read-only permission are created. Table 10-6 shows you some of the common default aliases, although the exact default aliases installed depend upon the software you've installed. To see the contents of these directories, a user would type the full URL to see its contents, as in

http://www.imanexample.com/IASDocs

Alias	Description
/IASDocs	IIS documentation
/iisadmin	Internet Server Manager HTML administration
/ASPSamp	ASP samples
/Scripts	CGI script directory

Table 10-6.   Default Web Server Aliases

NOTE: Only the web server installs default aliases.

Secure Transactions—SSL

The Secure Sockets Layer (SSL) is a security protocol designed to ensure data moving between a browser and a server remains private. In theory, someone could intercept information—such as a credit card number—while it is in transit between the browser and the server. One solution to prevent information from being usable if it is intercepted is to encrypt it. The most widely implemented encryption system for the Web at present is a protocol known as the Secure Sockets Layer (SSL).

The IIS web server supports SSL. However, there are several steps involved in enabling this support. Here's a general list of what you'll need to do:

1. Generate a key pair file and a request file using the Internet Service Manager Key Manager or the keygen program.

2. Request an SSL certificate from VeriSign, Inc. See their website at **http://www.verisign.com**.

3. Install the certificate in IIS using the Key Manager or the setkey program.

4. Enable SSL on the server by using the Internet Service Manager to select the directories you want to secure, and setting the Require Secure SSL Channel option.

MIME Types

The Web allows you to publish information in many different formats. Each format type has its own MIME (Multipurpose Internet Mail Extension) type.

NOTE: In Apache, MIME types are added to the file named *mime.types.*

Adding a new MIME type to IIS involves the following:

1. Start the Registry editor. See the "Registry Entries" section for more information.

2. Open the *HKEY_LOCAL_MACHINE\SYSTEM\CurrentControlSet\ Services\InetInfo\Parameters\MimeMap* key.

3. Select Edit | Add Value.

4. Enter a new MIME type. Your value should appear similar to the following:

   application/pdf,pdf,,P

   The format for a MIME type is

   <mime type>, <filename extension>, <unused parameter>, <Gopher type>

NOTE: The Gopher type tells a client what to do when an item is selected from the menu. Table 10-7 shows a selection of Gopher types.

5. Close the Registry editor.

6. Restart IIS for the changes to take effect.

MAINTENANCE

Maintenance is the ongoing process of tweaking the web server after its initial installation and configuration. It consists of tasks such as tuning its performance, starting and stopping the server, monitoring files such as the error and access logs, and generating usage statistics for your website(s). Some general maintenance tips include

▼ Back up your web documents frequently. You might also consider putting them in a version control system.

■ Keep an eye on the size of the log files. The busier your web server is, the faster they will grow in size.

■ Log as little information as possible. Turn DNS lookup off and do lookups later with a script. Log referrer URLs sparingly, if you need to know the origin of a consistent bad file request in the error logs, for example. There are search engines such as Digital's AltaVista that can tell you who's linking to you.

▲ Scan your access and error log files regularly. Signs of suspicious activity might involve system commands or repeated attempts to access a password-protected document. Extremely long URL requests can indicate an attempt to overrun a program's input buffer.

Type	Description
0	Text file, usually ASCII
1	Directory listing
2	CSO email address server
3	Error
4	Macintosh BinHex file
5	DOS archive file, such as ZIP
6	UNIX UUEncoded file
7	Index search server
8	Telnet session
9	Binary file
:	Bitmap image
;	Movie file
<	Sound file
c	Calendar or calendar of events
g	GIF graphic file
h	HTML file
I	Image file
i	Inline text type
M	MIME file
P	PDF document
S	Sound file
T	3270 mainframe session

Table 10-7.   Gopher Types

Starting and Stopping Servers

In IIS, the various Internet servers run as servers under Windows NT. To start and stop any of these services (HTTP, FTP, Gopher, Index Server, etc.), you can use either the

Internet Services Manager or the Services applet. The easiest way is to use the Internet Services Manager.

Log Files and Reports

Log files give you a record of every event that has occurred with your server. To turn this raw information into a more usable form, you run a report.

IIS log files can be in either text or database format. You can run reports from commercial tools, like Crystal Reports, or create your own reporting tools and log formatting programs.

Log Files

Log files give you a record of every event that has occurred with your web server. IIS gives you the option of logging to either a file or an SQL/ODBC compliant database.

To enable logging:

1. Start the Internet Service Manager and double-click the computer name of your web server.

2. In the WWW Service Properties dialog, select the Logging tab, as shown in Figure 10-7.

3. Enable logging, and select the type of logging for your service. Example log file formats within IIS are shown in Table 10-8.

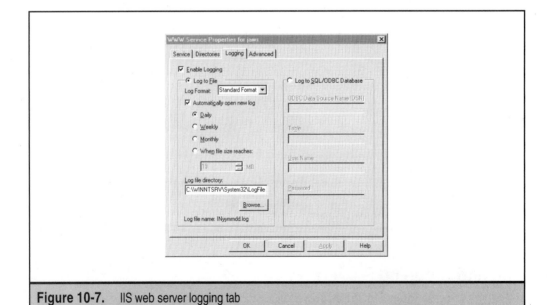

Figure 10-7. IIS web server logging tab

Name	Description
Common Log Format (CLF)	NCSA format. ASCII file where information is saved as a series of records. Each record is made up of fields, which are separated by spaces. Blank information is indicated by a dash.
European Microsoft Windows NT Academic Centre (EMWAC)	EMWAC servers were provided with Windows NT 3.5.1 Resource Kit.
Standard IIS format	IIS format. ASCII file where each line represents a single record. Each record is an event.

Table 10-8. Example Log Formats

The CONVLOG.EXE program converts text-based log files from IIS standard format to common log format (convlog -t ncsa *<logfilename>*) or EMWAC (convlog *<logfilename>*).

NOTE: Before converting, make a copy of the original log file.

Reports

Reports allow you to derive meaningful information from your web server logs. You can run custom reports from log information stored in databases, or use reporting tools such as Seagate Crystal Reports for IIS 3.0. Other sources for log analysis tools include Yahoo, at **http://www.yahoo.com/Computers_and_Internet/Software/Internet/World_Wide_Web/ Servers/Log_Analysis_Tools/**, and WebReference, at **http://www.webreference.com/ usage.html**. Table 10-9 lists URLs for reporting software.

Software	URL
Seagate Crystal Reports	**http://www.crystalinc.com/**
Actuate	**http://www.actuate.com/**
Corel Web.data	**http://www.corel.com/webdata/**

Table 10-9. Reporting Software

Performance Monitoring

The Performance Monitor is a standard Windows NT tool for tracking the status of various system resources. It allows you to monitor your system as it is being used and is useful when you need to determine where system performance is being affected.

NOTE: To check the status of connections, display information about the protocol being used, or display the port number used on the local machine. The *netstat* program is also useful.

To start the Performance Monitor:

1. Select Start | Programs | Administrative Tools (Common) | Performance Monitor.
2. The Performance Monitor window displays, as shown in Figure 10-8.

When IIS is installed, a number of related counters are automatically installed. Table 10-10 provides a listing of the major types. Using this tool, you can display chart, alert, log, and report information for your web server or other IIS services.

1. Start the Performance Monitor.
2. Select the Edit | Add to [Chart, Alert, Log, Report] option.
3. For the Object, select HTTP Service or Internet Information Services Global, as shown in Figure 10-9. IIS 3.0 objects are installed as you install each particular product; Table 10-10 describes some of the objects you may have on your system.
4. From the resulting counters, select the ones you want to use to generate displays.

Like any service, using the Performance Monitor can have an impact on your system performance. It uses system resources like memory and CPU cycles like any other program.

Security

Security is a very broad and important topic. In no way is this section a comprehensive treatment. It does however, provide you with some of the issues you may want to consider.

General Considerations

Site security typically includes a combination of firewalls and solid internal network security. This is a fairly common layered security approach. In theory, either method alone should protect your site; however, reality tends to do nasty things to theories.

A comprehensive approach to protecting a website generally means following best practices in a number of different areas. The National Computer Security Association,

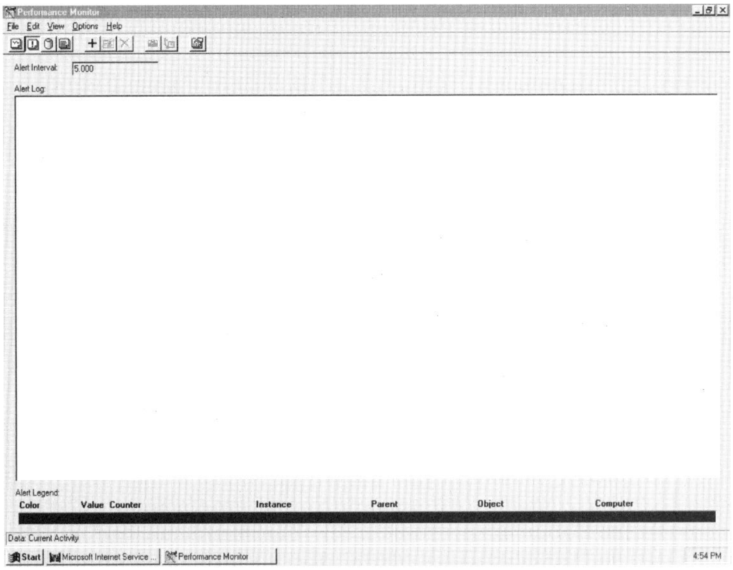

Figure 10-8. Performance Monitor window

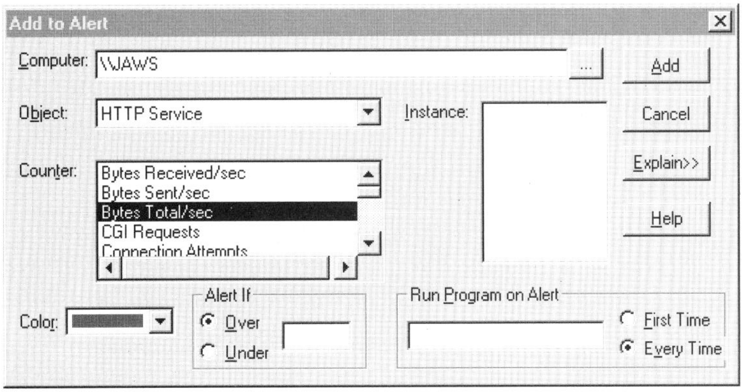

Figure 10-9. Selecting the web server object for monitoring

Object Name	Description
Internet Information Services Global	Monitors IIS performance as a whole. Items monitored are related to caching information (such as amount of cache used, cache flushes due to file or directory changes in the IIS directory tree, and cache hits) and bandwidth information
HTTP Service	Monitors web server performance. Items monitored include CGI requests, connection attempts, and number of users connected (broken down into anonymous and non-anonymous)
FTP Server	Monitors FTP server performance
Gopher Service	Monitors the Gopher server
Active Server Pages	Monitors the ASP server
NetShow On-Demand Service	Monitors NetShow On-Demand
Index Server provided with IIS 3.0 adds three objects: • Content Index • Content Index Filter • Http Content Index	• Monitors the Index Server performance • Monitors overall performance of individual index filters • Monitors performance of the interface between the web server and the Index Server

Table 10-10.   IIS 3.0 Performance Monitors

NCSA, is in the process of planning a certification process for websites that touches on a number of these areas. See NCSA at **http://www.ncsa.com** for more details.

NOTE: You may also want to take a look at RFC 1244, the Site Security Handbook—available at **gopher://ds1.internic.net/00/fyi/fyi8.txt**—for more information.

The guidelines being developed by NCSA are intended to ensure a basic level of security, rather than a hacker-proof one. They set minimum standards for logical and physical security issues that address such issues as hacking, intrusion, data loss, and tampering. While these guidelines may be more or less stringent than your site's needs, they can certainly be used as a starting point for developing your own security guidelines. A summary of the NCSA guidelines for a single server site is as follows:

▼   The website must withstand network-based attacks by means of a firewall, filtering router, or other appropriate security mechanism.

■   The Domain Naming Service (DNS) entries for all URL-referenced systems must be resolvable.

■   NIC handles must be authenticated and the NIC contact information must be accurate and contain at least two contacts.

■   The site must maintain logging. Access to logs must be limited to authorized personnel. Logs must be retained in a secure but retrievable format.

■   A standard encryption mechanism, such as SSL or SHTTP, must be used for sensitive data transmission.

■   CGI scripts and programs must be checked to ensure they don't intentionally or unintentionally compromise your system.

■   A person must be designated as the site's Client Executeable,"CxE," Evaluator. All client executables must be examined and evaluated as "harmless" to the user.

■   Pages that contain or accept sensitive data must be made non-cacheable. Users must be informed if any pages containing sensitive data will be cached to local storage.

■   The site must meet physical security requirements, such as access-controlled areas, roster of authorized personnel, suitable equipment, and emergency contact information.

■   The site must meet logical security requirements, such as secure password policies, webmaster contact, HTTPD server configured for least privilege, and separate development and production systems.

▲   If a transaction mechanism is in place, it must be documented, and the server's private key protected by a strong pass-phrase. Sensitive information must be periodically removed from the server. The OS and platform must be documented and integrity assured. Backups and Restore capabilities must be in place.

Specific Considerations

The following are some specific suggestions you might consider. While this list isn't intended to be all-inclusive, it does give you an idea of issues you may want to consider. For more suggestions, see the Windows NT Security Issues at **http://www.somarsoft.com/ security.htm** and the WWW Security FAQ at **http://www.genome.wi.mit.edu/WWW/ faqs/wwwsf1.html**.

▼ Use the NT File System (NTFS) as your file system. NTFS allows you to limit access to files and directories.

■ Check permissions on network shares.

■ Disable file mappings for *.bat* and *.cmd*.

■ Enable auditing. For websites connected to the Internet, the events to look at are Logon and Logoff, and File and Object Access for users logged on as IUSR.

■ Run only the services and protocols required by your system.

■ Don't overlook the built-in guest account. If you set up an FTP server, anyone can log into the guest account by entering any name/any password. Fix this by disabling the guest account under User Admin.

■ Run any HTTP servers, such as IIS, under an ordinary user account rather than the System account.

▲ Ensure remote Registry access is disabled except for administrators. In Windows NT Server 4.0, the *HKEY_LOCAL_MACHINE\SYSTEM\ CurrentControlSet\Control\SecurePipeServers\winreg* key is installed by default. If remote registry access is enabled, a user can change the registry of any workstation or server on which the user has an account. Usually, this means all servers in a domain environment, or on which the guest account is enabled.

NOTE: The key to disable remote access on NT 4.0 workstations is not installed by default, but it can be added.

SUMMARY

Microsoft's Internet Information Server provides an integrated environment for web services under Windows NT. It is a fairly easy system to install, configure, and manage. In this chapter, we looked at the various components that make up IIS, including several optional add-ons. We examined the installation and configuration process and looked at the various issues that you will face when managing an IIS system. Since IIS is very tightly coupled to Microsoft Windows NT Server, it is an obvious choice for a web server tool if you decide to use NT Server as your server platform.

WINDOWS
NT
Professional
Library

CHAPTER 11

UNIX Web Servers

Web growth over the past few years has been tremendous. As a result, web server applications are a very common type of server applications on both UNIX and Windows NT. If you are an experienced NT administrator who is having to also administer UNIX systems, you will probably encounter a UNIX-based web server before long. Unlike many Windows NT web servers—such as Microsoft IIS—which tend to be configurable through a GUI, many UNIX web servers are configured and administered via variables in configuration files.

NOTE: Although not covered in this chapter, Netscape web server configuration is more GUI-based.

In the UNIX world, there are a variety of web servers available. However, one of the most widely used web servers is the Apache web server. In fact, Apache is one of the most popular web servers even when compared to all other operating systems.

Since web servers are a very common UNIX application, it is very likely that you will run into an Apache web server if you do any serious UNIX administration. It would be impossible to cover all the details of all the different UNIX web servers that you might encounter in a single chapter. So, in the interest of providing practical information, we will discuss the Apache web server in detail.

WEB GROWTH

As you've probably heard (and experienced), the growth of the World Wide Web (WWW) has been phenomenal. Access to the Web really is worldwide: web servers and websites are in several hundred countries on all seven continents. You can find information available on almost any subject imaginable (and some you probably never thought of!). Companies, universities, governments, states, cities, schools, hospitals, museums, clubs, and individuals all maintain websites. The AltaVista search engine (**http://www.altavista.digital.com/**) alone reports that its robot has indexed over 31 million web pages on over 476,000 servers. And these figures don't include all the web servers and web pages contained within private intranets throughout the world!

Web servers, too, have had a growth explosion. Just a few years ago, there were roughly a dozen or so web servers. All were products of experimentation or research. Now, there are a multitude of web servers. Many are commercial, but there are many free web servers—such as Apache—that continue to be developed, supported, and used. Just how many different types of web servers are out there? Well, that depends on the platform that you're on. Table 11-1 gives you some idea of what's out there. These figures come from Yahoo's software listings (**http://www.yahoo.com/Computers_and_Internet/ Software/Internet/World_Wide_Web/Servers/**)—new servers and platforms are being added all the time.

NOTE: See WebCompare (**http://webcompare.iworld.com/compare/chart.html**) for a listing of web server software, platforms supported, and price.

As for the operating system of choice, UNIX currently holds the lead. Surveys from both AltaVista and WebCrawler show that UNIX is the most used web server platform. This isn't surprising, as the Internet cut its teeth on UNIX, which has a reputation for being a robust, highly scaleable, and flexible operating system that provides an excellent price-to-performance ratio.

Though UNIX still holds the lead, Windows NT is quickly catching up with its ease of use and decreasing cost. Microsoft is aggressively pursuing the UNIX market, citing Windows NT 4.0's increased scalability, performance, and reliability. Microsoft has also set out to provide integrated software solutions, from website creation to hosting and development.

OS Platform	Number of Web Servers Available
UNIX (various flavors)	55
Microsoft Windows/Windows 95	27
Microsoft NT	17
Apple Macintosh	16
IBM OS/2	6
Novell NetWare	5
IBM VM/CMS	4
Digital VMS	4
PERL	4
AS/400	1
IBM MVS	1
Amiga	1
BeOS	1

Table 11-1. Web Software Applications Available by Platform

NOTE: Some UNIX vendors, such as SunSoft (**http://www.sunsoft.com**) and SCO (**http://sco.com**), have also begun to offer more integrated software solutions.

When it comes to web server software, the numbers aren't quite as clear-cut. The top overall web servers are Apache, NCSA, and Netscape. Figure 11-1 shows a sample breakdown.

The web server software (and operating system) you select is likely to be influenced by a number of factors. For example, a commercial website that offers online purchasing or access to confidential information usually has different requirements from a site providing local television listings or an internal corporate site that is isolated from the outside Internet.

Overall, the percentage of NT-specific servers running either IIS, Website, WebsitePro, Purveyor, EMWAC, Commerce-Builder, Alibaba, or WebQuest, is around 20 percent.

NOTE: NT versions of Netscape or Navisoft Web servers are not included in this NetCraft total.

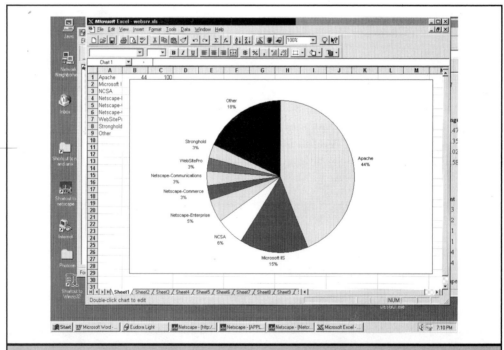

Figure 11-1. Web server software usage (information from NetCraft— http://www.netcraft.com/survey)

WHY APACHE?

There are a number of UNIX web servers to choose from, both commercial and free. Apache was selected for this chapter because of its widespread use. According to the NetCraft Web Server Survey (**http://www.netcraft.com/survey/**) Apache has consistently been the top web server in usage, found in roughly 40 percent of total sites surveyed. By comparison, the combined total of the other top web servers—from Microsoft, Netscape, and NCSA—is roughly 30 percent of the sites in the same survey.

NOTE: Some NetCraft figures are a compilation of multiple web server products offered by the same company. For example, Netscape is the sum of sites running Netscape-Enterprise, Netscape-FastTrack, Netscape-Commerce, Netscape-Communications, Netsite-Commerce and Netsite-Communications. Microsoft is the sum of sites running Microsoft-IIS, Microsoft-IIS-W, Microsoft-PWS-95, and Microsoft-PWS.

SECURE TRANSACTIONS

Before we go further, this is a good time to talk a little about secure transactions. Most of the information transmitted over the Internet isn't particularly confidential. However, there are times you may want to safeguard information..

For example, consider a current hot topic, credit card numbers on the Internet. When you place an order for goods or services from a website and enter a credit card number, the credit card number is transmitted across the Internet from the browser to the server. In theory, someone could intercept this information while it is in transit. One solution to prevent information from being usable if it is intercepted is to encrypt it. A good encryption scheme effectively scrambles the information and resists *cracking* (unscrambling by people who have no business seeing the information in the first place). The most widely implemented encryption system for the Web at present is SSL (Secure Sockets Layer).

SSL is an open, nonproprietary protocol developed by Netscape Communications. It uses industry-accepted RSA public key cryptography for authentication and encryption. The SSL protocol was designed to provide a data security layer between application protocols such as HTTP, Telnet, NNTP, or FTP and TCP/IP. SSL provides data encryption, server authentication, message integrity, and optional client authentication for a TCP/IP connection.

NOTE: Because SSL data transport requires encryption, you may find there are government-imposed restrictions on its use. Many governments—including the United States—have restrictions on the import, export, and use of encryption technology.

There are a number of commercial web servers that support SSL: several Netscape servers (**http://home.netscape.com/**), Thawte Sioux (**http://www.thawte.com/products/sioux/**), and IBM Connection Secure (**http://www.ics.raleigh.ibm.com/**), to name a few. While Apache doesn't support SSL, there is an Apache web server variant, called Stronghold, that does. Stronghold was formerly known as Apache SSL-US and is available for both UNIX and Windows NT from UK Web (**http://stronghold.ukweb.com**). SSL web servers require some additional steps that are not necessary for other types of web servers. Most notably, you must generate a public/private key pair, and register with a Certificate Authority (such as Verisign or Thawte). Although similar to Apache, this chapter does not address Stronghold installation and configuration.

SETTING UP A WEB SERVER

UNIX web servers are typically configured using configuration files. These files contain directives that control basic settings such as the server name and the directory locations of files such as the error log. In contrast, NT web servers, such as IIS and WebSite, are configured using a series of dialog boxes and wizards. A mixture of the two methods, the Netscape family of servers are configured via HTML forms, but maintain data in configuration files.

In general, setting up a web server involves the following steps:

1. Get the software.

2. Install the software.

3. Compile the software to create a web server. (Skip this step if you have a binary for your system.)

4. Configure the web server.

5. Run the web server.

6. Maintain the web server.

Getting the Software

You can get Apache from a number of different sources. You can download the latest release from the Apache website (**http://www.apache.org/**). You will also find a version of Apache on the CD-ROM included with this book.

If you download a binary distribution, you can go on to the "Installing Apache" section; otherwise, you will need to compile the source on your workstation.

Installing Apache

To install Apache, follow these steps:

1. Copy the source code package to a part of your file system. Free-space requirements vary among the different operating systems, and with the

specific options you want to include in your software. A general figure would be around 15MB of free space.

2. Unpack the software. This will create a directory called *apache_1.2.1/*. Within this directory, go to the *src/* subdirectory. A sample set of commands might look like this:

```
gunzip apache_1_2_1.tar.gz
tar -xvf apache_1_2_1.tar
cd src
```

Compiling Apache

Apache is known to compile on just about every UNIX variant: AIX, SunOS 4.1.*x*, Solaris 2.*x*, Linux, FreeBSD/OpenBSDI/NetBSD/BSDI, HP-UX, Ultrix, SCO, SGI Irix 5.*x* and 6.*x*, DEC OSF1, NeXT, Apple A/UX, UTS, UnixWare, Sequent, Apollo Domain/OS, QNX, and probably a few that haven't been tried yet. There's a port to OS/2, and a Windows NT port is rumored to be in the works.

If you have downloaded a binary for your system, you won't have to go through these steps; it has already been done for you. However, if you want to modify the functionality of your web server, you will need to recompile a new web server.

Compiling Apache is pretty straightforward:

1. Customize the *Configuration* file for your installation. In most cases, you should be able to skip this step: the configuration program has some intelligence built into it for detecting the platform and compiler on your system. If you have problems (i.e., you get error messages after running *Configure*), or know there are specific configuration changes you'd like to make (such as modules), you'll need to hand-edit this file. Run the *Configure* script. Run *make*.

2. After *make* finishes, you should have a web server executable called *httpd* in the Apache *src/* directory. You're now ready for the next step, which is configuring the web server behavior (see "Configuring Apache" later in this chapter).

The rest of this section gives you more details on the *Configuration* file, the *Configure* script, *make*, and modules.

Configuration File

The *Configuration* file is located in the Apache *src/* directory and is used by the *Configure* script to create a *MakeFile*. See the "Modules" section in this chapter for information about the default modules included with Apache.

Should you decide to edit the *Configuration* file by hand, the following are some of the main variables you should look at setting:

▼ Specify which C compiler you're using (probably *gcc*)

■ Uncomment the configuration for your operating system (including appropriate settings for the AUX_CFLAGS and AUX_LIBS variables)

▲ Modify the modules to be compiled as needed (see the "Modules" section for more information).

Configure Script

This file doesn't need any configuration; all you need to do is run it. The *Configure* script is a simple Bourne shell script that takes the *Configuration* file and creates two files—*MakeFile* and *modules.c*. The *MakeFile* created will be specifically targeted to your platform, with any necessary runtime defines set, and with any modules you've chosen compiled together. It also creates a *modules.c*, which contains information about which modules to link together at compilation time.

make

Like *Configure,* all you have to do with *make* is run it. After it finishes, you should have an executable program in your Apache *src/* directory called *httpd*. This file, *httpd,* is your web server program. At this point, you're ready to begin the server configuration (see the "Configuring Apache" section in this chapter).

Modules

Apache has a *modular* architecture that makes it possible for you to add or remove web server functionality without a lot of hassle. Most of the code that comes as part of an Apache distribution is in the form of modules. This gives you a great deal of flexibility in customizing the functionality of your web server, especially as your web server needs change over time.

Important points to keep in mind when selecting modules are

▼ The more modules included in the build, the more memory the compiled server will use.

■ Module placement is important: modules are listed in the *Configuration* file in reverse priority order. Later modules can override the behavior of those that come earlier.

■ Some modules are mutually exclusive.

■ Some modules may require extra linking.

▲ Apache 1.2 supports HTTP/1.1. Because of this, some older modules that process input via POST or PUT methods may not work correctly.

NOTE: HTTP/1.1 is a new standard that offers speed enhancements over HTTP/1.0 and new features such as hostname identification, content negotiation, persistent connections, chunked transfers, byte ranges, and support for proxies and caches. You can learn more by looking at RFC 2068, the HTTP/1.1 standard (**http://www.ics.uci.edu/pub/ietf/http/rfc2068.txt**), or at W3C's set of overviews (**http://www.w3.org/pub/WWW/Protocols/Overview.html**).

Default Modules   Modules packaged with your distribution are listed near the end of the *Configuration* file, which is located in the Apache *src/* directory. Unless there are specific changes you know you need to make, it's easiest to use the default settings. Following is an example listing of modules included in a default *Configuration* file. Module descriptions are provided with the Apache distribution. They are in HTML and are located in the Apache *htdocs/manual/mod/* directory.

NOTE: This example is from the *Configuration* file for the Apache version 1.2.1 distribution on the CD-ROM.

Not all modules provided with Apache are automatically compiled. Module names starting with a pound sign (#) are not included in the build. To include a default module, simply uncomment its entry in the *Configuration* file.

CAUTION: Before commenting or uncommenting default modules, make sure you understand what effect this will have on your server.

```
###############################################################
# Module configuration
#
# Modules are listed in reverse priority order --- the ones that come
# later can override the behavior of those that come earlier.  This
# can have visible effects; for instance, if UserDir followed Alias,
# you couldn't alias out a particular user's home directory.

# The configuration below is what we consider a decent default
# configuration.  If you want the functionality provided by a particular
# module, remove the "#" sign at the beginning of the line. But remember,
# the more modules you compile into the server, the larger the executable
# is and the more memory it will take, so if you are unlikely to use the
# functionality of a particular module you might wish to leave it out.
##
## Config manipulation modules
##
```

```
## mod_env sets up additional or restricted environment variables to be
## passed to CGI/SSI scripts.  It is listed first (lowest priority) since
## it does not do per-request stuff.

Module env_module            mod_env.o

## mod_dld defines commands that allow other modules to be loaded
## dynamically (at runtime).  This module is for experimental use only.

# Module dld_module          mod_dld.o

##
## Request logging modules
##

Module config_log_module   mod_log_config.o

## Optional modules for NCSA user-agent/referer logging compatibility
## We recommend, however, that you just use the configurable access_log.

# Module agent_log_module     mod_log_agent.o
# Module referer_log_module  mod_log_referer.o

##
## Type checking modules
##
## mod_mime maps filename extensions to content types, encodings, and
## magic type handlers (the latter is obsoleted by mod_actions).
## mod_negotiation allows content selection based on the Accept* headers.

Module mime_module           mod_mime.o
Module negotiation_module   mod_negotiation.o

##
## Content delivery modules
##
## The status module allows the server to display current details about
## how well it is performing and what it is doing.  Consider also enabling
## STATUS=yes (see the Rules section near the start of this file) to allow
## full status information.  Check conf/access.conf on how to enable this.

# Module status_module        mod_status.o
```

```
## The Info module displays configuration information for the server and
## all included modules. It's very useful for debugging.

# Module info_module           mod_info.o

## mod_include translates server-side include (SSI) statements in text files.
## mod_dir handles requests on directories and directory indexes.
## mod_cgi handles CGI scripts.

Module includes_module      mod_include.o
Module dir_module           mod_dir.o
Module cgi_module           mod_cgi.o

## The asis module implemented ".asis" file types, which allow the embedding
## of HTTP headers at the beginning of the document.  mod_imap handles internal
## imagemaps (no more cgi-bin/imagemap/!).  mod_actions is used to specify
## CGI scripts which act as "handlers" for particular files, for example to
## automatically convert every GIF to another file type.

Module asis_module          mod_asis.o
Module imap_module          mod_imap.o
Module action_module        mod_actions.o

##
## URL translation modules.
##
## The UserDir module for selecting resource directories by user name
## and a common prefix, e.g., /~<user> , /usr/web/<user> , etc.

Module userdir_module       mod_userdir.o

## The proxy module enables the server to act as a proxy for outside
## http and ftp services. It's not as complete as it could be yet.
## NOTE: You do not want this module UNLESS you are running a proxy;
##       it is not needed for normal (origin server) operation.

# Module proxy_module        modules/proxy/libproxy.a

## The Alias module provides simple URL translation and redirection.

Module alias_module         mod_alias.o

## mod_rewrite allows for powerful URI-to-URI and URI-to-filename mapping,
```

```
## using regular expressions.

# Module rewrite_module       mod_rewrite.o

##
## Access control and authentication modules.
##
Module access_module       mod_access.o
Module auth_module         mod_auth.o

## The anon_auth module allows for anonymous-FTP-style username/
## password authentication.

# Module anon_auth_module     mod_auth_anon.o

## db_auth and dbm_auth work with Berkeley DB files - make sure there
## is support for DBM files on your system.  You may need to grab the GNU
## "gdbm" package if not and possibly adjust EXTRA_LIBS. (This may be
## done by Configure at a later date)

# Module db_auth_module      mod_auth_db.o
# Module dbm_auth_module     mod_auth_dbm.o

## msql_auth checks against an mSQL database.  You must have mSQL installed
## and an "msql.h" available for this to even compile.  Additionally,
## you may need to add a couple entries to the EXTRA_LIBS line, like
##
##   -lmsql -L/usr/local/lib -L/usr/local/Minerva/lib
##
## This depends on your installation of mSQL. (This may be done by Configure
## at a later date)

# Module msql_auth_module     mod_auth_msql.o

## "digest" implements HTTP Digest Authentication rather than the less
## secure Basic Auth used by the other modules.

# Module digest_module       mod_digest.o

## Optional response header manipulation modules.
##
```

```
## cern_meta mimics the behavior of the CERN web server with regards to
## metainformation files.

# Module cern_meta_module     mod_cern_meta.o

## The expires module can apply Expires: headers to resources,
## as a function of access time or modification time.

# Module expires_module       mod_expires.o

## The headers module can set arbitrary HTTP response headers,
## as configured in server, vhost, access.conf or .htaccess configs

# Module headers_module       mod_headers.o

## Miscellaneous modules
##
## mod_usertrack.c is the new name for mod_cookies.c.  This module
## uses Netscape cookies to automatically construct and log
## click-trails from Netscape cookies, or compatible clients who
## aren't coming in via proxy.
##
## You do not need this, or any other module to allow your site
## to use Cookies.  This module is for user tracking only

# Module usertrack_module       mod_usertrack.o

## The example module, which demonstrates the use of the API.  See
## the file modules/example/README for details.  This module should
## only be used for testing -- DO NOT ENABLE IT on a production server.

# Module example_module         modules/example/mod_example.o

## mod_browser lets you set environment variables based on the User-Agent
## string in the request; this is useful for conditional HTML, for example.
## Since it is also used to detect buggy browsers for workarounds, it
## should be the last (highest priority) module.

Module browser_module       mod_browser.o
```

Adding a new module involves a few more steps; see "Adding a New Module" later in this chapter for more information.

Table 11-2 provides a listing of standard Apache modules. For more information on these modules, see the official Apache website (**http://www.apache.org/docs/mod/**) or the Apache Module Registry (**http://www.zyzzyva.com/module_registry/**).

Filename	Module	Description
mod_access.c	Access Control Module	Controls per-directory access for server document tree
mod_actions.c	Action Module	Performs action based on assigned MIME type
mod_ai_backcompat.c	MIT AI Lab Scripting	Early CGI-like kludge
mod_alias.c	Alias/Redirect Module	Directory Aliasing and Redirects
mod_asis.c	As-Is Module	Send filetypes without adding headers
mod_auth.c	Authorization Module	Basic user authentication
mod_auth_anon.c	Anonymous Access Control	Much like anon-FTP access, for user tracking
mod_auth_db.c	DB Authentication	User authentication using DB format database
mod_auth_dbm.c	DBM Authentication	User authentication using DBM format database
mod_auth_msql.c	Access control with mSQL database	Uses an mSQL database rather than a flat file
mod_browser	Environment variables based on User-Agent	Apache 1.2 and up. Set environment variables based on User-Agent strings
mod_cern_meta.c	CERN Meta File	CERN Meta File Emulation
mod_cgi.c	CGI Module	CGI execution compliant with CGI/1.1 spec
mod_cookies.c	Cookie Module	Cookie generation and tracking. In Apache 1.2 and up, replaced by mod_usertrack

Table 11-2.   Standard Apache Modules by Filename

Filename	Module	Description
mod_digest.c	Digest Authentication	Module Cookie generation and tracking
mod_dir.c	Directory Module	Directory index generation on the fly
mod_dld.c	Dynamic Loader Module	Dynamically load Apache modules
mod_env.c	Environment Module	Pass environment variables to CGI/SSI scripts
mod_example.c	API Example Module	Apache 1.2 and up. Demonstrates Apache API. (Not recommended for use in a production server.)
mod_expires.c	Expires Module	Apache 1.2 and up. Apply Expires: headers to resources
mod_headers.c	HTTP Header Module	Apache 1.2 and up. Add arbitrary HTTP headers to resources
mod_imap.c	Imagemap Module	Handle imagemap files
mod_include.c	Include Module	Server side includes
mod_info.c	Info Module	Server and module configuration information
mod_log_agent.c	Log User Agent	Log user agent from browser
mod_log_common.c	Common Log Module	Standard logging Common Log Format (CLF). In Apache 1.2 and up, replaced by mod_log_config
mod_log_config.c	Config Log Module	User-configurable log module
mod_log_referer.c	Log Referer	Log referer
mod_mime.c	MIME Module	Handle MIME types
mod_negotiation.c	Negotiation Module	Content negotiation of MIME types
mod_rewrite.c	URI Module	Apache 1.2 and up. URI-to-filename mapping using regular expressions

Table 11-2. Standard Apache Modules by Filename (*continued*)

Filename	Module	Description
mod_proxy.c	Proxy Module	Proxy support for Apache
mod_status.c	Server Status Module	Provides server status information
mod_userdir.c	Userdir Module	Controls filesystem mapping of user directories
mod_usertrack.c	User Tracking	Apache 1.2 and up. User tracking using Cookies. Replaces mod_cookies.c

Table 11-2. Standard Apache Modules by Filename (*continued*)

ADDITIONAL MODULES   There are a number of additional modules you may want to add to your web server. Table 11-3 lists a sampling of these modules. You can find modules and instructions for linking modules to core Apache code at the official Apache website (**http://www.apache.org/dist/contrib/modules/**). For additional information on modules, the Apache Module Registry (**http://www.zyzzyva.com/module_registry/**) provides listings of core Apache modules as well as additional modules contributed by other developers.

Module Type and Name	Description
Authentication	
mod_auth_msql (mSQL) mod_auth_pg95 (Postgres95) mod_auth_dbi (DBI)	Usernames and password can be stored in either ASCII flat file (included in the default distribution) or database format
mod_auth_external.c	Lets you call an external program for username and password verification
mod_auth_kerb.c	Kerebos-based authentication for mutual tkt or principal/passwd

Table 11-3. Example Custom Modules

Module Type and Name	Description
mod_auth_anon	Anonymous FTP-style access to authenticated areas, where users give an anonymous username and a real email address as password. (Included but not enabled in the default Apache 1.2 distribution.)
mod_auth_nis.c	NIS/passwd authorization using normal user IDs
mod_auth_dce.c	DCE authentication and secure DFS access
Counters	
mod_counter.c mod_cntr	Some server-side scripting languages, such as PHP/FI, can also provide access counters
Faster CGI	
mod_perl mod_perl_fast	Builds a PERL interpreter into the Apache executable
mod_fastcgi	Implements FastCGI on Apache
mod_pyapache.c	Builds a Python Interpreter into the Apache executable
Access control	
mod_auth_uid.c	Disallows serving web pages based on UID/GID
mod_access.c	Allows or denies access to a user/domain pair
mod_bandwidth.c	Limits bandwidth based on number of connections

Table 11-3.   Example Custom Modules (*continued*)

NOTE: To write your own modules, Apache provides specifications on its API. See the Apache Registry (**http://www.zyzzyva.com/module_registry/reference**) for links.

Adding a New Module

The steps for adding a new module are similar to installing Apache itself.

1. Get the module source code file and place it in the Apache *src/* directory.

2. Add the module definition to the *Configuration* file in the Apache *src/* directory. You'll add a line that looks something like this:

```
Module     <name_module>     <mod_something.o>
```

▼ *<name_module>* must match the name listed in the module's source code. You'll find this name in the module file itself, usually near the end of the file.

▲ *<mod_something.o>* is the filename of the module, with the final *.c* replaced by *.o.*

3. Recompile Apache (see "Compiling Apache" earlier in this chapter).

4. Restart the server (see the "Maintenance" section later in this chapter).

CONFIGURING APACHE

After you've installed your web server, you'll want to configure it. As we mentioned earlier, most UNIX web servers use separate configuration files to customize web server settings. Apache (and NCSA) use three files—*httpd.conf, srm.conf,* and *access.conf*—to configure web server behavior.

NOTE: The mime-types file is used to specify what MIME types are associated with which suffixes.

httpd.conf	Server configuration file specifying essential information the server needs to run
srm.conf	Resource configuration file specifying how resources should be handled when they are requested by a client
access.conf	Access configuration file specifying who has access to directories and files

The *srm.conf* and *access.conf* files are where you will make the most server configurations. The locations of both of these files are referenced by the *httpd.conf* file: the location of the *srm.conf* file is set by the ResourceConfig directive, and *access.conf* file is set by the AccessConfig directive.

All configuration files are located in the Apache *conf/* directory. In a new installation, files have a "-dist" extension. Before configuring, it's a good idea to make copies of all the files, saving them without the "-dist" extension, then edit the new files. The "-dist" files will then be your reference and backup copies.

Before configuring the server, there are some decisions you need to make regarding where web server directories and files should live on your system. You'll need to know these in order to make any necessary changes to the configuration files. The main directories you need to decide on are the following:

▼ Server root

■ Document root

▲ Log files

The *server root* is the subdirectory where you unpacked the Apache files. It contains the *conf/*, *src/*, *cgi-bin/*, and other server-related files and subdirectories. The default location is */usr/local/etc/httpd*; however, you can move it wherever you want. To change the default location, update the *ServerRoot* directive in the *httpd.conf* file.

NOTE: If the server *(httpd)* crashes, the core file will be in the server root directory.

The *document root* is the subdirectory where HTML and related files (such as images) will live. The default location is */usr/local/etc/httpd/htdocs*. Because users will have access to these files, the document root should be in a different location (its own directory) outside of the server root directory.

TIP: For security reasons, you should set file permissions in the document and server root directories such that only trusted users can make changes. Many sites create a "www" group and a "www" user for this purpose. Only trusted Web authors in the "www" group would be able to change files in the document root directory; only the official website administrator, the "www" user, would be able to change files in the server root directory.

Logfiles, by default, are stored in the Apache *logs/* directory. As these files grow dynamically, you may want to put them in a different location with a good amount of free space. How much free space? That depends on how much traffic the website(s) supported by your web server generate(s).

httpd.conf

The *httpd.conf* file sets basic system-level information about your web server. It contains the directory location of the *server root* (ServerRoot directive). If you are not the system administrator at the site where you're installing this web server, you might want to get that person's assistance.

Table 11-4 shows a selection of directives you might find useful from this file

Directive	Description
ServerAdmin <email address>	Specifies the email address used when the server sends error messages in response to failed requests. No default
ServerRoot <directory_path>	Specifies the directory in which all server-associated files reside. Default is */usr/local/etc/httpd*
User <username>	Specifies the user (UID) and group (GID) you want the server process to run as. Default is *nobody*
PidFile <filename>	Specifies the location of the file where the server should place the process ID (PID) of the server when running standalone. Default is *logs/httpd.pid*

Table 11-4.   Useful *httpd.conf* Directives

TIP: Apache treats *httpd.conf, srm.conf,* and *access.conf* the same way. You can create a single config file out of the three. To do this, append the contents of *srm.conf* and *access.conf* to *httpd.conf.* To prevent Apache from complaining about missing *srm.conf* and *access.conf* files, edit the AccessConfig and ResourceConfig variables so that they point to */dev/null.* The edited lines in *httpd.conf* would then look like this:

```
AccessConfig    /dev/null
ResourceConfig  /dev/null
```

srm.conf

The *srm.conf* file specifies how your web server handles resources such as HTML files. For initial configuration, this file contains the directory location of the *document root* (DocumentRoot directive*).*

Table 11-5 shows a selection of directives you might find useful from this file.

access.conf

The *access.conf* file controls how the contents of directories are accessed. Table 11-6 shows a selection of directives you might find useful from this file.

Directive	Description
AccessFileName <filename>	Specifies the file name for access control files. Default is *.htaccess*
Alias <symbolic_path> <real_path>	Creates a virtual name or directory by mapping a virtual pathname in a URL to a real path on your server
DocumentRoot <directory_path>	The main location for HTML and related files for the web server
ScriptAlias <symbolic_path> <real_path>	Provides a way to create a virtual *cgi-bin* directory. You can give users their own *cgi-bin* access without giving them access to the main *cgi-bin* directory located in the server root directory
UserDir <directory_name>	Specifies the Web directory name the server looks for in a user's home directory. Default is *public_html*
Redirect <pathname> <url>	Tells the server to forward clients that request a given directory or document to a new location

Table 11-5. Useful *srm.conf* Directives

Directive	Description
AllowOveride <options ... >	Specifies the level of control per-directory access has in overriding the global access defaults defined by the *access.conf* file
AuthName	Specifies a realm name for protection. Once a user has entered a valid username and password, any other resources within the same realm name can be accessed with the same username and password. This can be used to create two areas that share the same username and password

Table 11-6. Useful *access.conf* Directives

Directive	Description
AuthType	Tells the server what protocol to use for authentication. *Basic* authentication transmits passwords across the Internet unencrypted, so they could be intercepted. The Digest method is intended to address this issue. *Digest* authentication makes the sending of passwords across the Internet more secure by encrypting the password. It works exactly the same as Basic authentication as far as the end-user and server administrator are concerned. The use of Digest authentication will depend on whether browser authors write it into their products. Apache can already do Digest authentication, when compiled with the mod_digest module (supplied with the Apache distribution)
AuthUserFile	Tells the server the location of the *user* file created by *htpasswd*. A similar directive, *AuthGroupFile*, can be used to tell the server the location of a groups file
allow (or) *deny from* <*hostnames ...* >	Specifies what hosts can access a given directory
require	Specifies which authenticated users have access to a given directory

Table 11-6.   Useful *access.conf* Directives (*continued*)

Configuration Options

Apache is a highly configurable web server. Its modular structure makes it easy to add or remove functionality, while its configuration files give you a great deal of control over how that functionality is implemented.

This section discusses a selection of server configurations you may elect to make to your server. While it is not intended to be comprehensive, it does give you an idea of the types of configurations you are able to make.

User Directories

Many sites allow users to manage their own web pages from their home directories. This is usually the case when you see a URL that looks like **http://some.place.com/~jdoe**. This means there is a directory called *jdoe* that contains a subdirectory that matches the User directive in the *srm.conf* file.

By default, this is enabled in Apache; the subdirectory name is *public_html*. You can set this to be "www" or anything else you want. (Just notify your users!) If you don't want to allow users to have their own web pages, set the User directive to DISABLED.

NOTE: Users do not have default *cgi-bin* access within their *public_html* directory.

User Authentication

User authentication lets you restrict documents to people with valid usernames and passwords only. Before the user can view web pages, they must enter a valid username and password.

Setting up user authentication involves these steps:

1. Create a file containing the usernames and passwords.

2. Configure the server to specify what resources are protected and which users are allowed (after entering a valid password) to access those resources.

3. Create *.htaccess* file (or *.htgroup* file) and put it in the directory to be protected; or, create a *<Directory>* listing in *access.conf*.

4. Restart the server.

CREATING A USERNAME AND PASSWORD FILE   The password file(s) you create for web server access are similar to UNIX password files in that they contain usernames and encrypted passwords. Since there isn't a link between valid UNIX users and valid users for your server, you can specify any username you want.

NOTE: In Apache 1.2, you can restrict pages by username and password, and also let users from particular domains access the pages without giving a password. This is implemented with the *Satisfy* directive. Restrictions can be applied to individual files with *<File>*, and to files that match a regular expression.

To create password files, Apache is distributed with a program called *htpasswd* in the *source/* directory. This program will automatically generate an encrypted password for each username and password you enter.

Creating a password file is pretty straightforward. For example, to create a new user file called *users*, and add the username "dgunter" with the password "alti2ude," you would type

```
htpasswd -c users dgunter
```

The *-c* argument tells *htpasswd* to create a new *users* file. When you run this command, you will be prompted to enter a password for dgunter and to confirm it by entering it again. Other users can be added to the existing file in the same way, except that the *-c* argument is not needed. The same command can also be used to modify the password of an existing user.

After adding a few users, the */usr/local/etc/httpd/users* file might look like this:

```
dgunter:G1UJqVPOCD7U2
pixieg:NXD9tmO9GQqcU
kara:/14YDay8cnQVY
```

The first field is the username, and the second field is the encrypted password.

CONFIGURING THE SERVER   To get the server to use the usernames and passwords in the *username* and *password* file, you need to configure a realm. A *realm* is a section of your site that is to be restricted to some or all of the users listed in the *password* file. Once the user has entered a valid username and password, they have access to all the resources in that realm. If there is more than one realm with the same name, users will have access to those resources as well, unless access is limited via the *require* directive.

The directives to create the protected area can be placed in a *.htaccess* file in the directory concerned, or in a *<Directory>* section in the *access.conf* file.

TIP: Because Apache will search through every subdirectory of a directory that is *.htaccess*-enabled, this can cause a significant disk access load if you don't limit the search. To limit *.htaccess* searches to specific directories, create a <Directory> section for each *.htaccess*-containing directory, and use the *AllowOverride* directive. You can set up <Directory> sections in *access.conf* or even *srm.conf*. For example, say you needed a *.htaccess* file only in the */htdocs/company /finance/sales/4Q/bonuses* subdirectory. You might put something like this in your *access.conf* file:

```
<Directory /htdocs>
Options All
AllowOverride None
</Directory>
<Directory /htdocs/company/finance/sales/4Q/bonuses>
Options All
AllowOverride All
</Directory>
```

Make sure the *access.conf* file allows user authentication to be setup in a *.htaccess* file. This is controlled by the AuthConfig override. To allow authentication directives to be used in a *.htaccess* file, the *access.conf* file must include the following:

```
AllowOverride AuthConfig
```

HTACCESS   After you've created a password file, create a file named ".htaccess." Place the *.htaccess* file in the directory to be protected. All subdirectories of the protected directory will also be protected.

NOTE: Apache 1.2 will also let you protect individual files. You can also assign users to groups; the process is similar to setting up user-based access.

The *.htaccess* file should contain the following lines:

```
AuthName <realm_name>
AuthType Basic
AuthUserFile /usr/local/etc/httpd/my_users
require valid-user
```

These directives tell the server where to find the usernames and passwords and what authentication protocol to use. The server now knows that this resource is restricted to valid users.

NOTE: The *require* directive tells the server what usernames are valid for particular access methods; this may be a file of containing valid usernames or individual usernames separated by spaces. The *valid-user* tells the server that any username in the specified password file (set by the *AuthUserFile* directive) can be used. To restrict access to specific users within the password file, type "user," then the username(s), separated by spaces. For example:

```
require user dgunter zippy
```

The server can also be configured for DBM authentication. Its setup is similar to that for user authentication. For more information, see the Apache Week information on DBM User Authentication (**http://www.apacheweek.com/features/dbmauth**).

Imagemaps

Imagemaps are pictures that allow users to access different documents by clicking on different areas of an image. There are two types of imagemaps: server-side and client-side. Server-side imagemaps are processed by the web server and require some server configuration to enable them. Client-side imagemaps are processed by the user's browser and don't require any web server configuration or processing.

SERVER-SIDE IMAGEMAPS   The imagemap module included with Apache (mod_imap) allows you to do server-side imagemaps. This module is part of the core Apache distribution and is compiled by default. However, before using imagemaps you will need to configure the server to enable imagemaps. To do this, uncomment the following line in the *srm.conf* file:

```
AddHandler imap-file map
```

This specifies that files with a ".map" extension are imagemap files.

NOTE: When you change a configuration file, you must restart the server for the changes take effect. See the section "Starting, Stopping, and Restarting Apache" later in this chapter for more information.

To use imagemaps, follow these steps:

1. Create a map file that specifies the sections of the image that are "hot."

2. Add code to an HTML file to tell the browser which image and map file to use. For example:

```
<A HREF="/global_sites/world.map"><IMG SRC="/graphics/world.gif" ISMAP></A>
```

See Apache Week (**http://www.apacheweek.com/features/imagemaps**) and NCSA's tutorial on imagemaps (**http://hoohoo.ncsa.uiuc.edu/docs/tutorials/imagemapping.html**) for more information.

CLIENT-SIDE IMAGEMAPS   In client-side imagemaps, all information needed for the imagemap is contained within the same HTML file. No server configuration is necessary. See the SpyGlass client-side imagemap tutorial (**http://www.spyglass.com/ techspec/tutorial/img_maps.html**) for more information.

CGI

The Common Gateway Interface (CGI) is a specification that says how servers should talk to a script or program and how the script or program formats its reply for use by the server. CGI itself is not a language; it describes a protocol that can be used to write programs for use with a web server in any language.

As far as server configuration issues are concerned, CGI scripts can be executed out of a server root directory called *cgi-bin* without any special configuration. However, access to this directory is usually restricted. Other solutions for providing CGI access for your users include setting up *ScriptAlias*es or adding a CGI MIME type with AddType. Both of these methods are covered in this section.

CAUTION: All CGI programs, both scripted and compiled, are potentially insecure. The level of security required for a site varies widely. Some sites require users to submit their script or program to a webmaster who checks that the code doesn't contain security holes before it can be used. Other sites restrict CGI access to trusted users, who are responsible for checking their own code.

Although CGI has been a standard solution, there are other options. As an alternative to CGI, many scripting languages can be built into Apache as modules. This makes executing the scripts much more efficient, since an interpreter does not need to be started for every request. This is true in such cases as PERL (mod_perl.c) and Python. However, this method does present some risk, as users have the potential to cause damage to your system either intentionally or unintentionally.

SCRIPTALIAS   ScriptAlias is a directive in *srm.conf*. It tells the server you want to designate a directory (or directories) as script-only: that is, any time the server tries to retrieve a file from these directories, it will execute the file instead of reading it. For example:

```
ScriptAlias /cgi-bin/ cgi-bin/
```

This will make any request to the server that begins with *cgi-bin/* be fulfilled by executing the corresponding program in *ServerRoot/cgi-bin/*.

NOTE: You may have more than one ScriptAlias directive in *srm.conf* to designate different directories as CGI.

The advantages of using ScriptAlias are ease of administration, centralization, and slight increase in speed. However, many system managers don't want anything as dangerous as a script in the file system. Another disadvantage is that anyone wishing to create scripts must either have their own entry in *srm.conf* or must have write access to a *ScriptAlias* directory.

ADDTYPE Another method of allowing CGIs is to specify a "magic" MIME type that tells the server to execute files instead of sending them. This is done using the *AddType* directive in either *srm.conf* or in a per-directory *access.conf* file. The advantage (and disadvantage) of this setup is that scripts may be absolutely anywhere.

NOTE: Given the potential dangers of poorly written CGI, you probably don't want to make CGI's available everywhere. Per-directory access gives you more control over which directories can execute CGI's.

For instance, to designate all files ending in *.cgi* as scripts, use the following directive:

```
AddType application/x-httpd-cgi .cgi
```

Alternatively, you could add *.sh* and *.pl* after *.cgi* to allow automatic execution of shell scripts and PERL scripts, respectively. Note that you must have Options ExecCGI activated in the directory in which you create scripts.

SSIs

Server Side Includes (SSI) allow users to create simple, dynamic pages. The HTML author embeds special SSI variables, such as the current date or time, or even another file, in their HTML file. When the page is accessed, the server processes the file and substitutes any variables with actual values.

NOTE: Apache 1.2 extends SSI (xSSI) to include additional variables and conditional codes.

If a server had to look at every HTML file for SSIs, it would slow down access; by default, this capability is off. To turn it on, you need to tell Apache which documents contain the SSI commands. One method is to use a special file extension such as *.shtml*, which tells the server to process the file. This would be configured as follows:

```
AddHandler server-parsed .shtml
AddType    text/html    shmtl
```

The *AddHandler* directive tells Apache to process every *.shtml* file for SSI commands. This occurs whether there are any SSI commands in the file or not. The *AddType* directive makes sure that the resulting content is marked as HTML, so the browser displays it properly.

Another method of telling the server which files include SSI commands is to set the execute bit on HTML files and then set the *XBitHack* directive. Any file with a content type of text/html (i.e., an extension *.html*) and the execute bit set will be checked for SSI commands.

For either method, the server also needs to be configured to allow SSIs. This is done with the *Options Includes* directive, which can be placed in either the global *access.conf* or a local *.htaccess* file.

NOTE: For *.htaccess*, also enable *AllowOverride Options*.

MAINTENANCE

Maintenance is the ongoing process of tweaking the web server after its initial installation and configuration. It consists of tasks such as reconfiguring the server, tuning its performance, starting and stopping the server, monitoring files (such as the error and access logs), and generating usage statistics for your website(s). Some general maintenance tips include

▼ Back-up your web documents frequently. You might also consider putting them in a version control system like RCS.

■ Keep an eye on the size of the log files. The busier your web server is, the faster they will grow in size.

■ Rotate log files daily. Summarize your log files frequently so you don't have to keep disks full of old logs hanging around.

■ Log as little information as possible. Turn DNS lookup off and do lookups later with a script. Log referrer URLs sparingly—for example, if you need to know the origin of a consistent bad file request in the error logs. There are search engines that can tell you who's linking to you, such as Digital's AltaVista.

■ Scan your access and error log files regularly. Signs of suspicious activity might involve system commands (*rm*, *login*, *chmod*, etc.) or repeated attempts to access a password-protected document. Extremely long URL requests can indicate an attempt to overrun a program's input buffer.

▲ Read the WWW Security FAQ (**http://www.genome.wi.mit.edu/WWW/faqs/ wwwsf1.html**) for good, up-to-date information on setting up and maintaining web servers with as few security holes as possible.

Starting, Stopping, and Restarting Apache

To start the server, run the *httpd* program by typing

```
httpd
```

You may notice that there a several *httpd* processes running at the same time. There is a parent process and a number of child processes automatically spawned by the parent process. You stop or restart Apache by sending the parent *httpd* process a signal. Which process is the parent? It's easy to tell, because its PID is automatically written to the *httpd.pid* file.

NOTE: The location of the *httpd.pid* file is set by the PidFile directive in *httpd.conf*.

There are three signals you can send to Apache:

▼ TERM

■ HUP

▲ USR1

The TERM signal causes Apache to stop running. All child processes are killed first, then the parent exits, and the server is no longer running. For example:

```
kill -TERM 'cat /usr/local/etc/httpd/logs/httpd.pid'
```

The HUP signal causes Apache to re-read its configuration files and re-open any log files. Like TERM, all child processes are killed; however, the parent process remains alive. After the configuration and log files are dealt with, new children are created, and the server continues serving hits. For example:

```
kill -HUP 'cat /usr/local/etc/httpd/logs/httpd.pid'
```

The USR1 signal causes Apache to re-read configuration files and re-open log files without dropping connections in progress, as currently happens with a HUP restart. The parent process advises the child processes to exit after their current request, or exit immediately if they have no current requests. The parent re-reads its configuration files and re-opens any log files. As each child dies off, it is replaced by a new one, which begins serving new hits. For example:

```
kill -USR1 'cat /usr/local/etc/httpd/logs/httpd.pid'
```

CAUTION: Don't use this signal unless you are using Apache 1.2b9 or greater. The code for USR1 was unstable in previous versions.

Log Files

Currently, if you want the server to rotate its log files and start logging somewhere else, you send it a HUP. Unfortunately, this also has the effect of killing whatever transfers are currently in progress. For many sites, this only occurs once a week when logs are rotated and, thus, can effectively be ignored. However, sites with large files may be more worried about this problem, as users may be part of the way through a huge download when they get disconnected.

A solution is to log to another process rather than a file, using the "|" prefix for the log filename. As an example of this, you'll find a sample program called *rotatelogs.c* in the Apache *support/* directory.

CAUTION: Anyone who can write to the directory where Apache is writing a log file can almost certainly gain access to the UID that the server is started as, which is normally root. Don't give people write access to a directory where the logs are stored without being aware of the consequences.

For a listing of log file analysis tools, check out Yahoo (**http://www.yahoo.com/ Computers_and_Internet/Software/Internet/World_Wide_Web/Servers/Log_Analysis_Tools/**).

Security

Security is a very broad and important topic. In no way does this section provide a comprehensive treatment of security. It does, however, provide you with some of the issues you may want to consider.

General Considerations

Site security typically includes a combination of firewalls and solid internal network security. This is a fairly common, layered security approach. In theory, either method alone should protect your site; however, reality tends to do nasty things to theories.

A comprehensive approach to protecting a website generally means following best practices in a number of different areas. The National Computer Security Association, NCSA, is in the process of planning a certification process for websites that touches on a number of these areas. See NCSA (**http://www.ncsa.com**) for more details.

> ***NOTE:*** You may also want to take a look at RFC 1244, the Site Security Handbook (**gopher://ds1.internic.net/00/fyi/fyi8.txt**), for more information.

The guidelines being developed by NCSA are intended to ensure a basic level of security, rather than a hacker-proof one. They set minimum standards for logical and physical security issues, which address such issues as hacking, intrusion, data loss, and tampering. While these guidelines may be more (or less) stringent than your site's needs, they can certainly be used as starting point for developing your own security guidelines. A summary of the NCSA guidelines for a single-server site are as follows:

1. The website must withstand network-based attacks by means of a firewall, filtering router, or other appropriate security mechanism.

2. The Domain Naming Service (DNS) entries for all URL-referenced systems must be resolvable.

3. NIC handles must be authenticated, and the NIC contact information must be accurate and contain at least two contacts.

4. The site must maintain logging. Access to logs must be limited to authorized personnel. Logs must be retained in a secure, but retrievable, format.

5. A standard encryption mechanism, such as SSL or SHTTP, must be used for sensitive data transmission.

6. CGI scripts and programs must be checked to ensure they don't intentionally or unintentionally compromise your system.

7. A person must be designated as the site's "CxE Evaluator." All client executables must be examined and evaluated as "harmless" to the user.

8. Pages that contain or accept sensitive data must be made non-cacheable. Users must be informed if any pages containing sensitive data will be cached to local storage.

9. The site must meet physical security requirements, such as access-controlled areas, roster of authorized personnel, suitable equipment, and emergency contract information.

10. The site must meet logical security requirements, such as secure password policies, webmaster contact, HTTPD server configured for least privilege, and separate development and production systems.

11. If a transaction mechanism is in place, it must be documented, and the server's private key protected by a strong passphrase. Sensitive information must be periodically removed from the server. The OS/Platform must be documented and integrity assured. Backups and Restore capabilities must be in place.

Specific Considerations

The following are some specific suggestions you might consider. For more suggestions, see the WWW Security FAQ (**http://www.genome.wi.mit.edu/WWW/faqs/wwwsf1.html**).

▼   Set file permissions in the document and server root directories such that only trusted users can make changes. Many sites create a "www" group and a "www" user for this purpose. Only trusted web authors in the "www" group would be able to change files in the document root directory; only the official website administrator, the "www" user, would be able to change files in the server root directory.

■   When Apache starts, it opens the log files as the user who started the server before switching to the user defined in the *User* directive. Anyone who can write to the directory where Apache is writing a log file can almost certainly gain access to the UID that the server is started as, which is normally root. Don't give people write access to a directory where the logs are stored without being aware of the consequences.

■   CGI scripts run with the UID of the server child process. The default ID is "nobody." For this reason, you may want to consider "nobody" an untrusted user, and set its permissions so that it doesn't have read permission on sensitive files, or write permission in critical areas.

■   Don't require Apache to use DNS for any parsing of the configuration files. If Apache has to use DNS to parse the configuration files, your server may experience reliability problems, or even denial and theft of service attacks.

■   Some SSI commands, like *#exec*, let a user execute programs that could be a security risk. You might want to consider limiting this capability. The Includes NOExec option lets SSI commands work, except for those which would execute a program.

■   Unless you take steps to change it, if the server can find its way to a file through normal URL mapping rules, it can serve it to clients. Sometimes this default access can cause problems. For instance, consider the following example:

```
# cd /; ln -s / public_html
Accessing http://localhost/~root/
```

This would allow clients to walk through the entire file system. To work around this, add the following block to your server's configuration:

```
<Directory />
    Order deny,allow
    Deny from all
 </Directory>
```

This will prevent default access to file system locations. Add appropriate *<Directory>* blocks to allow access only in those areas you wish. For example:

```
<Directory /usr/local/users/*/public_html>
    Order deny,allow
    Allow from all
</Directory>
<Directory /usr/local/etc/httpd>
    Order deny,allow
    Allow from all
</Directory>
```

SUMMARY

Currently, there are a variety of UNIX web servers available. One of the most widely used is Apache. One of the reasons for its popularity is its flexibility. Its modular structure makes it easy to add or remove functionality, while its configuration files give a webmaster a great deal of control over how the web server functions. In this chapter, we have examined Apache in detail, including how to download the source distribution and compile it on your UNIX system. We then looked at the specifics of configuring Apache, including the syntax of its major configuration files. In addition, we examined various security issues, user authentication processes, log file management, and other maintenance tasks that you will encounter. Apache is a very robust web server with an extremely large installed base. If you find yourself needing to install a UNIX-based web server, you owe it to yourself to evaluate Apache.

WINDOWS
NT
Professional
Library

CHAPTER 12

Other Network Servers

O ver the past few years, the World Wide Web has completely changed how we view information services provided over a network. Now, by using the World Wide Web, a wide variety of different services are available to the user's desktop. However, there are still several network services that operate outside the realm of the common web server. Many of these other network servers are not widely discussed in the detail that web services are examined, even though desktop web browsers can act as clients for several of these services. In this chapter, we will look at some of the common network servers that run outside of a web-server environment. As with most things with an Internet heritage, many of these services grew up on a UNIX platform. However, all are currently available on both UNIX and NT platforms.

USENET NEWS AND NNTP

As a system or network administrator, you are almost guaranteed to have read and posted to Usenet news at some point in the past. If you are from a UNIX environment, you may have even managed an NNTP server at some point. If so, please bear with us for a moment while we introduce Usenet.

Usenet news was originally developed at Duke University in 1979 as an experiment attempting to devise a system where UNIX systems could exchange text-based messages. These text messages are called *articles* and are grouped into categories, known as *newsgroups*, based on topic. As the software grew out of the experimental stage and was released to the Internet at large, Usenet grew in popularity. In 1986, new software that provided an implementation of the Network News Transport Protocol (NNTP), defined in RFC 977, was released. NNTP allowed Usenet sites to migrate from UUCP to a direct TCP/IP connection for transferring news articles.

Usenet now carries hundreds of thousands of articles every day, categorized into tens of thousands of newsgroups. Each user of Usenet news uses client software known as a *news reader*, which allows a user to browse and read articles and to post new articles to the group of his or her choice.

NNTP Servers on UNIX

Since Usenet news was developed, there have been several different versions of news server software released for the UNIX platform. Currently, the most widely used is the *InterNetNews* system, or INN for short.

INN is a complete Usenet news system that handles posting messages and transferring and receiving messages from remote hosts. It was originally developed by Rich Salz and is now maintained by the Internet Software Consortium (ISC). The ISC's website can be found at **http://www.isc.org**.

It isn't possible to completely cover all the setup and configuration information that you need to install INN in this chapter. For complete details of how to install and configure INN, refer to the documentation that comes with the INN software distribution. Both the software and documentation are on the CD-ROM included with this book.

NNTP Servers on NT

Windows NT is just beginning to make inroads into the NNTP server arena. NNTP servers have traditionally run on UNIX systems, and the choices of NNTP servers for NT are currently quite limited. The most popular UNIX NNTP server, INN, has not been ported to NT, and there are no current plans to do so.

MetaInfo NewsChannel

There are a few commercial offerings available in the NT news server market. MetaInfo sells an NT-based news server called *NewsChannel*, which stacks up quite nicely against the competition. NewsChannel provides graphical setup and install wizards that simplify the installation process. In addition to providing a fully NNTP-compliant server, NewsChannel provides remote management features and access control. NewsChannel also assigns permission on either a user or group basis and has access control features that are enabled on a newsgroup-by-newsgroup basis. NewsChannel's access control features are very robust, enabling you to control access to your news server from a variety of parameters. For example, NewsChannel allows you to control access by user name and password, IP address, subnet, host name, and DNS domain. For more information about MetaInfo's NewsChannel news server, see their website at **http://www.metainfo.com**.

Netscape News Server

Netscape provides its own commercial news server in the form of the *Netscape News Server*. The Netscape News Server is integrated with Netscape's *SuiteSpot* server software suite and is available on a variety of platforms. The Netscape News Server is a fully NNTP-compliant news server, however, it doesn't appear to have the extensive access control features found in MetaInfo's NewsChannel. For example, the Netscape News Server does not support NT account and group ID validation for access control, nor does it appear to provide the same level of IP address, subnet, and domain name validation. For more information on the Netscape News Server, see their website at **http://www.netscape.com**.

DNEWS

The *DNEWS* NNTP server is available from NetWin, Ltd., an Auckland, New Zealand company. In addition to running on Windows NT, this news server software runs on a wide variety of platforms, including Linux and BSDI. DNEWS is a robust news server package. NetWin allows you a four-week free trial of their DNEWS software. For more information on DNEWS, including downloading the free trial software, see NetWin's website at **http://netwinsite.com**.

Using NNTP Servers Internally

Companies can benefit from using news servers internal to their corporate intranet for announcements and collaboration. Since the Usenet news paradigm allows you to read and respond to messages and follow subjects by topic, it makes an excellent system for interactive communications with employees and clients. You can establish an NNTP server that provides your clients and customers with discussion areas for your products and services. For example, if you provide software support services, you might opt to create a set of support newsgroups available to your customers.

By creating a set of corporate newsgroups, you can communicate information to employees without the overhead of maintaining web pages for information delivery. For example, if you wish to communicate company news and announcements, you can create a set of moderated newsgroups that only a specific person within your organization can post messages to. You can also facilitate corporate support of other activities within your organization by creating additional newsgroups that employees can use to meet and discuss different topics.

In general, depending on your organization, using an NNTP server to provide access to internal newsgroups can be beneficial both for client communication and for employee participation in discussions of various topics, which can allow you to build virtual communities within your organization.

ANONYMOUS FTP

One of the most common tasks in everyday network computing is downloading files to your local computer, or copying files from one computer to another over a network. The chances are, even if you didn't know it, that you have used the *File Transfer Protocol* (FTP) to copy files. The File Transfer Protocol component of the TCP/IP protocol suite has been around a long time, and it provides a way for transferring both binary and ASCII files between computers. A special configuration known as *Anonymous FTP* allows users to transfer files from computers on which they do not have an account.

Many sites provide anonymous FTP servers in order to distribute software or to act as public archives. With many people from all over the world accessing these archives, there needed to be a convention to allow unknown users access to certain file areas, while still maintaining adequate system security. Anonymous FTP was devised as a way to solve this problem.

Currently, anonymous FTP can be invoked either by a dedicated FTP client, or from most web browsers. With a web browser, you typically just make a connection using "ftp://" instead of "http://" as the URL designator. The web browser will handle logging into the anonymous FTP server behind the scenes. With a dedicated FTP client, you open a connection to a specific anonymous FTP server and log in with the user name *anonymous*. By convention, the password is your complete Internet email address.

NOTE: Virtually all large anonymous FTP sites, and most small sites as well, log all accesses and transfers from their server.

Properly configured anonymous FTP servers allow read-only access to a very specific part of the file system. Since access is controlled and logged, they provide a safe and effective way to distribute software, text, or binary files both for internal company use and for distribution to the Internet at large. However, FTP servers must be properly configured in order to provide a safe environment for file distribution. Incorrectly configured FTP servers can provide malicious users access to system files or passwords and can provide an avenue for uploading and exchanging pirated copies of software.

Configuring Anonymous FTP on UNIX

Like most things related to TCP/IP and the Internet, anonymous FTP grew up in the UNIX world. Most of the large FTP sites are still hosted on UNIX systems. In fact, many companies are using low cost or freeware UNIX operating systems such as Linux and BSDI UNIX for dedicated servers, including anonymous FTP servers. In any case, UNIX and anonymous FTP are going to be around for a while.

Creating the Password File Entry

The first step in configuring anonymous FTP under UNIX is to add the *ftp* entry to the */etc/passwd* file. Edit the password file and add a line similar to

```
ftp:*:500:500:Anonymous FTP User:/home/ftp:/bin/true
```

Adding this line to the password file turns on anonymous FTP access. As with all password file entries, the fields are separated by a colon character. The first field indicates that the user name is *ftp*, which enables anonymous FTP access. The second field is the password field. By using an asterisk character in the password field, you prevent anyone from being able to interactively log in as the user *ftp* and get to a UNIX shell. In this example, the user ID (UID) and group ID (GID) are both set to 500. On your system, you should assign a unique UID to the *ftp* user. You should also create a separate, unique *ftp* group in the */etc/group* file. The home directory in this example is set to */home/ftp*, but it can be set to whatever directory you are using for your FTP archive.

CAUTION: When choosing the location of the FTP home directory, make sure that there are no system directories located under it in the directory hierarchy.

The last field in the ftp password file entry sets the shell for the *ftp* user to be */bin/true*. This is not an interactive shell and thus provides an extra level of security should the *ftp* user manage to attempt an interactive login.

Creating the FTP Directory Hierarchy

The second step in setting up anonymous FTP access is to create the FTP directory hierarchy and set the file permissions properly. Choose a location for the home directory for anonymous FTP so that it does not sit above any system directories. A common path to the anonymous FTP root directory is */home/ftp*. Create the directory in the desired location and set both the owner and group to something other than *ftp*.

CAUTION: No directory in the anonymous FTP directory hierarchy should ever be owned by the *ftp* user or have group access set to the *ftp* group.

Set the owner of the */home/ftp* directory to be *root* and its group to be a system group, such as *sys*. Set the permissions on the */home/ftp* directory so that the owner has read, write, and execute permissions, and group and others have only read and execute permissions. Looking at the directory permissions and ownership should show something like

```
# ls -ld /home/ftp
drwxr-xr-x   2 root      sys        1024 May 14 15:35 /home/ftp
#
```

Next, create the *etc*, *bin*, and *pub* directories under the */home/ftp* directory. The ownership, group, and permissions for the *pub* directory should be the same as the */home/ftp* directory. For the *bin* and *etc* directories, set the ownership and group to be the same as */home/ftp*, but set the permissions to be execute only. Looking at the directory permissions and ownership in the */home/ftp* directory should show something like

```
# ls -l /home/ftp
d--x--x--x   2 root      sys        1024 May 14 15:35 bin
d--x--x--x   2 root      sys        1024 May 14 15:35 etc
drwxr-xr-x   2 root      sys        1024 May 14 15:36 pub
#
```

Adding Programs and Configuration Files

The next step is to add the necessary programs and configuration files to the anonymous FTP directory tree. In order to list the contents of directories, users will need access to the *ls* program. To install a copy of *ls* in the anonymous FTP area, copy the *ls* program into the */home/ftp/bin* directory. It should have the same ownership and group as the */home/ftp* directory, and its permissions should be set to execute only. So, the permissions and ownership for *ls* should be

```
# cd /home/ftp/bin
# ls -l ls
```

```
---x--x--x   1 root     sys        36792 Aug 19  1996 ls
#
```

You also need to provide a very simple version of the *passwd* and *group* files in the anonymous FTP area. These files are used by anonymous FTP to show the user name and group name of the files in the anonymous FTP area. They are not used in any way to authenticate or log in anonymous FTP users.

> *CAUTION:*   You should never use your real password and group files in the anonymous FTP area!

Since these files are only going to be used to fill in the user and group names displayed by *ls*, you can just create them from scratch. Change directory to the *etc* directory in the anonymous FTP area and create the password and group files here. Both files should have minimal entries. For example, your password file could look like

```
root:*:0:0:The Boss::
ftp:*:500:500: Anonymous ftp::
```

And your group file could look like

```
sys:*:10:
ftp:*:500:
```

These files should be owned by *root* and have read-only permission set for everyone. If you want even more security, you can usually get away with not even using the dummy password and group files. Anonymous FTP only uses them to keep from displaying numbers instead of user and group names. As such, virtually all UNIX anonymous FTP systems will work fine without them.

The *pub* Directory

The *pub* directory is where you will place files that you want anonymous FTP users to be able to transfer. This directory, and all directories below it, should have read and execute permission set for users. Do not set write permission for group and other users on these directories, as anonymous FTP users could then upload programs into your anonymous FTP area.

Providing an Incoming Directory

Some anonymous FTP sites provide an incoming directory that is world-writable, with the intent that users can contribute software to the FTP archive. In general, this is a bad idea and can cause you real problems. By having a directory with world-write access, malicious users can upload pirated software and essentially use your FTP server as a covert, pirate BBS. Also, users will occasionally upload huge amounts of data, which will cause the disk holding your anonymous FTP area to fill up, leading to a denial of service attack. We recommend that you do not provide write access in your anonymous FTP area, and that you check all your directory permissions carefully to insure the safety of your FTP site.

Configuring Anonymous FTP on NT

Under Windows NT 3.51, the FTP server component of the Microsoft TCP/IP network software ran as a network service. Under Windows NT 4.0, the FTP server is managed as a component of the NT Internet Information Server (IIS).

NOTE: For more information on the Microsoft Internet Information Server, see Chapter 10.

All components of IIS, including FTP, are managed with the Internet Service Manager tool. To configure the FTP service, start the Internet Service Manager and double-click on the FTP service. This brings up the FTP properties dialog box, as shown in Figure 12-1.

The Service Tab

The FTP properties dialog box has several tabs that allow configuration of different parts of the FTP server. In the Service tab, you can set FTP so that it runs on a different port

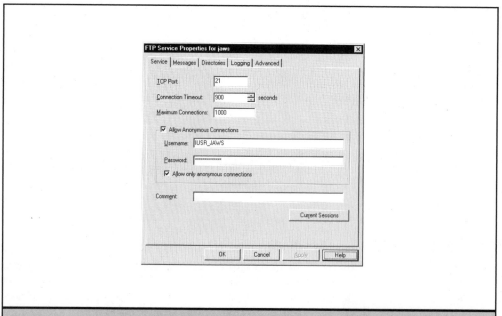

Figure 12-1. The FTP properties dialog box in the Internet Service Manager tool

from the default, set a specific session time-out value, and set the maximum number of connections.

The Service tab also allows you to configure the FTP server to accept anonymous connections. To enable anonymous connections, you must select the checkbox labeled "Allow Anonymous Connections." The user name and password fields are for a local account to be used to authenticate anonymous FTP connections to the FTP server. If you only want to allow anonymous connections, and disable any FTP connections with valid NT user names and passwords, select the checkbox labeled "Allow only anonymous connections."

At the bottom of the Service tab, there is a button labeled "Current Sessions." Clicking this button will list all currently connected FTP sessions. To disconnect a particular user, simply select the user and click Disconnect. To disconnect all FTP sessions at once, click the "Disconnect All" button.

The Messages Tab

Clicking the Messages tab displays the Messages configuration portion of the FTP properties dialog box, as shown in Figure 12-2. The Messages Tab allows you to provide informational messages to users who connect to your FTP site. You can enter three different types of messages for your FTP site:

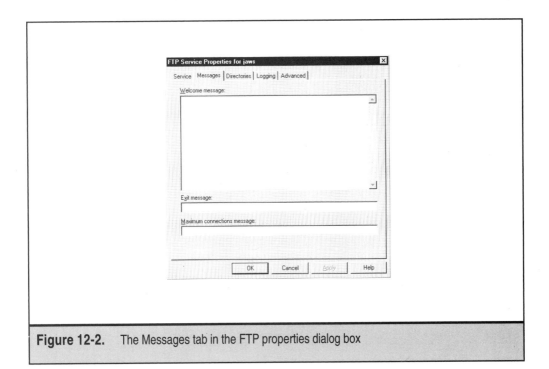

Figure 12-2.   The Messages tab in the FTP properties dialog box

▼ **Welcome message** This message is displayed when a user connects to your
site. It can be lengthy and is usually used to point out policies and the location
of informational files for the user.

■ **Exit message** This is a brief message that is displayed when a user exits your
FTP site.

▲ **Maximum connections message** This message is displayed if the maximum
number of simultaneous connections to your FTP site has been reached, and a
user is not permitted to make a new connection.

The Directories Tab

Selecting the Directories tab displays the Directories configuration portion of the FTP
properties dialog box, as shown in Figure 12-3. This configuration tab allows you to add
new directories to the FTP server's configuration and assign them an alias. In addition,
the Directories tab allows you to determine which format the FTP server will use when
listing the files in a directory. Depending on your selection, the FTP server will display
directory listings in either a UNIX-based format or a DOS-based format.

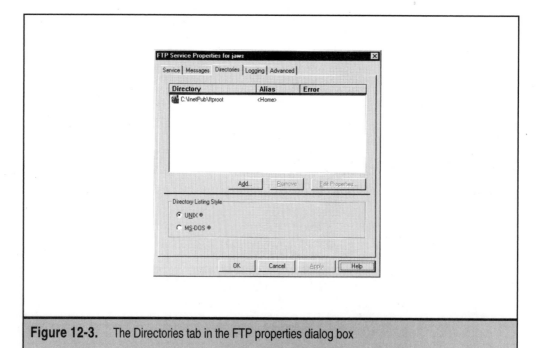

Figure 12-3.   The Directories tab in the FTP properties dialog box

The Logging Tab

Selecting the Logging tab in the FTP properties dialog box brings up the Logging configuration property sheet, as shown in Figure 12-4. This tab allows the administrator to configure how the FTP service logs accesses. You can opt to log all accesses to a file, in which case you can specify both the directory for log files and how often the FTP service will open a new log file. Or, instead of logging to a file, you can choose to log to an SQL or ODBC database. If you choose database logging, you must supply the data source name, table name, user name, and password for the database.

The Advanced Tab

The Advanced tab in the FTP properties dialog box, as shown in Figure 12-5, allows you to configure access control and network bandwidth usage. This tab allows you to decide if computers are granted or denied access by default, and then to enter IP addresses that are exceptions to the policy. You can also choose to limit the bandwidth used by the NT FTP server to a specific maximum amount, in order to keep from overloading your network.

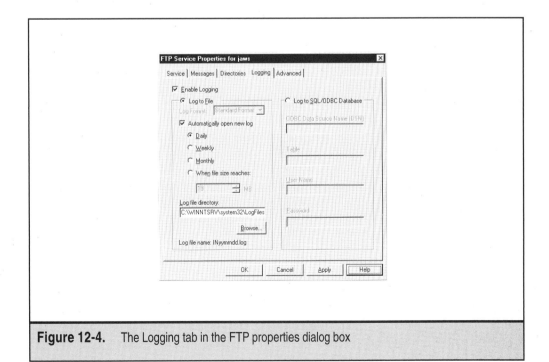

Figure 12-4. The Logging tab in the FTP properties dialog box

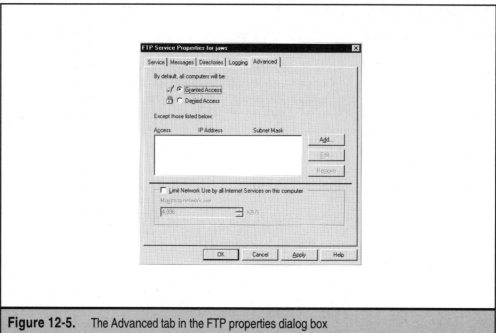

Figure 12-5.   The Advanced tab in the FTP properties dialog box

SECURE SHELL

Connecting over a network and performing sensitive tasks, such as system administration, has some inherent risks. When you send passwords over a network, they can be compromised. Hosts and addresses can be spoofed, allowing commands to be issued from unauthorized sources. One tool that can help solve these problems is the *Secure Shell (ssh)*.

The *ssh* software is designed to function as a replacement for the UNIX *rlogin, rsh,* and *rcp* commands. It provides strong authentication and encryption in order to protect the integrity of the data stream. The *ssh* software is available in both a public domain form and as a commercial product. The public domain software is available on the Web from **ftp://ftp.cs.hut.fi/pub/ssh/**. This version currently runs under most variants of UNIX. A very detailed FAQ covering *ssh* is available from **http://www.uni-karlsruhe.de/~ig25/ssh-faq/**. The commercial version of *ssh*, known as *F-Secure,* is distributed by Data Fellows. Two versions of F-Secure are available: a client version, F-Secure SSH Client, that runs under Windows 3.1, 95, NT, Macintosh, and UNIX; and a server version, F-Secure SSH Server, that runs under UNIX. For more information on the commercial version of *ssh*, see the Data Fellows website at **http://www.datafellows.com**.

NETWORK TIME PROTOCOL

Computer clocks will tend drift over time, causing different computers in your organization to have different values for the current time. Depending on your computing environment, you may need to make sure that computer clocks are always set accurately. Most computer operations groups use automated processes that are started at a specific time. If the computers in your organization rely heavily on processes that must be time synchronized, you might want to consider using a Network Time Protocol client to set your computer clocks.

The Network Time Protocol (NTP) is a network protocol that is used to synchronize computer clocks with a reference time. If you are synchronizing clocks over a wide area network, accuracy is usually within the tens of milliseconds range. With NTP, you have the option of configuring your own NTP server to use for synchronization. Since having an NTP primary server requires either a radio or satellite receiver or a dedicated modem, most people choose to connect to a public NTP server for NTP time data.

Clients for NTP are available for most versions of UNIX. For an NT client, you will have to compile it from the NTP source code. Full details about NTP, including the source for clients and servers, can be found at **http://www.eecis.udel.edu/~ntp/**.

MICROSOFT NETMEETING

The NetMeeting product from Microsoft is a bit different from other network software that you may have encountered. NetMeeting is a type of collaboration software, designed for corporate communication in order to allow a group of people to work together effectively over the Internet. NetMeeting supports a variety of communications and collaboration media, including voice and video conferencing, data conferencing via application sharing, group whiteboarding, text chat, and file transfer.

The idea behind NetMeeting is that you can use the Internet as a means for group interactivity, even if the participants are in different locations. You can conduct conference calls, video conferences, sales presentations, design meetings, and distance learning by using the various collaboration tools in NetMeeting.

Currently, NetMeeting only runs under Microsoft Windows 95 and Microsoft Windows NT 4.0. Installation and configuration of NetMeeting, while guided by setup wizards, has many options. For more information on NetMeeting, see the Microsoft NetMeeting website at **http://www.microsoft.com/netmeeting/**.

NOTE: Microsoft provides a NetMeeting Resource Kit in the form of a 330-page white paper. This resource kit is in Microsoft Word format and is available for download from Microsoft's website.

SUMMARY

There are a variety network services that run outside the confines of a web server. In this chapter, we have examined some of the most popular types of network software that you may find useful. NNTP news servers provide threaded, discussion group messaging and are useful for internal discussion groups, client feedback, and technical support. In addition, NNTP is the backbone protocol for the world-wide Usenet news system.

Anonymous FTP provides a way for system administrators to create software and information archives and make them available to the public. Configuring an anonymous FTP server requires attention to detail, in order to avoid common configuration problems that could lead to security breaches in your system. We examined the specifics, in detail, of how to install and configure anonymous FTP servers on both UNIX and NT platforms.

In addition to anonymous FTP and NNTP, we examined some of the other network service software available. These other services include the Network Time Protocol for computer clock synchronization, the *ssh* secure shell for secure network access, and Microsoft's NetMeeting collaboration server. As you would expect, not all of these services are available for both NT and UNIX, though the vast majority are. By analyzing your environment and system requirements, you, as the system administrator, can select appropriate tools from the wide variety of services that are available and apply them to your environment in an effective manner.

CHAPTER 13

Desktop Applications

Networks are growing bigger and more heterogeneous as time passes. This is due to the fact that, while new solutions to technical problems appear at a dizzying rate, old solutions may still work acceptably. Glass-house mainframe shops with character-based terminals may want to keep their mainframe and dumb terminal network: it's reliable, does many things well, and is already in place. On the other hand, a character-based, dumb terminal can't do anything other than talk to a mainframe. Most users want, and in fact need, the more sophisticated applications available in today's computing environment.

OPERATING SYSTEMS VS. DESKTOP APPLICATIONS

Windows networking with Windows NT approaches the ease of networking Apple has had for years with AppleTalk: building a small Windows NT-only network is still more complicated than just plugging in the cables, but it's not that difficult to construct. UNIX has evolved as the predominant operating system in the largest computer network of all: the conglomeration of systems, networks, and connectivity that is known as the Internet. Therefore, much of the networking effort over the last three decades or so has gone into either improving UNIX's networking functionality or in enhancing other operating systems to network into UNIX systems. Much of Microsoft's networking effort has been to extend Windows NT to better work with UNIX and thereby "the Internet," as different portions of this book have discussed.

However, users are not so much enamored with a given operating system as they can be with the applications on the operating systems. Users want to use applications to write, draw, or calculate. Users generally interact with operating systems in similar ways: they create, edit and delete files; they view listings of files in directories or folders; and they may copy or move files around in the directories. Users also manipulate files in other ways: attaching files to be included with electronic mail messages, outputting the files via a printer or other device, and so on.

Most often, users of modern systems today use a GUI (graphical user interface) to interact with a given operating system. DOS had the Windows GUI, until it was incorporated with the OS in Windows NT; the Apple Macintosh operating system, also a GUI, has been reviled by some for not having a command-line interface at all; and the different versions of UNIX have had several windowing systems, including the many versions of X Windows, Sun's OpenWindows, and the Common Desktop Environment (CDE).

Users who must deal with multiple operating systems are occasionally limited by the following details:

▼ Not all applications are available on all operating systems;

■ If they are available, the multiple versions may not be available on their network;

■ Sometimes applications that claim cross-platform compatibility are less than accurate, or are accurate only with a restricted subset of functionality; and

▲ Having multiple platforms can lead to its own logistical nightmare of needing to maintain multiple workstations for EACH user.

Much of this book has focused on specific areas of integrating UNIX and Windows NT systems in order for them to play nice with each other: printing, electronic mail, file systems, and so on. This chapter will focus on ways to allow users to share the same desktop, or the same functionality, from different places in the network.

First, this chapter will discuss X Windows, which is the basis for many of the windowing systems available for UNIX, and which has also been ported to many other operating systems. That topic will be followed by a discussion of means to provide access to X Windows-based applications to users of Windows NT desktop workstations, then the view will reverse and we'll look at ways to make Windows NT desktops available across the enterprise network. This chapter will then close with an overview of several tools, many comparatively low-level, that help provide veteran UNIX users with much of the same functionality they are accustomed to having in UNIX environments.

X WINDOWS

The X Windows System was originally developed at the Massachusetts Institute of Technology in order to help answer the needs of research and engineering computer users for graphics capability. X is a graphical user interface (GUI) system that is capable of running on top of many other operating systems. X is available for almost every form of UNIX, Windows, Macintosh OS, OS/2, and many other operating systems, as well as being the underlying basis for such offshoots as the G-Windows GUI for the OS-9 and OS-9000 operating systems. This section will discuss some of the history and architecture of X, and then discuss some of the options for making X available on PC-based platforms, including PC X servers and yet another Web tie-in.

X Windows History and the X Consortium

The first release of the major form of X, known as X version 11, was in 1987. The X Consortium was formed in 1988 to further the development of the X Windows System and was charged with its major goal: to promote cooperation between all participants in the computer industry for the creation of standardized software interfaces for all layers in the X Windows System environment. MIT for many years provided a vendor-neutral, central position for leading the development efforts of X, and later split off the X Consortium as a formal organization. Gone were the days of the sometimes heroic, ad hoc efforts to support X that existed until that time.

Release Six of X, referred to as X11R6, was released in 1994. In 1995, the X Consortium was named as the prime contractor for leading development of the next releases of the Common Desktop Environment (CDE) and Motif. At the beginning of 1997, the X Consortium transferred responsibility for the X Windows System to the Open Group, and was subsumed into the Open Group. This occurred largely due to a feeling that the original goal of the X Consortium was largely completed: the X windowing environment is widespread and no longer needs a full-scale industry consortium for nurturing.

The Open Group continues their existing work of publishing, testing, and branding products that conform to international standards, and now includes X as one of their responsibilities. For more information on the Open Group, their World Wide Web URL is **http://www.opengroup.org**. The next section of this chapter will discuss the architecture of X.

The Server Is the Client and the Client Is the Server

The X11 network windowing system has been one of the most popular desktop environments in the history of computing, given its wide availability. Almost all UNIX platforms developed since 1990 have some form of graphical display system available, based upon the X11 protocol. Some of the major reasons for the ubiquity of X in the UNIX world are the same as for sendmail's widespread popularity as a Mail Transport Agent:

▼   Flexibility

■   Portability

▲   Source code is available free and without limitations

For other environments, such as the Macintosh and Windows operating systems, X ports have been commercially available for some time now.

Architecture

X was designed from the beginning of its history to be platform- and kernel- (and therefore vendor-) independent. The X11 protocol is modeled after a network packet transmission model, with the X client and the display being the two ends of the connection, and an X server between the two. What confuses people about the X architecture is that X's client/server definition feels at odds with the way everyone else uses the term client/server. In general, the client is the server and the server is the client. Figure 13-1 provides an illustration of this behavior.

An X client opens a network socket appropriate for the intended display and writes X protocol packets to that particular socket. The X server accepts the packets and responds to the requests from the X client by drawing to the defined display. The user operates the input devices (keyboard and mouse) to send information to the X server, which then translates the user's input into X protocol packets and sends them to the appropriate X client. In addition to this, X clients may communicate with other X clients by setting values called *properties* on the X server. This distributed architecture of X provides several advantages: although the X client (a database application, for example) and the X server may run on the same workstation, they do not have to. In some cases, it may increase performance to run the X client and the X server on different workstations. Also, since the X client and server communicate using X protocol, there is no requirement that the two run on the same operating system or processor type. Only the X server application

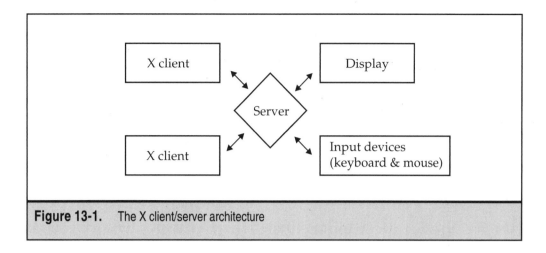

Figure 13-1.   The X client/server architecture

has to be aware of the hardware it is running on. Separating the client and server portions thereby improves portability and reuse of applications code.

The Common Desktop Environment

The Common Desktop Environment is a standard desktop for UNIX and is intended to provide consistent cross-platform services to users, application developers, and systems administrators. Introduced in 1995, CDE was jointly developed and licensed by Hewlett-Packard, IBM, Novell, and SunSoft under the COSE (Common Open Software Environment) initiative. Other participants in the CDE development effort include Hitachi, Fujitsu, Digital Equipment Corporation, and SCO. CDE was developed under the Open Group's Pre-Structured Technology (PST) process, a multi-vendor technology development program.

CDE 2.1, released in early 1997, integrated the Motif 2.0 GUI, X Windows System, and CDE to help standardize application presentation in distributed multiplatform environments. By incorporating some Motif 2.0 user interface objects, or *widgets*, the style guides for CDE and Motif converged with the 2.1 release. Standard features of the CDE, as shown in Figure 13-2, include a floating toolbar that is user- or system-configurable to incorporate launch buttons for any application.

For more information, the Common Desktop Environment FAQ has been included in this book as Appendix B.

X Terminal

An X terminal is a dumb terminal with just enough computing capability to run an X server. A GUI version of an ASCII character-based dumb terminal, an X terminal can be designed with no internal hard disk, and may be no more than a CPU, enough RAM, boot ROM that looks for a remote server to download the X server from, and a monitor, keyboard, and mouse. X terminals may use the Trivial File Transfer Protocol (TFTP) to

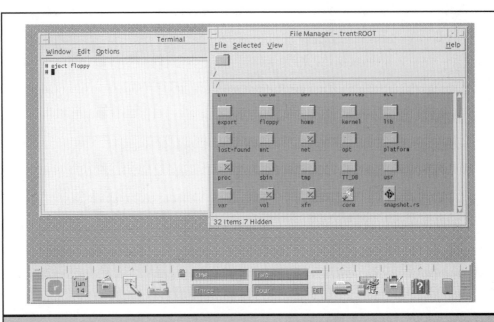

Figure 13-2.   The Common Desktop Environment GUI provides a standardized cross-platform GUI for many operating systems

download an X server from a specified remote host have the X server software embedded in ROM on the motherboard; or they may be a small workstation (that is to say, with a hard disk and perhaps a CD-ROM or floppy drive) that is dedicated to running the X server software. The rest of the network provides all other computing resources—data storage and lookup, processing of requests, and so on. The X terminal is merely responsible for drawing the windows on the monitor. Communication over the network is typically handled via a TCP/IP stack.

NOTE: If an X terminal is starting to sound like a simplified Network Computer (NC) design, that's a good analogy. NCs, however, do not require X, and do include Java as part of the Network Computer Reference Platform specification. NCs are considered by some as a low-cost upgrade to current ASCII character-based dumb terminals and X terminals.

PC X Servers

Character-based terminals are becoming extinct, and dedicated X terminals running UNIX applications are being replaced, in many cases, with PCs running networked terminal packages. PCs allow users to run personal productivity applications while attaining network terminal connectivity. Traditionally, UNIX systems provide large business or scientific application access, while the personal computing software market provides personal productivity applications such as word processing, spreadsheets, and contact managers.

PC X server software packages can run alongside (in separate windows) the native PC desktop, or replace the native desktop, converting the PC into an X terminal. These X Windows products, such as Hummingbird's Exceed, WRQ's Reflection X, and AGE Logic's XoftWare, allow users to run UNIX X Windows applications from a UNIX host on the PC desktop by providing a Motif or Open Look-based X Windows GUI, with functionality such as cut and paste, XDCMP compliance, shape extension, and other X protocol support.

With the Broadway extensions to the X protocol (see the following section), viewing and controlling X applications through a web browser (with the Broadway plug-in module) becomes possible. While requiring an X server and a web browser on both the local desktop workstation and the remote server, Broadway does allow identical access to X applications from either Windows or UNIX desktops. Some vendors in the PC X server market, including WRQ and Hummingbird, plan to incorporate the Broadway specifications in their products.

However, running an X server application alongside your regular PC's operating system may require a hardware upgrade, such as 16MB or more of additional RAM. Some PC X servers may crash or fail to release memory, especially if running with (and not instead of) the native operating system. Also, while X servers have improved significantly since their early releases, a dedicated X terminal is likely to exhibit superior performance to an X server running on a general-purpose PC workstation.

Broadway

In 1995, it was possible to joke about using Netscape's Navigator web browser as an operating system. Today it's much less of a joke: many different Internet technologies are grafting themselves onto the Web by means of the "plug-in" module technology for the major web browsers. One of these is the X Consortium's final project, *Broadway*, released as X11R6.3. This section will discuss the general design of Broadway, including the ability to access X clients (do you remember what a client is in X vocabulary?) via the Web through a web browser.

Broadway was the X Consortium's attempt to merge variations of some of the more common X protocol extensions into a vendor-neutral format. Broadway is intended as an extension to, rather than a replacement for, current X applications, and is designed to be compatible with unmodified X11 applications. Broadway introduced a wide array of features to the X group of protocols, discussed in the following sections.

X.FAST   The X.Fast Extension is a protocol for using X applications over a low-speed network, including dial-up lines, or across the Internet. Traditionally X11 exhibited good performance in 10MB/second Ethernet environments, but performed poorly over slower serial lines or modems. X.Fast achieves its goal through additional capabilities, including protocol data compression and caching.

REMOTE X   Remote X is a new Multiple Internet Message Extension (MIME) type, which allows integration with web browsers to allow X clients to be launched by and displayed within the browser using a plug-in module. As with other MIME types, the web server being used must be properly configured to understand the RX MIME type. Also, the X client must include the RX capability as well. Many extensions were made to X's security model, allowing a more secure use of the remote capabilities of X over a wide area network (WAN) or the Internet.

NETWORK PRINTING   A Print Extension protocol operates through the X protocol. Previous to Broadway, printing through X client applications required a separate mechanism through the UNIX file system. With the XPRINT service, a client application can print directly to a network printer. A platform-neutral solution, XPRINT works with either UNIX or Windows NT systems, as well as raster device, PostScript level 2, and PCL printers.

PROXY MANAGEMENT   A proxy management protocol allows the X server to use proxy services such as running an application through a firewall using TCP or UDP network ports.

NETWORK AUDIO   A network audio component allows users to play and record audio across a network, as well as to synchronize the audio with other events or applications, thus allowing both voice annotation of documents and teleconferencing.

For more information on X11R6.3 (Broadway), see **http://www.x.org/consortium/broadway.html**.

WINDOWS ON UNIX

The previous section of this chapter addressed the possibility of bringing X Windows to the Windows NT desktop. However, what if the situation were reversed, and you had many UNIX workstations in your network, but wanted to bring Windows NT to those users? One option would be to supply each UNIX user with a Windows NT workstation and double the size of the network, either by simply adding additional hubs where possible, or by building a second network for the Windows NT machines. (You *did* plan for expansion when you laid out the network configuration, right? It would be easier now if you had.) While a valid technical solution, this option may be precluded on the grounds of cost, or a majority of the users may simply not have enough room in their workspaces to add another workstation. One possible solution to this issue is a remote Windows NT server. This section will present some of the benefits and costs associated with remote Windows NT service, and discuss some other options, such as emulators.

Remote Windows NT Servers

By careful license agreements and judicious modification of the Windows NT source code, third-party vendors have extended Windows NT to allow remote display over networks. Products such as Citrix's WinFrame, ExodusTech's NTerprise, Insignia Solutions' NTrigue, and Tektronix's WinDD all use a modified Windows NT Server operating system to provide Windows NT remote access in much the same way as the X protocol is defined: the remote server handles application processing, while the local client (an X server) performs graphical updates and screen management. A protocol called Intelligent Console Architecture (ICA), which was created by Citrix and licensed to the other vendors, provides a network communications mechanism similar to the X client/server protocol model.

The ICA desktop client starts a remote session with a Windows NT server and displays either individual applications in separate windows or a full Windows NT desktop inside a window on the local X desktop. The remote Windows NT desktop appears almost exactly as if you were on a Windows NT Server directly. Since a remote user has to log in to Windows NT just as if they were at a local Windows NT workstation, separate user profiles, desktop views, and access controls are maintainable by the remote Windows NT server. The rest of this section will discuss some of these remote Windows NT servers.

Citrix WinFrame

Citrix was the first vendor to design remote Windows NT access with ICA. The original intent behind WinFrame was to provide Windows NT to a low-end X Windows workstation. As a logical extension of Citrix's concept, Wyse Technology's NC is almost a Windows version of an X terminal. Built around WinFrame, Wyse's minimal computer runs only the ICA client software, and requires a dedicated WinFrame server for everything else, making it considerably smaller than the Microsoft and Intel NetPC standard hardware specification (described in Chapter 14).

WinFrame runs the Program Manager as a single X window, with a maximum resolution of 800×600 pixels. More information on WinFrame may be found on the World Wide Web at **http://www.citrix.com/winframe.htm**.

ExodusTech's NTerprise

Like WinFrame, NTerprise currently operates at the level of Windows NT 3.51; Windows NT 4.0 versions are not available at the time of this writing. However, NTerprise differs from WinFrame in a few respects. WinFrame runs the Program Manager as a single X window, and to work with Windows NT applications, the user uses the Program Manager and therefore needs to understand the basics of the Windows NT GUI. NTerprise, on the other hand, runs NT under the X Windows manager, and can operate several different X windows on a single user's desktop. To take the matter further, NTerprise can use icons on the X desktop linked directly to a Windows NT application, isolating the user on X entirely from Windows NT and never requiring the user to work through the Microsoft Windows Program Manager. More information on NTerprise may be found on the World Wide Web at **http://www.exodustech.com**.

Insignia Solutions NTrigue

The Insignia NTrigue client is essentially an X server for your local workstation. Insignia chose to incorporate Citrix's WinFrame ICA system into its NTrigue for WinFrame product. HDS, which is producing a NC system based on its X terminal line, includes NTrigue clients with its NCs, and Sun announced NTrigue as a solution for providing Windows NT for their JavaStation NCs. More information on NTrigue may be found on the World Wide Web at **http://www.insignia.com/NTRIGUE/**.

Tektronix WinDD

Tektronix was originally a display and X terminal vendor. Tektronix initially designed WinDD to provide Windows NT access for its line of X terminals, then expanded the supported client platforms by incorporating the ICA protocol into its product. WinDD, like WinFrame, is a remote Windows NT application that displays the Windows NT desktop in a single X window on the UNIX desktop. More information on WinDD may be found on the World Wide Web at **http://www.tek.com/Network_Displays/Products/WinDD.html**.

Cautions for Using Remote Windows NT

In many cases, a remote Windows NT server may be a much better solution for deploying Windows NT to 200 UNIX users. It is almost certainly better than purchasing and installing 200 Windows NT workstations, with the attendant support costs. A single remote Windows NT server used as an applications server may fulfill the business needs. This is especially true if the users only need Windows NT for one or two applications, such as Microsoft Excel or Lotus Notes. However, there are some cautions to consider before choosing a remote Windows NT server.

First, remote Windows NT servers have high memory requirements. For reasonable performance, one calculation would be 32MB (for the server) + (the number of concurrent users × the amount of memory your users would need for a typical Windows NT workstation). The vendors claim their products will run in lower per-user memory environments than for real workstations, suggesting four to ten megabytes per user. For example, suppose you wanted to support 35 simultaneous connections. The equation would be

32 + (35 × 10) = 382MB recommended on the server

Obviously, given the server's intended use, a multiprocessor server (up to NT 4.0's limit of four processors) can also improve performance for multiple users.

Second, the remote Windows servers all work by *modifying* the Windows NT operating system, ranging from the low end of 25 or so dynamic link libraries (DLLs) to approximately 1000. While common applications such as Microsoft Office are likely to run (if for no other reason than the remote NT vendors will test their products against common products first), rare, esoteric, or custom applications would be less than likely to run, if at all.

Finally, as of this writing, no remote Windows NT server supports Microsoft NT 4.0: they all operate at NT Server 3.51, and only on the Intel processor. This may or may not be an issue for your users.

Windows Emulators for UNIX

Sun provides a Windows emulator of sorts for Solaris called Wabi. Wabi requires that you install Microsoft Windows into the Wabi environment. Upgrading Wabi requires that you reinstall Windows afterwards. These significant barriers to upgrading aside, Wabi is certified by Sun to run many of the common Windows-based applications, including Lotus SmartSuite and Microsoft Office. For more information on Wabi, see Sun's World Wide Web presence at **http://www.sun.com/**, or Sun's information page about Wabi at **http://www.sun.com/software/Products/PC-Integration-products/ support/wabi2.0-questions/1info.html**.

A freeware Windows emulator available for UNIX is named WINE, which stands for either WINdows Emulator, or Wine Is Not an Emulator. WINE has been tested to run on Intel 80386 processors and up—on Linux, NetBSD, FreeBSD and Unixware, and SCO OpenServer. WINE runs under X, so you will need X on whatever UNIX platform you are attempting to run WINE on. Still in active and fluid development, it is currently not recommended for any use other than experimentation. More information may be found on the World Wide Web at **http://www.asgardpro.com/wine/index.html**.

OTHER TOOLS

Many UNIX users are accustomed to working close to the operating system. If they need a new tool such as a new command, they write it, or write a script around an existing command. A variety of tools are available that should be comfortable to UNIX users working in a Windows NT environment. This section will present remote access tools similar to telnet, then look at a suite of similar low-level tools from a particular vendor, and close with an examination of scripting capabilities under Windows NT.

rsh and ssh

Remote login access is sometimes a useful tool. Many people are familiar with the telnet client in Windows NT. While Microsoft does not supply a telnet server in Windows NT, a telnet client is supplied. By modern standards, telnet and related applications are a primitive way to communicate between two host machines. However, telnet and these related primitive techniques have an advantage in that they are almost universally available across almost every platform. This section will examine the r^* set of UNIX commands for remote access of other systems, and the ssh application for more secure access.

rsh

The *r** group of UNIX commands (*rlogin, rsh,* and *rcp*) all provide remote execution of commands on a UNIX workstation or server, similar to telnet. *rlogin* uses the login service to connect to another workstation, using the TCP/IP protocol. Some configuration is required for UNIX systems that you wish to access: the two relevant files are */etc/hosts.equiv* and *$USER/.rhosts*. The */etc/hosts.equiv* file contains names of hosts, or machines that are considered to be the same as the local machine for security purposes. For example, consider two workstations named GRAPHICS and ADMIN. If the */etc/hosts.equiv* file on GRAPHICS contains the hostname ADMIN, then any user who has an account on ADMIN (and is logged into ADMIN) can issue an *rlogin* command to GRAPHICS and connect to GRAPHICS without needing to reenter a password, because ADMIN is defined as a trusted host.

The *$USER/.rhosts* file is located in a specific user's home directory and contains sets of user IDs matched with hostnames. To illustrate the difference between the two, consider the example given in the preceding paragraph. If Jeff has a userid of jeff and has an account on both GRAPHICS and ADMIN, then the two example files (shown in Table 13-1), if present on the GRAPHICS workstation, allow Jeff to *rlogin* from ADMIN.

The difference between the two is that the */etc/hosts.equiv* example allows all users with accounts on both ADMIN and GRAPHICS to *rlogin* to GRAPHICS, but the */usr/jeff/.rhosts* file allows only Jeff to *rlogin* to the GRAPHICS workstation.

NOTE: Caution should be applied whenever implementing any remote access method. For example, if the */usr/jeff/.rhosts* file contained a second line reading "john ADMIN," then the user with the ID john (with an account on both ADMIN and GRAPHICS) could also rlogin to GRAPHICS without a password. But when John does log in, he has Jeff's permissions and privileges on GRAPHICS. John can then create, edit, or delete files, send mail to others, and in general do anything Jeff could. This is exactly as safe as handing someone your house or apartment key— it depends on who the someone is.

While not officially distributed by Microsoft as part of NT Server 4.0, the RSHSVC (rsh service) is the server side for the TCP/IP utility RSH.EXE, and works the same way as UNIX's *rsh* daemon. Both UNIX and Windows NT rsh clients may communicate with the Windows NT rsh service.

File	Content
/etc/hosts.equiv	ADMIN
/usr/jeff/.rhosts	jeff ADMIN

Table 13-1. */etc/hosts.equiv* and *$USER/.rhosts*

RSHSVC is distributed on the Windows NT Resource Kit.

Installing Windows NT rsh service

To install the rsh service:

1. Copy RSHSETUP.EXE, RSHSVC.EXE, and RSHSVC.DLL to *%SystemRoot%\System32* directory, where *%SystemRoot%* is where Windows NT was installed on the system (often in C:\WINNT).

2. Type the command

    rshsetup %SystemRoot%\system32\rshsvc.exe %SystemRoot%\System32\rshsvc.dll

3. Type the command

    net start rshsvc

To stop the remote shell service, type the command

net stop rshsvc

Windows NT rsh Configuration

You need to have *.RHOSTS* files in the %SystemRoot%*System32\drivers\etc* directory. The *.RHOSTS* file should have one or more of the following type of entries. Each line should be in the following format:

```
<H1>    <user1> [<user2> <user3> ....]
```

where H1 is the name of the host machine from which an rsh client can be run, and user1 and so forth, are names of the users that are permitted to access the remote shell service from the H1 machine. If a host machine name is not part of the *.RHOSTS* file and a user attempts an rsh client connection from that machine, or the user is not associated with the host machine, an "Access Denied" message is returned by the rsh service. The service will also refuse a connection from any host machine with an unresolvable IP address.

NOTE: Microsoft cautions against using the rsh service or client to run interactive commands, such as for editing files.

ssh

One major security concern over telnet is that passwords are sent over the network "in the clear," or unencrypted, between the two endpoints. It is not difficult to set up an application or other tool to watch every packet of information going over the network and filter the traffic for "telnet fred" and "password: whatever" pairs. ssh is intended as a secure version of rsh and may be used as a replacement for rsh and telnet, with the addition of encryption for communication. The traditional UNIX *r** commands are vulnerable to several kinds of attacks, and the X Windows System also has a number of severe vulnerabilities. ssh (Secure Shell) is a program that allows a user to

▼ Log into another computer over a network

■ Execute commands in a remote machine

▲ Move files from one machine to another

Intended as a replacement for *rlogin, rsh,* and *rcp,* ssh provides strong authentication and securer communication over insecure channels. ssh never sends passwords in the clear. Established *$USER/.rhosts* and */etc/hosts.equiv* files are still usable: changing over to ssh is mostly transparent for users on these systems. If an ssh connection is attempted to a remote site that does not have an ssh server, the ssh client may fall back to use rsh.

ssh protects against interception of clear text passwords and other data by intermediate hosts and spoofing of several kinds—including IP spoofing (where a remote host sends out packets that pretend to come from another, trusted host), DNS spoofing (where an attacker forges name server records), and X spoofing (listening to X authentication data and spoofing a connection to the X11 server). ssh also protects against manipulation of data by people in control of intermediate hosts between the two ends of the ssh session.

NOTE: ssh does have an option to use encryption of type "none." This is included only for debugging purposes and is not recommended for use.

However, ssh will not help you with anything that compromises your host's security in some other way. Once an attacker has gained root privileges on a given machine, he or she can then subvert ssh usage on that machine as well.

ssh currently runs on most flavors of UNIX and OS/2. A commercial Windows and Macintosh port has been written by Tatu Ylonen, the original author of ssh. The connection configuration screen of the Windows client is shown in Figure 13-3.

For more information, the ssh FAQ website is at **http://www.uni-karlsruhe.de/~ig25/ssh-faq/**.

TCP/IP Tools

The Exceed suite from Hummingbird Communications provides a wide assortment of X TCP/IP tools. The Exceed connection settings window of the X server is shown in Figure 13-4.

The Inetd service is part of the Exceed TCP/IP suite (see Chapter 14). Many TCP/IP tools familiar to UNIX users are found here: a finger client, an FTP client (which supports drag-and-drop), a Usenet newsreader, a telnet client (supporting VT52, VT100, and VT320 emulations), an LPR (Line Print Request, for UNIX network printing), a whois client, a Network Time Protocol client, a 3270 terminal emulator, and many others. A variation of BASIC is included for use in scripting work with Exceed applications, and in developing local X clients.

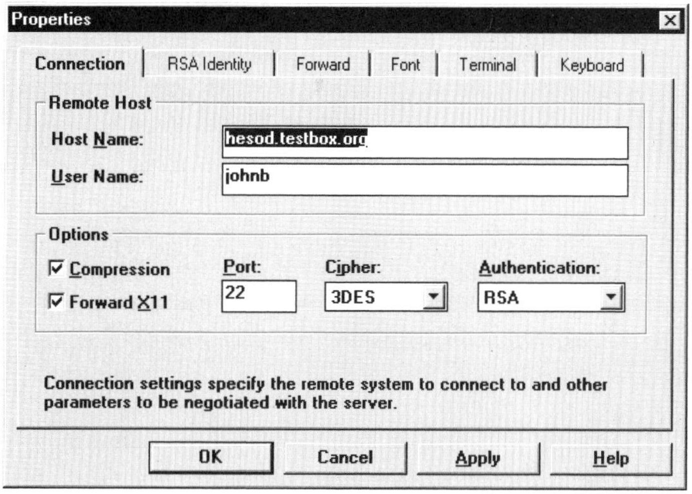

Figure 13-3.   The ssh Windows client allows secure connections to UNIX hosts running a ssh server

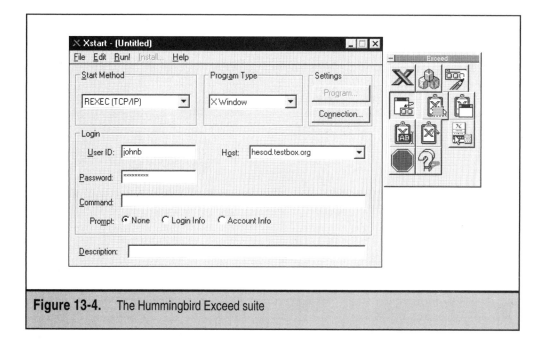

Figure 13-4.   The Hummingbird Exceed suite

The Inetd daemon runs as a service under Windows NT, and, like its UNIX counterpart, can be set to launch any application if a request is made through a particular port. Most of the tools may run in either a graphic mode or a command-line output mode. For example, Figure 13-5 shows the traceroute tool in graphic mode, and Figure 13-6 shows the tool with the same trace results in text mode. More information may be found on the Hummingbird website at **http://www.hummingbird.com**.

Scripting

For UNIX users who are very comfortable with their operating system and with programming methodology, there are a variety of scripting options for users to extend their capabilities by causing one command to trigger several commands. This section will mention some of the scripting options available on Windows NT and UNIX alike.

Shell

Most versions of UNIX have several shells available. A shell displays a command-line prompt, either over the entire screen or within a window of a GUI. Commands entered at a shell prompt are passed to the shell executable, which performs the commands and returns the output. The *bash* (for Bourne-Again SHell) UNIX shell has been ported to the Windows NT environment and is available as part of a GNU package at **ftp://ftp.cygnus.com/pub/gnu-win32/**.

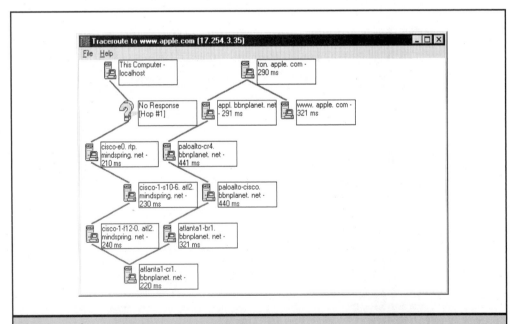

Figure 13-5. The Exceed traceroute tool in graphic mode

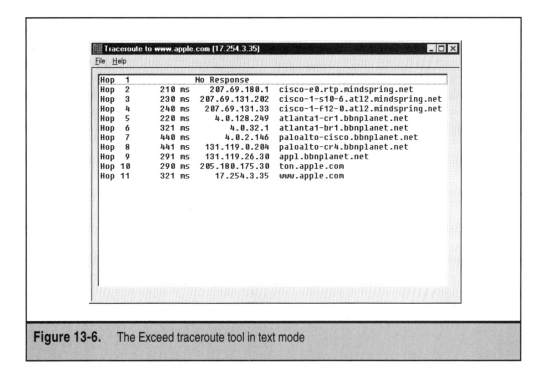

Figure 13-6.   The Exceed traceroute tool in text mode

A version of the C shell has also been ported for use under Windows 95 and Windows NT. A demonstration version is available at several archives, including **ftp://wuarchive.wustl.edu**. The filename to look for is **csh-x86.zip** for the Intel processor, but the application has also been compiled for the other processors Windows NT is available on.

perl

What is there to be said about perl that everyone doesn't already know that is appropriate outside of a "secrets of the perl masters" book? perl is an interpreted language that is optimized for scanning arbitrary text files, extracting information from those text files, and printing reports based on that information.

Reminiscent of some of the other languages—such as C, sed, awk, and sh—perl expression syntax is similar to C expression syntax. As a result of it having been ported to many platforms, perl is widely used where shell scripting would have occurred, because perl scripts are often more portable than most shell scripts. perl is widely used for Common Gateway Interface (CGI) scripts for use with World Wide Web servers.

More information on perl may be found on the World Wide Web at **http://www.perl.com/perl/**.

A Frequently Asked Questions (FAQ) file about perl for Windows NT is available at **http://www.endcontsw.com/people/evangelo/Perl_for_Win32_FAQ.html**.

Python

Python is an interpreted, interactive, object-oriented scripting language. Often compared to Tcl, perl, Scheme, or Java, Python has features such as modules, classes and exceptions, and very high-level dynamic data types and dynamic typing. Interfaces exist to many system calls and libraries, as well as to various windowing systems including X11, Motif, Tk, and MFC. Python has been ported to many flavors of UNIX, as well as Windows, DOS, OS/2, Macintosh, Amiga, and so on. More information on Python is available at **http://www.python.org/**. Information and the software for the Windows port of Python are available at **http://www.python.org/ftp/python/pythonwin/**.

Tcl/Tk

Sun Microsystems is providing active support for porting the Tcl scripting language and the Tk GUI toolkit to multiple platforms. As of this writing, Tcl/Tk runs on several flavors of UNIX, Windows 95 and NT 3.51, and the Macintosh OS. While the language is free, Sun has already released a commercial product called Tcl Plugin, which allows the running of Tcl scripts within a web browser. Current plans from Sun include incorporating Tcl into a web server, which will then be extended for system management functions and using Tcl scripts as an alternative to SNMP to intelligently report management information to a central management console. Predictably, future plans include porting the Tcl interpreter (which is presently developed in C) in Java, to allow use of Tcl in Java-enabled or Java-only environments.

SUMMARY

This chapter has tried to present some of the options for providing a Windows NT or UNIX desktop view to the other group of users without having to provide a duplicate network. For example, the main benefit of using a remote Windows NT server is the elimination of the need to support Windows workstations in addition to X terminals and UNIX workstations. System management costs may be reduced because there aren't 200 Windows NT workstations (added to the existing network of 200 UNIX workstations) to install, maintain, and upgrade; there is just one large remote Windows NT server. On the other hand, others argue that this trend of the centralization of remote windowing servers and using Network Computers is retrograde to the distributed trend of client/server computing, and a return to the days of the glass-house mainframe Information Systems department.

While a centralized system may be easier to manage from one location, centralized systems have one salient disadvantage: everyone stops whenever the mainframe has a problem. Using a distributed model and locally cached files, users can continue working if a central server goes down. This absolute centralized dependency is why mainframes aren't allowed to go down. Client/server computing has introduced an expectation that

"Oh, part of the system went down again, it happens all the time." Multiprocessor servers, RAID arrays, and clustering are all attempts to provide for a zero-time failover for modern operating systems. In the meantime, users will attempt to use what they have or can acquire for their real needs, which in most cases involve the applications that run on one or more of the extant operating systems, rather than the underlying operating systems.

CHAPTER 14

Systems and Network Management

System and network management, or administration, is a dauntingly huge set of tasks, and is often defined solely by example. Many computer professionals cannot give a clear and concise definition of the profession's characteristics, but much like the old definition of pornography, they know it when they see it.

System and network administration covers many unrelated tasks that all tend to circle around the issue of making services available to a user's desktop computer. Sometimes the users move from workstation to workstation, and need a single login distributed across a network. Sometimes the users take their workstations with them, working primarily from laptops. Whether the user is in one place or many, he or she wants a wide variety of services, which grow as the technology advances.

A DAY IN THE LIFE OF AN ADMINISTRATOR

The list of things an administrator may be asked to look after on any given day can be long and varied. Typical tasks system administrators are asked to perform include many from the following list:

▼ Backups/restores

■ Database administration

■ Desktop applications support

■ Disaster recovery

■ Electronic mail

■ Hardware support

■ OS support

■ Performance tuning

■ Software distribution support

■ Software installation and configuration

■ System analysis

■ Third-party hardware troubleshooting

▲ User training

This chapter will discuss some of the resources, possibilities, and trends available to system administrators faced with a heterogeneous UNIX and Windows NT environment. First, this chapter will discuss some basics of system and network administration, relevant regardless of the platform or operating system you are working with. Secondly, the system tools contained within Windows NT will be covered, followed by an explanation of the Simple Network Management Protocol. This chapter will close with coverage of two current trends: the Network Computer, and the advent of Web-based extensions to system and network management applications.

BASICS

Whatever your network consists of, be it an all-Solaris network, a mixed HP-UX and Windows network, or Macintosh workstations connected to NetWare file servers, some basic concepts are appropriate wherever you are and whatever you are asked to manage.

Know What You've Got

There are a couple of sub-areas to this. You need to know if you have 80 servers or 130 servers running Windows NT (don't laugh—answering that question was the first task assigned a newly hired administrator at a local company, because no one in the operations center knew). Knowing the network's composition provides a foundation for several of the other tasks: primarily, what operating systems to provide support for (if ten of 100 servers are Solaris and no one on staff is comfortable supporting Solaris, get someone trained or hired).

Secondly, it's hard to identify improvements in performance when you don't know what performance level you started from. For example, a directive is given to improve network throughput. Where's the bottleneck? Is the network sluggish only in mid-afternoon on workdays? Can existing components of the network be reorganized to improve performance, or do large portions of the network need replacement? Or consider this possibility: your facility is a Usenet news server node. This morning you were told to calculate the expansion of your site's storage necessary to maintain a 30-day inventory of all Usenet traffic. How do you start answering the question (after first laughing hysterically)?

Have Backups

For most organizations, their most significant investment is not in their network, or even their people—it's in the intellectual capital their people have created. To minimize productivity losses from the death of a given user's workstation and that user losing the last week's work, you can use a central file server. This allows you to set up a backup plan for that single file server, instead of providing backups for all workstations. On the other hand, it does focus your possible points of failure from many little ones to one big one. Also, backups should be kept in a secure offsite location, and rotated as frequently as appropriate to the organization. Backups become more complicated to accomplish across heterogeneous systems, and are discussed in Chapter 4.

Identify Points of Failure

When a portion of the network fails, what other portions does it affect? One firm had high-quality workstations, with all users operating from a central file server, and adequate network bandwidth to allow decent performance. Every workstation also had its own uninterruptible power supply (UPS). In a glaring oversight, the central file server wasn't on a UPS, so when the local power grid blanked out, the file server crashed. All the workstations survived the power outage, but they couldn't accomplish any work because their files were unavailable until the file server was restarted.

Have a Disaster Recovery Plan

In addition to helping identify performance bottlenecks, knowing what's on your network can help you recover from "unscheduled downtime incidents." Disaster recovery plans should be scaled to meet the needs of your organization. For some organizations, merely having a backup of important data is enough for them to feel secure. For others, having a complete network specification to replicate the entire information system center, and periodically rehearsing "rebuild the center from nothing," is considered necessary. For others, maintaining a complete center in another location as a backup site is necessary. This last level of disaster readiness is often found in telecommunication firms, where downtime is measured in the hundreds of thousands of dollars per minute, or in the military, where most naval vessels maintain a secondary command center in case the first one is destroyed.

For administrators, distributed access to management applications can allow faster response to perceived problems. One important trend in this area is the rapid growth of Web-enabled interfaces for system management applications.

Plan for Expansion

Systems should grow and change appropriately to the needs of the users and the organization. In the case of a change (either up or down) in the number of users, procedures should be in place for adding or removing users from the system and access to services, files, and so on. This includes such issues as planning the network by subnetting IP addresses to easily allow for expansion. Several tools exist that attempt to aid administrators in user and network management and configuration.

WHAT'S IN WINDOWS NT

Windows NT provides a wide range of networking and administrative services. One of the important limitations of a default Windows NT installation is that support for TCP/IP services is not automatically installed. Installing TCP/IP services from Microsoft (or other vendors) can provide great functionality to a Windows NT system in a heterogeneous network. This section will discuss the server-side services or daemons available for use with Windows NT.

Windows NT Server-Side Services

Windows NT server-side services are processes that tend to be started up at boot time, and do not require a user to log in and start them. These services are therefore counterparts to daemon processes under UNIX. With a default installation of Windows NT's support for TCP/IP package, you receive a minimal set of these low-level clients, including FTP and TFTP, telnet (VT52 and VT100/ANSI emulation), finger, remote execute (REXEC) and remote shell (RSH), and several network-related diagnostic commands, including ping. Installing the Simple TCP/IP service in Windows NT adds a few more client tools, including the perennial message of the day command, which allows an administrator to display a message to each user when he or she logs in that day.

NOTE: Most administrators tend to use the message of the day function for one of two types of messages: to announce system changes such as "The system is going down tonight at midnight for one hour," or for chatty, joking, quote-of-the-day messages. However, many users gloss over the message of the day, treating it much the way television watchers treat commercials—by looking at it without actually reading it.

Microsoft's TCP/IP Server-Side Services

When you install TCP/IP on Windows NT Server, no server-side services install by default—you have to install individual services separately. Many server-side services are included on the NT Server 4.0 installation media. The following services are discussed elsewhere in this book. Some of the TCP/IP services available include the following:

▼ TCP/IP Printing—provides an LPD (Line Printer Daemon), allowing access to and from UNIX and other systems that support TCP/IP printing.

■ Internet Information Server—provides several content-publishing protocols, including HTTP for the World Wide Web, FTP for file transfer, and Gopher (an older text file search and retrieval protocol using menus for navigation).

■ Dynamic Host Configuration Protocol—provides dynamic IP address assignments to compatible systems.

▲ Domain Name Service—provides IP name to IP address mapping, so a server can be reached using the address **webserver.testbox.org**, instead of having to remember 192.168.100.110.

Windows NT Administration and the Inet Daemon Server Suite

Administration of Window NT workstations and servers has become a major issue with many network managers. Although Microsoft's RAS and SMS provide a functional suite of services, their administrative functionality is limited when compared with UNIX systems. To gain control of peripherals and provide interoperable file and print services, enterprise administrators have implemented third-party TCP/IP application suites.

Enterprise system administrators can address some of the administration limitations of Windows NT by implementing the UNIX Inet daemon suite. Some TCP/IP products for Windows NT have been optimized by incorporating several important aspects of UNIX, such as the Inet daemon. The Inet daemon server suite was created to improve the efficiency of UNIX and TCP/IP by reducing the number of processes activated during system startup, many of which are not continuously required. *Inetd* (the InterNET service Daemon) continuously runs as an active process waiting for client connection requests. Upon receiving the request, Inetd starts up the appropriate server daemon (telnetd, FTPd, etc.), thereby conserving server and/or workstation resources.

Complete Inetd server suites are only provided by a few developers of TCP/IP application suites for the Windows NT workstation and server. A full Inet daemon server suite provides the Windows NT platform with much of the functionality of a UNIX workstation, enabling the PC desktop or server to provide client/server TCP/IP functions. This facilitates peer-to-peer connectivity among NT workstations and workgroups using TCP/IP applications.

The Inetd service can provide a valuable management utility, enabling network managers and administrators to telnet into a Windows NT workstation or server and execute remote operations or scripts. The value and functionality of Inetd is often underestimated and overlooked because it is a background service and is integrated into the UNIX operating system along with the TCP/IP protocol suite. A short table of Inetd functionality is included in Table 14-1. More information on third-party applications is provided in Chapter 13.

Windows NT Server's Built-In Utilities

Windows NT Server provides a number of basic utilities for system administration tasks. While many of these utilities are minimally functional, they are present. This section will provide a short overview of the system management utilities included in Windows NT Server. These applications may be found by default in the Administrative Tools folder. If other Windows NT services such as DNS, RAS, or DHCP are installed, the administrative utilities for those will also be found in this folder.

Backup

Windows NT's Backup utility provides for backing up both NTFS and FAT volumes, either local or NFS-mounted, to a tape drive. Backup can target an entire volume, a directory, or an individual file. It can also span backup media across multiple tapes and provides verification of the backup. Other useful concepts include logging its actions to log files and the ability to back up the local server's Windows NT Registry. The backup utility's weakest feature is in the area of scheduling. The Windows NT Schedule service must be used in order to perform an unattended backup.

Disk Administrator

The Disk Administrator provides for many functions related to disk formatting. Volumes may be formatted as either FAT or NTFS, primary and extended partitions may be modified, and disk configurations may be restored. The Disk Administrator is also used to define disk duplexing, mirroring, and striping. However, a note of caution is in order: as with FDISK under DOS, you can do serious damage to your drive configuration using the Disk Administrator.

Inetd Service	Function
Finger server	Services client inquiries as to who is logged on
FTP server	Supports FTP client file transfer
Gopher server	Supports gopher client searches and menus
LPD server	Supports PC-client, UNIX Line Printer Requests
New Talk server	Supports (New Talk) UNIX chat facility
Bootp server	Supports remote TCP/IP configurations
RSH server	Supports requests to execute commands on a remote system
Talk server	Supports (Old Talk) UNIX chat facility
Telnet server	Services Telnet client (virtual terminal) sessions
TFTP server	Provides file transfer for diskless workstations
Trival name server	Services host-to-IP address translations (name resolution)
Time server	Synchronizes client time with other NFS servers
HTTP server	Enables broadcasting of web pages
Exec Server	Provides remote execution services
Login server	Provides remote login services
Timed server	Provides the time of day

Table 14-1. TCP/IP Server Suite and Functions

Event Viewer

The Event Viewer serves as Windows NT Server's log file monitor. The three primary system log files you view with Event Viewer are the following:

▼ System Log—alerts and events from device drivers, processes, and services

■ Security Log—security-audit events such as logons, system restarts, and shutdowns

▲ Application Log—application alerts and system messages

The Event Viewer allows you to view the preceding logs remotely for other Windows NT installations on the network. A log file may be exported in plain or comma-delimited format for transporting into a database, or for saving in Event Viewer .EVT file format.

License Manager

It is amazing how many businesses are operating with more copies of software applications than they have purchased. The License Manager is used to enforce network compliance with software license restrictions. In addition to allowing restrictions on a per-client or per-server basis, the utility allows monitoring of usage statistics for each user. Such monitoring can reduce the expenses for software applications by determining the appropriate number of licenses needed for purchase.

Migration Tool for NetWare

The Migration Tool for NetWare is designed to import NetWare user accounts, groups, and files into a Windows NT environment. The operative word here is "designed." The best feature of this utility is that the detailed log file records every action taken on both nodes of the migration effort, so you can correct the errors. One irritating feature is that user passwords do not migrate. Future versions of this utility may improve, possibly after the Novell Directory Service (NDS) is ported to Windows NT.

Network Client Administrator

The Network Client Administrator is intended to ease the connection of a non-networked OS to an NT Server. Another limited utility, the Network Client Administrator, presently only supports DOS clients and does not include Network Interface Card (NIC) support.

Performance Monitor

If it can't be measured, it's hard to optimize. The Performance Monitor provides literally hundreds of measurements for system and network activities and objects. The graphical display may be customized on a per-target basis: you may choose which measurements to display for each system or group of systems.

Server Manager

The Server Manager is used to administer and maintain Windows NT domains. Adding or removing computers to or from a domain, promoting Backup Domain Controllers (BCDs) to Primary Domain Controller (PDC) status, and synchronization of BDCs with the PDC are all done through this tool. Server Manager is also used for viewing connected users and managing shares.

System Policy Editor

A policy is a means to control and manage system configurations, user profiles, and user desktop settings. The System Policy Editor is used to define policies for everyone (global), server-specific, or individual users. Since policies override Registry settings, be careful—working in this tool can be almost as dangerous as directly editing the Registry in some cases.

User Manager for Domains

The User Manager for Domains allows an administrator to create, edit, and delete users and groups within the domain. Default options such as home directory location, RAS access, and group membership are all defined through this tool. User Manager for Domains also may be used to set system-level policies, including user password parameters, user access rights, and auditing of system-level events such as startup and shutdown.

Windows NT Diagnostics

This final tool supplies general information for both local hardware and operating system as well as other Windows NT installations on the network. The Diagnostics tool identifies device and card settings such as IRQ and DMA parameters, monitor resolution supported by the video cards, and so on.

SNMP

The Simple Network Management Protocol (SNMP) is a protocol designed to give a user the capability to remotely manage a computer network by polling and setting terminal values and monitoring network events. SNMP operates under the TCP/IP (Transport Control Protocol/Internet Protocol) communication stack.

SNMP Components

SNMP acquires MIB (Management Information Base) information from a network. Following a hierarchical tree structure, the most general information available about a network is at the top of the tree. As an MIB browser descends each branch of the tree, the information gets progressively more detailed into a specific network area, with the final nodes of the tree being the most specific.

For example, a device may be a parent category in the tree, with serial and parallel devices as its children. The value of these may be 4, 3, and 1, respectively. The numbers in this example correspond to the number of devices attached (listed in reverse order here): 1 parallel + 3 serial = 4 total devices. While the ISO definition of an MIB only contains a single tree structure, a point on the tree allows attachment of vendor-specific information. Examine Figure 14-1 for a partial diagram of the MIB tree.

Not all branches are shown in this diagram. The top is, obviously, the top. The second level contains the ISO branch (1) and two others. Below the ISO branch is the Organization branch (3), which has the U.S. Department Of Defense (6) as a subordinate

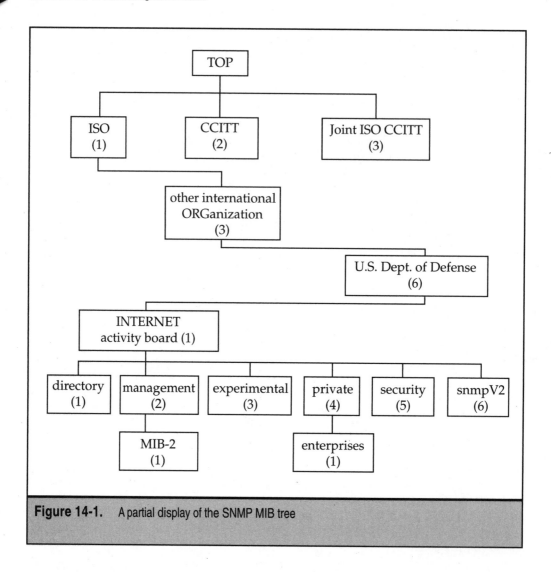

Figure 14-1.   A partial display of the SNMP MIB tree

branch. Below that is the INTERNET activity board branch (1). MIB paths are written separated by periods, so the Internet branch may be described by the sequence

```
1.3.6.1
```

or by the appropriate abbreviations of

```
iso.org.dod.internet.
```

The two most common branches are shown. The generic branch is

```
1.3.6.1.2.1 (iso.org.dod.internet.management.mib)
```

and the enterprise-specific branch is

```
1.3.6.1.4.1 (iso.org.dod.internet.private.enterprises)
```

For a manufacturer-specific example, the MIB branch containing all IBM entries is

```
1.3.6.1.4.1.2 (iso.org.dod.internet.private.enterprises.ibm)
```

SNMP requires three components: the MIB, an agent, and a manager. The agent runs on each node on the network to collect network and terminal information. The manager is located on the host computer on the network and polls the agents for requested information.

SNMP Requests for Comment

For the most precise definitions of SNMP, Table 14-2 presents some of the most relevant Requests for Comment (RFCs) from the IETF.

RFC 1089	SNMP over Ethernet
RFC 1155	Structure and Identification of Management Information for TCP/IP-based internets
RFC 1157	A Simple Network Management Protocol
RFC 1158	Management Information Base for Network Management of TCP/IP-based internets: MIB-II
RFC 1212	Concise MIB Definitions
RFC 1213	Management Information Base for Network Management of TCP/IP-based internets: MIB-II
RFC 1908	Coexistence between SNMPv1 and SNMPv2

Table 14-2.   SNMP-Related RFCs

SNMP Tools

A simple tool made for Windows NT to query MIB variables is the command line program SNMPUTIL.EXE from the Microsoft Windows NT 4.0 Resource Kit. An MIB browser written in Java is available over the World Wide Web from **http://www.adventnet.com/snmpagent**, and an SNMP-to-HTML gateway named MIBMaster is available from Equivalence at **http://www.ozemail.com.au/~equival**.

NETWORK COMPUTERS

The concept of Network Computers (NCs) was originally evangelized by Oracle and Sun as a low-cost alternative to the PC or workstation for people who didn't use the processing power of the workstation. Estimates of a single desktop PC's total purchase, installation, and support costs vary, but run as high as $42,000 over a five-year period. A working definition of the term "network computer" used in this section is almost any computing hardware that's smarter than a dumb terminal, but not as complicated or expensive as a PC. This section will discuss the initial Network Computer Reference Profile, the more detailed NetPC specification, and other issues for system managers to consider.

Network Computer Reference Profile

The initial Network Computer Reference Profile was hardware-neutral and does not impose many limitations on implementations. By being hardware-neutral, the Network Computer Reference Profile concentrates on software and protocols, such as

- ▼ Networking protocols (TCP/IP, NFS, FTP, telnet, SNMP, BOOTP and DHCP),
- ■ Multimedia protocols (JPEG, GIF, WAV, and AU),
- ■ Web-related protocols (HTTP and Java), and
- ▲ Electronic mail protocols (SMTP, IMAP4, and POP3) for email.

In general, Network Computers are expected to work best in the following specific situations:

- ▼ Users who work with only a limited set of programs
- ■ Users who share machines or work in different locations from day to day
- ■ Users at remote locations (difficult to provide adequate support)
- ■ Tasks that revolve around data stored centrally instead of local data
- ▲ As replacements for older, text-based terminals

NCs are not necessarily intended simply to save money by not buying desktop PCs or workstations for people who need only limited functionality. NCs are also aimed to replace dumb, character-based terminals currently still in use. While an NC costs more than a VT-100 terminal, an NC will have terminal emulation and will provide more capabilities, including the ability to use Windows applications and other GUI-based software.

NetPC

Like the NC, the NetPC is targeted at a class of task-oriented business users who do not require the same level of flexibility offered by traditional PCs. Advantages over traditional PCs include a sealed-case design for less customization by the end-user, smaller desktop footprint, the lack of a floppy drive, centralized administration capability, and flexibility for deploying either thin Web-style applications or traditional applications.

The NetPC definition is a specification for a low-maintenance PC system that was designed with networking in mind. In short, a NetPC is a Windows-based desktop box that runs on an Intel/PC-based architecture, but is not intended as a minimally configured low-powered system. Deployed in sealed boxes, NetPCs are intended to have all management, upgrading, and software installation deployed remotely from a server. Individual end users are not intended to alter the NetPC's hardware or software configuration.

The NetPC hardware specification includes

▼ CPU: Pentium 100MHz or equivalent

■ 16MB RAM minimum

■ Internal hard disk as cache

■ 640 × 480 pixels at 8 bits/pixel (VGA)

■ Audio device (type unspecified)

■ Plug-and-Play BIOS support by only using 32-bit PCIbus slots

■ No expansion slots

■ Network interface (Ethernet, Token Ring, V.34 modem, ISDN, ATM, T1)

■ Keyboard, pointing device/mouse

■ Locked/sealed case

▲ Optional hardware additions, including an IDE floppy drive, CD-ROM drive, PCMCIA card slots, and the Universal Serial Bus (USB) and the Firewire high-speed bus for peripherals.

For software, the NetPC specification includes the following:

▼ A Microsoft Windows operating system (either Windows 95 or NT)

■ Microsoft Windows 95 and NT-standard compatible device drivers

■ Machine-encoded, unique identification numbers

- Built-in network-management agent software and integration with Web-Based Enterprise Management (WBEM)
- Automatic pre-boot device driver configuration
- Automatic system/software scanning for policy compliance
- Diagnostic tools for monitoring and predicting component failure
- System-level trouble-ticketing software
▲ Remote wake utility

NOTE: Microsoft intends to include Plug and Play automatic configuration of PCIbus cards as part of Windows NT 5.0.

Microsoft is not claiming the NetPC acquisition price will be significantly less than a traditional PC, but sees the overall savings as coming from a reduction in support costs.

Sun's JavaStation

Many in the computer industry want what NCs promise: heterogeneous environments where applications and data can be shared across platforms consisting of PCs, Macs, UNIX workstations, 3270 terminals, and NCs.

In the hardware department, the JavaStation has the following specifications:

▼ 100 MHz microSPARC II CPU
- 8 to 64MB RAM
- 10/100BaseT Ethernet
- Remote deployment possible through PPP (point-to-point protocol), modem support, and flash memory
- SVGA (800 × 600) and XVGA (1024 × 768)
- Boots over the network from a server, or from flash memory (optional)
▲ PS2 keyboard and mouse ports

The JavaStation runs the JavaOS environment. JavaOS is a small operating environment that executes Java applications directly on the JavaStation hardware without requiring a separate host operating system. JavaOS consists of a small Java kernel, an embedded Java Virtual Machine (JVM), window and graphics extensions, and a suite of networking protocols. Optimized for size, JavaOS may boot and launch the HotJava browser in 2.5MB of memory. While JavaOS is not a traditional operating system—because it does not include such traditional operating system features as a file system, virtual memory, or multiple address spaces—it does include a GUI, is multi-threaded, supports a password-protected login feature, includes several device drivers, and communicates using standard network protocols.

Administrators can configure JavaOS, after a user logs in and passes authentication, to boot directly into a custom Java application. This allows the JavaStation to act as a dedicated terminal for many of the uses currently fulfilled by character-based terminals. Alternatively, the device may launch into the HotJava Browser, the HotJava Views "webtop," or a Windows emulation application such as Insignia's NTrigue or Citrix's WinFrame.

Table 14-3 presents a comparison of the Network Computer Reference specification with the NetPC and JavaStation definitions.

Network Computers: Why Bother?

If your company is already using centralized databases and application servers, then NCs fit well into such an infrastructure. This may also be well suited for IS departments that

Feature	NCRef1	NetPC	JavaStation
Network Interface	Various (Serial, Ethernet, ATM)	Various (Serial, Ethernet, ATM)	10MB/100MB Ethernet
CPU	Various	Intel x86 family, Pentium 100MHz	100MHz microSPARC II
Memory (RAM)	typical 8MB	16MB	8MB to 64MB
Operating System	Non-specific	Windows	JavaOS
Disk	Not required	Yes	No
Local File System	Not Applicable	DOS FAT	Not Applicable
Network File System	NFS, WebNFS, FTP	CIFS, Windows Networking	NFS, WebNFS, FTP
Network Protocols	TCP/IP protocols	Microsoft-derived TCP/IP protocols (SMB), some standard TCP/IP protocols	TCP/IP protocols
Management Environment	SNMP	Microsoft/Intel software package based on DMI and WBEM	SNMP

Table 14-3.   The NC Reference and Two Implementations

have grown up with terminal-based access to mainframe data and applications. In fact, the general concept of network computers is very similar to that of terminal networks, with the significant difference that NCs have sufficient computing power to participate as active members in client/server architectures. For terminal-based users, NCs offer the same functionality as IBM3270, IBM5250, VT100, and other terminal types, but provide more options for future expansion. On the other hand, terminal-based users may be initially resistant at having to learn a GUI to get to their familiar terminal interface.

NCs will work best in specific situations, such as for users who work with only a few applications, who share machines, or who work at remote locations where it is difficult to provide technical support. NCs also will fit in well for users performing tasks that revolve around central data stores, acting as an upgrade for older character-based terminals that will be better capable of working in the growing number of intranet environments. Since NCs are not designed to the needs of power users, don't force them to use an NC. Let them use a workstation adequate to their assigned tasks. The more knowledgeable users will often act as their own technical support anyway (admittedly, this is sometimes a mixed blessing for the official system support groups, as knowledgeable users can occasionally cause significantly more havoc when they reach their personal threshold of incompetence).

THE WEB EATS THE NETWORK

The World Wide Web has experienced explosive growth since its beginnings in 1992, with millions of users using the Web for a seemingly infinite variety of uses. Part of the Web's growth has come from extending the Web to encompass some of the older formats of information on the Internet, such as Usenet newsgroups, and from the ability of most web browsers to act as FTP clients as well. Other areas of the Web's growth have arisen from the fact that HTML forms are a simple and highly platform-independent way of creating a distributed client/server application. It is therefore unsurprising to observe the numbers of system and network administration tools that have appeared to allow access to administrative functions via a web browser. The addition of Java as an Internet standard language and platform has merely increased this trend, especially with Sun's introduction of JMAPI (Java Management API). This section will deal with some of the Web-based management approaches that have appeared and are expected to appear in the near future.

Before beginning this section, it is necessary to define what Web-based management is and is not, in order to reduce confusion. Web-based management is the use of World Wide Web server and browser technology for viewing, identifying, and reporting enterprise-scale network and systems management data. Web-based management technology can be used to monitor and sometimes configure the following types of network parameters: LAN traffic, UNIX host IP addresses, router congestion, or mainframe network throughput, to name a few examples. Web management, however, refers to a different problem space: the tools and functions required to manage web servers, firewalls, and related content and subsystems.

This section will begin by discussing the beginnings of this trend in developing browser interfaces for viewing systems and network status. It will then move into a discussion of new standards such as Sun's Java Management API and the Web-Based Enterprise Management standard.

The Browser Interface

A widespread development among network management application vendors has been the addition of web browser interfaces as an alternative access method to their existing management strategies. Most network management platforms, such as HP OpenView, SunNet Manager, and IBM's NetView for AIX, were designed primarily to be used by network engineers and administrators.

Other members of the business now want access to the information available from the enterprise's network management applications. A remote administrator needs to identify points of failure rapidly, without physically traveling about the corporate network. A user wants to identify the source of a delay, whether it is a temporary or systemic bottleneck. Senior management personnel want to know the network's status because of its effect on the business's financial status. For many of these users, full administrator access is unnecessary, if not an actual danger: Having a control in reach increases the odds that that control will be triggered, either by intention, ignorance, or accident.

Corporate savings arise from the reduction of calls or other contacts users make to the help desk or call center. Instead of calling technical support when the network is perceived as being slow, users can investigate network delays on their own, and not interrupt the support staff in the middle of trying to solve the failure. To satisfy many of these users, system and network administrators want to offer viewer access to some subgroup of the information available in their network management applications. As a well-known and widespread user interface, a web browser is an appropriate choice for providing a monitoring window on the network's status. The view-only browsing nature of the HyperText Transport Protocol behavior also provides a "look, but don't touch" one-way window into the network. Some users, such as the remote LAN administrator, may need to interact with the network or system components in order to manage those components.

Tribe, a router manufacturer, produced one of the earliest examples of Web-based management, providing a tool for viewing and configuring its routers, built from web forms, as early as 1995. With WebManage, administrators could configure ports, protocols and users, as well as get a snapshot of current router activity. Unlike logging into the router through telnet, passwords were transmitted in encrypted form. As a device connected to the Internet almost by definition, WebManage also provided direct links to Tribe's online manuals, technical support, and FTP server. Figure 14-2 presents a control page of the WebManage application.

Other network management software vendors started adding browser interfaces to many of their products, from management frameworks to routers. Hewlett-Packard ships a free web viewer for the main component of Hewlett-Packard's OpenView. Cisco

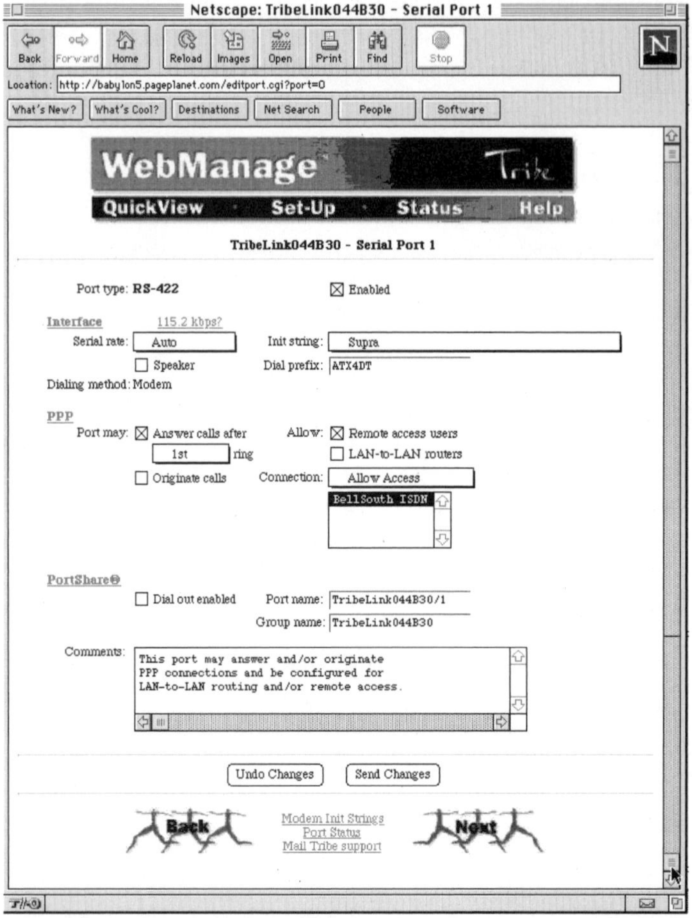

Figure 14-2. Tribe's WebManage allowed router management over the World Wide Web

includes a web server with its operating system for Cisco routers, allowing users to view as well as configure the status of routers and switches from a browser.

Turner View

One early and successful example of this trend was Turner Broadcasting Systems. TBS created a web browser interface for its network management application, allowing its information support staff to view status information without requiring the expense of an X terminal or workstation.

Named Turner View, their assembled solution is comprised of Hewlett-Packard Co.'s OpenView management framework, Seagate Software's NerveCenter for event management and filtering, and several internally developed applications correlating the pieces. Administrators use a web browser to view an OpenView log to identify the status of a single node or larger portions of the network.

IPSwitch's What'sUp is a scalable network monitor that runs on Windows 95 or Windows NT servers, and can be used for monitoring a wide variety of components of the network. In addition, the What'sUp Gold version incorporates a small, self-contained World Wide Web server that allows the remote monitoring of network data from anywhere that can reach the What'sUp server. Figure 14-3 shows an example of a remote view of a node on a network.

For more information, visit IPSwitch's World Wide Web site at **http://www.ipswitch.com**.

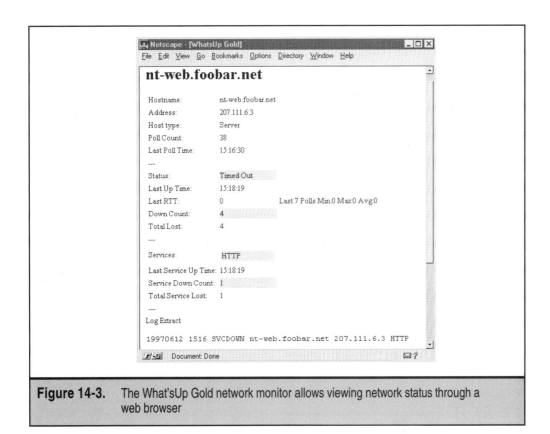

Figure 14-3.   The What'sUp Gold network monitor allows viewing network status through a web browser

NetID

Isotro's NetID allows network administrators in remote locations to administer aspects of their networks, including IP addressing and DNS and DHCP administration. Using a Sybase or Oracle database to provide a central storage of identifier information, administrators may access the database either through a NetID Admin Tool GUI or a web browser. Existing identifier information, such as DNS zone information files, UNIX host files, BOOTP tab files, and others, may be imported into the database. The DNS server is automatically updated at configurable intervals as DNS records in the database are modified. A World Wide Web interface is provided, which allows administrators to add, modify, and delete IP address and domain name data. Customizable profiles allow users to control the format of the displayed data.

Web Administration for Microsoft Windows NT Server

The Web Administration for Microsoft Windows NT Server package allows remote administration of Microsoft Windows NT Server using existing web browsers. The package does not allow control identical to that of working at a Windows NT computer, in that it doesn't support the complete range of administrative tools described in the "Windows NT Server's Built-In Utilities" section of this chapter. Still, the package does allow several tasks to be performed from non-Windows NT workstations. The Web Administration package can be installed on a server running Windows NT Server and Microsoft Internet Information Server. Servers must support Basic Authentication or Windows NT Challenge Response security. If the browser you use supports Secure Sockets Layer (SSL) encryption of a session, the server side of the Web Administration process also supports SSL.

You may install the Web Administration software on any server that runs Windows NT Server 4.0 and Microsoft Internet Information Server (IIS). IIS is required because the Web Administration tool is an ISAPI.DLL, and the IIS service is required to make the API calls into ISAPI.DLL (other web servers do not support the ISAPI.DLLs). Installing the Web Administration software on the server causes the server to publish web pages that include forms you can use to administer that particular server. Accessing the Web Administration pages is accomplished by entering the URL **http://<your_server_name>/ntadmin/ntadmin.htm** and beginning your work.

The administrative interface is a set of HTML pages designed to resemble the normal look of the Windows NT administrative tools. Some of the sections of the web interface include the following:

▼ The Account Management section allows you to view, create, disable, edit and delete user accounts and properties, as well as change user passwords. You can also view, create, edit and delete groups, and add workstations to that domain.

■ The Share Management section gives an administrator the ability to view, create, and change permissions for shares for all installed file services.

■ The Session Management section allows administrators to view and delete current sessions, and to send pop-up broadcast messages to current logged-in users.

■ The Server Management section allows remote administrators to shut down the server and view and change server services and driver configuration. The system, application, and security log event files may be viewed, and the current server configuration may be viewed and saved to a file.

▲ The Printer Management section allows administrators to view print queues and their current jobs, and to pause or delete entire print queues or specific print jobs.

Web-Related Initiatives

As described in "The Browser Interface" section of this chapter, web browsers and web forms are used primarily for viewing system and network status, with limited control capabilities. Most management applications have interfaces, methods of information gathering, and report formats that are often radically different from each other. This inconsistency causes administrators to have to launch separate applications for different components of the system and network. While these low-level applications or agents don't communicate with each other, they can often report information to a framework. A framework is a larger management application that is traditionally used to see an overview of a network's status. There are two industry initiatives intended to aid integration of system and network monitoring and management tools: Sun's Java Management API, and the Web-Based Enterprise Management consortium. This section will discuss these two evolving initiatives.

Sun's Java Management API

Sun's Java Management API (JMAPI) is part of Sun's Java Standard Extension API framework, providing a set of extensible objects and methods for building applets that can manage a network. JMAPI uses remote method invocation (RMI) as its remote communication mechanism. For a loose analogy, RMI can be categorized as the Java version of remote procedure calls (RPCs).

Backed by a wide range of networking and management companies, JMAPI is intended to assist developers in writing applets, or small Java applications, that can be downloaded across Internet links. This dynamic loading of code as required allows administrators to perform diagnostic functions from any device, even if that device is not attached to an SNMP management workstation. With the object-oriented nature of Java, the applets will aid in establishing relationship links between management applications and network components to more rapidly identify the true cause of a system or network failure.

Sun's engineers have used the JMAPI to build a web interface for Solaris' JumpStart automatic configuration technology. The web-enabled software includes different APIs for installation, configuration, registration, and licensing, and can also perform uninstalls, reinstalls, or upgrades. Sun has stated the long-term plan is to Java-enable the entire suite of Solstice Solaris administration tools, although it has been confirmed that a command line interface will remain part of Solaris.

Other companies are developing Java applications for other management uses. Applets have been developed that allow remote administrators with a web browser to view all applications running on a server. The applet dynamically updates, and allows administrators to find state information and shut down or pause an application as needed. Other Java applets can be used to display a real-time graph of transaction processing rates. More information on JMAPI is available at **http://java.sun.com/APIext/JMAPI**.

WBEM

The Web-Based Enterprise Management (WBEM) industry initiative establishes an architecture that supports the management of an enterprise across a network. The WBEM architecture is intended to define the structures and conventions required to access information about objects being managed, and to centralize information for analysis and support, as well as to provide location-transparent access to managed objects for remote administrators' control. The WBEM group intends to define an umbrella set of standards that merges DMI, HTTP, and SNMP into an architecture that can be viewed and modified by any standard web browser. WBEM was designed to be compatible with major existing management protocols, including SNMP, DMI, and CMIP. A wide range of companies, including Cisco, Compaq, Intel, and Microsoft, are participating in the WBEM initiative, many of whom are also working with JMAPI. WBEM also defines a new protocol for access of management information, in order to allow management solutions to be platform independent and physically distributed across the enterprise. This protocol is known as the HyperMedia Management Protocol (HMMP).

HMMP   HMMP provides management services across platform boundaries by defining a common network access model, schema, and security model. HMMP is a transport-independent protocol that uses a request-response paradigm to represent management activities. In a familiar client/server model, a client makes requests concerning a management task. An HMMP server processes the requested task and returns the appropriate response. An HMMP server may act as a client of yet another server in order to complete the task the first client requested of it.

HMOM AND HMMS   HyperMedia Object Manager (HMOM) is a software development technology that enables WBEM-compliant applications to manage network elements as objects. HyperMedia Management Schema (HMMS) was designed as an extensible data model of the managed network environment. The HMMS portion of WBEM was rejected by the Desktop Management Task Force, and its inclusion in WBEM is presently in limbo. More information on the WBEM initiative is available on the World Wide Web at **http://wbem.freerange.com**.

Web-based Management Tradeoffs

As shown, web-based management strategies are becoming common. Some of the advantages of such an approach are presented here:

▼ Universal viewing of management applications—Administrators do not have to use an X terminal or a UNIX workstation to view a management framework application.

■ Low cost—A PC or Macintosh desktop equipped with a browser costs much less than a typical X terminal or UNIX workstation configured to run a management framework. Also, with many current management products adding a web interface, any current investment in hardware or applications licenses and training is not wasted.

■ Ease of use—Administrators will require less training because the browser metaphor is familiar to most people. The ease of use translates to a shorter learning curve before an administrator becomes productive.

■ Reduced external technical support costs—Management applications can often require extensive training and experience before an administrator becomes productive. Management applications themselves also may require significant configuration and support costs.

■ Reduced external technical support costs—Users can check the state of the network themselves. This can reduce call volume to the organization's help desk.

▲ Better interoperability—An administrator can use a browser to switch between multiple management applications at various levels. A browser can also access vendors' help sites on the Internet, allowing the vendor to update and correct the documentation quickly.

However, some perceive problems with aspects of Web-based management, citing the following:

▼ Decreased security.

■ Inconsistency between Java Virtual Machines (JVMs), causing applets to work differently or not at all on different platforms.

■ Java is still an immature language.

▲ The proliferation of Java applets on networks will create other management concerns besides security, such as bandwidth and version-management issues.

For example, users may tire of downloading Java applets. Caching Java applets on a local machine may reduce this problem, but the JVM environments do not presently include a method of controlling the version of the Java applets cached on the local machine. Many feel that the security issues with browser-based management are no worse than traditional approaches, given that much current system management occurs over a telnet session, with logins and passwords passed in unencrypted ASCII format over the network. As for Java being an immature language in comparison to more mature object-oriented programming languages, such as Smalltalk, that is true now. However,

Sun's commitment to move their administration tools into Java implies they and others will continue to improve the usefulness of the language.

SUMMARY

System and network management is becoming more difficult all the time. With the rapid growth of networks, administrators are constantly asked to make different computer systems communicate with each other—preferably seamlessly, transparent to the user, reliably, inexpensively, and "get it done today." Various attempts have been made to extend portions of networks outwards, with varying degrees of success and general acceptance: NFS for file services, TCP/IP printing, distributed login capability offered earlier by the Open Software Foundation's Distributed Computing Environment (DCE) (and more recently offered to an extent by Windows NT), the Common Desktop Environment (CDE) GUI offered for most versions of UNIX and Windows NT, and so on. Some of these solutions are even free or inexpensive, as in the case of Samba for file and print services.

Network Computers are a current trend designed to reduce the high cost of information systems support. By being standardized and minimally configurable, they are supposed to be easier to manage than normal UNIX or PC workstations. However, Network Computers are not for everyone: few business facilities are going to completely replace their workstations with Network Computers. Network Computers may provide less savings than predicted, as many businesses already have standardized their workstation configurations by job level and expected use, in order to realize quantity savings on bulk ordering as well as making the administrators' jobs easier. While Network Computers may be even easier than standardized PC workstations to set up and maintain, they may not realize as drastic a savings as predicted for all adopters.

One of the true enemies of system administration is time: no time to keep up with system security notices, to perform routine tasks, and to solve problems before they become critical nightmares. Since distance takes time to travel, good distributed system and network management tools that allow fast remote diagnosis and reconfiguration or repair without having to physically travel from a given location save the travel time. That is, if the travel time saved is not outweighed by the time spent on evaluating, acquiring, installing, and learning the distributed management tool. Some of the higher-end distributed system management tools are reported to have a horrifically steep learning curve before competence is attained. There is also a tradeoff of simplicity versus detail, in that if a picture is clear and simple enough to take in at a glance, it's likely that important information may have been filtered out along with the noise. However, distributed management tools will continue to evolve and improve.

APPENDIX A

sendmail Frequently Asked Questions

Last updated May 12, 1997
Copyright 1996, by Brad Knowles, all rights reserved
(*reprinted with permission*)

This FAQ is edited and maintained by Brad Knowles, **brad@etext.org**. The official archive for all FAQs posted to **news:news.answers** is **ftp://rtfm.mit.edu/pub/usenet/ news.answers/**, with many known mirrors. On this site, the latest version of this FAQ can be found in **ftp://rtfm.mit.edu/pub/usenet/news.answers/mail/sendmail-faq/**. Since this server tends to be extremely busy, as an alternative, you might want to try using **http://www.imc.org/sendmail-faq-1** and **http://www.imc.org/sendmail-faq-2** instead.

If you don't have access to FTP or WWW, this FAQ can be retrieved by sending Internet email to **mail-server@rtfm.mit.edu** with an empty subject line (it gets ignored) and the command "send usenet/news.answers/mail/sendmail-faq/part*" as the body of the message (omitting the quotes, of course).

As an alternative, you might want to try sending Internet email to **info@imc.org** with an empty subject line (it gets ignored) and "send sendmail-faq-*" as the body of the message (again, omitting the quotes).

Additional alternative access methods are detailed within.

The intent is to ultimately make this document more web-friendly (in that all original work is done in SGML), and, using sgml-tools (was the linuxdoc-sgml package), automatically generate both the HTML and ASCII text versions, automatically posting the ASCII version to **comp.mail.sendmail** as appropriate.

In the meanwhile, all pseudo-HTMLized versions of this FAQ are considered unsupported. We cannot be held responsible for what someone else's program does to this document in an attempt to make it more web-friendly. Nevertheless, the Landfield Hypertext Usenet FAQ Archive seems to work well, and if you must access the **comp.mail.sendmail** FAQ via the Web, try slinging over to **http://www.landfield.com/ faqs/mail/sendmail-faq/**.

Comments/updates should be sent to **sendmail-faq@etext.org**.

Table of Contents

PART ONE

0. TO DO

1. COPYRIGHT NOTICE/REDISTRIBUTION REQUIREMENTS

2. INTRODUCTION/MISCELLANEOUS

2.1 What is this newsgroup?
2.2 What is the scope of this FAQ?
2.3 Where can I find the latest version of this FAQ?
2.4 How do I access **comp.mail.sendmail** by email?
2.5 Where can I ask email-related DNS questions?

PART TWO

4. GENERAL SENDMAIL ISSUES

4.1 Should I use a wildcard MX for my domain?

4.2 How can I set up an auto-responder?

4.3 How can I get sendmail to deliver local mail to *$HOME/.mail* instead of into */usr/spool/mail* (or */usr/mail*)?

4.4 Why does it deliver the mail interactively when I'm trying to get it to go into queue-only mode?

4.5 How can I solve "config error: mail loops back to myself" messages?

4.6 Why does my sendmail process sometimes hang when connecting over a SLIP/PPP link?

4.7 How can I summarize the statistics generated by sendmail in the syslog?

4.8 How can I check my *sendmail.cf* to ensure that it's re-writing addresses correctly?

4.9 What is procmail, and where can I get it?

4.10 How can I solve "cannot alias non-local names" errors?

5. VENDOR/OS-SPECIFIC SENDMAIL ISSUES

5.1 Sun Microsystems SunOS/Solaris 1.*x*/2.*x*

5.1.1 How can I solve "line 273: replacement $3 out of bounds" errors?

5.1.2 How can I solve "line 445: bad ruleset 96 (50 max)" errors?

5.1.3 Why does version 8 sendmail (< 8.7.5) sometimes hang under Solaris 2.5?

5.1.4 Why can't I use SunOS/Solaris to get email to certain large sites?

5.2 IBM AIX

5.2.1 The system resource controller always reports sendmail as "inoperative." What's wrong?

5.2.2 Why can't I use AIX to get email to some sites?

5.2.3 Why can't I get sendmail 8.7.1 to use MX records with AIX 3.2.5?

6. ADDITIONAL INFORMATION SOURCES (RFC 1807 bibliography format)

6.1 Reference Material Devoted Exclusively to sendmail

6.2 Reference Material with Chapters or Sections on sendmail

6.3 Reference Material on Subjects Related to sendmail

6.4 World Wide Web Index Pages on sendmail

6.5 World Wide Web Index Pages on Internet Email in General

6.6 Online Tutorials for sendmail

6.7 Online Archives of Mailing Lists and Usenet Newsgroups Relating to Internet Email

7. THANKS!

Q0—TO DO LIST

▼ Make the FAQ more web-friendly by writing it in SGML and using sgml-tools (was the linuxdoc-sgml package) to automate the generation of the HTML and ASCII text versions.

■ Index

■ Additional net resources (web pages, anonymous ftp sites, etc.)

■ Larger, more clearly written annotated bibliography (including RFCs and comments/corrections for books specific to sendmail)

▲ Reorganize by platform/version of sendmail (All Sun questions in one section, all AIX questions in another, etc.)

Q1—COPYRIGHT NOTICE/REDISTRIBUTION REQUIREMENTS

The entire contents of this document are copyright 1996 by Brad Knowles, all rights reserved.

This document may be freely distributed for non-profit purposes (including, but not limited to: posting to mailing lists, Usenet newsgroups, and World Wide Web pages; inclusion on CD-ROM or other distribution media; and insertion into text retrieval systems), so long as it is the latest version available at the time, all parts are distributed together, and it is kept completely intact without editing, changes, deletions, or additions. Non-profit redistribution in accordance with these guidelines does not require contact with or approval from the copyright holder.

Redistribution of this document for profit without express prior permission is not allowed. At the very least, expect to provide the copyright holder a free copy of the product (exactly as it would be sold to customers, all distribution media intact), or a percentage of the gross revenue from said product and sufficient proof that the integrity and completeness requirements set for non-profit distribution will be met.

In the event that the copyright holder discovers a redistributed version that is not in compliance with the above requirements, he will make a good-faith effort to get it corrected or removed, and failing that, at least note its deprecated status in a new version. Legal action will likely be taken against redistribution for profit that is not in compliance with the above requirements.

Q2.1—What is this newsgroup?

The Usenet newsgroup **news:comp.mail.sendmail** is dedicated to the discussion of the program named "sendmail" in all its various forms. It is most commonly found on computers running a flavor of the Operating System known as UNIX, or derived from UNIX.

This program has been ported to other OSes, but those versions have typically been ported by a particular vendor and are considered proprietary. There are many versions of sendmail, but the original author (Eric Allman) is continuing development on a particular version typically referred to as "Version Eight," or sometimes just "V8." This is considered by many to be the One True Version. This is also the version that this FAQ is centered around.

If you have a question that amounts to, "How do I send mail to my friend?", then you're in the wrong newsgroup. You should first check with your System or E-Mail Administrator(s), BBS SysOp(s), etc., before you post your question publicly, since the answer will likely be very highly dependent on what software and hardware you have. You also don't want to embarass yourself publicly, nor do you want to annoy the kinds of people who are likely to be the counterparts of your System or E-Mail Administrator(s), BBS SysOp(s), etc. If asking them doesn't do you any good, make sure you read this FAQ and the other mail-related FAQs at the archive sites listed below.

If you have a question about another program similar to sendmail (technically referred to as an "SMTP MTA"), an SMTP Gateway package, or a LAN email package, then you should see if there is another group in the **news:comp.mail** hierarchy that more closely matches the particular program you want to ask a question about. For example, the SMTP MTA known as Smail has **news:comp.mail.smail** dedicated to it. The Mail User Agent (MUA) Eudora has two newsgroups dedicated to it (**news:comp.mail.eudora.mac** and **news:comp.mail.eudora.ms-windows**), depending on which hardware platform you use. If there isn't a more appropriate newsgroup, try **news:comp.mail.misc**. Again, make sure your question isn't already addressed in one of the mail-related FAQs or other available documentation. See the IMC website (more info below) for a good list of mail-related FAQs.

If you have a question about an older or vendor-proprietary version of sendmail, be prepared for a lot of answers that amount to, "Get V8." Version 8 isn't a panacea, but it does solve many problems known to plague previous versions, as well as having many new features that make it much easier to administer large or complex sites. In many cases, it makes at least possible what was previously virtually impossible, and relatively easy the previously difficult.

There are, of course, many alternative programs that have sprung up in an attempt to answer one or another weakness or perceived fault of sendmail, but so far, none of them have had the kind of success it would require to unseat it as the de facto standard program for sending Internet mail. Obviously, this forum should not be used to discuss the merits of any of the alternative programs versus sendmail. These kinds of discussions should be taken to **news:comp.mail.misc**, or you should agitate to get a new newsgroup or newsgroup hierarchy created where that sort of thing is acceptable (or even the norm, such as a **news:comp.mail.advocacy** or **news:comp.mail.mta.advocacy** newsgroup).

Q2.2—What is the scope of this FAQ?

This FAQ is strongly centered around version 8 sendmail, for many reasons. First and foremost, this is the area of most interest on the part of the maintainer of this FAQ. Secondly, version 8 is where most of the additional development is being concentrated.

Version 8 sendmail is also the best documented of all SMTP MTAs, by virtue of the book by Bryan Costales (see entry sendmail-faq//book/ISBN/1-56592-222-0 in Q6.1).

Other versions of sendmail get mentioned in passing, and some interesting interactions between version 8 and various OSes are also covered.

This FAQ is aimed primarily at the experienced UNIX System Administrator/Postmaster/DNS Domain Administrator. If you're looking for introductory texts, see the references in Q6.1.

Where I've provided URLs, I've generally tried to keep them exactly as they should be entered, without line breaks or anything else. This may make them or the surrounding text ugly, but hopefully they'll be easier to cut-and-paste, or just click on once I've got an HTMLized version. However, this has not been possible in the bibliography section, since I'm trying to adhere to RFC 1807 guidelines, and they explicitly require lines to be no longer than 79 characters. In those cases, I've tried to break the lines at relatively obvious and innocuous places.

Q2.3—Where can I find the latest version of this FAQ?

▼ I post changes as they occur to my sendmail FAQ support page at **http://www.his.com/pub/brad/sendmail/**.

■ The ASCII text of my private version can be found at **ftp://ftp.his.com/pub/brad/sendmail/sendmail-faq/part***, while the latest "single part" version before the split can be found at **ftp://ftp.his.com/pub/brad/sendmail/sendmail-faq/old**. I don't have an HTMLized version yet, but when I do, I will put in a link to it from my support page as well as updating this document.

■ The official version (as posted to **news:news.answers**) is in **ftp://rtfm.mit.edu/pub/usenet/news.answers/mail/sendmail-faq/**.

▲ The Internet Mail Consortium **http://www.imc.org** maintains an archive of email-related FAQs and many other documents. On their site, the latest version of this FAQ can be found in **http://www.imc.org/sendmail-faq-1** and **http://www.imc.org/sendmail-faq-2**.

Unfortunately, the parser for the Ohio State semi-official pseudo-HTMLized version tends to misinterpret the way I provide URLs, so I no longer support it or provide the URL for this FAQ at that site. However, Kent Landfield has put together an alternative web archive of Usenet FAQs, and it appears to parse things in a more sensible manner.

The root of the Landfield FAQ archive is at **http://www.landfield.com/faqs/**, and the **comp.mail.sendmail** FAQ can be found at **http://www.landfield.com/faqs/mail/sendmail-faq/**.

▼ The Landfield Usenet Hypertext FAQ Archive supports full text searching with multiple ways to access Usenet's Frequently Asked Question postings. Hyperlinks are enabled wherever possible to make references easy to follow. A full set of FAQ statistics is also available.

■ If you don't have access to FTP or WWW, this FAQ can be retrieved by sending Internet email to **mail-server@rtfm.mit.edu** with an empty subject line (it gets ignored) and the command "send usenet/news.answers/mail/ sendmail-faq/ part*" as the body of the message (omitting the quotes, of course).

▲ Since this server tends to be extremely busy, as an alternative, you might want to try sending Internet email to **info@imc.org** with an empty subject line (it gets ignored) and "send sendmail-faq-*" as the body of the message (again, omitting the quotes).

Well-known mirrors for the FAQs archived at **rtfm.mit.edu** can be found at:

Continent	URL
North America	**ftp://mirrors.aol.com/pub/rtfm/usenet/**
	ftp://ftp.uu.net/usenet/news.answers/
	ftp://ftp.seas.gwu.edu/pub/rtfm/
	http://www.landfield.com/faqs/
Europe	**ftp://ftp.uni-paderborn.de/pub/FAQ/**
	ftp://ftp.Germany.EU.net/pub/newsarchive/news.answers/
	ftp://ftp.sunet.se/pub/usenet/
	http://www.cs.ruu.nl/cgi-bin/faqwais/
	http://www.lib.ox.ac.uk/internet/news/faq/by_group.index.html
Asia	**ftp://nctuccca.edu.tw/USENET/FAQ/**
	ftp://hwarang.postech.ac.kr/pub/usenet/news.answers/
	ftp://ftp.hk.super.net/mirror/faqs/
Australia	**ftp://ftp.info.au/usenet/FAQs/**

▼ Additional information on how to get access to various Internet resources by email can be found in Bob Rankin's Internet-by-Email FAQ, **ftp://rtfm.mit.edu/ pub/usenet/news.answers/internet-services/access-via-email**.

■ To get the latest edition of this document sent to you by return email, send a message to one of these addresses:

To: **mail-server@rtfm.mit.edu** (for US, Canada, and South America)

Enter only this line in the BODY of the note:

  send usenet/news.answers/internet-services/access-via-email

To: **mailbase@mailbase.ac.uk** (for Europe, Asia, etc.)

Enter only this line in the BODY of the note:

    send lis-iis e-access-inet.txt

Q2.4—How do I access comp.mail.sendmail by email?

Send email to **mxt@dl.ac.uk** with the command "sub comp-news.comp.mail.sendmail full-US-ordered-email-address" as the body of the message (with your correct address in place of the "full-US-ordered-email-address," and omitting the double quotes in all cases of this example).

E-mail you want posted on **comp.mail.sendmail** should be sent to **comp-mail-sendmail@dl.ac.uk**.

Q2.5—Where can I ask email-related DNS questions?

Depending on how deeply they get into the DNS, they can be asked here. However, you'll probably be told that you should send them to the Usenet newsgroup **news:comp.protocols.tcp-ip.domains** (DNS in general) or to the Info-BIND mailing list (if the question is specific to that program).

Q2.6—How can I subscribe to these?

For **news:comp.protocols.tcp-ip.domains**, you have to be on Usenet. They don't have a news-to-mail gateway yet (I'm working on this), but they do have a FAQ, and it can be found at **ftp://ftp.njit.edu/pub/dns/Comp.protocols.tcp-ip.domains.FAQ**.

Questions from all levels of experience can be found on this newsgroup (as well as people to answer them), so don't be shy about asking a question you think may be too simple.

For the Info-BIND mailing list, send email to **bind-request@vix.com** with an empty subject (it gets ignored) and the command "subscribe" as the body of the message. Submissions should be sent to **bind@vix.com**.

Note that this list is now moderated, and anything you post to it may get material added, deleted, or changed by the moderator. He reserves the right to reject any postings (and possibly unsubscribe the poster) if he deems them inappropriate.

Q2.7—Which version of sendmail should I run?

If you're concerned at all about the security of your machines, you should make sure you're at least running a recent release of version 8 sendmail (either from your vendor, or the public version detailed in 1.8).

Check the CERT Alerts and Summaries (details in 1.13) to make sure that you're running a version that is free of known security holes. Just because the sendmail program provided by your vendor isn't listed doesn't mean that you're not vulnerable, however. If your particular vendor or version isn't listed, check with your vendor and on the appropriate Internet mailing lists and Usenet newsgroups to verify.

If nothing else, the most recent public version is usually a pretty good bet, although you should check **news:comp.mail.sendmail** to see if anyone has posted recent comments that haven't yet been folded into a new release.

That said, you need to look at what the primary function is for the machine. If its primary function is to run some CAD/CAM package on the desk of an engineer, then there's probably not much sense in replacing the vendor-supplied version of sendmail (assuming it's secure, according to the CERT Alerts and Summaries). Just set the machine up to forward all outbound mail to a central mail relay, and then worry about making that central mail relay the best it can be.

Also arrange to have all their inbound mail pass through a central Mail eXchanger (probably the same machine as the central Mail Relay), for the same reasons.

If the primary function for a machine is to act as that central Mail Relay/Mail eXchanger, then I *strongly* recommend the best version of sendmail you can get, and in my opinion that is the latest release of version 8. IDA sendmail is also pretty good, but virtually everything it does, version 8 does better, and version 8 has the additional advantage of having continued development as well. On a central mailhub, recent versions of IDA sendmail are the oldest sendmail that I'd even consider leaving in place instead of replacing with version 8.

However, keep in mind that version 8 still hasn't been ported (so far as we know) to some of the older (and perhaps more esoteric) platforms, and if you're stuck using one of them, you may not have much choice.

Recently, some vendors have started shipping (or announced that they will soon ship) version 8 sendmail pre-configured for their machines. Unfortunately, in most cases this means you get a pre-compiled binary and a *sendmail.cf* file (that may need a bit of tweaking), but not much else of the "standard" version 8 sendmail installation kit. Silicon Graphics (SGI) is known to already be shipping version 8 sendmail in this fashion, and both Hewlett-Packard and Sun Microsystems have announced that they soon will be (Sun has a patch today that can be applied to upgrade many machines to an older release of version 8 sendmail).

This may be suitable for desktop machines forwarding all their mail to a central Mail Relay and receiving all their mail from a central Mail eXchanger, but I personally believe that this is not likely to be suitable for the central Mail Relay/Mail eXchanger itself. In that case, I recommend you get and install the latest version and get the m4 macros, the on-line documentation, the source code, etc.

Q2.8—What is the latest release of sendmail?

For version 8 sendmail, there are three release trees. For those people who, for whatever reason, are unable or unwilling to upgrade to version 8.8.z, releases of version 8.6 and 8.7 sendmail are still available. As of this writing, the most recent release of version 8.6 sendmail is 8.6.13, and the most recent release of version 8.7 sendmail is 8.7.6.

For the most recent releases of 8.6 and 8.7 sendmail, there is a version number difference between the sendmail program itself and the associated configuration files. This is okay. The security-related bug fixes that were made only required changes to the sendmail program itself and not the configuration files, so only the version number of the sendmail program itself was incremented.

The most recent release of version 8.8 sendmail is 8.8.5. On machines exposed directly to the Internet, you should either already be running 8.8.5 sendmail or plan on upgrading to it in the immediate future. This release is considered "mature," has security fixes included that will not be found in any previous release, and therefore supercedes all previous releases.

There is no further support for previous releases of sendmail.

Q2.9—Where can I find it?

By anonymous FTP from **ftp.sendmail.org** in */pub/sendmail*, or (in URL form) via **ftp://ftp.sendmail.org/pub/sendmail/**. If you care, there should be files in this directory that end with the extension ".sig" which you can check with PGP to make sure that corresponding archives haven't been modified. You'll need to have the PGP key of Eric Allman on your public keyring to be able to verify these archives with their associated .sig files.

Current releases of sendmail can also be found at **ftp://ftp.cs.berkeley.edu/ucb/src/sendmail/**.

There are no other known official version 8 sendmail mirrors.

Check the sendmail home page at **http://www.sendmail.org/** for late-breaking updates and other useful information.

If you want to be notified regarding future updates to sendmail and other items of potential interest, you may want to subscribe to the sendmail-announce mailing list. Address your subscription requests to **majordomo@lists.sendmail.org** with "subscribe sendmail-announce" as the body of the message.

Q2.10—What are the differences between Version 8 and other versions?

See *doc/changes/changes.{me,ps}* in the distribution. See also RELEASE_NOTES at the top level.

Q2.11—What's the best platform for running sendmail?

Generally speaking, I adhere to the old axiom that you should choose what software you want to run first, then choose the platform (hardware and OS) that best runs this software. By this token, if sendmail is the software, then a recent version of BSD UNIX would probably be best, since sendmail was developed at UC Berkeley on BSD UNIX. FreeBSD and BSD/OS are two known implementations of BSD UNIX for Intel-based PCs (among other hardware platforms), and this would make them the most "native" OSes for sendmail. FreeBSD is freely available by anonymous ftp or on CD-ROM, and BSD/OS is a commercial product.

However, not everyone has this kind of "luxury." If you're on a homogenous network (i.e., completely composed of only one type of hardware and OS), then you should probably be running the same OS as the rest of the machines on the network, regardless of the axiom stated above. You may have other problems, but you should at least be able to get some local support on the OS for your machine.

Either way, if the primary function of the machine is to handle "large" quantities of mail (for whatever value you define "large" to be), I strongly recommend getting the latest stable release of version 8 sendmail.

You may be surprised to find that it is easier for you to support only one version of sendmail across all the various platforms than it is to try to support multiple versions of sendmail, each unique for their particular platform. In that case, the easy solution is to put version 8 sendmail everywhere, and not have to worry about vendor-specific problems with older versions.

For more information on BSD UNIX in general, see the Usenet newsgroups under **news:comp.unix.bsd**, **news:comp.bugs.4bsd**, **news:comp.os.386bsd**. For more information on BSD/OS, see the BSD newsgroups mentioned above, or the BSD/OS Home Page at **http://www.bsdi.com/**. For more information on FreeBSD, see the Usenet newsgroups under **news:comp.unix.bsd.freebsd**, or the FreeBSD Home Page at **http://www.freebsd.org/**.

Q2.12—What is BIND, and where can I get the latest version?

BIND stands for "Berkeley Internet Name Daemon" and is the Internet de-facto standard program for turning host names into IP addresses.

The BIND Home Page is at **http://www.isc.org/bind.html**, which provides pointers to the most recent release of BIND. Note that BIND 4.9.5-P1 is the most recent "production version," and BIND 8.1 (the next major release; skipping 5.x-7.x) is a "release candidate" as of version 8.1T3B. See the BIND 8.1T3B announcement at **ftp://ftp.isc.org/isc/bind/src/testing/t3b-ann.asc** for more information.

Note that there are bugs in older resolver libraries, which can cause problems getting to large sites (that list more than five IP addresses for a particular name), or represent a huge security hole as they do not check the returned data to see if it will fit in the amount of space pre-allocated for it.

If at all possible, you should get the most recent "release" version of BIND and make a serious attempt to integrate it into your configuration, since virtually all vendor-provided resolver libaries are woefully out of date.

Q2.13—What is smrsh, and where can I get it?

From **ftp://info.cert.org/pub/tools/smrsh/README**:

"smrsh is a restricted shell utility that provides the ability to specify, through a configuration, an explicit list of executable programs. When used in conjunction with sendmail, smrsh effectively limits sendmail's scope of program execution to only those programs specified in smrsh's configuration."

smrsh has been written with portability in mind, and uses traditional UNIX library utilities. As such, smrsh should compile on most UNIX C compilers.

The purpose for restricting the list of programs that can be executed in this manner is to keep mail messages (either through an alias or the *.forward* file in a user's home directory) from being sent to arbitrary programs which are not necessarily known to be sufficiently paranoid in checking their input, and can therefore be easily subverted (this is related to, but different from, the *etc/shells* feature discussed in Q3.11).

More information regarding the CERT-CC can be found at their web site, **http://www.cert.org**. For more information on CERT Alerts and CERT Summaries, see **ftp://info.cert.org/pub/cert_advisories/** and **ftp://info.cert.org/pub/cert_summaries/**, respectively.

You can find smrsh in the most recent sendmail source archive, as well as **ftp://info.cert.org/pub/tools/smrsh/**. Other very useful programs can be found in **ftp://info.cert.org/pub/tools/**.

Q2.14—What is smap, and where can I get it?

smap (and smapd) are tools out of the Trusted Information Systems (TIS) Firewall Toolkit (fwtk). They were originally written by firewall expert Marcus Ranum under contract to TIS, and TIS is continuing what maintenance there is. The toolkit may be found at **ftp://ftp.tis.com/pub/firewalls/toolkit/**. Support questions regarding the toolkit may be sent to **mailto:fwall-support@tis.com**, while you may join their mailing list **mailto:fwall-users@tis.com** by sending electronic mail to **mailto:fwall-users-request@tis.com**.

The concept of smap and smapd is that sendmail is a huge, monolithic setuid root program that is virtually impossible to verify as being "correct" and free from bugs (historically, sendmail has been rather buggy and an easy mark for system crackers to exploit, although with the advent of version 8 sendmail, this becomes much more difficult). In contrast, smap and smapd are very small (only a few hundred lines long), and relatively easy to verify as being correct and functioning as designed (however, as you will see later, we can question their design). According to the theory, it is therefore safer and "better" to run smap and smapd as "wrappers" around sendmail, which would no longer need to be run setuid root.

Unfortunately, smap and smapd have a few problems of their own, and don't appear to have been updated since late March, 1996. There have been conflicting reports of incompatibilities between smapd and sendmail 8.7.*y* (both cannot be run on the same machine, although if you're running sendmail 8.6.*x* and smap/smapd on the local machine, people on the outside can still use sendmail 8.7 to talk to you).

For further information on smap and smapd, see the documentation that comes with the TIS Firewall Toolkit.

For more information on firewalls, see the Firewalls FAQ at **http://www.v-one.com/newpages/faq.htm**.

Q2.15—What is TCP-Wrappers, and where can I get it?

TCP-Wrappers is another security enhancement package. The theory is that you take programs being run under inetd (see *etc/inetd.conf*), and, before you run the program to do the real work (ftpd, telnetd, etc.), you first run the connection attempt through a package that checks to see if the IP address of the source packet is coming from a host known to be either good or bad (you may filter connection attempts by source host name, domain name, raw IP address, port they are attempting to connect to; and either allow known good connections through, thus refusing unknown connections, or accept all connections except those known to be bad).

```
tcsh: getwd: can't stat .
tcsh: Trying to start from "/home/b/bknowles"
tcsh: Trying to start from "/"
tcsh: getwd: can't stat .
tcsh: Trying to start from "/home/b/bknowles"
tcsh: Trying to start from "/"
```

The practice of TCP-Wrappers actually follows the theory quite well. It is a very useful and important tool in the System Administrator's Bag of Things To Help You Secure Your Machine From Crackers, Spammers, Junkmailers, and Other Undesirables. However, it only works for programs that communicate via TCP packets (not UDP, such as NFS) started up out of inetd. It does not work for RPC-based services, and programs that start up a daemon outside of inetd and just leave it running obviously don't benefit beyond the initial connection that gets the daemon started (however, see the FTP URL below for other packages that can help secure RPC and portmapper-based services).

However, most sendmail installations tend to start up a daemon and leave it running at all times. If you did run sendmail out of inetd, you'd lose the benefit of the load average checking code that is executed only in daemon mode, and for systems that handle a lot of mail, this is vitally important.

You can get TCP-Wrappers from **ftp://ftp.win.tue.nl/pub/security/**, a site that has a whole host of other useful security tools, such as securelib, portmap, satan, cops, crack, etc. You can also find pointers to many other useful security tools at **http://ciac.llnl.gov/ciac/SecurityTools.html**, and the COAST Archive at **http://www.cs.purdue.edu/homes/spaf/hotlists/csec.html** is a veritable cornucopia of all things security related. The SANS 1996 Network Security Roadmap at **http://www.sans.org/roadmap/** has much useful information and pointers to many other useful resources.

For the adventurous, you can get a source patch for version 8 sendmail (created for 8.7.6, but, with work, applicable to older releases) that will take the core TCP-Wrappers code and integrate it into the daemon, so that you get the best of both worlds. However, this isn't as smoothly integrated as it should be, is not for the faint-of-heart, and is certainly not officially supported by the orginal author of sendmail (Eric Allman). This functionality is integrated in a different fashion into version 8.8.5 sendmail.

You should be able to find the unsupported patch at **ftp://ftp.win.tue.nl/pub/security/sendmail-tcpd.patch**.

Q2.16—Why won't db 1.85 build on my machine?

The db 1.85 package as available from **ftp.cs.berkeley.edu** provides Irix support up to Irix 4.05F, but 5.{2,3} need a slightly patched version, as does HP-UX 10.20. Some vendors also provide db standard with their OS (DEC UNIX 4.0, for example).

A tarball incorporating these changes for Irix 5.*x* is available at **ftp://ftp.his.com/pub/brad/sendmail/irix5.tar.gz**. This will extract into *./db.1.85/PORT/irix.5.2*, with a symbolic link created from *./db.1.85/PORT/irix.5.3* to this same directory. Make sure you extract this archive into the same directory where you extracted the db 1.85 archive as available from **ftp.cs.berkeley.edu**. (See Q3.5 for more information on getting the db 1.85 package). An ASCII context diff of this same patch is at **ftp://ftp.his.com/pub/brad/sendmail/irix4-5.diff**.

A version of db 1.85 that has supposedly been patched to compile under Irix 6.2 has been made available at **http://reality.sgi.com/ariel/db-1.85-irix.tar.Z**, but I haven't had a chance to download and check it out yet.

The context diffs required to get db 1.85 working under HP-UX 10.20 are available at **ftp://ftp.his.com/pub/brad/sendmail/hpux.10.20.diff**. A tarball incorporating these changes is available at **ftp://ftp.his.com/pub/brad/sendmail/hp-ux.10.20.tar.gz**. This will extract into *./db.1.85/PORT/hpux.10.20*, so make sure you extract this archive into the same directory where you extracted the db 1.85 archive as available from **ftp.cs.berkeley.edu**.

Q2.17—What is makemap, and where can I get it?

The program "makemap" is used to build the databases used by version 8 sendmail, for things like the UserDB, mailertables, etc.

It is distributed as part of the basic operating system from some vendors, but source code for it is also included at the root level of the sendmail archive (at least, it is for sendmail 8.6.12 and 8.7.5, and presumably will continue to be as newer releases come out). However, it is not considered a "supported" part of version 8 sendmail. Just like the other source provided in the archive, the Makefile will likely need some tweaking for your specific site.

It turns out that Irix 5.3 doesn't appear to have the dbm or ndbm libraries, but to compile makemap.c, you need to have -DNDBM on the "DBMDEF=" line (some necessary things are defined only in */usr/include/ndbm.h*). Try just leaving off "-lndbm" from the "LIBS=" line in the Makefile for makemap.

If you plan on using makemap with db 1.85 on an SGI machine running a version of Irix later than 4.*x*, see Q2.16 for some additional steps to get db 1.85 compiled on your machine.

Q3.1—How do I make all my addresses appear to be from a single host?

Using the m4 macros, use

```
MASQUERADE_AS(my.dom.ain)
```

This will cause all addresses to be sent out as being from the indicated domain.

On your mailhub/mailhost/Domain Mail eXchanger, you may need to add "my.dom.ain" to the *sendmail.cw* file or the "Cwhost.my.dom.ain" line in the *sendmail.cf* file.

If you're using version 8.7 sendmail (or newer), and you want to hide this information in the envelope as well as the headers, use

```
FEATURE(masquerade_envelope)
```

Q3.2—How do I rewrite my From: lines to read "First_Last@My.Domain"?

There are a couple of ways of doing this. This describes using the "user database" code. This is still experimental, and was intended for a different purpose—however, it does work with a bit of care. It does require that you have the Berkeley "db" package installed (it won't work with DBM).

First, create your input file. This should have lines like

```
loginname:mailname      First_Last
First_Last:maildrop     loginname
```

If your login name is "john" and your full name is "John Q. Public," then this would be

```
john:mailname              John_Q_Public@your.domain.goes.here
John_Q_Public:maildrop     john
```

The words "mailname" and "maildrop" must be typed in literally, just as they appear. Install this file in (say) */etc/userdb*. Create the database:

```
makemap -d btree /etc/userdb.db < /etc/userdb
```

You can then create a config file that uses this. You will have to include the following in your *.mc* file:

```
define(confUSERDB_SPEC, /etc/userdb.db)
  FEATURE(notsticky)
```

Version 8.7 sendmail changes the semantics of this feature such that notsticky is turned on by default, and if you want the old (8.6) behaviour, you instead define

```
FEATURE(stickyhost)
```

You also need to make sure that you have the "ik" flags specified on the affected mailer definition.

Note: The program "makemap" is discussed in further detail in Q2.17. The UserDB feature is discussed further on pp. 643-645 of *sendmail, 2nd Ed.* by Costales.

Q3.3—Why are you so hostile to using full names for email addresses?

Because full names are not unique. For example, the computer community has two Andy Tannenbaums and two Peter Deutsches. At one time, Bell Labs had two Stephen R. Bournes with offices a few doors apart. You can create alternative addresses (e.g., Stephen_R_Bourne_2), but that's even worse—which one of them has to have their name desecrated in this way? And you can bet that one of them will get most of the other person's email.

So-called "full names" are just an attempt to create longer versions of unique names. Rather than lulling people into a sense of security, I'd rather that it be clear that these handles are arbitrary. People should use good user agents that have alias mappings, so that they can attach arbitrary names for their personal use to those with whom they correspond (such as the MH alias file).

Even worse is fuzzy matching in email—this can make good addresses turn bad. For example, Eric Allman is currently (to the best of our knowledge) the only "Allman" at Berkeley, so mail sent to **Allman@Berkeley.EDU** should get to him. But if another Allman ever appears, this address could suddenly become ambiguous. He's been the only Allman at Berkeley for over fifteen years—to suddenly have this "good address" bounce mail because it is ambiguous would be a heinous wrong.

Directory services should be as fuzzy as possible (within reason, of course). Mail services should be unique.

Q3.4—So what was the user database feature intended for?

The intent was to have all information for a given user (where the user is the unique login name, not an inherently non-unique full name) in one place. This would include phone numbers, addresses, and so forth. The "maildrop" feature is because Berkeley does not use a centralized mail server (there are a number of reasons for this that are mostly historic), and so we need to know where each user gets his or her mail delivered—i.e., the mail drop.

UC Berkeley is (was) in the process of setting up their environment so that mail sent to an unqualified "name" goes to that person's preferred maildrop; mail sent to "name@host" goes to that host. The purpose of "FEATURE(notsticky)" is to cause "name@host" to be looked up in the user database for delivery to the maildrop.

Q3.5—Where do I find this user database (UserDB) code?

The user database code is part of the sendmail V8 distribution. However, it depends on your installing the db library from the package at **ftp://ftp.cs.berkeley.edu/ pub/4bsd/db.1.85.tar.gz**. If you install this library, edit the Makefile to include the right option (-DNEWDB), and then make sendmail again, you get a binary which has the database features described in the book and the documentation provided in the sendmail source archive.

If you're using SGI Irix above 4.*x*, see Q2.16 for the patches you will need to get db 1.85 working on your machine.

Q3.6—How do I get the user database to work with Pine or with FEATURE(always_add_domain)?

The basic incompatibility with Pine and the user database option is in how Pine writes From addresses in the header. Most MUAs write the From address as "From: user", while Pine, for reasons given in its documentation, write the From address as "From: user@FQDN" (FQDN=fully qualified domain name). Using the m4 feature macro "always_add_domain" has the same effect. Because of this difference, the user database does not rewrite these headers.

One solution to this problem is to make the following change in the sendmail.mc file compiled by m4 into your */etc/sendmail.cf* (or wherever your sendmail.cf file is located) after you have the user database option installed and working with other MUAs:

Early in the section(s) where you are setting configuration variables, add the following:

```
# Define our userdb file for FQDN rewrites
Kuserdb btree -o /etc/userdb.db
```

And a bit later, before the "MAILER()" entries, but after other configuration options have been set:

```
LOCAL_RULE_1
#########################################################
### Local Ruleset 1, rewrite sender header & envelope ##
#########################################################
#Thanks to Bjart Kvarme <bjart.kvarme@usit.uio.no>
S1
R$-              $1 < @ $j . >                    user => user@localhost
R$- < @ $=w . > $*    $: $1 < @ $2 . > $3 ?? $1    user@localhost ?
R$+ ?? $+         $: $1 ?? $(userdb $2 : mailname $: @ $)
R$+ ?? @          $@ $1                        Not found
R$+ ?? $+         $>3 $2                       Found, rewrite

#NOTE    ^^^^^^^^^^^^^^    ^^^^^^^^^^^^^^^^^^^^^^^^^
#       Use Tab Characters  Use Tab Characters in these regions
# to make three columns (the line with "mailname" only has 2
columns).
```

Now the user database should re-write messages sent with Pine or anything else that causes local users to have their address be fully qualified (both header and envelope sender will be properly re-written). If this still does not work for you, try adding the following to either the system-wide pine.conf, pine.conf.fixed, or your personal .pinerc:

```
user-domain=localhost
```

This has been known to help solve the problem for some people. However, a more elegant (read: m4-based) solution for version 8 sendmail users has yet to be created.

Q3.7—How do I manage several (virtual) domains?

If you want to provide mailservice to several domains and be able to add identical names across different domains, as in this example:

```
user@a.dom.ain    mb1@dom.ain
user@b.dom.ain    mb2@dom.ain
user@c.dom.ain    mb@outer.space
```

you may accomplish this by using an external database in conjunction with minor Ruleset rewriting in sendmail.cf. Many ISPs (Internet Service Providers) have asked me, and here's a general solution (you may combine it with userdb's if you need to):

1. **Make a textfile**. (I usually make one for each domain and concatenate them before database-compilation) with the following structure:

   ```
   user@a.dom.ain    mb1@dom.ain
   user@b.dom.ain    mb2@dom.ain
   user@c.dom.ain    mb@outer.space
   ```

   The LHS (Left Hand Side) is the mail-address of a particular user, and the RHS is the corresponding mailbox. An example that might apply to the real world:

   ```
   webmaster@josnet.se       wm.list@eowyn.josnet.se
   webmaster@client1.se      joe@client1.se
   webmaster@client2.se      anne@another.provider.se
   webmaster@client3.se      joe@client3.se
   joe@client1.se            c1_joe@mail.josnet.se
   joe@client3.se            joeuser
   ```

   Note that you have to spell out the complete email-address in the LHS entry. The RHS entry may be either a local address (for example, 'johan,' if that account exists) or a complete email-address on another system (or a domain that the server recognizes as local, for that matter).

2. **Compile the textfile into a database:**

```
makemap hash mbt.db <mbt
```

You may you use other lookup-methods than hash (btree, for example). The resulting database is *mbt.db* in this example, and the input is the textfile *mbt*.

3. **Add a few lines in sendmail.cf:**

A. In the beginning (typically in the "local info" section or together with the user database option in the "options" section):

```
# Declare mbt as a hash-lookup database:
Kmbt hash /etc/mail/mbt.db
```

B. In the Ruleset 98 (local part of ruleset 0) section, add

```
# Use mailboxtable-database:
R$+ < @ $+ . >   $: $1 < @ $2 > .
R$+ < @ $+ > $*  $: $(mbt $1@$2 $: $1 < @ $2 > $3 $)
R$+ < @ $+ > $*  $: $(mbt $2 $: $1 < @ $2 > $3 $)
RERROR $*        $#error $: $1
R$+ < @ $+ > .   $: $1 < @ $2 . >
```

If you have any other rewrite rules in ruleset 98, these should be able to either go after or before the existing rules, but you may have to do some experimenting to find out which placement works best.

4. **The next-to-last line of these rules lets you have an alias file, like**

```
joe@somedom.com     joe
jim@somedom.com     jim@othersite
somedom.com         ERROR "No such user"
```

and still have mail addressed to unknown users at that domain bounce properly. You can also do a form of redirects, such as

```
fred@somedom.com    ERROR "This user has moved to fred@otherdom.com"
```

5. **Test with sendmail -bv and/or sendmail -bt.**

6. **Restart sendmail.** You must do this in order to have the daemon reread the *sendmail.cf.*

NOTE: Alternate sets of instructions and/or kits can be found at **http://www.westnet.com/ providers**, **http://hub.org/softdocs/Sendmail-VD**, **ftp://samson.oslo.uninett.no/pub/unix/sendmail/**, and **http://jos.net/projects/mbt/**. None of these has been tested by the maintainer of this FAQ, but they are believed to work correctly. Which you use is a matter of your personal aesthetics.

If you're using version 8.8 sendmail, you can make use of the new "virtual user table" feature (for one thing, it won't require that you add new rewrite rules to your sendmail configuration, as the previous example does).

1. **Put "FEATURE(virtusertable)" in your sendmail.mc file.**

2. **By default, sendmail will build tables out of /etc/virtusertable.** If you want to change this, put something like

```
define('VIRTUSER_TABLE', '-o hash /usr/local/lib/virtusertable')dnl
```

in your sendmail.mc file.

3. **Construct the virtusertable file like so:**

```
info@foo.com      foo-info
info@bar.com      bar-info
@baz.org       jane@elsewhere.net
@somedom.com      error : 5.5.0 User unknown
```

(Contrast with steps 1 and 4 in the previous example using regular mailertables).

4. **Compile the textfile into a database:**

```
makemap hash /etc/virtusertable.db </etc/virtusertable
```

You may you use other lookup-methods than hash (btree, for example). Make sure that this database type matches what is defined for the table in step 2.

5. **Put all the domains listed on the LHS of these aliases in your sendmail.cw file, or on the Cw line in your sendmail.cf.**

6. **Recompile your sendmail.cf from your sendmail.mc and test it.**

7. **Once you are satisfied, move it into place and restart sendmail.**

Note that the virtusertable is only referenced for inbound mail (more accurately, only for controlling delivery). If you want to rewrite mail addresses from your virtual domain users as they pass through your system, you'll also need to make comparable modifications to the genericstable (used for rewriting).

Q3.8—There are four UUCP mailers listed in the configuration files. Which one should I use?

The choice is partly a matter of local preferences and what is running at the other end of your UUCP connection. Unlike good protocols that define what will go over the wire, UUCP uses the policy that you should do what is right for the other end; if they change, you have to change. This makes it hard to do the right thing, and discourages people from updating their software. In general, if you can avoid UUCP, please do. If you can't avoid it, you'll have to find the version that is closest to what the other end accepts. Following is a summary of the UUCP mailers available.

uucp-old (obsolete name: "uucp")

This is the oldest, the worst (but the closest to UUCP) way of sending messages across UUCP connections. It does bangify everything and prepends $U (your UUCP name) to the sender's address (which can already be a bang path itself). It can only send to one address at a time, so it spends a lot of time copying duplicates of messages. Avoid this if at all possible.

uucp-new (obsolete name: "suucp")

The same as above, except that it assumes that in one rmail command you can specify several recipients. It still has a lot of other problems.

uucp-dom

This UUCP mailer keeps everything as domain addresses. Basically, it uses the SMTP mailer rewriting rules.

Unfortunately, a lot of UUCP mailer transport agents require bangified addresses in the envelope, although you can use domain-based addresses in the message header. (The envelope shows up as the From_ line on UNIX mail.) So ...

uucp-uudom

This is a cross between uucp-new (for the envelope addresses) and uucp-dom (for the header addresses). It bangifies the envelope sender (From_ line in messages) without adding the local hostname, unless there is no host name on the address at all (e.g., "wolf") or the host component is a UUCP host name instead of a domain name ("somehost!wolf" instead of "some.dom.ain!wolf").

Examples:

We are on host grasp.insa-lyon.fr (UUCP host name "grasp"). The following summarizes the sender rewriting for various mailers:

Mailer	Sender	Rewriting in the envelope
uucp-{old,new}	wolf	grasp!wolf
uucp-dom	wolf	wolf@grasp.insa-lyon.fr
uucp-uudom	wolf	grasp.insa-lyon.fr!wolf
uucp-{old,new}	wolf@fr.net	grasp!fr.net!wolf
uucp-dom	wolf@fr.net	wolf@fr.net
uucp-uudom	wolf@fr.net	fr.net!wolf
uucp-{old,new}	somehost!wolf	grasp!somehost!wolf
uucp-dom	somehost!wolf	somehost!wolf@grasp.insa-lyon.fr
uucp-uudom	somehost!wolf	grasp.insa-lyon.fr!somehost!wolf

If your only contact with the external world is through UUCP, you'll probably want to recompile sendmail with support for DNS turned off (if your host architecture supports a service switch file that sendmail understands, it will use the service switch however you've got it configured, even if you've compiled sendmail with DNS support turned off; so make sure the service switch file is also properly configured).

Using "FEATURE(nodns)" probably won't completely satisfy you, as more recent releases of version 8 sendmail really, REALLY, want to know what their canonical hostname is, and will go to great lengths to figure this out from the DNS. But if you don't have any nameservers, this can obviously add significant amounts of time to process startup as sendmail repeatedly tries (and fails) to find this information. It then becomes doubly important to have the proper Fully Qualified Domain Name (FQDN) listed first in your /etc/hosts file or in the file used to build your NIS/NIS+ table (or whatever you use). For more information on "FEATURE(nodns)," see the RELEASE_NOTES file for sendmail versions 8.7.1 and later (search for "FQDN"), as well as *sendmail*, page 741 (page reference correct as of first edition, first printing).

Q3.9—How do I fix "undefined symbol inet_aton" and "undefined symbol _strerror" messages?

You've probably replaced your resolver with the version from BIND 4.9.3. You need to compile with -l44bsd in order to get the additional routines.

Q3.10—How do I solve "collect: I/O error on connection" errors?

There is nothing wrong. This is just a diagnosis of a condition that had not been diagnosed before. If you are getting a lot of these from a single host, there is probably some incompatibility between 8.*x* and that host. If you get a lot of them in general, you may have network problems that are causing connections to get reset.

Note that this problem is sometimes caused by incompatible values of the MTU (Maximum Transmission Unit) size on a SLIP or PPP connection. Be sure that your MTU size is configured to be the same value as what your ISP has configured for your connection. If you are still having problems, then have your ISP configure your MTU size for 1500 (the maximum value), and you configure your MTU size similarly.

Although it seems like a problem of this sort would affect all of your connections, that is not the case. You may encounter this problem with only a small number of sites with which you exchange mail, and it may even affect only certain size messages.

Q3.11—Why can't my users forward their mail to a program?

I just upgraded to version 8 sendmail, and now, when my users try to forward their mail to a program, they get an "illegal shell" or "cannot mail to programs" message, and their mail is not delivered. What's wrong?

In order for people to be able to run a program from their .forward file, version 8 sendmail insists that their shell (that is, the shell listed for that user in the passwd entry) be a "valid" shell, meaning a shell listed in */etc/shells*. If */etc/shells* does not exist, a default list is used, typically consisting of */bin/sh and /bin/csh*.

This is to support environments that may have NFS-shared directories mounted on machines on which users do not have login permission. For example, many people make their file server inaccessible for performance or security reasons; although users have directories, their shell on the server is */usr/local/etc/nologin* or some such. If you allowed them to run programs anyway, you might as well let them log in.

If you are willing to let users run programs from their .forward file even though they cannot telnet or rsh in (as might be reasonable if you run smrsh to control the list of programs they can run), then add the line

```
/SENDMAIL/ANY/SHELL/
```

to */etc/shells*. This must be typed exactly as indicated, in caps, with the trailing slash.

NOTA BENE: DO NOT list */usr/local/etc/nologin* in */etc/shells*—this will open up other security problems.

IBM AIX does not use */etc/shells*—a list of allowable login shells is contained, along with many other login parameters, in */etc/security/login.cfg*. You can copy the information in the "shells=" stanza into a */etc/shells* on your system, so sendmail will have something to use. Do NOT add "*/usr/lib/uucp/uucico*," or any other non-login shell, into */etc/shells*.

Also note that there are some weird things that AFS throws into the mix, and these can keep a program from running or running correctly out of *.forward* files or the system-wide aliases.

See also "smrsh" in Q2.13.

Q3.12—Why do connections to the SMTP port take such a long time?

I just upgraded to version 8 sendmail, and suddenly connections to the SMTP port take a long time. What is going wrong?

It's probably something weird in your TCP implementation that makes the IDENT code act oddly. On most systems, version 8 sendmail tries to do a "callback" to the connecting host to get a validated user name (see RFC 1413 for detail). If the connecting host does not support such a service it will normally fail quickly with "Connection refused"; but certain kinds of packet filters and certain TCP implementations just time out.

To test this (pre-8.7.*y* sendmail), set the IDENT timeout to zero, using

```
define('confREAD_TIMEOUT','Ident=0')dnl
```

in the .mc file used by m4 to generate your sendmail.cf file. Alternatively, if you don't use m4, you can put "OrIdent=0" in the configuration file (we recommend the m4 solution, since that makes maintenance much easier for people who don't understand sendmail re-write rules, or after you've been away from it for a while). Either way, this will completely disable all use of the IDENT protocol.

For version 8.7.*y* sendmail (and above), you should instead use

```
define('confTO_IDENT','0s')dnl
```

Another possible problem is that you have your name server and/or resolver configured improperly. Make sure that all "nameserver" entries in */etc/resolv.conf* point to functional servers. If you are running your own server, make certain that all the servers listed in your root cache are up to date (this file is usually called something like "*/var/namedb/root.cache*"; see your */etc/named.boot* file to get your value). Either of these can cause long delays.

Q3.13—Why do I get "unknown mailer error 5 — mail: options MUST PRECEDE recipients" errors?

I just upgraded to version 8 sendmail and suddenly I get errors such as "unknown mailer error 5 — mail: options MUST PRECEDE recipients." What is going wrong?

You need OSTYPE(systype) in your *.mc* file, where "systype" is set correctly for your hardware and OS combination—otherwise the configurations use a default that probably disagrees with your local mail system. See cf/README for details.

If this is on a Sun workstation, you might also want to take a look at the local mailer flags in the Sun-supplied *sendmail.cf* and compare them to the local mailer flags generated for your version 8 *sendmail.cf*. If they differ, you might try changing the V8 flags to match the Sun flags.

Q3.14—Why does version 8 sendmail panic my SunOS box?

Sendmail 8.7.*y* panics SunOS 4.1.3_U1 (at least for $1<=y<=3$) and SunOS 4.1.3, and sendmail 8.6.*x* seems fine on both machines (at least for $9<=x<=12$).

The problem is that a kernel patch is missing, specifically 100584-08 (4.1.3), 102010-03 (4.1.3_U1), or 102517 (4.1.4). This should be available from your hardware vendor through your support contract or their online support facilities (including being available on the SunSolve CD).

Q3.15—Why does the "From" header gets mysteriously munged when I send to an alias?

"It's not a bug, it's a feature." This happens when you have an "owner-list" alias and you send to "list." V8 propagates the owner information into the envelope sender field (which appears as the "From" header on UNIX mail or as the Return-Path: header) so that downstream errors are properly returned to the mailing list owner instead of to the sender. In order to make this appear as sensible as possible to end users, I recommend making the owner point to a "request" address—for example:

```
list:        :include:/path/name/list.list
owner-list:      list-request
list-request:       eric
```

This will make a message sent to "list" come out as being "From list-request" instead of "From eric."

Q3.16—Why doesn't MASQUERADE_AS (or the user database) work for envelope addresses as well as header addresses?

Believe it or not, this is intentional. The interpretation of the standards by the version 8 sendmail development group was that this was an inappropriate rewriting, and that if the rewriting were incorrect, at least the envelope would contain a valid return address.

If you're using version 8.7.*y* sendmail (or later), you can use

```
FEATURE(masquerade_envelope)
```

in your *sendmail.mc* file to change this behaviour.

Q3.17—How do I run version 8 sendmail and support the MAIL11V3 protocol?

Get the re-implementation of the mail11 protocol by Keith Moore from **ftp:// gatekeeper.dec.com/pub/DEC/gwtools/** (with contributions from Paul Vixie).

Q3.18—Why do messages disappear from my queue unsent?

When I look in the queue directory, I see that qf* files have been renamed to Qf*, and sendmail doesn't see these. What's wrong?

If you look closely, you should find that the Qf files are owned by users other than root. Since sendmail runs as root, it refuses to believe information in non-root-owned qf files, and it renames them to Qf to get them out of the way and make it easy for you to find. The usual cause of this is twofold: first, you have the queue directory world writable (which is probably a mistake—this opens up other security problems) and someone is calling sendmail with an "unsafe" flag, usually a -o flag that sets an option that could compromise security. When sendmail sees this, it gives up setuid root permissions.

The usual solution is to not use the problematic flags. If you must use them, you have to write a special queue directory and have them processed by the same uid that submitted the job in the first place.

Q3.19—When is sendmail going to support RFC 1522 MIME header encoding?

This is considered to be a MUA issue rather than an MTA issue.

Quoth Eric Allman:

"The primary reason is that the information necessary to do the encoding (that is, 8->7 bit) is unknown to the MTA. In specific, the character set used to encode names in headers is *NOT* necessarily the same as used to encode the body (which is already encoded in MIME in the charset parameter of the Content-Type: header). Furthermore, it is perfectly reasonable for, say, a Swede to be living and working in Korea, or a Russian living and working in Germany, and want their name to be encoded in their native character set; it could even be that the sender was Japanese, the recipient Russian, and the body encoded in ISO 8859-1. If all I have are 8-bit characters, I can't choose the charset properly.

"Similarly, when doing 7->8 bit conversions, I don't want to throw away this information, as it is necessary for proper presentation to the end user."

Q3.20—Why can't I get mail to some places, but instead always get the error "reply: read error from name.of.remote.host"?

This is usually caused by a bug in the remote host's mail server, or Mail Transport Agent (MTA). The "EHLO" command of ESMTP causes the remote server to drop the SMTP connection. There are several MTAs that have this problem, but one of the most common server implementations can be identified by the "220 All set, fire away" greeting it gives when you telnet to its SMTP port.

To work around this problem, you can configure sendmail to use a mailertable with an entry telling sendmail to use plain SMTP when talking to that host:

```
name.of.remote.host        smtp:name.of.remote.host
```

Sites which must run a host with this broken SMTP implemetation should do so by having a site running sendmail or some other reliable (and reasonably modern) SMTP MTA act as an MX server for the problem host.

There is also a problem wherein some TCP/IP implementations are broken, and if any connection attempt to a remote end gets a "connection refused," then **all** connections to that site will get closed. Of course, if you try to use the IDENT protocol across a firewall (at either end), this is highly likely to result in the same apparent kind of "read error."

The fix is simple—on those machines with broken TCP/IP implementations, do not attempt to use IDENT. When compiling newer releases of version 8 sendmail, the compiler should automatically detect whether you're on a machine that is known to have this kind of TCP/IP networking problem, and make sure that sendmail does not attempt to use IDENT. If you've since patched your machine so that it no longer has this problem, you'll need to go back in and explicitly configure sendmail for support of IDENT, if you want that feature.

Q3.21—Why doesn't "FEATURE(xxx)" work?

When creating m4 Master Config (".mc") files for version 8 sendmail, many "FEATURE()" macros simply change the definition of internal variables that are referenced in the "MAILER()" definitions.

To make sure that everything works as desired, you need to make sure that "OSTYPE()" macros are put at the very beginning of the file, followed by "FEATURE()" and "HACK()" macros, local definitions, and, at the very bottom, the "MAILER()" definitions.

Q3.22—How do I configure sendmail to not use DNS?

In situations where you're behind a firewall, or across a dial-up line, there are times when you need to make sure that programs (such as sendmail) do not use the DNS at all.

With version 8.8, you change the service switch file to omit "DNS" and use only NIS, files, and other map types as appropriate. With previous releases of version 8 sendmail, you need to recompile the binary and make sure that "NAMED_BIND" is turned off in *src/conf.h*.

Note that you'll need to forward all your outbound mail to another machine as a "relay" (one that does use DNS, and understands how to properly use MX records, etc.), otherwise you won't be able to get mail to any site(s) other than the one(s) you configure in your */etc/hosts* file (or whatever).

Q3.23—How do I get all my queued mail delivered to my UNIX box from my ISP?

Assuming you're running sendmail or some other SMTP MTA on some sort of a UNIX host, and your ISP uses version 8.8 sendmail and they queue all mail for your domain (as opposed to stuffing it all in one file that you need to download via POP3 or somesuch), something like the following script should do the trick:

```
#!/bin/sh
telnet mail.myisp.com. 25 < __EOF__
EHLO me.mydomain.com
ETRN mydomain.com
QUIT
__EOF__
```

Note that this is indented for readability, and the real script would have column position #1 of the file be the first printable character in each line. Of course, you'll have to fill in the appropriate details for "mail.myisp.com", "mydomain.com", etc. If this script doesn't work, you may have problems with "here" documents being fed as standard input to commands (like telnet). In that case, you'll need to build a similar script using "expect." For more information on expect, see **http://expect.nist.gov** and the book *Exploring Expect:*

A Tcl-Based Toolkit for Automating Interactive Applications (**http://www.ora.com/catalog/ expect/noframes.html**).

If your ISP doesn't use version 8.8 sendmail, you may have to cobble together alternative solutions. They may have a "ppplogin" script that is executed every time your machines dials them up, and if so, you may be able to have them modify this script so as to put a "sendmail -qRmydomain.com" in it (which is effectively what the "ETRN" command does, but in a safer fashion). Alternatively, they may have a hacked finger daemon, so that you'd put "finger mydomain.com@theirhost.theirdomain.com" in your script. Or, they may have some other solution for you. However, only they would be able to answer what solutions they have available to them. Obviously, the easiest and most "standard" solution is to have them upgrade their system to the most recent stable release of version 8.8 sendmail.

Comments/updates should be sent to **sendmail-faq@etext.org**.
Copyright 1996, by Brad Knowles, all rights reserved
End of **comp.mail.sendmail** Frequently Asked Questions (FAQ), part 1 of 2

****

Q4.1—Should I use a wildcard MX for my domain?

If at all possible, no.

Wildcard MX records have lots of semantic "gotcha's." For example, they will match a host "unknown.your.domain"—if you don't explicitly test for unknown hosts in your domain, you will get "config error: mail loops back to myself." See RFCs 1535, 1536, and 1912 (updates RFC 1537) for more detail and other related (or common) problems. See also *DNS and BIND* by Albitz and Liu. They can also cause your system to add your domain to outgoing FQDNs in a desperate attempt to get the mail to where it's supposed to go, but because *.your.domain is valid due to the wildcard MX, delivery to not.real.domain.your.domain will get dumped on you, and you may even find yourself in a loop as the domain keeps getting tacked on time after time after time (the "config error: mail loops back to myself" problem). Wildcard MX records are just a bad idea, plain and simple. They don't work the way you'd expect, and virtually no one gets them right. Avoid them at all costs.

Q4.2—How can I set up an auto-responder?

This is a local mailer issue, not a sendmail issue. Depending on what you're doing, look at procmail (see Q4.9), ftpmail, or Majordomo. The latest version of Majordomo can be found at **ftp://ftp.greatcircle.com/pub/majordomo/**. It is written in Perl and requires either Perl 4.036, and appears to run with only minor tweaks under 5.001a or later. Make sure to check out the web interface for Majordomo called "Mailserv" at **http://iquest.com/ ~fitz/www/mailserv/** or "LWGate" at **http://www.netspace.org/users/ dwb/lwgate.html**.

The latest versions of Perl (both 4.*x* and 5.*x*) can be found in **http://www. metronet. com/perlinfo/src/**. More information about Perl can be found at **http://www.metronet. com/perlinfo/perl5.html**. The latest version of ftpmail can be found at **ftp://src.doc.ic. ac.uk/packages/ftpmail** or any **comp.sources.misc** archive (volume 37).

Q4.3—How can I get sendmail to deliver local mail to HOME/.mail instead of into */usr/spool/mail* (or */usr/mail*)?

Again, this is a local mailer issue, not a sendmail issue. Either modify your local mailer (source code will be required), or change the program called in the "local" mailer configuration description to be a new program that does this local delivery. One program that is capable of doing this is procmail (see Q4.9), although there are probably many others as well. You might be interested in reading the paper "HLFSD: Delivering Email to your $HOME," available in the Proceedings of the USENIX System Administration (LISA VII) Conference (November 1993). More information is at **ftp://ftp.cs.columbia.edu/pub/hlfsd/ README.hlfsd**, while the actual archive of the papers is at **ftp://ftp.cs.columbia.edu/ pub/hlfsd/hlfsd-paper.tar.gz** (tar archive, gzip'ed).

Q4.4—Why does it deliver the mail interactively when I'm trying to get it to go into queue-only mode?

Or, I'm trying to use the "don't deliver to expensive mailer" flag, and it delivers the mail interactively anyway. I can see it does it: here's the output of "sendmail -v foo@somehost" (or Mail -v or equivalent).

The -v flag to sendmail (which is implied by the -v flag to Mail and other programs in that family) tells sendmail to watch the transaction. Since you have explicitly asked to see what's going on, it assumes that you do not want to auto-queue, and turns that feature off. Remove the -v flag and use a "tail -f" of the log instead to see what's going on. If you are trying to use the "don't deliver to expensive mailer" flag (mailer flag "e"), be sure you also turn on global option "c"—otherwise it ignores the mailer flag.

Q4.5—How can I solve "config error: mail loops back to myself" messages?

I'm getting these error messages:

```
553 relay.domain.net config error: mail loops back to myself
554 <user@domain.net>... Local configuration error
```

How can I solve this problem?

You have asked mail to the domain (e.g., domain.net) to be forwarded to a specific host (in this case, relay.domain.net) by using an MX record, but the relay machine doesn't recognize itself as domain.net. Add domain.net to */etc/sendmail.cw* (if you are using FEATURE(use_cw_file)) or add "Cw domain.net" to your configuration file.

IMPORTANT: When making changes to your configuration file, be sure you kill and restart the sendmail daemon (for ANY change in the configuration, not just this one):

```
kill 'head -1 /etc/sendmail.pid'
sh -c "'tail -1 /etc/sendmail.pid'"
```

NOTA BENE: kill -1 does not work with versions prior to 8.7.*y*! With version 8.8.*z* sendmail, if the daemon was started up with a full pathname (i.e., "/usr/lib/sendmail -bd -q13m"), then you should be able to send it a HUP signal ("kill -1," or, more safely, "kill -HUP") and have it reload itself (version 8.7.*y* sendmail cannot do this safely, and represents a security risk if it's not replaced with version 8.8.3 or later).

Q4.6—Why does my sendmail process sometimes hang when connecting over a SLIP/PPP link?

I'm connected to the network via a SLIP/PPP link. Sometimes my sendmail process hangs (although it looks like part of the message has been transferred). Everything else works. What's wrong?

Most likely, the problem isn't sendmail at all, but the low-level network connection. It's important that the MTU (Maximum Transfer Unit) for the SLIP connection be set properly at both ends. If they disagree, large packets will be trashed, and the connection will hang.

Q4.7—How can I summarize the statistics generated by sendmail in the syslog?

This question is addressed on pages 445-449 of *sendmail, 2nd Ed* (see page 319 of first edition) by Bryan Costales (see entry sendmail-faq//book/ISBN/1-56592-222-0 in Q6.1). An updated version of this syslog-stat.pl script (so that it understands the log format used in version 8 sendmail) is at **ftp://ftp.his.com/pub/brad/sendmail/syslog_stats**. The updated version of ssl has been uploaded to the SMTP Resources Directory (in **ftp://ftp.is.co.za/networking/mail/tools/**), as well as **ftp://ftp.his.com/pub/brad/ sendmail/ ssl**. There is also another program (written by Bryan Beecher) at **ftp://ftp. his.com/pub/brad/sendmail/smtpstats**. If you're interested in summarizing POP statistics, there is **ftp://ftp.his.com/pub/brad/sendmail/popstats**, also written by Bryan Beecher. To see what else is available today, check the Comprehensive Perl Archive Network, **ftp://ftp.funet.fi/pub/languages/perl/CPAN/CPAN** or ftp://ftp.cis.ufl.edu/ pub/ perl/ **CPAN/CPAN** for the site nearest you.

For the scripts themselves, look under **CPAN/scripts/mailstuff/** at any CPAN site. For more information, see the **comp.lang.perl.** FAQs at **ftp://ftp.cis.ufl.edu:/pub/perl/ faq/FAQ** or **ftp://rtfm.mit.edu/pub/usenet-by-hierarchy/comp/lang/perl/**. There is also the "Sendmail Statistics Project," which has a web page at **http://www.josnet.se/ projects/ssp/**. Although they have examples online of what the output might look like, it now appears that this project is either dead or at least indefinitely on hold. Still, you may be able to talk to the authors in order to get what code from them you can.

If you're interested in using these kinds of tools to help you do some near-real-time monitoring of your system, you might be interested in MEWS (Mail Early Warning System). From the README:

If you've ever written a perl script to parse sendmail log files looking for errors, MEWS might be of interest to you. If you've ever thought about writing a perl script to munge sendmail log files, cringed a little and hurriedly came up with an excuse not to do it, read on.

If you don't have a Solaris 2.5 machine, you can probably stop reading here.

The Mail Early Warning System (MEWS) gives postmasters immediate notification of trouble spots on your mail backbone. It only works with sendmail.

To explain it in a nutshell, whenever sendmail returns a 4xx or 5xx SMTP code, with the MEWS modifications, it also sends the code over UDP to a daemon which then replays the error message to interested parties. The man pages go into a little bit more detail.

If this sounds like something you might be interested in getting more details about, you can find the MEWS archive at **ftp://ftp.qualcomm.com/pub/people/eamonn/ mews.tar.Z**.

Q4.8—How can I check my sendmail.cf to ensure that it's re-writing addresses correctly?

The recommended program for this is "checksendmail" by Rob Kolstad. Old versions of this are available on various archive sites, but currently, the only way to get the most recent version (which has been updated to understand version 8.7 long option name syntax, as well as now supporting both Perl 4.x and Perl 5.x) is from Rob himself. The latest archive will be made publicly available (most likely through the SMTPRD run by Andras Salamon; see Q6.5, entry sendmail-faq//online/index/14) as soon as it is received.

Q4.9—What is procmail, and where can I get it?

The program "procmail" is a replacement for the local mailer (variously called /bin/mail, /usr/bin/mail, mail.local, rmail, etc.). It has been ported to run on virtually every UNIX-like OS you're likely to run into, and has a whole host of features. It is typically about 30% faster performing the job of the local mailer than programs such as /bin/mail or /usr/bin/mail, it has been hammered on widely to make it extremely secure (much more so than most local mailers) and very robust. Procmail is also capable of helping you put a quota on a user's mailbox through the standard UNIX quota mechanism (see Q4.3). In short, whatever you've got, you're almost guaranteed that procmail is better (if nothing else, the author has been able to focus lots of time and energy into making it the best and fastest tool available, while most system vendors just throw something together as fast as they can and move on to the whole rest of the OS).

However, this only begins to scratch the surface of what procmail is capable of. Its most important feature is the fact that it gives you a standard way to create rules (procmail calls them "recipes") to process your mail before the messages get put into your mailbox, and for that feature alone, it is one of the most important tools any administrator can have in their repertoire. By filtering out or automatically dealing with 80% of your daily cruft, it lets you spend more time on the hard 20%. Note that recent releases of version 8 sendmail natively support using procmail as an alternate local mailer (see "FEATURE(local_procmail)" for version 8.7 and above). They also support procmail as an additional local mailer, if you're concerned about flat-out replacing your current local mailer with procmail (see "MAILER(procmail)" in version 8.7 and above).

You can also install procmail as a user and run it out of your .forward file, although this tends to be a bit slower and less efficient. The latest version of procmail can be found at **ftp://ftp.informatik.rwth-aachen.de/pub/packages/procmail/**. Procmail is also the core to a mailing list management package called "SmartList," so if you've already got procmail, adding SmartList may be a good option. Some listowners prefer Majordomo, Listserv, or one of those other programs, but SmartList has more than a few adherents as well. Your personal tastes will dictate whether you swear by SmartList or at it.

Q4.10—How can I solve "cannot alias non-local names" errors?

I upgraded from my vendor's sendmail to the latest version, and now I'm getting these error messages when I run "newaliases":

```
/etc/aliases: line 13: MAILER-DAEMON... cannot alias non-local names
/etc/aliases: line 14: postmaster... cannot alias non-local names
```

How can I solve this problem?

Your local mailer doesn't have the "A" flag specified. Edit the Mlocal line in *sendmail.cf* and add "A" to the flags listed after "F=". Better yet, if you're running a recent version of sendmail that uses m4 to generate *.cf* files from *.mc* files, regenerate your *sendmail.cf* and see if that fixes the problem. Remember to install the new *sendmail.cf* and restart the sendmail daemon.

Q5.1.1—How can I solve "line 273: replacement $3 out of bounds" errors?

When I use sendmail V8 with a Sun config file, I get lines like

```
/etc/sendmail.cf: line 273: replacement $3 out of bounds
```

the line in question reads

```
R$*<@$%y>$*        $1<@$2.LOCAL>$3         user@ether
```

What does this mean? How do I fix it?

V8 doesn't recognize the Sun "$%y" syntax, so as far as it is concerned, there is only a $1 and a $2 (but no $3) in this line. Read Rick McCarty's paper on "Converting Standard Sun Config Files to Sendmail Version 8," in the contrib directory (file "converting.sun.configs") in the latest version 8 sendmail distribution, for a full discussion of how to do this.

Q5.1.2—How can I solve "line 445: bad ruleset 96 (50 max)" errors?

When I use sendmail V8 on a Sun, I sometimes get lines like:

```
/etc/sendmail.cf: line 445: bad ruleset 96 (50 max)
```

What does this mean? How do I fix it?

You're somehow trying to start up the old Sun sendmail (or sendmail.mx) with a version 8 sendmail config file, which Sun's sendmail doesn't like. Check your /etc/rc.local, any procedures that have been created to stop and re-start the sendmail processes, etc. Make sure that you've switched everything over to using the new sendmail. To keep this problem from ever happening again, try the following (make sure you're logged in as root):

```
mv /usr/lib/sendmail /usr/lib/sendmail.old
ln -s /usr/local/lib/sendmail.v8 /usr/lib/sendmail
mv /usr/lib/sendmail.mx /usr/lib/sendmail.mx.old
ln -s /usr/local/lib/sendmail.v8 /usr/lib/sendmail.mx
chmod 0000 /usr/lib/sendmail.old
chmod 0000 /usr/lib/sendmail.mx.old
```

Assuming, of course, that you have installed sendmail V8 in *usr/local/ lib/sendmail.v8*.

Q5.1.3—Why does version 8 sendmail (< 8.7.5) sometimes hang under Solaris 2.5?

In moving from Solaris 2.4 to Solaris 2.5, the kernel changed its name and is now in /kernel/genunix instead of /kernel/unix, so _PATH_UNIX in *conf.h* is pointing to the wrong place. If you can't upgrade to the latest release of sendmail 8.8.z, the next best thing to do is change _PATH_UNIX in *conf.h* (in the solaris2 part) to point to the generic interface /dev/ksyms, like so:

```
#    define _PATH_UNIX    "/dev/ksyms"
```

Q5.1.4—Why can't I use SunOS/Solaris to get email to certain large sites?

This is most likely a problem in your resolver libraries (DNS, /etc/hosts, NIS, etc.). Older Sun (and Solaris?) resolver libraries allocated enough room for only five IP addresses for each host name, and if any program ever ran across a name with more than five IP addresses for it, the program would crash. For example, this would keep you from getting mail to CompuServe, since (at the time of this writing) they list eleven IP addresses for mx1.compuserve.com (one of the named MXes for compuserve.com). This will affect you even if you use version 8 sendmail, since it's a problem in the resolver libraries, and not in sendmail itself. You should either get patches to the resolver libraries from Sun, or the latest version of BIND (see Q2.12), and install their resolver library routines. Between the two, installing BIND is a bit more work, but it typically gives you much more up-to-date code to help you resist attacks to your systems, more capable programs to be used for serving the DNS (including support for IPv6 and several other features), and some very useful utility programs.

Q5.2.1—The system resource controller always reports sendmail as "inoperative." What's wrong?

When I use version 8 sendmail on an IBM RS/6000 running AIX, the system resource controller always reports sendmail as "inoperative," even though it's actually running. What's wrong?

When running as a daemon, sendmail detaches from its parent process, fooling the SRC into thinking that sendmail has exited. To fix this, issue the commands

```
kill 'head -1 /etc/sendmail.pid'
chssys -s sendmail -f 9 -n 15 -S -a "-d99.100"
# use "-d0.1" in sendmail 8.6.x
startsrc -s sendmail -a "-bd -q30m"
# your sendmail args may vary
```

Now the SRC should report the correct status of sendmail. If you are using version 8.6.*x*, use "-d0.1" instead of "-d99.100" (the debug options changed somewhat in version 8.7). In 8.6.*x* a side-effect of the "-d0.1" option is that a few lines of debug output will be printed on the system console every time sendmail starts up. For more information, read up on the System Resource Controller, the lssrc command, and the chssys command in the online AIX documentation.

Q5.2.2—Why can't I use AIX to get email to some sites?

When I use IBM's sendmail on an IBM RS/6000 running AIX trying to get to certain sites, it seems that I can get to some of them and not others. What's wrong?

There are two possible problems here:

1. Your version of sendmail is not configured to recognize MX records in the DNS. Search through your *sendmail.cf* looking for "OK MX" or "OK ALL." Older configurations had this line commented out, and this will cause mail from you to some sites to fail (because those sites have MX records, but no A records in their DNS for the specific Fully Qualified Domain Name you're trying to mail to). For more information, see the comp.unix.aix FAQ, **ftp://rtfm.mit.edu/ pub/usenet/news.answers/aix-faq/**.

2. There is a negative caching bug in AIX 3.2.5 with /usr/sbin/named executables that are less than 103000 bytes long. Ask your IBM representative to give you PMP 3251, or the most recent patch that fixes this problem for your particular configuration and version of the OS.

Q5.2.3—Why can't I get sendmail 8.7.1 to use MX records with AIX 3.2.5?

IBM, in their infinite wisdom, provided a header file that would easily mis-compile. This resulted in the struct{} for the DNS query to be mis-allocated, and MX processing would barf.

Fix 1) Upgrade to 8.7.5—this has a code fix for this problem.

Fix 2) Install the BIND 4.9.4 libraries and include files and tweak the Makefile.AIX to use them—I **think** these Get It Right (if not, at least it'll die during compile rather than failing weirdly at runtime).

Fix 3) Hack Makefile.AIX to pass a -DBIT_ZERO_ON_LEFT to cause the headers to use the right #ifdefs.

Q6—ADDITIONAL INFORMATION SOURCES

This probably isn't in strict RFC 1807 format, but I'm getting closer. Unfortunately, the format detailed in RFC 1807 was never intended to be used in this fashion, so I'm doing a bit of square-peg fitting into round holes. Note that the publisher ids that I've assigned should not be misconstrued to imply that I have actually published all these documents, it's just that I need some sort of reasonable entry for the RFC 1807 "ID" field, and in lieu of information to the contrary indicating what the actual publishers have registered, I have assigned my own, independant, "third-party" IDs. Hopefully, the bibliographic entries below make it obvious who the real publishers of the various documents are.

6.1 Reference Material Devoted Exlusively to sendmail

BIB-VERSION:: CS-TR-v2.1
ID:: sendmail-faq//online/reference/1
ENTRY:: March 23, 1996
TYPE:: Reference manual, available online in printable format
REVISION:: April 8, 1997; Updated "CONTACT" information

TITLE:: Sendmail Installation and Operation Guide
AUTHOR:: Allman, Eric
CONTACT:: Eric Allman **eric@Sendmail.ORG**
DATE:: November 19, 1995
PAGES:: 69
RETRIEVAL:: Contents of manual is in doc/op/op.ps of sendmail source archive
KEYWORD:: version 8.7.5 sendmail
LANGUAGE:: English
NOTES:: {g|n}roff "me" macro format version is in doc/op/op.me
See: URL: **http://www.sendmail.org/**
ABSTRACT::

The documentation, written by Eric Allman himself, comes with the sendmail distribution. The file in doc/op/op.me (nroff "me" macro format) may have a different number of pages depending on the type of device it is printed on, etc.

Eric provides his free consulting in the form of continuing development on sendmail, and occasional posts to **comp.mail.sendmail**. Please don't be so rude as to ask him to provide further free consulting directly to you. If you (or your company) are willing to compensate him for his consulting time, he may be willing to listen. At the very least, you should make sure you've exhausted all other courses of action before resorting to adding another message to the thousands he gets per day. Check the sendmail home page at **http://www.sendmail.org/** for late-breaking updates and other useful information.

If you want to be notified regarding future updates to sendmail and other items of potential interest, you may want to subscribe to the sendmail-announce mailing list. Address your subscription requests to **majordomo@lists.sendmail.org** with "subscribe sendmail-announce" as the body of the message.

END:: sendmail-faq//online/reference/1

BIB-VERSION:: CS-TR-v2.1
ID:: sendmail-faq//book/ISBN/1-56592-222-0
ENTRY:: March 23, 1996
REVISION:: April 8, 1997; Updated entire entry re: 2nd Ed.
TYPE:: Reference book, hardcopy
TITLE:: sendmail
AUTHOR:: Costales, Bryan
AUTHOR:: Allman, Eric
CONTACT:: Bryan Costales **bcx@BCX.COM**
O'Reilly & Associates, Inc.
103 Morris Street, Suite A
Sebastapol, CA 95472
Order by phone: 800-998-9938 (US/Canada inquiries)
800-889-8969 (US/Canada credit card orders)
707-829-0515 (local/overseas)

DATE:: January, 1997
PAGES:: 1021
COPYRIGHT:: Copyright (c) 1997 O'Reilly & Associates, Inc. All rights reserved.
LANGUAGE:: English
NOTES:: See: URL: **http://www.ora.com/catalog/sendmail2/**
ABSTRACT::

The definitive reference for version 8 sendmail (specifically, version 8.8). If you can have only one book on the subject of sendmail, this one is it. Bryan provides his consulting to the world in the form of his book, unless you're willing to compensate him for his services as well. Like Eric, you should make sure you've exhausted all other courses of action before you spend any of his valuable time.

END:: sendmail-faq/ /book/ISBN/1-56592-222-0

BIB-VERSION:: CS-TR-v2.1
ID:: sendmail-faq/ /book/ISBN/1-55558-127-7
ENTRY:: March 23, 1996
TYPE:: Reference book, hardcopy
REVISION:: Sep 9, 1996; fixed typo
TITLE:: Sendmail: Theory and Practice
AUTHOR:: Avolio, Frederick M.
AUTHOR:: Vixie, Paul A.
CONTACT:: Fred Avolio **fma@al.org**, Paul Vixie **vix@al.org**
Digital Press
225 Wildwood Avenue
Woburn, MA 01801, USA
Ordering Info: voice 1 800 366 2665
fax 1 800 446 6520
DATE:: 1994
PAGES:: 262
COPYRIGHT:: Copyright (c) by 1995 Butterworth-Heinemann
LANGUAGE:: English
NOTES:: See: URL: **http://www.vix.com/vix/smtap/**
ABSTRACT::

Centers more on IDA sendmail (at least partly because version 8 didn't exist when they began the book). Written more like a college sophomore- or junior-level textbook. While you'll probably never let the Costales book out of your grubby little hands (especially if you do much work with version 8 sendmail), this is a book you'll probably read once or maybe twice, learn some very valuable things, but then likely put on a shelf and not read or reference again (unless you have to write up a bibliographic entry for it). Makes a better introduction to sendmail for management types, especially if you don't want them getting their hands on too much "dangerous" technical information. Also a **lot** smaller and less imposing. If possible, I recommend getting both, but if you can only get one, get Costales—unless you're going to be working exclusively with IDA sendmail, in which case Avolio & Vixie will probably be more useful.

Note that Paul Vixie is extremely busy working on further development of BIND, the Internet de facto standard program for serving the DNS, upon which all Internet services depend, mail being only one of them. Like Eric and Bryan, he's also very busy. Unless you're willing to compensate him for his services, please let him get real work done.

END:: sendmail-faq//book/ISBN/1-55558-127-7

6.2 Reference Material with Chapters or Sections on sendmail

BIB-VERSION:: CS-TR-v2.1
ID:: sendmail-faq//book/ISBN/0-13-151051-7
ENTRY:: March 23, 1996
TYPE:: Reference book, hardcopy
REVISION:: May 23, 1996; Updated abstract
TITLE:: Unix System Administration Handbook, Second Edition
AUTHOR:: Nemeth, Evi
AUTHOR:: Snyder, Garth
AUTHOR:: Seebass, Scott
AUTHOR:: Hein, Trent R.
CONTACT:: **sa-book@admin.com**
Prentice-Hall, Inc.
Upper Saddle River, New Jersey 07458
DATE:: January, 1995
PAGES:: 780
COPYRIGHT:: Copyright (c) 1995 by Prentice Hall PTR
LANGUAGE:: English
NOTES:: See: URL: **http://www.admin.com/**
ABSTRACT::

Still the best hands-on UNIX System Administration book around. Covers far more than just sendmail, but the sixty-four pages (pages 455-518 in the third printing) it does devote are very well written and quite useful. Also provides a version of Rob Kolstad's checksendmail script on the accompanying CD-ROM.

Note that Eric Allman and Marshall Kirk McKusick wrote the Foreword for the Second Edition. This should give you at least an inkling as to how essential this book is, even for experienced UNIX administrators.

END:: sendmail-faq//book/ISBN/0-13-151051-7

BIB-VERSION:: CS-TR-v2.1
ID:: sendmail-faq//book/ISBN/0-201-58629=0
ENTRY:: March 23, 1996
TYPE:: Reference book, hardcopy
REVISION:: March 27, 1996; Changed ID format to include ISBN,
moved URL to NOTES field from OTHER_ACCESS field,
also updated ABSTRACT
REVISION:: March 29, 1996; Updated ID, PAGES, COPYRIGHT, and ABSTRACT
TITLE:: Practical Internetworking With TCP/IP and UNIX
AUTHOR:: Carl-Mitchell, Smoot
AUTHOR:: Quarterman, John S.
CONTACT:: **tic@tic.com**
Addison-Wesley Publishing Company
Computer Science & Engineering Division
One Jacob Way
Reading, MA 01867
USA
Orders: voice: 800-822-6339 (USA)
fax: 617-942-1117
DATE:: 1993
PAGES:: 476
COPYRIGHT:: Copyright (c) 1993 by Addison-Wesley Publishing
Company, Inc.
LANGUAGE:: English
NOTES:: See URL: **http://heg-school.aw.com/cseng/authors/mitchell/
practical/practical.html**
ABSTRACT::

Devotes 50 pages (most of chapter 8) to discussion of sendmail. As far as TCP/IP networking books go that also happen to discuss sendmail, it seems well-written and clear (better than I recall Hunt's book being), but rather dated in the face of books devoted to the topic and all the recent development activity in the sendmail community. Forget about the references, though. The newest sendmail-related reference listed is dated 1983, ten years before the date on this book and most certainly wildly out-of-date now. There are other books written on the subject of Internetworking with TCP/IP (most notably Comer), but this particular book seems to have a unique mix of theory (if perhaps a bit dated) and practical advice. Other books tend to have lots of one or the other, or split their theory and nitty-gritty details into separate books in a series (like Comer).

Assuming that an update will be coming out soon, it probably deserves a place on the shelf of most System or Network Administrators, right next to *Internetworking with TCP/IP* by Comer, *Managing Internet Information Services* by Liu, et. al., *DNS and BIND* by Albitz and Liu, *Unix System Administration* by Nemeth, et. al., and last, but certainly not least, *sendmail* by Costales. However, it deserves this place more because of the non-sendmail-related material, as opposed to what sendmail-related material there is.

END:: sendmail-faq/ /book/ISBN/0-201-58629-0

BIB-VERSION:: CS-TR-v2.1
ID:: sendmail-faq/ /book/ISBN/0-937175-82-X
ENTRY:: March 23, 1996
TYPE:: Reference book, hardcopy
REVISION:: April 8, 1997; updated URL in NOTES section
TITLE:: TCP/IP Network Administration
AUTHOR:: Hunt, Craig
CONTACT:: O'Reilly & Associates, Inc.
103 Morris Street, Suite A
Sebastapol, CA 95472
Order by phone: 800-998-9938 (US/Canada inquiries)
800-889-8969 (US/Canada credit card orders)
707-829-0515 (local/overseas)
DATE:: August, 1992
PAGES:: 502
LANGUAGE:: English
NOTES:: See: URL: **http://www.ora.com/catalog/tcp/**
ABSTRACT::

The book I learned sendmail from when there was no other book in print that even
mentioned the name. Here primarily for historical purposes, especially with respect to
the sending of Internet mail and the DNS. Some of the other TCP/IP networking stuff is
relevant, but this book is getting more and more dated as time goes by.

END:: sendmail-faq/ /book/ISBN/0-937175-82-X

6.3 Reference Material on Subjects Related to sendmail

BIB-VERSION:: CS-TR-v2.1
ID:: sendmail-faq/ /book/ISBN/1-56592-236-0
ENTRY:: March 23, 1996
TYPE:: Reference book, hardcopy
REVISION:: April 8, 1997; Updated entire entry for 2nd Ed.
TITLE:: DNS and BIND
AUTHOR:: Albitz, Paul
AUTHOR:: Liu, Cricket
CONTACT:: O'Reilly & Associates, Inc.
103 Morris Street, Suite A
Sebastapol, CA 95472
Order by phone: 800-998-9938 (US/Canada inquiries)
800-889-8969 (US/Canada credit card orders)

707-829-0515 (local / overseas)
DATE:: January, 1997
PAGES:: 418
COPYRIGHT:: Copyright (c) 1997 O'Reilly & Associates, Inc. All rights reserved.
LANGUAGE:: English
NOTES:: See: URL: **http://www.ora.com/catalog/dns2/**
ABSTRACT::

As definitive as Costales is on sendmail, this book is on the subject of the Domain Name System (DNS) and the most common server software for the DNS, namely, BIND. The second edition has been updated to reflect the changes in BIND up through version 4.9.4, but even the first edition still stands the test of time as the one book **every** DNS/Domain Administrator should have on their shelf. The second edition is just that much better. Since the sending of Internet mail is so very heavily dependant on the DNS, it obviously also belongs on the shelf of any Postmaster or System Administrator whose site does Internet email. That means virtually every administrator of every site on the Internet.

END:: sendmail-faq//book/ISBN/1-56592-236-0

BIB-VERSION:: CS-TR-v2.1
ID:: sendmail-faq//book/ISBN/1-56592-153-4
ENTRY:: April 8, 1997
TYPE:: Reference book, hardcopy
TITLE:: Using & Managing UUCP
AUTHOR:: Ravin, Ed
AUTHOR:: O'Reilly, Tim
AUTHOR:: Dougherty, Dale
AUTHOR:: Todino, Grace
CONTACT:: O'Reilly & Associates, Inc.
103 Morris Street, Suite A
Sepastapol, CA 95472
Order by phone: 800-998-9938 (US/Canada inquiries)
800-889-8969 (US/Canada credit card orders)
707-829-0515 (local / overseas)
DATE:: September, 1996
PAGES:: 424
LANGUAGE:: English
NOTES:: See: URL: **http://www.ora.com/catalog/umuucp/**
ABSTRACT::

Replaces *Managing UUCP and Usenet* by Todino and O'Reilly as the definitive book for using, installing, and managing UUCP. The general assumption with version 8 sendmail is that virtually no one uses UUCP to send email anymore, but if that assumption isn't true for you, then you probably need this book.

END:: sendmail-faq//book/ISBN/1-56592-153-4

6.4 World Wide Web Index/Resource Pages on sendmail

BIB-VERSION:: CS-TR-v2.1
ID:: sendmail-faq//online/index/10
ENTRY:: March 23, 1996
TYPE:: Online sendmail index
REVISION:: March 27, 1996; moved URL from RETRIEVAL field to OTHER_ACCESS field
TITLE:: comp.mail.sendmail FAQ Support Page
AUTHOR:: Knowles, Brad
CONTACT:: Brad Knowles **brad@etext.org**
OTHER_ACCESS:: URL: **http://www.his.com/~brad/sendmail/**
LANGUAGE:: English
ABSTRACT::

Support Page for this FAQ.

END:: sendmail-faq//online/index/10

BIB-VERSION:: CS-TR-v2.1
ID:: sendmail-faq//online/index/17
ENTRY:: March 25, 1996
TYPE:: Online sendmail index
REVISION:: March 27, 1996; moved URL from RETRIEVAL field to OTHER_ACCESS field
TITLE:: comp.mail.sendmail Most Frequently Asked Questions Support Page
AUTHOR:: Assman, Claus
CONTACT:: Claus Assmann **ca@informatik.uni-kiel.de**
OTHER_ACCESS:: URL: **http://www.informatik.uni-kiel.de/~ca/email/english.html**
LANGUAGE:: English
ABSTRACT::

Most Frequently Asked Questions on **comp.mail.sendmail** and their answers. Also has some links to a few other resources.

END:: sendmail-faq//online/index/17

BIB-VERSION:: CS-TR-v2.1
ID:: sendmail-faq//online/resources/22
ENTRY:: November 24, 1996
TITLE:: IICONS Sendmail Resources
AUTHOR:: Caloca, Paul
CONTACT:: Paul Caloca **pcaloca@iicons.com**
COPYRIGHT:: Copyright (c) 1996 Paul Caloca. All Rights Reserved.
OTHER_ACCESS:: URL: **http://www.iicons.com/sendmail/index.html**
LANGUAGE:: English
ABSTRACT::

Provides information on how to compile sendmail and the NEWDB db.1.85 for Solaris 2. Also has a section on which Sun patches update Solaris 2 to BIND 4.9.3. Has pointers to some non-Sun/Solaris sendmail resources, especially including CERT Advisories related to sendmail.

END:: sendmail-faq//online/index/22

6.5 World Wide Web Index Pages and Other Reference on Internet Email in General

BIB-VERSION:: CS-TR-v2.1
ID:: sendmail-faq//online/index/12
ENTRY:: March 23, 1996
TYPE:: Online general Internet email index
REVISION:: March 27, 1996; moved URL from RETRIEVAL field to OTHER_ACCESS field
TITLE:: Internet Mail Consortium web site
CORP-AUTHOR:: Internet Mail Consortium
CONTACT:: **info@imc.org**
OTHER_ACCESS:: URL: **http://www.imc.org/**
LANGUAGE:: English
ABSTRACT::

If it has to do with Internet email, you'll probably find it here, or a link to it from here. They have or have information on email-related Usenet FAQs, RFCs, Internet Drafts (documents that are in the process of becoming RFCs), IETF Working Groups, security standards, and are running a few email-related mailing lists. Tends to be focussed on the standards issues. If you care about Internet email, you should make it your duty in life to check this site frequently.

END:: sendmail-faq//online/index/12

BIB-VERSION:: CS-TR-v2.1
ID:: sendmail-faq//online/index/13
ENTRY:: March 23, 1996
TYPE:: Online general Internet email index
REVISION:: August 20, 1996; updated URL
TITLE:: Email References
AUTHOR:: Wohler, Bill
CONTACT:: Bill Wohler **wohler@worldtalk.com**
OTHER_ACCESS::
URL:**http://www.worldtalk.com/html/msg_resources/email_ref.html**
LANGUAGE:: English
ABSTRACT::

The most exhaustive index site I know of for Internet email-related documents outside of the Internet Mail Consortium. Also has pointers to other organizations that relate to Internet email, such as the Electronic Messaging Association and the European Electronic Messaging Association. Tends to be focused on the server and standards issues.

END:: sendmail-faq//online/index/13

BIB-VERSION:: CS-TR-v2.1
ID:: sendmail-faq//online/index/14
ENTRY:: March 23, 1996
TYPE:: Online general Internet email index
REVISION:: June 28, 1996; added acronym for SMTPRD
TITLE:: SMTP Resources Directory (SMTPRD)
AUTHOR:: Salamon, Andras
AUTHOR:: Knowles, Brad
CONTACT:: Andras Salamon **smtprd@dns.net**
OTHER_ACCESS:: URL: **http://www.dns.net/smtprd/**
LANGUAGE:: English
ABSTRACT::

Another good index site, but still very much in the early phases of gestation. Based very heavily on the DNS Resources Directory, also by Andras Salamon, at **http://www.is.co.za/dnsrd/**. A well-rounded site, for the amount of material it covers so far.

END:: sendmail-faq//online/index/14

BIB-VERSION:: CS-TR-v2.1
ID:: sendmail-faq//online/index/15
ENTRY:: March 23, 1996
TYPE:: Online general Internet email index
REVISION:: March 27, 1996; moved URL from RETRIEVAL field to
OTHER_ACCESS field
TITLE:: E-Mail Web Resources
AUTHOR:: Wall, Matt
CONTACT:: Matt Wall **wall+@cmu.edu**
OTHER_ACCESS:: URL: **http://andrew2.andrew.cmu.edu/cyrus/email/email.html**
LANGUAGE:: English
ABSTRACT::

Another good index site, tends to be more focused on client-side and LAN email packages. Also lists some email services, which no one else that I've seen appears to have taken the time to catalog. Excellent side-by-side feature comparison of various MUAs and their compliance with various Internet protocols.

END:: sendmail-faq//online/index/15

6.6 Online Tutorials for sendmail

BIB-VERSION:: CS-TR-v2.1
ID:: sendmail-faq//online/tutorial/9
ENTRY:: March 23, 1996
TYPE:: Online sendmail tutorial
REVISION:: March 27, 1996; moved URL from RETRIEVAL field to
OTHER_ACCESS field
TITLE:: Sendmail V8: A (Smoother) Engine Powers Network Email
AUTHOR:: Reich, Richard
CONTACT:: Richard Reich **richard@reich.com**
DATE:: February 8, 1996
COPYRIGHT:: Copyright (c) 1995 The McGraw-Hill Companies, Inc. All Rights
Reserved.
OTHER_ACCESS:: URL: **http://www.unixworld.com/unixworld/archives/95/tutorial/008/008.txt.html**
LANGUAGE:: English
NOTES:: UnixWorld Online: Tutorial: Article No. 008
ABSTRACT::

Good technical introduction. Some useful references. Notably does not reference this FAQ as a place to get more information.

END:: sendmail-faq//online/article/9

BIB-VERSION:: CS-TR-v2.1
ID:: sendmail-faq//online/tutorial/16
ENTRY:: March 23, 1996
TYPE:: Online sendmail tutorial
REVISION:: March 27, 1996; moved URL from RETRIEVAL field to
OTHER_ACCESS field
TITLE:: Sendmail—Care and Feeding
AUTHOR:: Quinton, Reg
CONTACT:: Reg Quinton **reggers@julian.uwo.ca**
Computing and Communications Services
The University of Western Ontario
London, Ontario N6A 5B7
Canada
DATE:: March 24, 1992
OTHER_ACCESS:: URL: **ftp://ftp.sterling.com/mail/sendmail/
uwo-course/sendmail.txt.Z**
LANGUAGE:: English
NOTES:: Postscript version also available. See **ftp://ftp.sterling.com/mail/
sendmail/uwo-course/sendmail.ps.Z**
ABSTRACT::

Dated. Only here until I find better.

END:: sendmail-faq//online/tutorial/16

BIB-VERSION:: CS-TR-v2.1
ID:: sendmail-faq//online/tutorial/21
ENTRY:: March 27, 1996
TYPE:: Online sendmail tutorial
TITLE:: Explosion in a Punctuation Factory
AUTHOR:: Bryan Costales
CONTACT:: Becca Thomas **editor@unixworld.com**
DATE:: January 1994
COPYRIGHT:: Copyright (c) 1995 The McGraw-Hill Companies, Inc. All Rights Reserved.
OTHER_ACCESS:: URL: **http://www.unixworld.com/unixworld/archives/
94/tutorial/01/01.txt.html**
LANGUAGE:: English
ABSTRACT::

Good introduction on how sendmail re-write rules work.

END:: sendmail-faq//online/article/21

6.7 Online Archives of Mailing Lists and Usenet Newsgroups Relating to Internet Email

BIB-VERSION:: CS-TR-v2.1
ID:: sendmail-faq//online/archive/18
ENTRY:: March 25, 1996
TYPE:: Online Usenet newgroup archive
REVISION:: March 27, 1996; moved URL from RETRIEVAL field to
OTHER_ACCESS field
TITLE:: DejaNews
OTHER_ACCESS:: URL: **http://www.dejanews.com**
LANGUAGE:: English
NOTES:: Archives/indexes only Usenet news.
ABSTRACT::

The first, and still most focused, Usenet news archive/index site. Others archive/index news as well as other things, but none that I've seen do it better.

Go to "Power Search" then "Query Filter" if you wish to restrict the newsgroups you search on to something like just comp.mail.sendmail and not all newsgroups.

END:: sendmail-faq//online/archive/18

BIB-VERSION:: CS-TR-v2.1
ID:: sendmail-faq//online/archive/19
ENTRY:: March 25, 1996
TYPE:: Online Usenet newgroup archive
REVISION:: March 27, 1996; moved URL from RETRIEVAL field to
OTHER_ACCESS field
TITLE:: AltaVista
OTHER_ACCESS:: URL: **http://www.altavista.digital.com**
LANGUAGE:: English
NOTES:: Archives/indexes Usenet news and World Wide Web pages.
ABSTRACT::

One of the leading indexes of World-Wide Web pages, and their archive/index of Usenet news is obviously secondary.

END:: sendmail-faq//online/archive/19

BIB-VERSION:: CS-TR-v2.1
ID:: sendmail-faq//online/archive/20
ENTRY:: March 25, 1996
TYPE:: Online Usenet newgroup archive
REVISION:: April 8, 1997; additional information based on experience
TITLE:: InReference
OTHER_ACCESS:: URL: **http://www.reference.com**
LANGUAGE:: English
ABSTRACT::

Had promise to be the best Usenet news/publicly accessible mailing list index/archive site in the world. The best minds that were working on the project have since left, and the difference is visible. You'll probably be happier with DejaNews instead.

END:: sendmail-faq//online/archive/20

BIB-VERSION:: CS-TR-v2.1
ID:: sendmail-faq//online/archive/21
ENTRY:: May 24, 1996
TYPE:: Online archive of spam/junkmail
TITLE:: list-managers spam discussion archives
AUTHOR:: Gilman, Al
CONTACT:: Al Gilman **asgilman@access.digex.net**
OTHER_ACCESS:: URL: **http://www.access.digex.net/~asgilman/spam/**
OTHER_ACCESS:: URL: **ftp://www.access.digex.net/~asgilman/spam/**
LANGUAGE:: English
ABSTRACT::

These collections of past mail from the list-managers discussion list can be retrieved by ftp or HTTP. For anonymous ftp, open **ftp.digex.net** and cd to */pub/access/asgilman/spam*. For http, Go to **http://www.access.digex.net/~asgilman/spam/**. In this directory you will find, *inter alia*, two files which are mail folders:

```
spam       -- collects examples of spams
spam-NOT   -- collects discussion of spam countermeasures
```

END:: sendmail-faq//online/archive/21

Q7—THANKS!

Special thanks to:

Eric Allman

The core of the material here comes from his FAQ for version 8.6.9 sendmail. I couldn't even have gotten started were it not for him. And if he hadn't written sendmail, there obviously wouldn't even be a FAQ. Heck, there might not even be an Internet.

Paul Southworth

Provides FAQ posting services, useful comments on various sections, and the mailclient-faq. I couldn't have kept doing this were it not for his help.

Ed Ravin

Virtually all the material regarding the use of sendmail on AIX is his, and most of it has been carried over verbatim.

Thanks also to: Neil Hoggarth, Andras Salamon, Johan Svensson, Christopher X. Candreva, Bill Wohler, Matthew Wall, Henry W. Farkas, Claus Assmann, Curt Sampson, Rebecca Lasher, Jim Davis, David Keegel, Betty Lee, Alain Durand, Walter Schweizer, Christophe Wolfhugel, Al Gilman, Valdis Kletnieks, John Gardiner Myers, Paul DuBois, Adam Bentley, Dave Sill, Dave Wreski, Paul Caloca, Eamonn Coleman, Michael Fuhr, Betty Lee, Derrell Lipman, Era Eriksson, Richard Troxel, and the readers and posters of comp.mail.sendmail.

End of comp.mail.sendmail Frequently Asked Questions (FAQ), part 2 of 2

****

APPENDIX B

Common Desktop Environment (CDE) Frequently Asked Questions

Last updated June 9, 1997
(*reprinted with permission*)
Version: 1.6
Last modified date: 06/09/97
Maintained-by: Aditya Talwar (**cosc4hf@menudo.uh.edu**)

Objective: This FAQ will attempt to provide answers to overcome day-to-day snags encountered in using CDE desktop.

The following is a list of questions that are frequently asked about CDE (Common Desktop Environment) in the **comp.unix.cde** newsgroup. You can help make it an even better-quality FAQ by writing a succinct contribution or update it by sending an email to me.

My Employer/account is *not* responsible for the contents of this FAQ. Since CDE is a joint venture between several UNIX vendors, this document may not contain the latest or most accurate information on all platforms and versions at all times. Whenever time permits I'll try my level best to keep the information in this document updated.

To get the initial structure of the CDE FAQ going, I have added some questions; please send me what you think should be useful over here. I'll try my best to keep this FAQ updated and post it on a weekly schedule initially, and then lengthen the interval later. Thanks for your help in advance! (Please bear in mind this is still in primitive form.)

The first indexed, HTML, WWW version of this FAQ is available at **http://www.pobox.com/~burnett/cde/index.html**.

+ added questions?
* updated answers?

1. General

1.1) What is CDE? Why should I use CDE?
1.2) What are the current platforms and versions of CDE?

2. More Info

2.1) What WWW/FTP sites contain CDE information?
2.2) What books should I read for CDE?
2.3) Where can I look for more information for setting up my desktop?

3. Desktop Setup

3.1) How can I change my default window manager in CDE?
3.2) How can I change my keyboard settings in CDE?
3.3) Is there a .mailcap/.mime types file for dtmail? Where can I find it?
3.4) What if I have login problems? How to see the errors?
3.5) Why can't some applications, like Netscape, etc., start up in workspaces other than my login workspace?

3.6) Would someone please tell me how to access a floppy while in CDE 1.0.2?

3.7) One question I see a lot is, "How to deal with multiple heads?"

3.8) How do I change keyboard repeat rate?

3.9) I'm new to CDE. I'm running it on a Sun with Solaris 2.5. The lock icon on the control panel doesn't work.

3.10) How do I use arrow keys to switch between workspaces?

3.11) How to use xv under CDE to create smaller icons?

+3.12) I have recently installed CDE on my Solaris 2.5.1 server. I would like to have CDE throw up the login screen at boot time on my console, but miss the console messages that are normally displayed there.

+3.13) Does anyone know how to switch between desktops without having to use the TAB key?

+3.14) When I log on to CDE in HP-UX, I want certain applications automatically started, like a dtterm running a certain script, etc. How can this be done?

+3.15) Why does xsetroot not work?

+3.16) How do I disable "Open Terminal" on the File Manager?

+3.17) How do I replace the clock on the front panel with a digital clock?

+3.18) Where are all of the f.<functions> in dtwm documented? If you say the dtwm man page, I will ask you to find f.goto_workspace, f.next_workspace, etc. I can't find any reference to them in the dtwm man pages?

+3.19) How do I get an application to display in a particular workspace? For example: xterm -xrm "???" What goes inside the quotes?

+3.20) Is there an equivalent .xinitrc file in CDE which can be edited so apps get launched on startup?

+3.21) Maybe we're backward or something, but our Sun w/s are not configured to give users access to */usr*. All docs talk about copying some file from */etc/dt* to */usr/dt* and modifying it, which doesn't work in our environment.

+3.22) What are the advantages of dtterm over xterm? The only one I can think of is that it is already installed as the default. Apart from that, cut-and-paste requires more effort than with xterm, and it is not identified as VT100 compatible when logging in to remote systems (I'm getting tired of typing "export TERM=vt100" and "SET/TERM=vt100"). Before I give up on it, are there some features I'm overlooking?

4. Application Development

4.1) What are actions and datatypes in CDE?

4.2) How can I reload new actions and datatypes in CDE?

5. Troubleshooting

5.1) What directories/files can I look at to check for errors?
5.2) The lock button doesn't work, and .dt/errorlog shows "dtsession: Unable to lock display due to security restrictions."

6. Acknowledgements

1. GENERAL

*1.1) What is CDE? Why should I use CDE?

The Common Desktop Environment is a standard desktop for UNIX, providing services to end-users, systems administrators, and application developers consistently across many platforms.

CDE was originally developed under the COSE (Common Open Software Environment) initiative by Hewlett-Packard, IBM, Novell and SunSoft. Those companies were joined by Digital, Fujitsu, and Hitachi as sponsors of the CDE-Motif PST under the auspices of the Open Software Foundation (OSF). That project is developing the successors to CDE 1.0 and Motif 2.0, along with enhancements to X11R6 that will be included in the Broadway Release. The X Consortium is the Prime Contractor for the PST.

*1.2) What are the current platforms and versions of CDE?

All of the companies in 1.1 offer CDE in some form. In addition, TriTeal offers the Triteal Enhanced Desktop (TED), their CDE implementation, on several other platforms.

X Inside has just recently released a port of CDE for Linux and FreeBSD. WGS (Work Group Solutions) is selling it bundled with X Inside's Accelerated X server (which is needed for its CDE kit).

Each company productizes CDE in its own way, including defect repairs, platform-specific hardware/software support, and value-added features onto the common software base that is available to sponsors of the technology and licensees. This is similar to what has happened in the past with Motif and X11.

OSF licenses the common source base without modifications. The original COSE source was version 1.0.0; the CDE Maintenance Release was 1.0.10 (to avoid conflicts with sponsor-specific version numbers, e.g., 1.0.2 from Sun that comes with Solaris 2.5.1; the source base produced by the CDE-Motif CST will be version 2.1.0 and will include Motif 2.1.0 (so that the numbering schemes for CDE and Motif can be unified).

Therefore, it is very important for people to provide not only the version number but also the vendor when identifying the version of CDE that they are using.

2. MORE INFO

2.1) What WWW/FTP sites contain CDE information?

Action-definitions and the icons can be found at:

> **http://www.tm.bi.ruhr-uni-bochum.de/dt/**
> **ftp://ftp.tm.bi.ruhr-uni-bochum.de/pub/dt**

These directories are mirrors of our */etc/dt/appconfig*.

Does anybody know another resource of this kind on the Web or did anybody the same work as we did?

***ftp://ftp.frontec.se/pub/cde** is a great site for actions, icons which can be placed in */etc/dt*.

Any mail or upload in **ftp://ftp.tm.bi.ruhr-uni-bochum.de/incoming/dt** would be greatly appreciated.

> **http://www.austin.ibm.com/cgi-bin/CDE/faqtop** - AIX flavored FAQ
> **http://www.hp.com/wsg/ssa/cde.html**
> **http://www.hp.com/xwindow/windowmgrs/cde.html**

is the main descriptive page about HP-CDE. Use the site-specific search engine to look for "CDE." My last search turned up 154 documents that reference it on the HP Web site.

> ***http://www.partner.digital.com/www-swdev/pages/Home/TECH/CDE/cdedocs.html**

*Above seems to have a complete list of manuals for various CDE tasks as system administration, *programming, etc. in HTML format.

http://www.iac.net/~hollende/manual/hd_cde.html is the top of an elaborate description of how Hale & Dorr, a prestigious Boston law firm, has adapted CDE for use in their environment.

http://www.triteal.com/cde.html has the information about TED.

http://www.sun.com/cde/index.html has the description of the current CDE offering for Solaris from Sun.

http://www.osf.org/motif/CDE/cde.html contains information about licensing from OSF the CDE Maintenance Release that was produced by the CDE-Motif PST.

http://www.lib.ox.ac.uk/internet/news/faq/archive/cde-cose-faq.html is an old FAQ about CDE from the COSE days.

http://www.xinside.com/ is X Inside, Inc.'s Web site—we also have some screen shots up of CDE as well. Other versions floating around? Please let me know.

2.2) What books should I read for CDE?

A series of official documentation is available from Addison Wesley:

http://www.aw.com/devpress/series/cde.html

I found the Advanced Users and System Adminstrators guide most useful to get jump-started.

2.3) Where can I look for more information for setting up my desktop?

Make sure */usr/dt/man* is added to your $MANPATH. Section 4 of */usr/dt/man* contains useful setup information, e.g., dtfpfile, dtactionfile, dtdtfile, etc.

3. DESKTOP SETUP

3.1) How can I change my default window manager in CDE?

I asked if it were possible to add other window managers such as twm or fvwm to the CDE login. I did get a few responses saying that it could be done, but unfortunately no one knew how. Anyway, a search through Web Crawler revealed the following document:

http://www.chem.duke.edu/~watkins/altdesk.html

I'm running fvwm right now. All I had to do was put *Dtsession*wmStartupCommand: /home/orb/bin/sunos5/fvwm* in my *.Xdefaults* file. Just change the path to wherever you put fvwm.

3.2) How can I change my keyboard settings in CDE?

Try putting something like this in your *.dt/dtwmrc*:

```
Keys DtKeyBindings

{
    Meta<Key>space              icon|window          f.post_wmenu
    Meta<Key>Tab                root|icon|window     f.next_key
    Meta Shift<Key>Tab          root|icon|window     f.prev_key
    Meta<Key>Prior              root|icon|window     f.next_key
    Meta<Key>Next               root|icon|window     f.prev_key
```

```
Meta<Key>Down              root|icon|window      f.circle_down
Meta<Key>Up                root|icon|window      f.circle_up
Meta Ctrl Shift<Key>exclam root|icon|window      f.set_behavior
Meta<Key>F6                window                f.next_key transient
<Key>F11                   root|icon|window      f.next_workspace
Shift<Key>F11              root|icon|window      f.prev_workspace
}
```

You might need to change the key names—this is based on an HP keyboard. Under the above config, F11 will switch workspaces, and SHIFT F11 will switch backwards.

3.3) Is there a .mailcap/.mime types file for dtmail? Where can I find it?

dtMail, like most other CDE applications, uses the CDE database to figure out the MIME types. Look at the *Advanced User's and System Administrator's Guide* book that comes with CDE in the sections on Actions and DataTypes. These actions and datatypes allow you to do a lot more than just a MIME file and are not all that hard to work with. Just remember to reload the actions and restart the applications you are testing with.

3.4) What if I have login problems? How to see the errors?

If you cannot log in, from the log in session interface, choose the Options menu, then choose Failsafe login selection. Then log in. If there is an error, you can log in the following location and fix the problem:

$HOME/.dt/errorlog, $HOME/.dt/startlog, and */var/dt/Xerrors,* etc

3.5) Why can't some applications, like Netscape, etc., start up in workspaces other than my login workspace?

Some applications, like Netscape, are non-ICCCM compliant, i.e., they don't write their, command line to the WM_COMMAND property. This means they don't follow the -xrm resource setting and can't open in the workspace you want. I believe it will take some time for vendors to make their applications ICCCM/CDE complaint.

3.6) Would someone please tell me how to access a floppy while in CDE 1.0.2?

You can still use */usr/openwin/bin/filemgr* to manage floppies and CD-ROMs. Or you can use the volcheck(1) command and then do

```
dtaction Open /floppy/floppy0
```

Full support for removable media will be in CDE 1.1.

3.7) One question I see a lot is, "How to deal with multiple heads?"

mrz@nimba.NSD.3Com.COM (Matthew Zeier) writes:

> I have CDE configured to use two screens. The only problem is that I can not get CDE to display a second toolbar on my other screen. Without that, I don't quite know how to easily switch workspaces nor do I know how to change backdrops.

Running a second toolbar would require having a second dtwm running; I've never tried this, but I've talked to people who have. Some had problems, some seemed to work just fine. I've never bothered to try myself, since the following hacks are good enough for me.

1. Customize dtwm keystrokes to change workspaces. In ~/.dt/dtwmrc I have key bindings including the following:

```
Keys DtKeyBindings
{
    Meta<Key>Right          root|icon|window   f.next_workspace
    Meta<Key>Left           root|icon|window   f.prev_workspace
}
```

I then use meta and the left/right arrows to bang around the workspaces. This works on both screens.

2. Put the programs I use most often on the second screen in the dtwm root menu:

```
Menu DtRootMenu
{
    "Workspace Menu"              f.title
    "Xemacs"                      f.exec "xemacs"
    "Cmdtool"                     f.exec "/usr/openwin/bin/cmdtool"
    "Dtterm"                      f.exec "/usr/dt/bin/dtterm"
     no-label                     f.separator
    "Refresh"                     f.refresh
    "Minimize/Restore Front Panel" f.toggle_frontpanel
    "Next workspace"              f.next_workspace
     no-label                     f.separator
    "Restart Workspace Manager..." f.restart
    "Log out..."                  f.action ExitSession
}
```

This gives me a way to launch these apps on the second screen, since dtwm sets DISPLAY according to which screen you're on when you pick an app off the root menu. (You'll note this includes a dtterm, so I can always launch other applications via the shell.)

3. To set backdrops, just run dtstyle on the other screen, e.g.,

$ dtstyle -display :0.1

This gets the style manager running on the other screen; you can now set backdrops as normal. For those who *really* want a GUI gadget for changing the workspaces, check out the sample script in */usr/dt/examples/dtksh/DtWsTest1*. This is a dtksh script that uses the workspace management APIs to change the workspaces when buttons are clicked. It's just a sample, and a little rough, but it works. (I'd love to see somebody come up with a polished-up version of this.) [Note the sample scripts in */usr/dt/examples* are only loaded if you installed the "developer's" version of CDE on Solaris; I don't know about the other platforms.]

3.8) How do I change keyboard repeat rate?

To turn the autorepeat feature on or off, open the workspace menu, bring up the style manager, click on the kbd icon, and change the repeat rate.You can also do this from within a dtterm window: Options=>Global BlinkingCursor (Disabled | Enabled).

To change the keyboard repeat rate you need to pass some options to the Xserver (Xsun is the default for CDE). dtlogin will start the Xserver by first looking at */etc/dt/config/Xservers*. If it does not exist it will use */usr/dt/config/Xservers*. See dtlogin(1X) for more info. Copy */usr/dt/config/Xservers* to */etc/dt/config/Xservers* and add your preferences there. Then you must restart the Xserver for changes to take effect. The line to start the server should look something like this:

```
:0   Local local_uid@console root /usr/openwin/bin/Xsun :0 -nobanner
-ar1 350 -ar2 30
 # /etc/rc2.d/S99dtlogin stop
 # /etc/rc2.d/S99dtlogin start
```

from Xsun manpage ...
-ar1 milliseconds
Specify amount of time in milliseconds before a pressed key begins to autorepeat. The default is 500 milliseconds.
-ar2 milliseconds
Specify the interval in milliseconds between autorepeats of pressed keys. The default is 50 milliseconds.

3.9) I'm new to CDE. I'm running it on a Sun with Solaris 2.5. The lock icon on the control panel doesn't work.

This is a known problem with CDE and is being investigated. This is known to happen in an NIS+ environment.

3.10) How do I use arrow keys to switch between workspaces?

Take the following lines and add them to the "Keys DtKeyBindings" section of your *$HOME/.dt/dtwmrc* file:

```
<Key>F20              root|window|icon          f.next_workspace
<Key>F19              root|window|icon          f.prev_workspace
```

or something similar.

3.11) How to use xv under CDE to create smaller icons?

For the trivia file: The problem is caused by xv refusing to force itself to be drawn smaller than the window manager-recommended minimum size. To defeat that, add this to .Xdefaults:

```
Dtwm*xv*clientDecoration: none
```

This makes the main xv window borderless, but you can still move it in CDE's dtwm (by default, anyway) with ALT+mouse1drag.

3.12) I have recently installed CDE on my Solaris 2.5.1 server. I would like to have CDE throw up the login screen at boot time on my console, but miss the console messages that are normally displayed there.

A. Add the following to */etc/dt/config/Xconfig*:

```
Dtlogin._0.setup:       Xsetup_0
Dtlogin*grabServer:     False
```

B. Copy */usr/dt/config/Xsetup* to */etc/dt/config/Xsetup_0* and add to following line at the bottom:

```
( sleep 2; /usr/openwin/bin/xconsole -geometry 480x130-0-0 -daemon -notify
-verbose -fn fixed -exitOnFail )&
```

Then restart dtlogin.

+3.13) Does anyone know how to switch between desktops without having to use the TAB key?

The neat way to do this is to edit your *$HOME/.dt/dtwmrc* file and add the following lines in the Keys DtKeyBindings section:

```
<Key>F5       root|icon|window                f.goto_workspace ws0
<Key>F6       root|icon|window                f.goto_workspace ws1
<Key>F7       root|icon|window                f.goto_workspace ws2
<Key>F8       root|icon|window                f.goto_workspace ws3
```

If you don't have a dtwmrc file in the above directory, then copy the */usr/dt/config/C/sys.dtwmrc* to *$HOME/.dt/dtwmrc*.

+3.14) When I log on to CDE in HP-UX, I want certain applications automatically started, like a dtterm running a certain script, etc. How can this be done?

You can create a script in *~/.dt/sessions* called sessionetc. The script is executed at CDE startup, and in it, you can start up all those cde-unaware apps that cde can't start up itself. If necessary, you can also use *~/.dt/sessions/sessionexit* to execute commands at CDE exit time.

+3.15) Why does xsetroot not work?

Change backdrop to Transparent.

+3.16) How do I disable "Open Terminal" on the File Manager?

Create ACTION Terminal {EXEC_STRING dterror.ds "Unavailable"}, etc.

+3.17) How do I replace the clock on the front panel with a digital clock?

Anybody knows this ... forward me the answer!

+3.18) Where are all of the f.<functions> in dtwm documented? If you say the dtwm man page, I will ask you to find f.goto_workspace, f.next_workspace, etc. I can't find any reference to them in the dtwm man pages?

The dtwmrc man page has all this information. dtwmrc(4), to be precise.
>From the man page:

```
f.goto_workspace workspace
```

This function causes the workspace manager to switch to the workspace named by workspace. If no workspace exists by the specified name, then no action occurs. Note that adding and deleting workspaces dynamically can affect this function.

```
f.next_workspace
```

This function causes the workspace manager to switch to the next workspace. If the last workspace is currently active, then this function will switch to the first workspace. Etc., etc., etc.

+3.19) How do I get an application to display in a particular workspace? For example: xterm -xrm "???" What goes inside the quotes?

```
xterm -xrm "*workspaceList: ws0 ws1"
```

The workspace names can be either ws0, ws1, etc., or the Names entered in the labels on the front panel workspace switch. The application must copy the "-xrm" option to a WM_COMMAND property on the application's top level window. You can usually check whether an application does that by running "xprop WM_COMMAND" and clicking on the application's window. (The dtterm command is aware of workspaces and will obey the resource but does not have any WM_COMMAND property before the session manager asks it to update one.)

2. What is dtsmcmd, and where can I find documentation on it? Is it an undocumented function of CDE? A find was unable to find the binary, and a search through the man pages was fruitless as well.

It is an undocumented internal mechanism of the session manager.

3. Where are all of the f.<functions> in dtwm documented? If you say the dtwm man page, I will ask you to find f.goto_workspace, f.next_workspace, etc. I can't find any reference to them in the dtwm man pages. I checked the Sun, IBM, and TED versions and

found no reference to them. BTW, all the above versions understand f.goto_workspace, et al., even if they're not documented. (I found out about the functions from this newsgroup.)

They are all documented in "man dtwmrc."

+3.20) Is there an equivalent .xinitrc file in CDE which can be edited so apps get launched on startup?

Explore *$HOME/.dt*—you'll find a bunch of stuff in there. But the equivalent to *.xinitrc* for the *home* session would be *$HOME/.dt/sessions/home/dt.session.* You can, however, have more than one session, so you'll have to edit each one separately.

+3.21) Maybe we're backward or something, but our Sun w/s are not configured to give users access to */usr.* All docs talk about copying some file from */etc/dt* to */usr/dt* and modifying it, which doesn't work in our environment.

This is for system-wide configuration only! It affects *all* CDE users on that system. And it's not from */etc/dt* to */usr/dt*, but probably the other way around ... original copies are stored in */usr/dt*, but if you plan to modify them, copy them to */etc/dt*, so that an upgrade of CDE which would overwrite the files in */usr/dt* would not wipe out your customizations.

>For user customizations, I assume we can make these types of */usr/dt* changes in *$HOME/.dt*?

That's correct. Individuals who want to modify the behavior of CDE for their use only, should do it in *$HOME/.dt.*

+3.22) What are the advantages of dtterm over xterm?

The only one I can think of is that it is already installed as the default. Apart from that, cut-and-paste requires more effort than with xterm, and it is not identified as VT100 compatible when logging in to remote systems (I'm getting tired of typing "export TERM=vt100" and "SET/TERM=vt100"). Before I give up on it, are there some features I'm overlooking?

You can use the middle mouse button (if you have one) for pasting a selection. Putting the following line in *~/app-defaults/Dtterm* causes dtterm to set the TERM environment variable to vt100:

```
Dtterm*termName: vt100
```

Other examples of resources that I find useful are

```
Dtterm*kshMode: True
Dtterm*autoWrap: True
Dtterm*userFont: -*-lucida sans typewriter-medium-*-*-*-*-120-*
Dtterm*sunFunctionKeys: True        - if you are using a Sun machine
Dtterm*saveLines: 100s
Dtterm*loginShell: True
```

4. APPLICATION DEVELOPMENT

4.1) What are actions and datatypes in CDE?

Actions are modular programming methods by which CDE can automate desktop tasks like running applications or manipulating data files. You can create your own actions, data types, and icons for your local environment. If you are new to CDE, the following link is a good site and contains good examples, which are installed in /etc/dt of your machine: The complete thing is now accessible as **ftp://ftp.frontec.se/pub/cde**, just point it out.

And now, we want to see more! There just MUST be other guys sitting on resources like this! Maybe you should make an explicit request for such resources in **comp.unix.cde**?

—Michael

datatype (can someone give me a good definition?)

4.2) How can I reload new actions and datatypes in CDE?

There are two ways:
/usr/dt/bin/dtaction ReloadActions, or click on the Reload_Actions icon under the Desktop_Tools folder.

5. TROUBLESHOOTING

5.1) What directories/files can I look at to check for errors?

$HOME/.dt/errorlog
$HOME/.dt/startlog
/var/dt/Xerrors

+5.2) The lock button doesn't work, and .dt/errorlog shows "dtsession: Unable to lock display due to security restrictions."

Kevin Davidson, **tkld@cogsci.ed.ac.uk**, suggests creating Xlock.dt in *~/.dt/types* or */etc/dt/appconfig/types/C*, containing

```
----------------------------8<--snip-snip--8<----------------------------

## Replace broken LockDisplay action
## Built in one claims it cannot lock the screen...
ACTION LockDisplay
{
        LABEL    LockDisplay
        TYPE     COMMAND
        EXEC_STRING    xlock -remote
        WINDOW_TYPE    NO_STDIO
        DESCRIPTION    The LockDisplay action locks the workstation. \
                       You must know the user's or root password to \
                       unlock the workstation.
}
----------------------------8<--snip-snip--8<----------------------------
```

6. ACKNOWLEDGEMENTS

This is a rudimentary set of initial questions I have come up with to help the new user or the Guru to look for common problems and answers. Your contributions to enhance this document will be much appreciated. I have written some material in this document and shamelessly copied some of your USENET postings from the CDE newsgroup.

Acknowledgements for contributions go to:

Rich McAllister: **rfm@eng.sun.com**

Claus Oberste-Brandenburg: **cob@tm.bi.ruhr-uni-bochum.de**

Andrew Page: **page@cv.hp.com**

Brian Holtz: **holtz@netcord.Eng.Sun.COM**

Scott Raney: **raney@metacard.com**

Rick Beldin: **rbeldin@atl.hp.com**

Chris O'Regan: **chris@ECE.Concordia.CA**
Steven F. Burnett: **burnett@pobox.com**
Michael.Kolmodin: **Michael.Kolmodin@lule.frontec.se**
Amit Paul: **akpaul@leland.Stanford.EDU**
Ola Andersson: **mailto:rand@ling.umu.se**
Himanshu Gohel: **gohel@rad.usf.edu**
Mike Stroyan: **mike_stroyan@fc.hp.com**
Andy Warburton: **andyw@parallax.co.uk**

and many more ...

Aditya Talwar: **cosc4hf@menudo.uh.edu**

APPENDIX C

Samba Server HOWTO

> **NOTE:**   The information in this HOWTO was correct at the time it was written. The vast majority is still correct, and represents the best, unified explanation of Samba currently available. Please be aware that some URLs may have changed since this document was written.

Michal Jaegermann, **michal@ellpspace.math.ualberta.ca** v1.4, 10 June 1996

This document is a short-form guide to configuring Samba and getting it running in as short a time as possible. It also attempts to provide answers for some frequently asked questions, but is not a replacement for the full FAQ, the man pages or the Samba Guide.

1. PREFACE

Please send any corrections to **michal@ellpspace.math.ualberta.ca**. This document attempts to provide hints and answers for basic problems encountered when setting shared directories, print services, user accounts, and access control on the Samba server. Nothing here cannot be found in already existing documentation for Samba and/ or MS-Windows, but it may not always be easy to find, especially for folks not used to reading documentation. :-)

On the other hand, the full documentation is much more detailed and touches on many points not even mentioned here. There are many variations on this basic theme, and the author has seen only some of them.

Further, Samba itself develops and changes rather quickly, especially at present as we move towards version 2.0. It has become very popular and gains contributions and technical information from quarters previously unexpected. Therefore, these answers may not always be absolutely valid. They may also depend on specifics of your network and the version of Samba you are running, especially when it comes to browsing. Please contribute and correct at will!

1.1 Copyright Information

1.2 Standard Disclaimer

The author disavows any potential liability, either real or perceived, for the contents or use of this document. Any use of the concepts, examples, and/or any other content of this document is entirely at your own risk.

Microsoft is a registered trademark of Microsoft Corporation. All other products mentioned are trademarks of their respective companies.

1.3 Contributors

A direct contribution of these persons to the contents of this document is gratefully acknowledged:

▼ Maurice Hilarius, **maurice@ellpspace.math.ualberta.ca**

■ Dan Shearer, **Dan.Shearer@UniSA.edu.au**

▲ Andrew Tridgell, **Andrew.Tridgell@anu.edu.au**

2. GENERAL INFORMATION

2.1 What is Samba?

Samba is server software for computers running under UNIX or another UNIX-like operating systems with standard TCP/IP available. (Samba, as it stands right now, depends on UNIX file structure, permissions, system calls, and services. There was a talk about a port to VMS, and maybe something else, but the status is currently unknown.) It provides file and printer services for clients using some variants of SMB (Server Message Block) protocol. SMB is a "native" networking protocol used by MS-DOS based (in a very broad sense, including derivatives) clients. They include those from IBM, ICL, Microsoft, and even one particular Novell product.

In particular, clients are distributed with Windows for Workgroups, Windows 95, Windows NT (Microsoft), OS/2 Warp (IBM), and others. Even if you have a client already, please refer to the section "Where I will find client software?" for security and update issues.

Some of Samba's server cousins include DEC Pathworks, Microsoft LAN Manager/X, OS/2 Lan Manager, IBM LAN Server, Syntax Server, and Windows NT Server. Some clients, such as Windows 95/Workgroups or Warp Connect, can also act as low-volume servers with limited management facilities.

▼ SMB is becoming very popular, mainly owing to these factors: Windows 95 has dial-up access to PPP servers with an included service, and this service allows one to "browse" to public shares on the Internet.

■ Samba is "free" and this is a lot less expensive than Novell! (friendlier, too!)

■ With Samba, UNIX servers, well-connected to a global network, can speak in a "native" protocol of clients. It is much simpler to maintain one more protocol on a capable server than teach new tricks to multiple clients which were never meant to do something else.

▲ There is an established, well-tested way of doing SMB over TCP/IP, described in publicly available RFC 1001 and RFC 1002 documents. This means that SMB has a head start when it comes to Internet integration.

2.2 Where will I find server software?

Samba software is freely available "on the net." It was created, and is still actively developed, by Andrew Tridgell, **Andrew.Tridgell@anu.edu.au**. The main Samba site is

ftp://nimbus.anu.edu.au/pub/tridge/samba/

There are also various mirrors, which include

ftp://src.doc.ic.ac.uk/packages/samba
ftp://ftp.demon.co.uk/pub/unix/samba
ftp://sunsite.unc.edu/pub/Linux/system/Network/Samba/
ftp://choc.satech.net.au/pub/samba

If you would like Andrew to spend more time on the Samba code, then do not flood his private mailbox. If you have bug reports, contributions, patches, or technical questions for which you really cannot find answers elsewhere, e-mail to **samba-bugs@anu.edu.au**.

At the time of writing, the current version of Samba is 1.9.15p8 (released, for brave souls, there is 1.9.16alpha10), but this is not likely to stay long at that. :-)

2.3 Where will I find client software?

Together with Samba suite comes the smbclient program; so anything which can run the server may also become a client. If software on a machine you would like to connect to a Samba server did not include a client already, see the section "What is Samba?", then various free clients can be found at **ftp://ftp.microsoft.com/bussys/**.

Be sure to look carefully. Microsoft keeps both older and current versions of some things on line there, and you most definitely want the newer versions. Also, the client included with Windows for Workgroups has been superseded by a newer one at this site (V 3.12b). Finally, Microsoft has acknowledged a security bug in the versions earlier distributed, both with Windows for Workgroups and Windows 95. This bug may allow people to access shares using the UNIX smbclient program, and then cd ../ to access, possibly in a few steps, the whole disk that the share is on. More information is available from Microsoft at:

> http://www.microsoft.com/windows/software/w95fpup.htm
> http://www.microsoft.com:80/KB/PEROPSYS/windows/Q136418.htm

This can be fixed by downloading and installing with Microsoft's patches at

> http://www.microsoft.com:80/KB/SoftLib/MSLFiles/Wfwvsrvr.exe—Win 3.11
> http://www.microsoft.com/windows/download/vservupd.exe—Windows 95

Please note that they also have a similar Netware bug. See details at

> http://www.microsoft.com/windows/software/w95fpup.htm#Netware

Be sure to consult **http://lake.canberra.edu.au/pub/samba/docs/security.htm** for up-to-date information on possible other client security problems.

Lastly, not free (but maybe you still want to look at them) replacement stacks for all the Microsoft operating systems are sold by companies such as FTP Software (**http://www.ftp.com**) and Core Systems (**http://www.win.net/~core/**), who claim they, provide better quality and have more features. There are also proprietry network solutions such as Dec Pathworks which include an SMB client as well.

2.4 Where can I find more information on Samba?

There are WWW sites devoted to Samba. They include

> http://lake.canberra.edu.au/pub/samba
> http://www.choc.satech.net.au/pub/samba

Check also various WWW index sites for a "samba" keyword. Moreover, there are two mailing lists, **samba@listproc.anu.edu.au** and **samba-announce@listproc.anu.edu.au** to which you can subscribe. Discussions in the newsgroup **comp.protocols.smb** seem to concentrate mostly on Samba. Last, but not least, read the documents included with source distributions.

2.5 Where can I find details of SMB protocol?

Beyond the protocol description writeup included with Samba sources, and various bits and pieces one may fish out on assorted Microsoft servers, one of the better sources is Chapter 8 in *UNIX Networking*, ed. Kochan and Wood (Pipeline Associates, Inc., 1989, published by Hayden Books, ISBN 0-672-48440-4). This particular chapter was written by Martin R.M. Dunsmuir, Director of Xenix Development, Microsoft Corp. As for Microsoft servers, try this:

> **ftp://ftp.microsoft.com/developr/drg/SMB-info/smbpub.zip**
> **ftp://ftp.microsoft.com/developr/drg/SMB-info/smbhlp.zip**

and possibly other files in the same directory.

Another source of information can be found in X/Open publications. On-line catalog can be browsed at

> **http://www.xopen.org/public/pubs/catalog/**

Buying documents from X/Open is a pretty expensive proposition. For those of you used to thinking in terms of OSI model, Core SMB is an application layer service. The following diagram illustrates this mode with NETBIOS and SMB.

```
Application
-------------------> SMB Protocol
Presentation
Session
-------------------> Netbios
Transport
Network
Data Link
Physical
```

2.6 How can I install Samba on my UNIX machine?

Get sources, read instructions, configure, compile, install. For some flavours of OS (Linux, SCO, ...) it is possible to find already precompiled binaries. It still can be simpler to make your own as long as you have a compiler.

As distributed, the Samba software is installed in subdirectories of */usr/local/samba/*. This default can be changed at compile time if there are prevailing reasons for that. If needed, add entries in */etc/services* and */etc/inetd.conf* as described in the Samba documentation.

Make sure that the names of services (in UNIX and Internet Protocol sense, not Samba services) in these two files are exactly the same. This is especially important if some entries were already there.

These services use privileged ports, so you will need root access, or at least cooperation from root, to install the Samba server. On the UNIX side these ports could be moved, obviously, somewhere else. Unfortunately, the port numbers seem to be hardwired into Microsoft clients, even if they sometimes pretend that this is not the case, so it looks like you are forced to use defaults for proper operation.

3. EXPORTING FILES TO SMB CLIENTS

3.1 How do I post a share?

In MS-speak a "share" is a directory, its contents including subdirectories, which is made available to clients. To achieve that goal you include in your *smb.conf* file (*/usr/local/samba/lib/smb.conf in a default installation*) a section like this:

```
[newjunk]
    comment  = Just testing Samba
    path     = /usr/some/stuff
    public   = yes
    writable = no
```

After this, everybody able to log on from a client to the Samba server should be able to see the contents of stuff. By the way, many configuration parameters have multiple synonymous names. In particular, you may use "writeable" instead of "writable" with equal success.

The sample *smb.conf* from the distribution contains more examples, together with explanations in comments. In the longer run the *smb.conf* manpage is a required reading!

3.2 What about names?

Some old SMB clients will have problems with share names longer than eight characters. Not "eight plus three," but eight characters total. For portability, it is better to not overstep that limit. If you do, Samba will warn you, but it will work without trouble; something else may misbehave, however, such as older MS-DOS SMB clients.

3.3 How do I control an access?

The access to a file served by Samba is governed by both UNIX permissions and Samba configuration parameters. In other words, even if writable would be "yes" for a [newjunk] Samba share, one cannot write to a file *newfile.txt* without UNIX write permissions on it.

The paragraph above implies that users trying to access files via Samba server need valid logons on Samba server. This is indeed the case, with the possible exception of browsing public shares, which can be done from a valid guest account. For the latter to work you have to be able to connect with a guest account name or with an empty name. Try something like these from a client, if you must:

```
\\server\public%nobody
 \\server\public%
```

It may even work if your client is having a good day. See the section "User accounts" for more details.

Samba can also control access to a share with the help of the following lists:

▼ invalid users

■ valid users

■ read list

▲ write list

Lists may include names of individual accounts and/or groups (in the UNIX sense, with the @group syntax). In the above, "read" really means "read only," and "write" stands for "read and write." They override other Samba controls which can be given on a share. A User who shows up on both "read" and "write" lists will have a "write" access. On the other hand, somebody listed among "invalid users" will be not allowed to a share regardless what other lists and access properties say.

The requirements of UNIX permissions still remain in force. However, if, for a given share, Samba includes the specification

```
force group = thisgroup
```

then for the purposes of access to files from the share every valid user is automatically added to thisgroup. Similarly, force user = auser will change an accessing user name to auser. This is a big security hole when used imprudently. It should be pretty clear from the above that one may declare a share in *smb.conf* file as "public" and still limit the access to it by using UNIX permissions. You are strongly advised against it; this will present an unclear picture to client browsers and will be quite confusing during Samba maintenance. It is advisable to make your intentions explicit with the help of access lists.

3.4 How do I avoid making my files accessible to everybody in the world?

SMB networks rely heavily on broadcast, and LanManager clients do not really have a mechanism which would narrow a share availability only to particular targets. Therefore, if you are connected to some wider network, like the Internet, then, in the absence of a firewall machine, your public shares will be open to everybody on the Net who cares to mount them.

The Samba server can limit valid incoming connections, either globally or on a service-by-service basis, to hosts from allow hosts lists. For details, read the description on the manual page for *smb.conf*; but in particular, specifying a network/netmask pair, like in

```
allow hosts = 10.10.14.0/255.255.254.0
```

means that a host with IP numbers between 10.10.14.0 and 10.10.15.255 (a result of a "logical and" of IP with a netmask should give a subnetwork number) will be allowed.
Two caveats:

▼ The above does nothing to shield shares posted by non-Samba clients; they still can be guarded by individual passwords.

▲ The protection is not absolute, as IP numbers on TCP/IP packets can, and have been, spoofed; still, doing that is not exactly easy.

In summary: you should carefully consider the security implications of your network communications, but this aspect is far from being unique to Samba.

3.5 "Wild-card" services

To make the life of a system administrator a bit simpler, Samba provides some service templates which will be automatically filled in. One of these is the [homes] section, which may look like this:

```
[homes]
    writable = yes
```

A server will try to replace this with a service based on a connecting user name and with a path set to a user's home directory. This means that every user will actually see a different service located separately in a server file system, even if all of them look outwardly the same in a client browser. Each will be unique to the individual user. This service may include a path specification as well, if you wish, but, unless you want everybody to connect to the same directory, you had better use some Samba macros in the name, like

```
path = /smb/clients/%u.
```

Another service of this kind is [printers], which allows for succinct descriptions of all printers available on your server. It is described in more detail elsewhere in this document. See "Printing with Samba."
You may create your own patterns for services. For example, a specification like this:

```
[clientd]
    comment  = Client directories
```

```
path     = /smb/clients/%m
public   = no
writable = yes
```

will provide every client with a directory based on its name (the same for all users connecting from the given client, but this also can be separated by using more macros in path). Directories to which path will expand on a connection have to exist or you will get a "cannot change to a directory" error.

Another method for "template" services is to use the "copy" directive in *smb.conf*. Options from copied services can be amended or overridden.

3.6 How do I change options only for a particular user/clients?

The configuration file *smb.conf* may include other files with "include" directive, and names of included files may contain standard macros (with some exceptions like '%u', but '%U' should be ok).

If an included file does not exist it will be skipped. If your debug level is set high enough a relevant message will be written to your log files. In the current sources "high enough" means 1. It could be changed in *loadparm.c*.

For example, you want to check what happens on a connection from "buggy," but you do not want to overfill other logs with debug info. A line like

```
include %m.conf
```

in *smb.conf*, and a file *buggy.conf* which contains something like

```
debug level = 5
```

will do the trick.

Since standard macros also include '%L', which stands for a netbios server name; and, as one server may have multiple names, then the same server may be configured differently, depending on the name with which it was called.

3.7 How do I access client shares from a server?

The program smbclient (distributed with Samba) allows you to switch roles of a server and a client if the client posted some shares (thus becoming a server). It provides an ftp-like interface and a set of commands for listing, showing, and transferring files. Newer versions of smbclient can be talked into preserving case and long file names when talking to Windows 95 or NT machines. For Linux, one can find loadable smbfs file system and smbmount utility. It is possible to use it to include shares as subdirectories of a "normal" file system and use regular UNIX tools for operation on files. Starting with 1.3.*x* series of development kernels, smbfs is included with kernel sources. For earlier kernels, this is a separate module (look for "ksmbfs" on servers).

If your OS allows loadable file systems, then in principle smbfs could be ported to it, but somebody has to do it yet, such as you. :-)

4. USER ACCOUNTS

Really Dire Warning: Due to severe implementation bugs of the RC4 cipher as used by Microsoft, whatever is stored in Windows and Windows 95 .pwl files is crackable in a matter of seconds! I mean it literally. I do not know about NT one way or another. If you value your security, do not store there your "real" passwords—ever! At a minimum, one may disable "password caching" on Windows, but this, although supported and entirely possible, may be somewhat of an inconvenience to the users. The problem is that, by default, Windows caches network passwords in files with the .pwl extension in the windows directory of the user's system. This file contains encrypted versions of the passwords, but the encryption method used (RC4) has been implemented very poorly, so it is possible to break the encryption using a program which has been posted publicly on the Net. Of course, for someone to take advantage of this flaw, one would have to have physical or filesystem access to the .pwl files on a client machine.

Microsoft has acknowledged the problem, and has provided a patch for Windows 95 clients. This patch is supposed to fix the implementation problems, and also changes the cipher method to use a 128-bit key, rather than the previously used 32-bit key. This should also provide a better level of protection from "brute force" attacks. One may obtain further information about this bug, locations of patches, and other interesting reading on Microsoft security issues from:

http://www.c2.org/hackmsoft/

To my best knowledge, at the time of this writing the patch was available only for "US version" of Windows 95. A promised patch for "international" variants is still in the making. (One wonders about new RC4 width and U.S. cryptography export regulations, but this is pure speculation at this moment.)

4.1 How do I set accounts for Samba users?

Samba users need UNIX accounts on a Samba server. These accounts can be provided by the usual /etc/passwd mechanism or may be distributed with NIS ("yellow pages"). The server uses them to get the information about uid number and groups to which users belong. These accounts can be pretty minimal in the sense that Samba will be quite happy with an entry which has '*' in a password field and /bin/false for a shell ("real" UNIX logins with this type of account will be impossible, obviously enough). Still, one should be careful with this advice if you have real security concerns. On many machines (very popular on Linux systems), /bin/false is a shell script. This may provide a foothold to a determined attacker. It is advisable to replace it with a "true" compiled program (linked statically if you use shared libraries).

Tim Baverstock, **warwick@mmm.co.uk**, suggests to use */bin/passwd* instead of */bin/false*. That way account owners are free to modify passwords, without bothering sysadmin, by telnetting to a server. To do the same for passwords used by Samba, when you have them, make your smbpasswd program (usually located at */usr/local/samba/bin/smbpasswd*) into a "faux shell"; */bin/passwd* "shell" can be very handy for POP-only users, for example. In the later case, "*" in a password field is obviously counterproductive, and a true thing has to be there.

When checking access to services, Samba may need also its own password file. This happens only when you will set global configuration parameter encrypted passwords to "yes." Passwords in this file (*/usr/local/samba/private/smbpasswd* for a default installation) do not, or rather should not, have anything in common with UNIX passwords.

An ENCRYPTION writeup from the Samba distribution is required reading for this and provides detailed information. Pay attention to security issues.

Before compiling Samba with encryption support, you will need an extra DES crypt library. Sources can be found at

ftp://nimbus.anu.edu.au/pub/tridge/libdes/libdes.tar.92-10.13.gz

WARNING: due to U.S. Government regulations (ITAR), you cannot export this library (classified as munitions) from the U.S. to another country. It is totally immaterial that you imported it from abroad in the first place (and which is legal). The only exception to this rule is Canada, but Canada is also covered by regulations analogous to ITAR.

4.2 How do I put accounts into smbpasswd file?

Before trying any manipulations with this file, save a backup copy of it with the current information, maybe to *smbpasswd.old*. This file has a pretty strict format, and typing entries with an editor is not Great Fun. The script *mksmbpasswd.sh* will create a required skeleton from */etc/passwd* entries. Another method, which allows adding selected accounts to smbpasswd at any time, consists of listing them as arguments to the addtosmbpass (awk) program. Feed it the old (existing) smbpasswd information on stdin, and the resulting rewrite will be printed on stdout. When starting any empty file, use */dev/null* as input. An example usage may look like this:

```
addtosmbpass name1 name2 name3 name4 <smbpasswd.old> smbpasswd
```

If any of the argument names already occur in input, then those will be skipped and that information will not change. Another advantage is that addtosmbpass, if needed, will search for necessary information in NIS databases (if you run NIS authentication).

4.3 How do I change a Samba password?

If remote password changing works (this is the case only for some systems) and the password program is configured to affect the smbpasswd utility, then a user may use that. Otherwise, a user has to log on on the server and run smbpasswd there—similar to a normal passwd program; non-root users can change passwords only for themselves. If this is impossible, then the System Administrator has to perform this service for the user. This may be better if you don't want to see user passwords such as "wageslave" or "Chevrolet."

4.4 What security levels are available?

The default security is SHARE, which means that individual shares have their own access passwords. Clients authenticate themselves on every connection but do not send user names. Samba, being a UNIX creature, actually does only username/password checks. This means that it can fudge things a bit by guessing names, going through a list of a username configuration parameter, and checking against UNIX passwords (a detailed description in the *smb.conf* manual page is a required reading). Some clients do not allow for any other security.

From a UNIX point of view, a more natural security level is USER. Pairs username/password are validated once per session (unless the revalidate option on a share is set). Either */etc/passwd* or *smbpasswd* stores encrypted passwords. See "How do I set accounts for Samba users?" for more on that.

If you have a secure NT box on your network, then you may designate it as the password server. With SERVER setting access check looks to clients the same as with security USER but passwords are passed for checks to another SMB server on the network. Currently, Samba cannot act as a password server.

Starting with version 1.9.15p6, Samba distribution includes a longer writeup on SMB security levels. Please consult for more details.

4.5 Logging in from a client

When logging from a Windows client and with USER security, a user will be using two passwords—one to get an access to the network, and another to get shares from a server.

If these two passwords are the same, then the server will not ask for a password the second time; but it will accept an access as validated, and it will show immediately the shares to browse, and network mounts defined in Filemanager or Explorer will normally be established. If these passwords are different, then a user will not be able to browse before first login to a (known) share; the second password, stored in smbpasswd, will have then been supplied. See also "What security levels are available?"

Passwords are not stored on Windows machines in a manner which could be called secure, neither physically nor cryptographically. It may be highly advisable to use different passwords for login to Samba server, even if the method with two identical passwords is quite convenient.

Be also aware that screen-saver passwords on Windows side are usually trivial to bypass, leaving your unattended connections to a server much less secure than you may think. Publicly posted programs are available which will break a Windows screensaver password in the blink of an eye!

4.6 Why does my NT machine misbehave with USER security level?

If a server does not use "encrypted passwords," in the sense given by *smb.conf*, the NT box will not browse it; it will also repeatedly ask for passwords on every single connection. See also the encryption remarks in "How do I set accounts for Samba users?"

4.7 How do I share the same file/directory between a group of users?

This is particularly relevant if a group of users works on the same files and wants to share results. Set a special service available for these users, make one of them an owner—in the UNIX sense—of everything, and set the force user property on this service in the *smb.conf* file. Setting permissions that way will apply to all files and subdirectories of a chosen service. In such a setup, controlling who can write in a given moment to a file becomes essential. Samba allows for locking for a service. If this is not enough, then there is revision control software in the MS-DOS world (for example, "MKS Source Integrity," "PVCS"), but it costs real money. Depending on what, and how you are doing this, it may be money very well spent.

Another option would be to use software like RCS or CVS on the UNIX side. This would require logging to a UNIX host for checking files in and out. See, however, also magic script on *smb.conf* manual page.

5. FINDING MACHINES ON A NETWORK WITH SAMBA

Samba is basically using the *gethostbyname()* library function to convert names to IP addresses on your network. Some programs from the Samba suite will allow you to specify network name and IP address separately. This comes in handy when your name resolution software does not know how to handle it.

5.1 DNS or WINS?

DNS stands for "Domain Name Services," and it may range from a simple static */etc/hosts* table to a full-blown network of cooperating primary and secondary nameservers with authority over different segments of a network. It provides correspondence between machine names and their network addresses, and also allows "aliases" of machine names.

WINS is a poor DNS cousin used for SMB protocol-based networks. A table similar in function to */etc/hosts* is called lmhosts and may or may not be consulted—depending on your client. To find out more about this table, consult the section "How do I construct an lmhosts table?"

See also Windows help for what you can find. A location for lmhosts on Samba the server is set at compile time. In a default configuration it is */usr/local/samba/lib/lmhosts*.

There is no conflict between DNS, lmhosts, and WINS. Samba actually uses all, and you may run all three at the same time on your clients as well. Depending on the request, one or another will provide resolution. The order in which resorces will be searched by clients can be modified, at least for Windows 95, but this requires a direct edit of registry files (caution!). The Samba daemon handling WINS requests is called nmbd. Later versions of Samba also include the nmblookup program for SMB network searches. In any case, running both on your network may have advantages. If either the DNS or the WINS server on your network goes away, your clients will still be able to find the shares without fuss. This can be very useful, especially if the DNS gets flooded sometimes.

5.2 Why do my clients not browse my server shares?

Is your nmbd program running? Browsing will not happen without it. Current versions of nmbd run as daemons even when started by inetd, so it looks like that you may go ahead and start them in your startup scripts. On the other hand, if nmbd will die for some reasons, then inetd will attempt to restart it when needed, so leaving the nmbd entry in */etc/inetd.conf* may be to your advantage. One possible reason for nmbd failing to start is that your nmbd is newer than your documentation (an unfortunate but real possibility), and it refuses to start with some options which were once valid but are not anymore. Check "help" message and/or sources.

5.3 How do I split my clients between different netgroups?

The simplest way is to have different servers, each serving a separate netgroup. A server workgroup name can be specified in *smb.conf* file or given as an argument to nmbd. It may be a good idea to have clients from different netgroups belonging to different subnetworks, with different netmask/broadcast address pairs. Your broadcast packets will then have a more limited audience.

A single Samba server may belong to multiple netgroups. One way of achieving that is as follows. In DNS databases, give your server machine different aliases corresponding to netbios names under which the server will show up in different netgroups. Put into your *smb.conf* only the settings which are common for everybody, and a statement like

```
include /usr/local/samba/lib/L%.conf
```

For every netbios NAME, the group-specific configuration, including workgroup name and services for this group, goes into the *NAME.conf* file. Your server then looks differently depending on the name with which it was called.

5.4 How do I browse between subnetworks?

Put a Samba server on each subnetwork and list the other servers in each server lmhosts file. Making servers into master browsers (current version of Samba supports that) should help. But see also "Preface—introductory remarks."

5.5 How can I connect to Samba server via PPP or SLIP?

Once you establish a regular PPP or SLIP connection to your network (a machine handling incoming calls does not have to be your Samba server, but it might be), then explicit connections, with a fully specified UNC, to SMB shares should work; but a client will be still unable to browse. To achieve also the latter, place the Samba server, local to the subnet of the PPP or SLIP connection, as the first entry in the clients' lmhosts table. This ordering is really important. More about lmhosts can be found in the section "How do I construct an lmhosts table?" The table entry will require both #PRE and #DOM options.

An explanation for the curious. SMB protocol relies (much too heavily) on a broadcast. Point-to-point protocols, like SLIP or PPP, by their design, block broadcast packets. A trick with lmhosts provides a way around it.

5.6 How do I find who responds to SMB protocol?

If you have nmblookup program, try this on a server:

```
nmblookup -d2 '*'
```

Or, with older versions of Samba:

```
nmbd -L '*'
```

which has a similar effect. These commands broadcast only on your subnetwork, with a broadcast address derived from a network mask. From clients, the other SMB hosts should, hopefully, show up in your browser.

5.7 How do I construct an lmhosts table?

Documentation for the lmhosts file format is rather hard to find. It is loosely based on the 4.2 BSD hosts format. What is included here is for the reader's convenience and is a compilation from several sources, and does not claim to be complete and/or correct for all possible clients.

On the client side, the lmhosts file is used to match server names across remote networks connected by routers or gateways. You can also use the lmhosts file if WINS servers are not available on the network, or on a routed or bridged section. Use of lmhosts files on clients can substantially decrease the broadcast traffic on a network, even if WINS and DNS are running. Clients must have DNS usage enabled to use lmhosts.

Through the use of a well-managed lmhosts file propagated from the server, the administrator may easily handle updates to system mapping, and may also keep browser lists reasonably small and appropriate in content to the users. This also allows for routed browsing, even without WINS servers on the subnets. Useful modifiers in lmhosts for Microsoft Windows clients include

▼ **#PRE**   Added after an entry, causes that entry to be preloaded into the name cache. By default, entries are not preloaded, but are only parsed after WINS and name query broadcasts fail to resolve a name. #PRE must be appended for entries that also appear in #INCLUDE statements; otherwise, the entry in #INCLUDE is ignored.

■ **#DOM domain**   Added after an entry, associates that entry with the domain specified by domain. This keyword affects how the Browser and Logon services behave in routed TCP/IP environments. To preload a #DOM entry, you must also add the #PRE keyword to the line.

■ **#INCLUDE filename**   Forces the system to seek the given filename and parse it as if it were local. Specifying a Universal Naming Convention (UNC) filename allows you to use a centralized lmhosts file on a server. You may also include different lmhosts files from a server to selected clients. This is very useful for administration, as you may change and control share paths for clients centrally. You must add a mapping for the server before its entry in the #INCLUDE section and also append #PRE to ensure that it is preloaded (otherwise, the #INCLUDE will be ignored).

■ **G**   Denotes a broadcast address for a workgroup with a given name. An IP address of 0.0.0.0 will be replaced by our default broadcast address, but explicit addresses can also be given. Used when a workgroup spans several subnets or when including names of "external" workgroups.

■ **#BEGIN_ALTERNATE**   Used to group multiple #INCLUDE statements. Any single successful #INCLUDE statement causes the group to succeed.

■ **#END_ALTERNATE**   Used to mark the end of an #INCLUDE grouping.

▲ **\0xnn**   Support for nonprinting characters in NetBIOS names. A character specified this way has to be the last one in a string of a length 16 characters; the name should be padded with blanks if necessary. Enclose the NetBIOS name in double quotation marks and use \0xnn hexadecimal notation to specify a hexadecimal value for the character. This allows to hide custom applications. Names with non-printing characters will not show up in browsers, but still can be connected to when specified explicitly. However, LAN Manager 1.0 TCP/IP does not recognize the hexadecimal format, so you surrender backward compatibility to old LAN Manager servers if you use this feature.

The following example shows how all of these keywords are used:

```
0.0.0.0           mygroup    G     # defaults to our broadcast
102.54.95.255     mygroup    G     # more of "mygroup"
                                   # on another subnetwork
102.54.94.98      localserv        #PRE
102.54.94.97      trey        #PRE #DOM:networking      #net
102.54.94.102     "appname  \0x14"              #special app server
102.54.94.123     popular          #PRE        #source server
#BEGIN_ALTERNATE
#INCLUDE   \\localsrv\public\lmhosts      #adds LMhosts
#INCLUDE   \\trey\public\lmhosts          #adds LMhosts
#END_ALTERNATE
```

In the preceding example:

▼ The servers named localsrv and trey are preloaded so that they may be used later in an #INCLUDE statement in a centrally maintained lmhosts file.

■ The server named "appname \0x14" contains a special character after the 15 characters in its name (including blanks), so its name is enclosed in double quotes.

▲ The server named popular is preloaded, based on the #PRE keyword.

6. PRINTING WITH SAMBA

6.1 How do I set up basic print services?

Samba prints, in principle, by making a copy of your print data on a server and passing a resulting file as an argument to whatever is used for printing there. The simplest way to achieve that effect is to use a "canned" [printers] section in conjunction with load printers = yes directive, as described on the manpage for *smb.conf.*

There are a few details which have to be taken into account. If your server print command is lpr, then most likely you want to set printing = bsd in the configuration file. If this is lp, then printing = sysv. HP-UX and AIX have their own, hpux, and, respectively, aix printing styles.

If none of the above applies, or does not work as expected, you have to configure your print command, lpq command, and lprm command in an explicit manner. See also the section "I am getting only an initial fragment of my printout; why?" for more ideas.

Make also sure that the path given in print services points to a world writable directory, as Samba will copy the print data into there. Using your print spool directories here is not a good idea, as, on a properly configured system, this write access requirement is not satisfied.

Automatic configuration via [printers] section works only in the presence of an */etc/printcap*, or equivalent, file.

Sometimes (e.g., NEXTSTEP or Solaris) such a file does not exist. You may either provide a "dummy printcap" (basically only printer names are needed there) or configure print services by creating a configuration section for every printer. This can actually be preferable, even if */etc/printcap* does exist, especially if you need finer control of how the printers are configured. For example, if you do not want to show all your printers, or if you want to give access to some printers only from some machines (with the help of include), or by certain users only (valid users can be useful here).

See also load printers in the *smb.conf* man page. If you prefer to show globally as shares only some printers from your */etc/printcap* file, then you may want to use auto services list instead.

6.2 How do I show printer names less daunting than lp4js?

This can be a problem when there are multiple printers on a network, in multiple locations, and "what is what" is not clear from the names. If you specify your print services explicitly, then the matter is simple. Add a comment in your service, and it will show up in browsers. Otherwise, you may add comment strings in the */etc/printcap* file. For example, if your printer entry reads like:

```
lp4js|lp12|LaserJet on the third floor by the coffee machine:\
    .....(other stuff)...
```

then a name with blanks in it, the third one in this case, will be taken by Samba as a comment on the service. If such a name does not exist, then something else will be picked (hard to tell what ...). ATTENTION! Share names, legal across various subprotocols of SMB, cannot be longer than eight characters. If all names in your printcap entry are longer than that, then Samba will silently skip such entry, and the corresponding printer will remain hidden to your clients. This does not apply to printer shares specified explicitly in *smb.conf* (you will get complaints for names too long, but they will be there if your clients can handle them).

6.3 How do I test what I am sending to my printer?

Temporarily replace your print command with something like this:

```
print command = cat %s > /tmp/print.%m.$$ ; rm -f %s
```

This will create a "print" file marked by the name of a sending client and a writer process number. Now you may try to figure out if your printer will really like it. :-)

6.4 I have a printer on a client machine. Can I print from a server?

At least for Windows and NT it is possible to find software (commercial and not) which will make a printer connected to a client into a "regular" network printer. It can then be configured for any UNIX machine as a remote printer.

If you do not have such software, but a printer is exported by the client as a "share," you may use smbclient with the -P option to connect to it. The following sample shell script should get you started.

```
#!/bin/sh
# Print from Unix on a printer on SMB network.  An assumption is that
# 'printer' was posted as a passwordless "share"
#
client="myclient"    # client name here...
pshare="printer"     # and here printer share name
printfile="/tmp/smbspool.$$"

cat > $printfile
if [ -s $printfile ] ; then
   ( echo "translate" ; echo "print $printfile" ; echo "quit" ) \
   | smbclient \\\\$client\\$pshare -P -N
fi
rm -f $printfile
exit 0
```

Once you have something like that running you may add to your server a new printer, which "prints" on *dev/null*, and with this script as a default print filter for it. Details of doing that vary between different print models, so check your docs. Subsequently, you will use "normal" print commands from your server to print on your client printer (lpr -Psmb, or something like that); spooling and printing from stdin will work, etc. In such settings you may want to print with a command which creates a symbolic link to an original file (lpr -s in "bsd model"), especially for bigger files. Otherwise you will end up, for a short time, with three copies of your input (an original, a copy in a printer spool directory, and the "smbspool" copy to be sent on the network).

6.5 I am getting only an initial fragment of my printout; why?

Historically, print software, by default, was limiting the size of accepted input. Usually this would be something like 1MB, which is something like five hundred pages of straight text and looks reasonable enough. Nowadays, with graphic printouts (and even text is usually sent in a graphics mode as well), this no longer makes sense. You may change this limit by editing the value of mx in your */etc/printcap* or equivalent; :mx#0: means "no limit." You may still want to be careful with that, however, unless you have infinite amounts of storage and paper! Another possibility, if your print software allows it, is to print using a symbolic link instead of a copy into a printer spool directory. For example, with bsd-style print software,

```
print command = lpr -s -r -P %p %s
```

will do this, and it will remove the input file, placed by Samba, once it is done. This configuration can be to your advantage even with :mx#0:, since you avoid creating two copies (one by Samba, the other one in a spool directory) for potentially big data files. If you have a lot of clients printing big jobs, this may save you a lot of disk.

6.6 Why does my Postscript printer refuse to cooperate?

The output sent by Windows printer drivers is only "more-or-less" Postscript. Various Postscript interpreters try to deal with that but do not always succeed. Samba has postscript = True, which attempts to help. Unfortunately, this is not a good idea, globally, in [printers] section, if you have printers which are capable of Postscript and some non-Postscript printers and you are not configuring them individually, or you have printers like some HP models which would accept both Postscript and non-Postscript (HPGL) jobs.

A better approach is to try to configure your Windows printer drivers to not send the initial "control-D from hell." If you look at many of the Windows printer drivers, they send this as a default. Fortunately, this may be turned off! This will help with the most blatant standard violations, but alas, not always. For some examples, see the next question.

6.7 How do I make a NEXTSTEP server accept Windows output?

This is an example of "nearly Postscript but not quite" problems. The trouble is that some initialization and cleanup, which should be in the document header and trailer, is packed by Windows into the first and last page comments. NeXT normally prints in reverse page order (collated), and things do not happen at the right time, and, therefore, nothing works properly.

Here are possible suggestions for how do deal with this:

▼ In your printer "ppd" file, comment out the line *DefaultOutputOrder: Reverse by putting '%' after '*'. It works, but you will have to collate all your print jobs by hand (sigh ...).

■ Copy "ppd" to file with a slightly different name, comment out the "Reverse" line like above, provide a second, non-reversing, logical printer on the same physical device (possibly use niload for that), and print Windows jobs on it. We have not tested this in a real-life situation, but hopefully it should work.

■ Add a filter in print command to strip as much as you dare of the comments. Piping through a simple *sed '/^%%/d'* may work. The Postscript interpreter will be not able to reverse pages, and files will print. Check with Shon Vella, **shon@novell.com**, for details.

▲ Another variant of the above; not really required, but maybe with a better aesthetic appeal. Create a printer with */dev/null* for an output device and a filter like this:
sed '/^%%/d' | lpr
Export with Samba only this printer. (This uses a standard UNIX trick for adding filters to printers where you otherwise cannot, like to remote ones.)

On the other hand, Eugene Mah, **eugene@raddi.uah.ualberta.ca**, reports that he prints with a NEXTSTEP server by telling PCs that they print on an HP Laserjet III with Postscript and with postscript = yes in the configuration file. Your mileage may vary.

6.8 Can I make other UNIX peripheral devices available to my clients?

Why not? On the UNIX side, every peripheral device, for example a tape drive, looks like a file (possibly "special," with a limited set of valid operations on it). If you can export it as a Samba service writable to a client, then a client may type to it (or from it) on its side. A weird variation on backup services, and not one for the faint-of-heart.

7. OPTIMIZATION OF SAMBA SERVICES

Samba has a number of parameters which allow for tuning your SMB network. They may work to cross-purposes, and local requirements may differ, so you will have to experiment.

7.1 Memory usage

Keep also in mind that Samba spawns a new smbd process for every client connection, which does take some memory (you may count usually about 800K for the first client, plus some memory used for caching). How big the increments are may depend on how shared libraries are used, if at all. Also important is how good your OS is at overlapping the text part of different processes, etc. One of the possible optimizations may consist of adding more memory to a server or splitting the server's job between more machines. Normally, after about 25 active clients, this is advisable, unless your server has a lot of CPU and memory horsepower. Bear in mind, however, that if you have 50 possible clients, probably only a few of them may be logged into the server at any given time.

The rate with which clients gobble server memory, and the level where it is going to stop, depend to a great degree on how many open, and how big, directories are cached in memory. Some clients do not close directories when they are done, and memory usage grows and grows. You may change the MAXDIR constant in local.h to keep Samba from caching too much. An absolute minimum for a correct operation is 2, but with low values, complex operations on deep directory trees may fail. 64 is the default as of the 1.9.15p5 patchlevel of Samba. Andrew Tridgell wrote: "Note that samba does try to allow up to 256 open directories even if MAXDIR is much smaller. It does this by assuming the directory doesn't change on disk and "idling" then by noting only the path name in memory and reopening it when needed. This will fail if the client is deleting files in a directory that it has open from a previous search, then continuing the search in that directory. In this case the client can get confused. To combat this samba always idles the directory that is least recently used." Also, MAX_CONNECTIONS and MAX_OPEN_FILES have some memory impact, even when entries are not in use. These limits are per client and not server-wide.

7.2 Tuning

Check the *smb.conf* manual page for details, but here are some parameters (some of them are tune-up parameters in a rather broad sense) that you may want to read about:

- ▼ dead time
- ■ keep alive
- ■ max disk size
- ■ max connections
- ■ min print space
- ■ wide links
- ■ read raw
- ■ write raw
- ■ getwd cache
- ■ lpq cache time
- ■ read prediction
- ■ read size
- ▲ socket options

Available socket options, their behaviour, and interpretations may depend on the underlying sockets implementation. Consult your library documentation for details.

WINDOWS
NT
Professional
Library

APPENDIX D

Samba Frequently Asked Questions

P aul Blackman, **ictinus@lake.canberra.edu.au**, v 0.5

This is the Frequently Asked Questions (FAQ) document for Samba, the free and very popular SMB server product. An SMB server allows file and printer connections from clients such as Windows, OS/2, Linux and others. Current to version 1.9.16. Please send any corrections to the author.

Table of Contents:

1. General Information

2. Compiling and Installing Samba on a UNIX Host

3. Common Client Questions

3.6. Why are my file's timestamps off by an hour, or by a few hours?

3.7. How do I set the printer driver name correctly?

4. Specific client application problems

4.1. MS Office Setup reports "Cannot change properties of MSOFFICEUP.INI."

1. GENERAL INFORMATION

All about Samba—what it is, how to get it, related sources of information, how to understand the version numbering scheme, pizza details.

1.1. What is Samba?

Samba is a suite of programs which work together to allow clients to access a server's filespace and printers via the SMB (Server Message Block) protocol. Initially written for UNIX, Samba now also runs on Netware, OS/2 and VMS.

In practice, this means that you can redirect disks and printers to UNIX disks and printers from LAN Manager clients, Windows for Workgroups 3.11 clients, Windows NT clients, Linux clients and OS/2 clients. There is also a generic UNIX client program supplied as part of the suite which allows UNIX users to use an ftp-like interface to access filespace and printers on any other SMB servers. This gives the capability for these operating systems to behave much like a LAN Server or Windows NT Server machine, only with added functionality and flexibility designed to make life easier for administrators.

The components of the suite are (in summary)

▼ smbd, the SMB server. This handles actual connections from clients, doing all the file, permission and username work

■ nmbd, the Netbios name server, which helps clients locate servers, doing the browsing work and managing domains as this capability is being built into Samba

■ smbclient, the UNIX-hosted client program

■ smbrun, a little "glue" program to help the server run external

■ programs

■ testprns, a program to test server access to printers

■ testparms, a program to test the Samba configuration file for correctness

■ *smb.conf*, the Samba configuration file

■ smbprint, a sample script to allow a UNIX host to use smbclient to print to an SMB server

▲ documentation! DON'T neglect to read it—you will save a great deal of time!

The suite is supplied with full source (of course!) and is GPLed.

The primary creator of the Samba suite is Andrew Tridgell. Later versions incorporate much effort by many net.helpers. The man pages and this FAQ were originally written by Karl Auer.

1.2. What is the current version of Samba?

At time of writing, the current version was 1.9.16. If you want to be sure, check the bottom of the change-log file: **ftp://samba.anu.edu.au/pub/samba/alpha/change-log**

For more information, see "What do the version numbers mean?"

1.3. Where can I get it?

The Samba suite is available via anonymous ftp from **samba.anu.edu.au**. The latest and greatest versions of the suite are in the directory: */pub/samba/*.

Development (read "alpha") versions, which are NOT necessarily stable and which do NOT necessarily have accurate documentation, are available in the directory: */pub/samba/alpha*.

Note that binaries are NOT included in any of the above. Samba is distributed ONLY in source form, though binaries may be available from other sites. Recent versions of some Linux distributions, for example, do contain Samba binaries for that platform.

1.4. What do the version numbers mean?

It is not recommended that you run a version of Samba with the word "alpha" in its name unless you know what you are doing and are willing to do some debugging. Many, many people just get the latest recommended stable release version and are happy. If you are brave, by all means take the plunge and help with the testing and development—but don't install it on your departmental server. Samba is typically very stable and safe, and this is mostly due to the policy of many public releases.

How the scheme works:

1. When major changes are made the version number is increased. For example, the transition from 1.9.15 to 1.9.16. However, this version number will not appear immediately, and people should continue to use 1.9.15 for production systems (see next point.)

2. Just after major changes are made, the software is considered unstable, and a series of alpha releases are distributed, for example, 1.9.16alpha1. These are for testing by those who know what they are doing. The "alpha" in the filename will hopefully scare off those who are just looking for the latest version to install.

3. When Andrew thinks that the alphas have stabilized to the point where he would recommend new users install it, he renames it to the same version number without the alpha, for example, 1.9.16.

4. Inevitably, bugs are found in the "stable" releases and minor patch levels are released, which give us the pXX series, for example, 1.9.16p2.

So the progression goes

1.9.15p7 (production) 1.9.15p8 (production) 1.9.16alpha1(test sites only) : 1.9.16alpha20 (test sites only) 1.9.16(production) 1.9.16p1 (production)

The above system means that whenever someone looks at the samba ftp site, they will be able to grab the highest-numbered release without an alpha in the name and be sure of getting the current recommended version.

1.5. What platforms are supported?

Many different platforms have run Samba successfully. The platforms most widely used and thus best tested are Linux and SunOS.

At time of writing, the Makefile claimed support for

* SunOS * Linux with shadow passwords * Linux without shadow passwords * SOLARIS * SOLARIS 2.2 and above (aka SunOS 5) * SVR4 * ULTRIX * OSF1 (alpha only) * OSF1 with NIS and Fast Crypt (alpha only) * OSF1 V2.0 Enhanced Security (alpha only) * AIX * BSDI * NetBSD * NetBSD 1.0 * SEQUENT * HP-UX * SGI * SGI IRIX 4.*x*.*x* * SGI IRIX 5.*x*.*x* * FreeBSD * NeXT 3.2 and above * NeXT OS 2.*x* * NeXT OS 3.0 * ISC SVR3V4 (POSIX mode) * ISC SVR3V4 (iBCS2 mode) * A / UX 3.0 * SCO with shadow passwords.* SCO with shadow passwords, without YP * SCO with TCB passwords * SCO 3.2v2 (ODT 1.1) with TCP passwords * intergraph * DGUX * Apollo Domain / OS sr10.3 (BSD4.3)

1.6. How can I find out more about Samba?

There are two mailing lists devoted to discussion of Samba-related matters.There is also the newsgroup, **comp.protocols.smb**, which has a great deal of discussion on Samba. There is also a WWW site "SAMBA Web Pages" at **http://samba.canberra.edu.au/ pub/samba/samba.html**, under which there is a comprehensive survey of Samba users. Another useful resource is the hypertext archive of the Samba mailing list.

Send email to **listproc@samba.anu.edu.au**. Make sure the subject line is blank, and include the following two lines in the body of the message:

subscribe samba *Firstname Lastname*
subscribe samba-announce *Firstname Lastname*

Obviously you should substitute YOUR first name for "Firstname" and YOUR last name for "Lastname"! Try not to send any signature stuff; it sometimes confuses the list processor.

The samba list is a digest list—every eight hours or so it regurgitates a single message containing all the messages that have been received by the list since the last time and sends a copy of this message to all subscribers.

If you stop being interested in Samba, please send another email to **listproc@samba.anu.edu.au**. Make sure the subject line is blank, and include the following two lines in the body of the message:

> **unsubscribe samba**
> **unsubscribe samba-announce**

The From: line in your message MUST be the same address you used when you subscribed.

1.7. Something's gone wrong—what should I do?

*** IMPORTANT! *** # DO NOT post messages on mailing lists or in newsgroups until you have carried out the first three steps given here!

First, see if there are any likely-looking entries in this FAQ! If you have just installed Samba, have you run through the checklist in *DIAGNOSIS.txt*? It can save you a lot of time and effort.

Second, read the man pages for smbd, nmbd and *smb.conf*, looking for topics that relate to what you are trying to do.

Third, if there is no obvious solution at hand, try to get a look at the log files for smbd and/or nmbd for the period during which you were having problems. You may need to reconfigure the servers to provide more extensive debugging information—usually level 2 or level 3 provide ample debugging info. Inspect these logs closely, looking particularly for the string "Error:".

Fourth, if you still haven't gotten anywhere, ask the mailing list or newsgroup. In general, nobody minds answering questions, provided you have followed the preceding steps. It might be a good idea to scan the archives of the mailing list, which are available through the Samba website described in the previous section.

If you successfully solve a problem, please mail the FAQ maintainer a succinct description of the symptom, the problem and the solution, so I can incorporate it in the next version.

If you make changes to the source code, *please* submit these patches so that everyone else gets the benefit of your work. This is one of the most important aspects to the maintainence of Samba. Send all patches to **samba-bugs@samba.anu.edu.au**, not Andrew Tridgell or any other individual and not the samba team mailing list.

1.8. Pizza supply details

Those who have registered in the Samba survey as "Pizza Factory" will already know this, but the rest may need some help. Andrew doesn't ask for payment, but he does appreciate it when people give him pizza. This calls for a little organization when the pizza donor is twenty thousand kilometers away, but it has been done.

▼ Method 1: Ring up your local branch of an international pizza chain and see if they honour their vouchers internationally. Pizza Hut does, which is how the entire Canberra Linux Users Group got to eat pizza one night, courtesy of someone in the U.S.

■ Method 2: Ring up a local pizza shop in Canberra and quote a credit card number for a certain amount, and tell them that Andrew will be collecting it (don't forget to tell him). One kind soul from Germany did this.

■ Method 3: Purchase a pizza voucher from your local pizza shop that has no international affiliations and send it to Andrew. It is completely useless, but he can hang it on the wall next to the one he already has from Germany.

▲ Method 4: Air freight him a pizza with your favorite regional flavors. It will probably get stuck in customs or torn apart by hungry sniffer dogs but it will have been a noble gesture.

2. COMPILING AND INSTALLING SAMBA ON A UNIX HOST

2.1. I can't see the Samba server in any browse lists!

*** Until the FAQ can be updated, please check the file: **ftp://samba.anu.edu.au/pub/ samba/BROWSING.txt** *** for more information on browsing.

If your GUI client does not permit you to select non-browsable servers, you may need to do so on the command line. For example, under LAN Manager you might connect to the above service as disk drive M: thus:

```
net use M: \maryed
```

The details of how to do this and the specific syntax varies from client to client—check your client's documentation.

2.2. Some files that I KNOW are on the server doesn't show up when I view the files from my client!

2.3. Some files on the server show up with really weird filenames when I view the files from my client!

If you check what files are not showing up, you will note that they are files which contain uppercase letters or which are otherwise not DOS-compatible (i.e., they are not legal DOS filenames for some reason).

The Samba server can be configured either to ignore such files completely, or to present them to the client in "mangled" form. If you are not seeing the files at all, the Samba server has most likely been configured to ignore them.Consult the man page smb.conf(5) for details of how to change this—the parameter you need to set is "mangled names = yes".

2.4. My client reports "cannot locate specified computer" or similar.

This indicates one of three things: You supplied an incorrect server name, the underlying TCP/IP layer is not working correctly, or the name you specified cannot be resolved.

After carefully checking that the name you typed is the name you should have typed, try doing things like pinging a host or telnetting to somewhere on your network to see if TCP/IP is functioning OK. If it is, the problem is most likely name resolution.

If your client has a facility to do so, hardcode a mapping between the hosts IP and the name you want to use. For example, with Man Manager or Windows for Workgroups you would put a suitable entry in the file LMHOSTS. If this works, the problem is in the communication between your client and the netbios name server. If it does not work, then there is something fundamentally wrong with your naming and the solution is beyond the scope of this document.

If you do not have any server on your subnet supplying netbios name resolution, hardcoded mappings are your only option. If you DO have a netbios name server running (such as the Samba suite's nmbd program), the problem probably lies in the way it is set up. Refer to Section Two of this FAQ for more ideas.

By the way, remember to REMOVE the hardcoded mapping before further tests.

2.5. My client reports "cannot locate specified share name" or similar.

This message indicates that your client CAN locate the specified server, which is a good start, but that it cannot find a service of the name you gave.

The first step is to check the exact name of the service you are trying to connect to (consult your system administrator). Assuming it exists and you specified it correctly (read your client's doco on how to specify a service name correctly), read on:

▼ Many clients cannot accept or use service names longer than eight characters.

■ Many clients cannot accept or use service names containing spaces.

■ Some servers (not Samba though) are case-sensitive with service names.

▲ Some clients force service names into uppercase.

2.6. My client reports "cannot find domain controller," "cannot logon to the network" or similar.

Nothing is wrong—Samba does not implement the primary domain name controller stuff for several reasons, including the fact that the whole concept of a primary domain controller and "logging in to a network" doesn't fit well with clients possibly running on multiuser machines (such as users of smbclient under UNIX). Having said that, several developers are working hard on building it in to the next major version of Samba. If you can contribute, send a message to samba-bugs!

Seeing this message should not affect your ability to mount redirected disks and printers, which is really what all this is about.

For many clients (including Windows for Workgroups and LAN Manager), setting the domain to STANDALONE at least gets rid of the message.

2.7. Printing doesn't work.

Make sure that the specified print command for the service you are connecting to is correct and that it has a fully-qualified path (e.g., use "/usr/bin/lpr" rather than just "lpr").

Make sure that the spool directory specified for the service is writable by the user connected to the service. In particular, the user "nobody" often has problems with printing, even if it worked with an earlier version of Samba. Try creating another guest user other than "nobody."

Make sure that the user specified in the service is permitted to use the printer.

Check the debug log produced by smbd. Search for the printer name and see if the log turns up any clues. Note that error messages to do with a service ipc$ are meaningless—they relate to the way the client attempts to retrieve status information when using the LANMAN1 protocol.

If using WfWg, then you need to set the default protocol to TCP/IP, not Netbeui. This is a WfWg bug.

If using the LANMAN1 protocol (the default), then try switching to coreplus. Also note that print status error messages don't mean printing won't work. The print status is received by a different mechanism.

2.8. My programs install on the server OK, but refuse to work properly.

There are numerous possible reasons for this, but one MAJOR possibility is that your software uses locking. Make sure you are using Samba 1.6.11 or later. It may also be possible to work around the problem by setting "locking=no" in the Samba configuration file for the service the software is installed on. This should be regarded as a strictly temporary solution.

In earlier Samba versions there were some difficulties with the very latest Microsoft products, particularly Excel 5 and Word for Windows 6. These should have all been solved. If not, then please let Andrew Tridgell know.

2.9. My "server string" doesn't seem to be recognized. My client reports the default setting, eg., "Samba 1.9.15p4," instead of what I have changed it to in the smb.conf file.

You need to use the -C option in nmbd. The "server string" affects what smbd puts out, and -C affects what nmbd puts out. In a future version these will probably be combined and -C will be removed, but for now use -C.

2.10. My client reports "This server is not configured to list shared resources."

Your guest account is probably invalid for some reason. Samba uses the guest account for browsing in smbd. Check that your guest account is valid.

See also "guest account" in *smb.conf* man page.

2.11. Log message "you appear to have a trapdoor uid system."

This can have several causes. It might be because you are using a uid or gid of 65535 or -1. This is a VERY bad idea, and is a big security hole. Check carefully in your */etc/passwd* file and make sure that no user has uid 65535 or -1. Especially check the "nobody" user, as many broken systems are shipped with nobody set up with a uid of 65535.

It might also mean that your OS has a trapdoor uid / gid system.

This means that once a process changes effective uid from root to another user, it can't go back to root. Unfortunately, Samba relies on being able to change effective uid from root to non-root and back again to implement its security policy. If your OS has a trapdoor uid system this won't work, and several things in Samba may break. Less things will break if you use user- or server-level security instead of the default share level security, but you may still strike problems.

The problems don't give rise to any security holes, so don't panic, but it does mean some of Samba's capabilities will be unavailable. In particular, you will not be able to connect to the Samba server as two different uids at once. This may happen if you try to print as a "guest" while accessing a share as a normal user. It may also affect your ability to list the available shares, as this is normally done as the guest user.

Complain to your OS vendor and ask them to fix their system.

Note: The reason why 65535 is a VERY bad choice of uid and gid is that it casts to -1 as a uid, and the setreuid() system call ignores (with no error) uid changes to -1. This means any daemon attempting to run as uid 65535 will actually run as root. This is not good!

3. COMMON CLIENT QUESTIONS

3.1. Are any Macintosh clients for Samba?

lkcl - update 09mar97 - the answer is "Yes!". Thursby now have a CIFS Client / Server - see **http://www.thursby.com/**.They test it against Windows 95, Windows NT, and Samba for compatibility issues. At present, DAVE is at version 1.0.0.DAVE version 1.0.1 is in beta, and will be released in April 97 (the speed of finder copies has been greatly enhanced, and there are bug-fixes included).

Alternatives: There are two free implementations of AppleTalk for several kinds of UNIX machines, and several more commercial ones. These products allow you to run file services and print services natively to Macintosh users, with no additional support required on the Macintosh. The two free implementations are Netatalk (**http://www.umich.edu/~rsug/netatalk/**) and CAP (**http://www.cs.mu.oz.au/appletalk/atalk.html**). What Samba offers MS Windows users, these packages offer to Macs. For more info on these packages, Samba, and Linux (and other UNIX-based systems) see **http://www.eats.com/linux_mac_win.html**.

3.2. "Session request failed (131,130)" error.

The following answer is provided by John E. Miller:

I'll assume that you're able to ping back and forth between the machines by IP address and name, and that you're using some security model where you're confident that you've got user IDs and passwords right. The logging options (-d3 or greater) can help a lot with that. DNS and WINS configuration can also impact connectivity as well.

Now, on to "Scope IDs." Somewhere in your Win95 TCP/IP network configuration (I'm too much of an NT bigot to know where it's located in the Win95 setup, but I'll have to learn someday since I teach for a Microsoft Solution Provider Authorized Tech Education Center—what an acronym...) Note: It's under Control Panel | Network | TCP/IP | WINS Configuration—there's a little text entry field called something like "Scope ID."

This field essentially creates "invisible" sub-workgroups on the same wire. Boxes can only see other boxes whose Scope IDs are set to the exact same value—it's sometimes used by OEMs to configure their boxes to browse only other boxes from the same vendor and, in most environments, this field should be left blank. If you, in fact, have something in this box, that EXACT value (case-sensitive!) needs to be provided to smbclient and nmbd as the -i (lowercase) parameter. So, if your Scope ID is configured as the string 'SomeStr' in Win95 then you'd have to use smbclient -iSomeStr otherparms in connecting to it.

3.3. How do I synchronize my PC's clock with my Samba server?

To synchronize your PC's clock with your Samba server:

▼ Copy TIMESYNC.PIF to your Windows directory. TIMESYNC.PIF can be found at:

http://samba.canberra.edu.au/pub/samba/binaries/miscellaneous/timesync.pif

- ■ Add TIMESYNC.PIF to your Start Up group / folder.
- ■ Open the Properties dialog box for the program / icon.
- ■ Make sure the Run Minimized option is set in program.
- ■ Change the command line section that reads \ sambahost to reflect the name of your server.
- ▲ Close the Properties dialog box by choosing OK.

Each time you start your computer (or log in for Win95) your PC will synchronize its clock with your Samba server.

3.4. Problems with WinDD, NTrigue, WinCenterPro, etc.

All of the above programs are applications that sit on an NT box and allow multiple users to access the NT GUI applications from remote workstations (often over X).

What has this got to do with Samba? The problem comes when these users use filemanager to mount shares from a Samba server. The most common symptom is that the first user to connect gets correct file permissions and has a nice day, but subsequent connections get logged in as the same user as the first person to log in. They find that they cannot access files in their own home directory, but that they can access files in the first user's home directory (maybe not such a nice day after all?).

Why does this happen? The above products all share a common heritage (and code base, I believe). They all open just a single TCP-based SMB connection to the Samba server, and requests from all users are piped over this connection. This is unfortunate, but not fatal.

It means that if you run your Samba server in share-level security (the default), then things will definitely break as described above. The share level SMB security model has no provision for multiple user IDs on the one SMB connection. See *security_level.txt* in the docs for more info on share / user / server level security.

If you run in user- or server-level security, then you have a chance, but only if you have a recent version of Samba (at least 1.9.15p6). In older versions, bugs in Samba meant you still would have had problems.

If you have a trapdoor uid system in your OS, then it will never work properly. Samba needs to be able to switch uids on the connection, and it can't if your OS has a trapdoor uid system. You'll know this because Samba will note it in your logs.

Also note that you should not use the magic "homes" share name with products like these, as otherwise all users will end up with the same home directory. Use \ \ *server* \ *username* instead.

3.5. Problem with printers under NT

This info from Stefan Hergeth, **hergeth@f7axp1.informatik.fh-muenchen.de**, may be useful:

A network-printer (with ethernetcard) is connected to the NT-Clients via our UNIX-Fileserver (SAMBA-Server), like the configuration told by Matthew Harrell, **harrell@leech.nrl.navy.mil** (see WinNT.txt).

1. If a user has choosen this printer as the default printer in his NT-Session and this printer is not connected to the network (e.g. switched off) then this user has a problem with the SAMBA connection of his filesystems. It's very slow.

2. If the printer is connected to the network everything works fine.

3. When the smbd is started with debug level 3, you can see the NT spooling system try to connect to the printer many times. If the printer is not connected to the network this request fails and the NT spooler is wasting a lot of time to connect to the printer service. This seems to be the reason for the slow network connection.

4. Maybe it's possible to change this behavior by setting different printer properties in the Print-Manager-Menu of NT, but I didn't try it yet.

3.6. Why are my file's timestamps off by an hour, or by a few hours?

This is from Paul Eggert, **eggert@twinsun.com**:

Most likely it's a problem with your time zone settings.

Internally, Samba maintains time in traditional UNIX format, namely, the number of seconds since 1970-01-01 00:00:00 Universal Time (or "GMT"), not counting leap seconds.

On the server side, Samba uses the UNIX TZ variable to convert internal timestamps to and from local time. So on the server side, there are two things to get right.

1. The UNIX system clock must have the correct Universal time. Use the shell command "sh -c 'TZ=UTC0 date'" to check this.

2. The TZ environment variable must be set on the server before Samba is invoked.The details of this depend on the server OS, but typically you must edit a file whose name is */etc/TIMEZONE* or */etc/default/init*, or run the command *zic -l*.

3. TZ must have the correct value.

   a) If possible, use geographical time zone settings (e.g., TZ='America/ Los_Angeles' or perhaps TZ=':US/Pacific').These are supported by most popular UNIX OSes, are easier to get right, and are more accurate for historical timestamps. If your operating system has out-of-date tables, you should be able to update them from the public domain time zone tables at

   URL: **ftp://elsie.nci.nih.gov/pub/**.

b) If your system does not support geographical time zone settings, you must use a Posix-style TZ strings, e.g., TZ='PST8PDT,M4.1.0/2,M10.5.0/2' for US Pacific time. Posix TZ strings can take the following form (with optional items in brackets):

```
StdOffsetDst[Offset,Date/Time,Date/Time]
```

where

- "Std" is the standard time designation (e.g., "PST").

- "Offset" is the number of hours behind UTC (e.g., '8'). Prepend a "-" if you are ahead of UTC, and append ":30" if you are at a half-hour offset. Omit all the remaining items if you do not use daylight-saving time.

- "Dst" is the daylight-saving time designation (e.g., "PDT").

- The optional second "Offset" is the number of hours that daylight-saving time is behind UTC. The default is 1 hour ahead of standard time.

- "Date/Time,Date/Time" specify when daylight-saving time starts and ends.The format for a date is "Mm.n.d," which specifies the dth day (0 is Sunday) of the nth week of the mth month, where week 5 means the last such day in the month.The format for a time is hh:mm[:ss], using a 24-hour clock.

Other Posix string formats are allowed, but you don't want to know about them.

On the client side, you must make sure that your client's clock and time zone is also set appropriately. [I don't know how to do this.] Samba traditionally has had many problems dealing with time zones, due to the bizarre ways that Microsoft network protocols handle time zones. A common symptom is for file timestamps to be off by an hour. To work around the problem, try disconnecting from your Samba server and then reconnecting to it; or upgrade your Samba server to 1.9.16alpha10 or later.

3.7. How do I set the printer driver name correctly?

Question: On NT, I opened "Printer Manager" and "Connect to Printer". Enter "\ptdi270s1" in the box of printer. I got the following error message: You do not have sufficient access to your machine to connect to the selected printer, since a driver needs to be installed locally.

Answer: In the more recent versions of Samba you can now set the "printer driver" in *smb.conf*. This tells the client what driver to use. For example, I have

```
printer driver = HP LaserJet 4L
```

and NT knows to use the right driver. You have to get this string exactly right.

To find the exact string to use, you need to get to the dialog box in your client where you select which printer driver to install. The correct strings for all the different printers are shown in a listbox in that dialog box.

You could also try setting the driver to NULL like this:

```
printer driver = NULL
```

This is effectively what older versions of Samba did, so if that worked for you then give it a go. If this does work, then let me know and I'll make it the default. Currently, the default is a 0 length string.

4. SPECIFIC CLIENT APPLICATION PROBLEMS

4.1. MS Office Setup reports "Cannot change properties of "\MSOFFICE\SETUP.INI."

When installing MS Office on a Samba drive for which you have admin user permissions, i.e., admin users = username, you will find the setup program unable to complete the installation.

To get around this problem, do the installation without admin user permissions. The problem is that MS Office Setup checks that a file is read-only by trying to open it for writing.

Admin users can always open a file for writing, as they run as root. You just have to install as a non-admin user and then use "chown -R" to fix the owner.

Index

J

 K

▼ **L**

 M

O

P

HUMMINGBIRD SAMPLER CD OFFER

Hummingbird Communications Ltd. specializes in the development of enterprise internetworking software products and document distribution solutions that provide high performance access to internetwork-based information and applications.

Hummingbird products are sold and supported internationally by authorized resellers in more than 40 countries. The Company is headquartered in North York, Ontario, Canada, with offices in Mountain View, CA, Washington, DC, and Raleigh, NC in the United States; in Sydney, Australia; and in Geneva, Switzerland; Munich, Germany; Paris, France; and Maidenhead, United Kingdom in Europe.

This Hummingbird Sampler CD contains evaluation copies for Windows NT, Windows 95, and Windows for the Intel platform. Products include V5.1.3 of Exceed, Exceed 3D, NFS Maestro Client and Server, NFS Maestro SOLO and V1.0 of Hummingbird Mail Server. Documentation for all products is included in Hummingbird DigitalPaper format. The evaluation software expires 60 days from date of installation.

Since the manufacturing of this evaluation CD, it is possible that a new version of the software has been released. To receive the most current Hummingbird Sampler CD, or for product price and ordering information, please call your Hummingbird Reseller or Hummingbird Sales directly at:

Tel: 1 (416) 496-2200
Fax: 1 (416) 496-6357

In Europe:

Tel: +41 (22) 733 1858
Fax: +41 (22) 733 6403

E-mail: sales@hummingbird.com

You are invited to visit the Hummingbird Web Site (**www.hummingbird.com**) where current product information and evaluation copies of our product families are available.

A WORLD OF SOLUTIONS . . .

Receive more information and a current evaluation of the Hummingbird software product of your choice:

Attn: Hummingbird Sales

☐ **Exceed**

The award winning family of PC to UNIX internetworking products accommodate all popular PC operating environments including Windows, Windows 95, Windows NT, OS/2 and DOS.

☐ **HostExplorer**

Features high-performance TN3270E, TN5250 and VT420 terminal emulation delivering full-featured connectivity between PCs, mainframes and other hosts over standard-based TCP/IP networks.

☐ **Hummingbird NewsSeek**

A Web-enabled Usenet indexing engine that automates users' queries of hundreds of thousands of Usenet articles.

☐ **NFS Maestro**

A comprehensive family of high performance NFS, TCP/IP, and internetworking applications.

☐ **Common Ground**

The ultimate solution for document publishing on the Web. Publish and distribute electronic documents using your favorite applications.

☐ **Hummingbird Mail Server**

A highly integrated set of NT Services that provides robust, high-speed e-mail delivery and transmission based on open-system standards.

Simply complete and return the fax back to 1-416-496-6357, call 1-416-496-2200, or e-mail sales@hummingbird.com

Name: _____

Title: _____

Company: _____

Phone: _____

Fax: _____

Address: _____

State: _____

Zip Code: _____

E-mail: _____

ABOUT THE CD-ROM IN THIS BOOK

This CD-ROM contains a variety of tools designed to help you with the NT and UNIX integration process. Some of these tools are commercial demos, some are shareware, and some are freeware.

The contents of the CD-ROM are in the following directory structure:

Directory	Description
Apache	The UNIX-based Apache web server
FAQ	A series of FAQs for reference
INN	The INN news server
Mail	The Exchange SMTP Mail Migration tool
MetaInfo	Demo versions of MetaInfo's DNS for NT, NewsChannel Lite, and Sendmail servers
MibMaster	An SNMP agent viewer and modification tool
rsh	A remote shell client for Windows
rshd	A remote shell daemon for Windows NT
Samba	The Samba file and print sharing utility for UNIX
SOSSNT	The SOSSNT NFS server for Windows NT
TotalNet	Demo versions of TotalNet's advanced server for IRIX, Solaris, and HP-UX
Hummingbird	Evaluation copies of Exceed, Exceed 3D, NFS Maestro Client and Server, NFS Maestro SOLO v5.1.3, and Hummingbird Mail Server v1.0

Also included on the CD is the file *GPL.txt*, which is the GNU Public License required for distribution of certain free software packages.